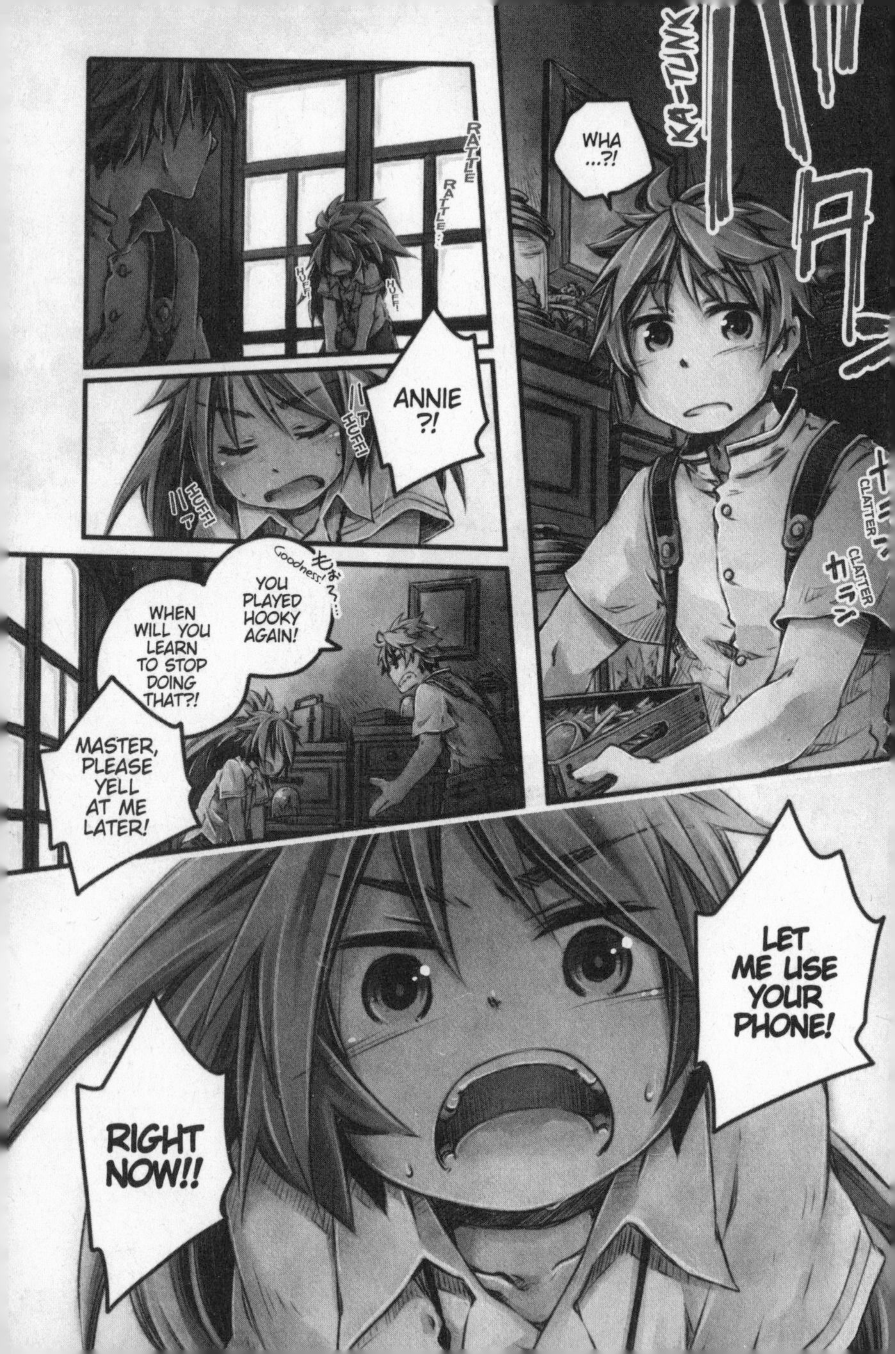
KA-TUNK
WHA ...?!
CLATTER
CLATTER
RATTLE
RATTLE...
HUFF!
HUFF!
ANNIE ?!
HUFF!
HUFF!
Goodness!
YOU PLAYED HOOKY AGAIN!
WHEN WILL YOU LEARN TO STOP DOING THAT?!
MASTER, PLEASE YELL AT ME LATER!
LET ME USE YOUR PHONE!
RIGHT NOW!!

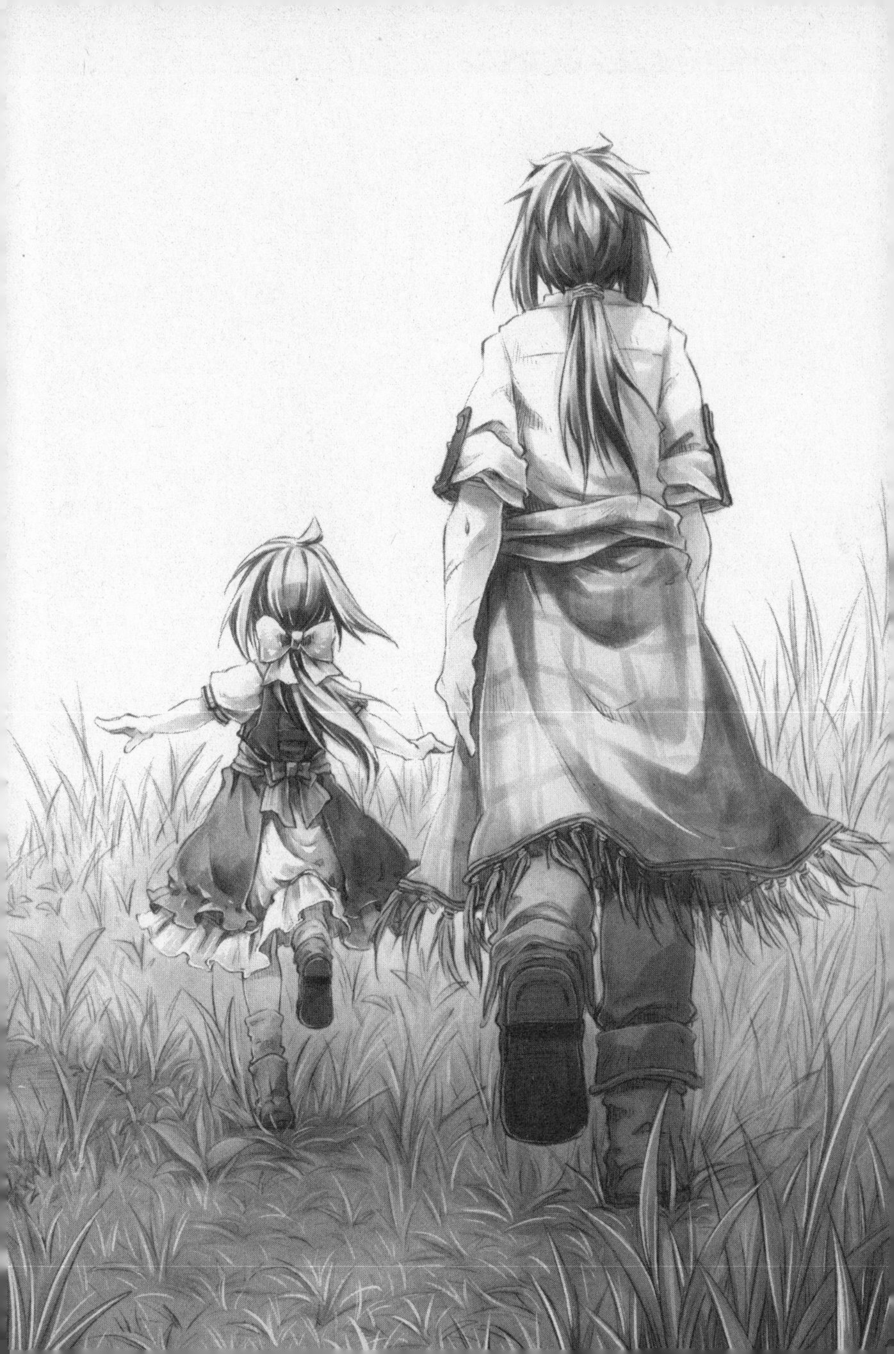

[Case 6: Kelpie (Part 2)]

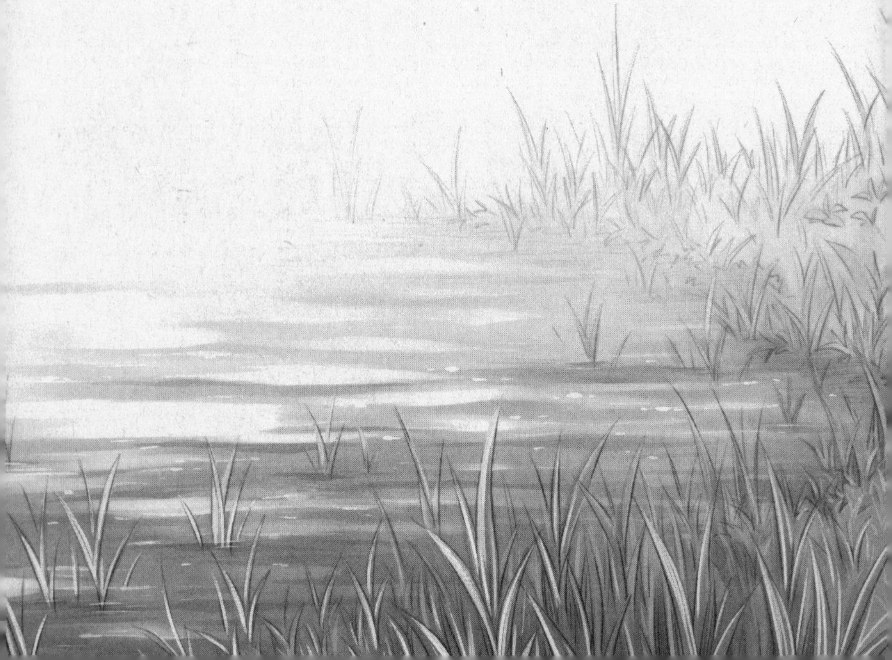

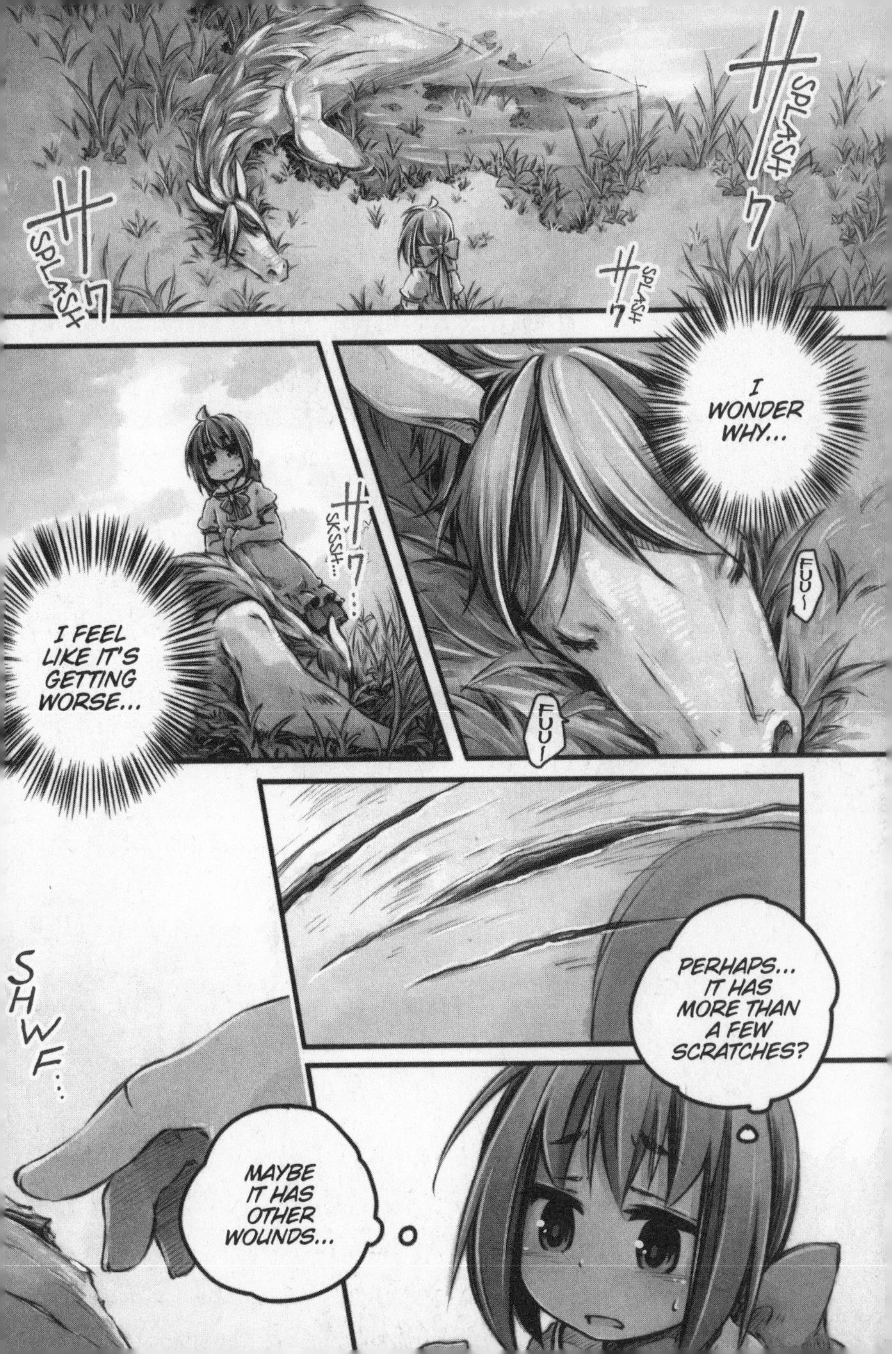
SPLASH
SPLASH
SPLASH
I WONDER WHY...
FUU~
FUU~
SKSSH...
I FEEL LIKE IT'S GETTING WORSE...
PERHAPS... IT HAS MORE THAN A FEW SCRATCHES?
SHWF...
MAYBE IT HAS OTHER WOUNDS...

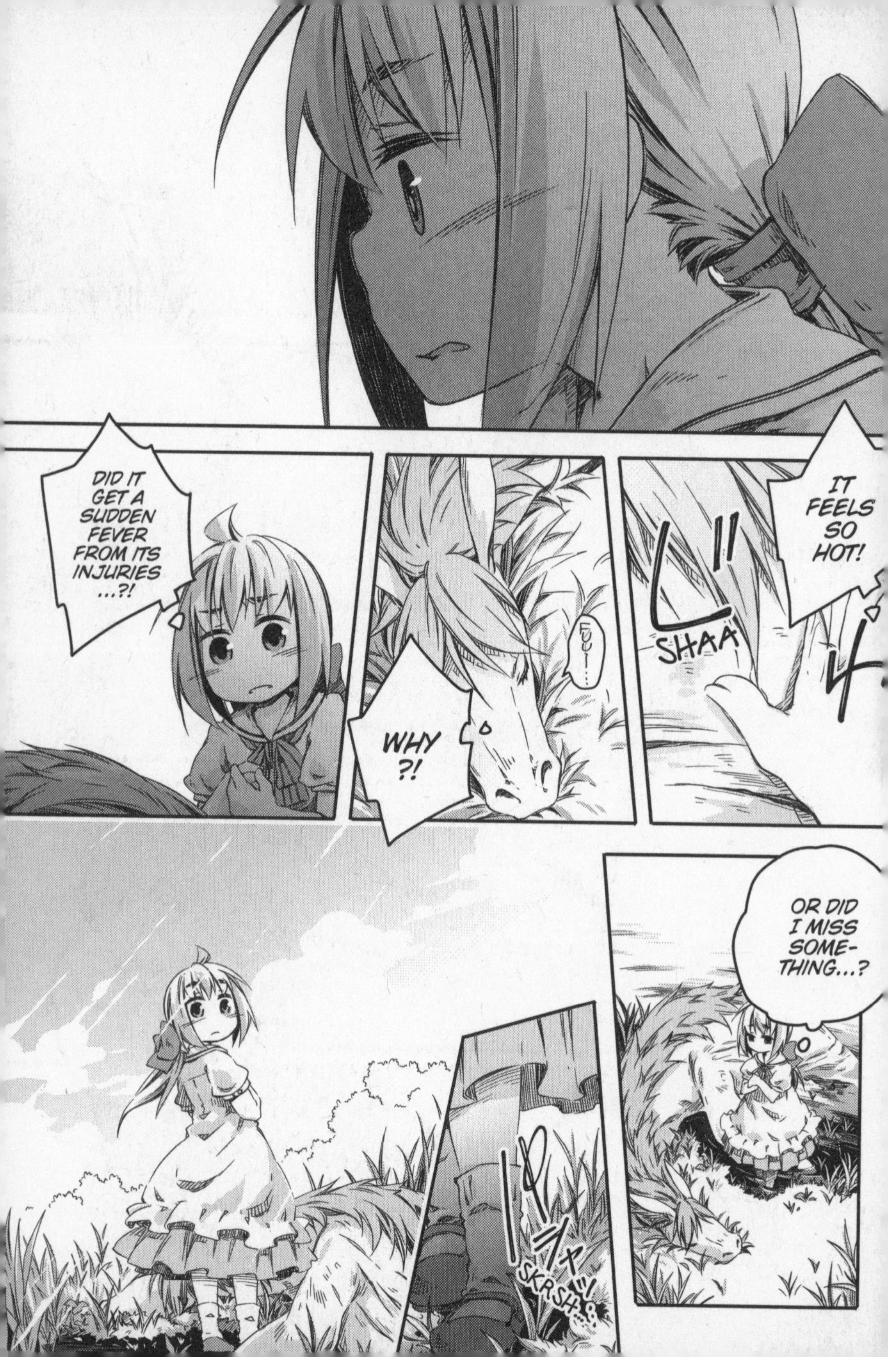
IT FEELS SO HOT!
SHAA
FUU-...
WHY?!
DID IT GET A SUDDEN FEVER FROM ITS INJURIES...?!
OR DID I MISS SOME-THING...?
SKRSH...

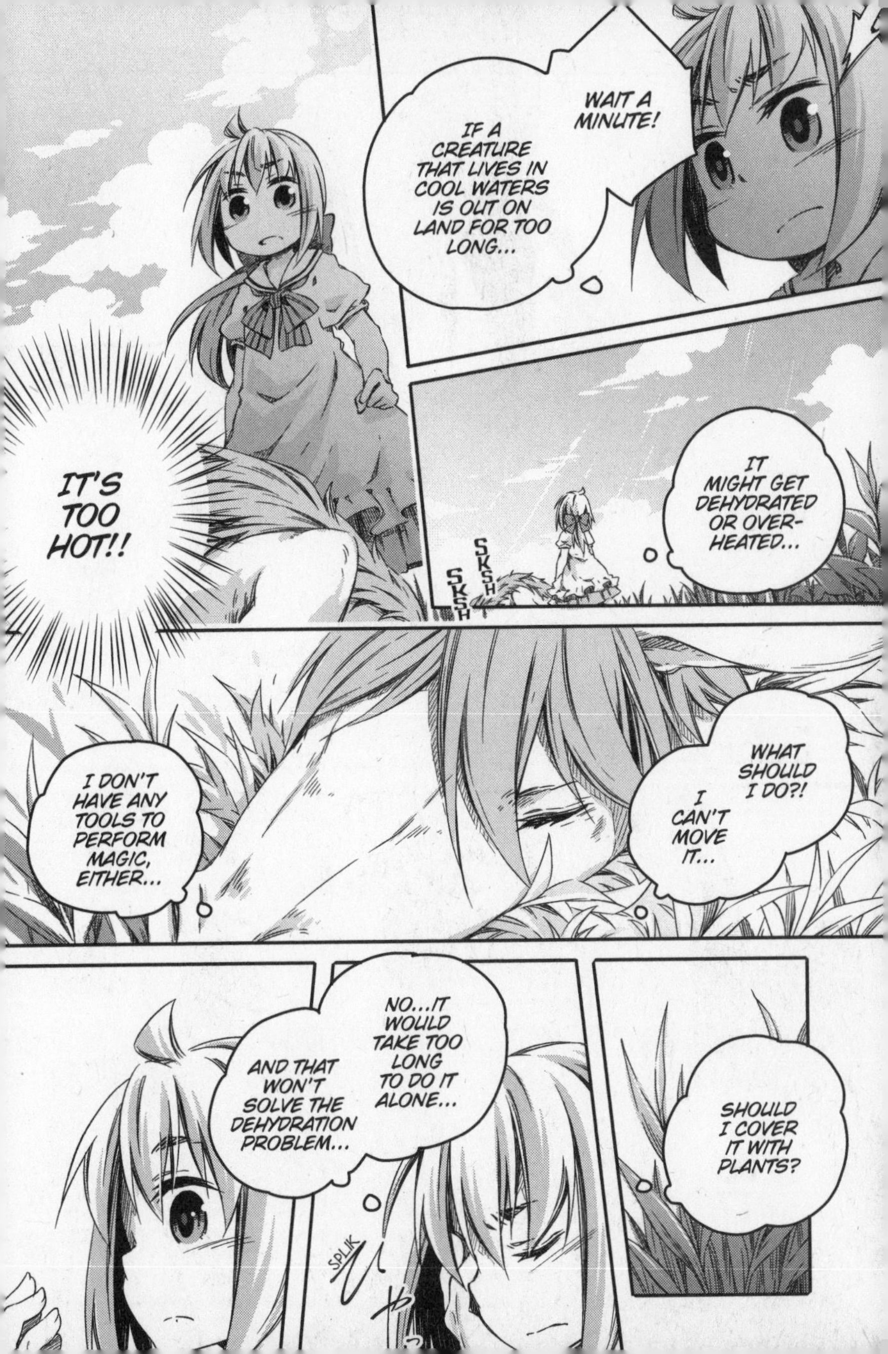
WAIT A MINUTE!
IF A CREATURE THAT LIVES IN COOL WATERS IS OUT ON LAND FOR TOO LONG...
IT MIGHT GET DEHYDRATED OR OVER-HEATED...
SKSH
SKSH
IT'S TOO HOT!!
WHAT SHOULD I DO?!
I CAN'T MOVE IT...
I DON'T HAVE ANY TOOLS TO PERFORM MAGIC, EITHER...
SHOULD I COVER IT WITH PLANTS?
NO...IT WOULD TAKE TOO LONG TO DO IT ALONE...
AND THAT WON'T SOLVE THE DEHYDRATION PROBLEM...
SPLIK

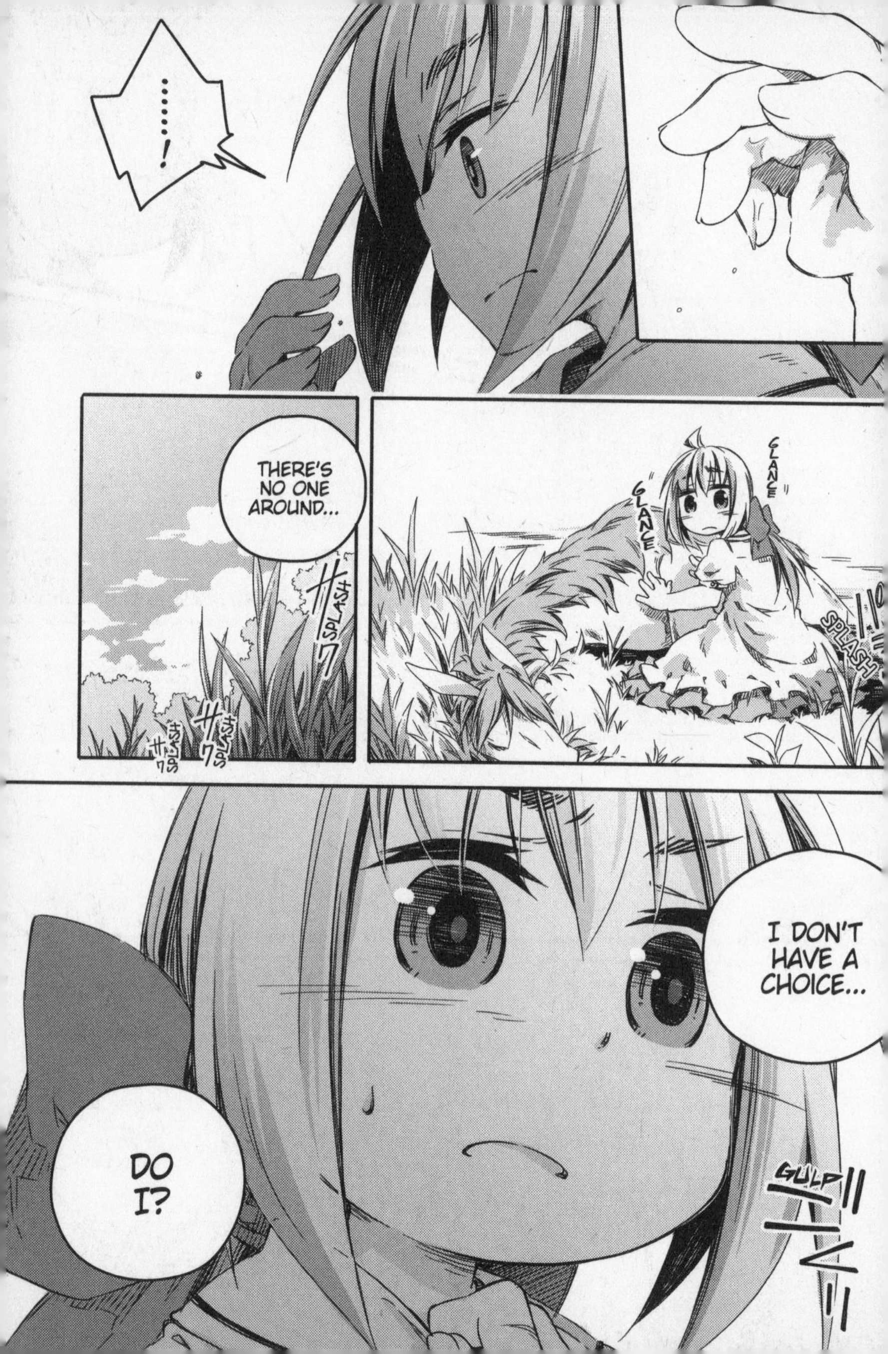
......!
GLANCE
GLANCE
SPLASH
THERE'S NO ONE AROUND...
SPLASH
SPLASH
SPLASH
I DON'T HAVE A CHOICE...
DO I?
GULP

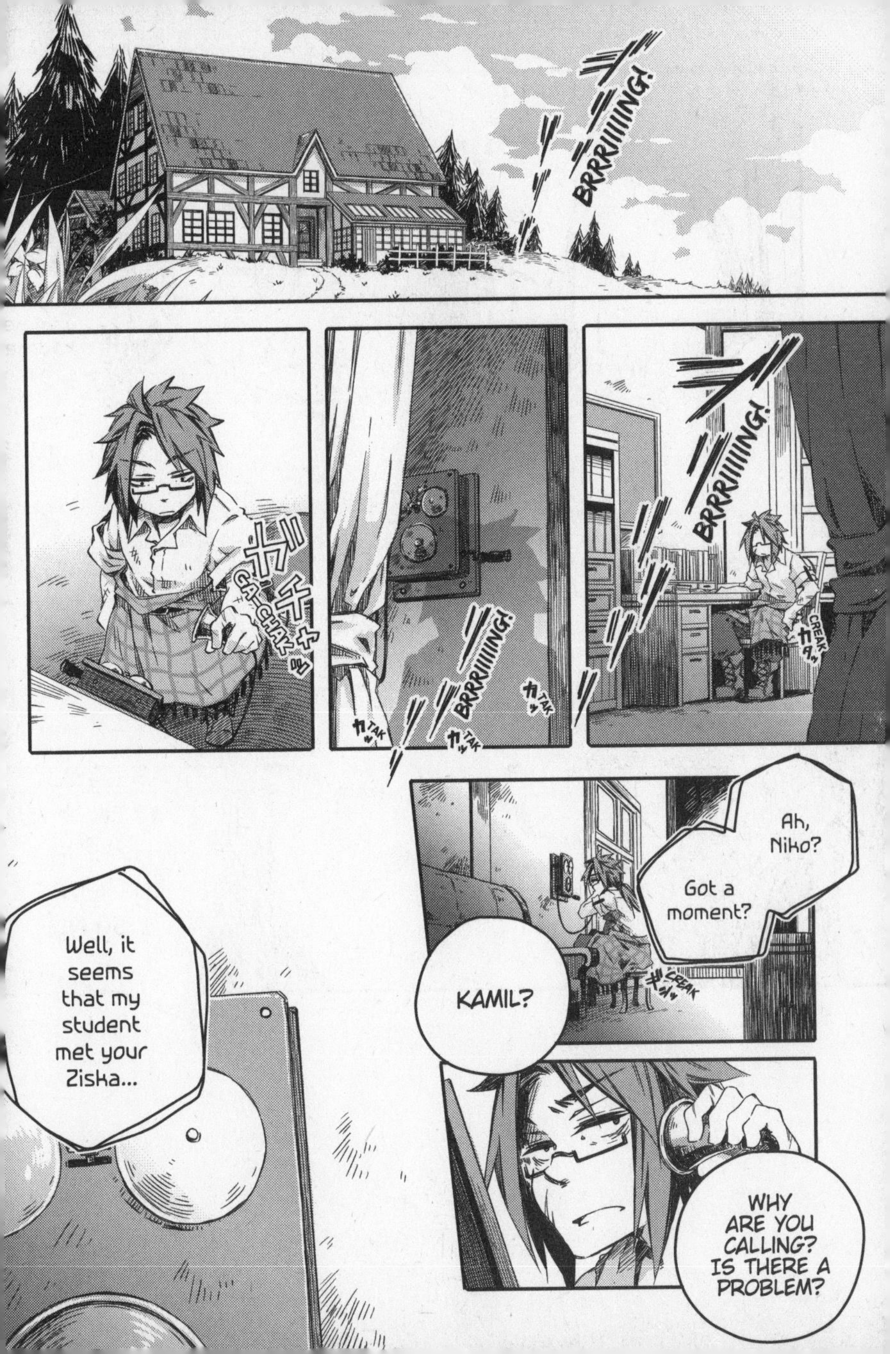
BRRRIIIIIING!
BRRRIIIIIING!
CREAK
カタッ
BRRRIIIIIING!
TAK
カッ
TAK
カッ
TAK
カッ
GA-CHAK
ガチャッ
Ah, Niko?
Got a moment?
KAMIL?
CREAK
ギシッ
WHY ARE YOU CALLING? IS THERE A PROBLEM?
Well, it seems that my student met your Ziska...

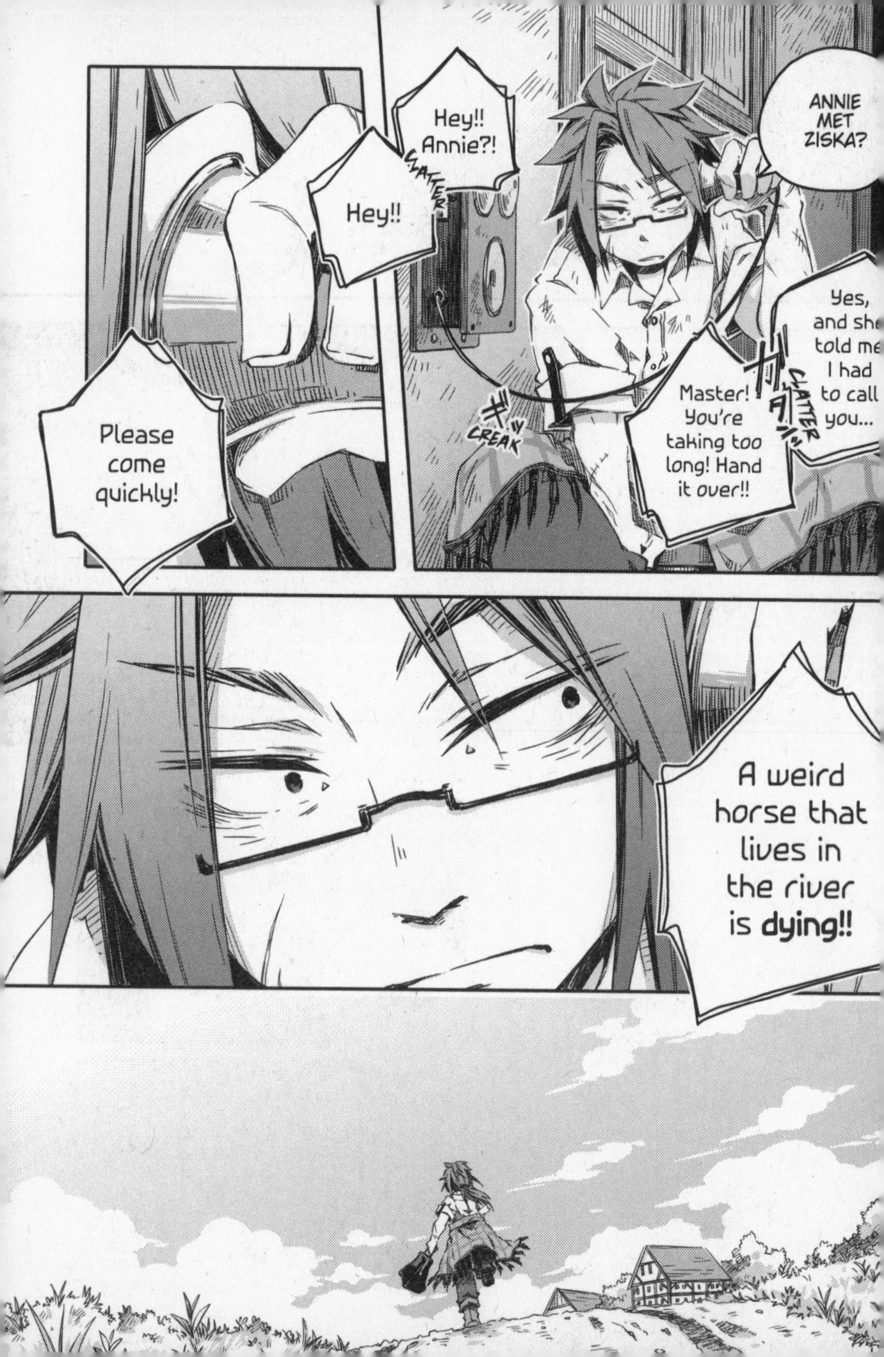
ANNIE MET ZISKA?
Yes, and she told me I had to call you...
Hey!! Annie?!
CLATTER
Hey!!
Master! You're taking too long! Hand it over!!
CLATTER
CREAK
Please come quickly!
A weird horse that lives in the river is **dying!!**

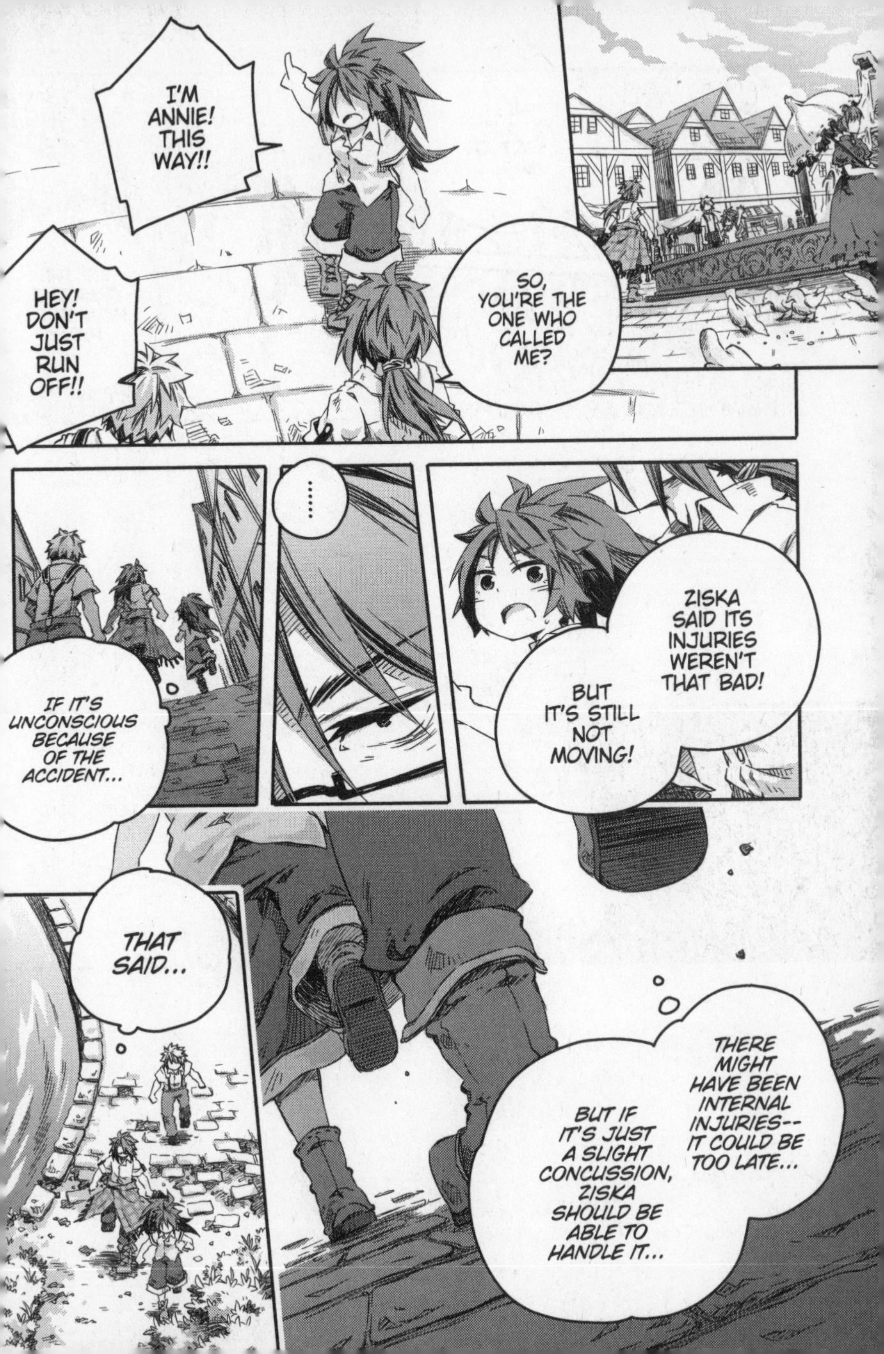
I'M ANNIE! THIS WAY!!
SO, YOU'RE THE ONE WHO CALLED ME?
HEY! DON'T JUST RUN OFF!!
ZISKA SAID ITS INJURIES WEREN'T THAT BAD!
BUT IT'S STILL NOT MOVING!
......
IF IT'S UNCONSCIOUS BECAUSE OF THE ACCIDENT...
THERE MIGHT HAVE BEEN INTERNAL INJURIES-- IT COULD BE TOO LATE...
BUT IF IT'S JUST A SLIGHT CONCUSSION, ZISKA SHOULD BE ABLE TO HANDLE IT...
THAT SAID...

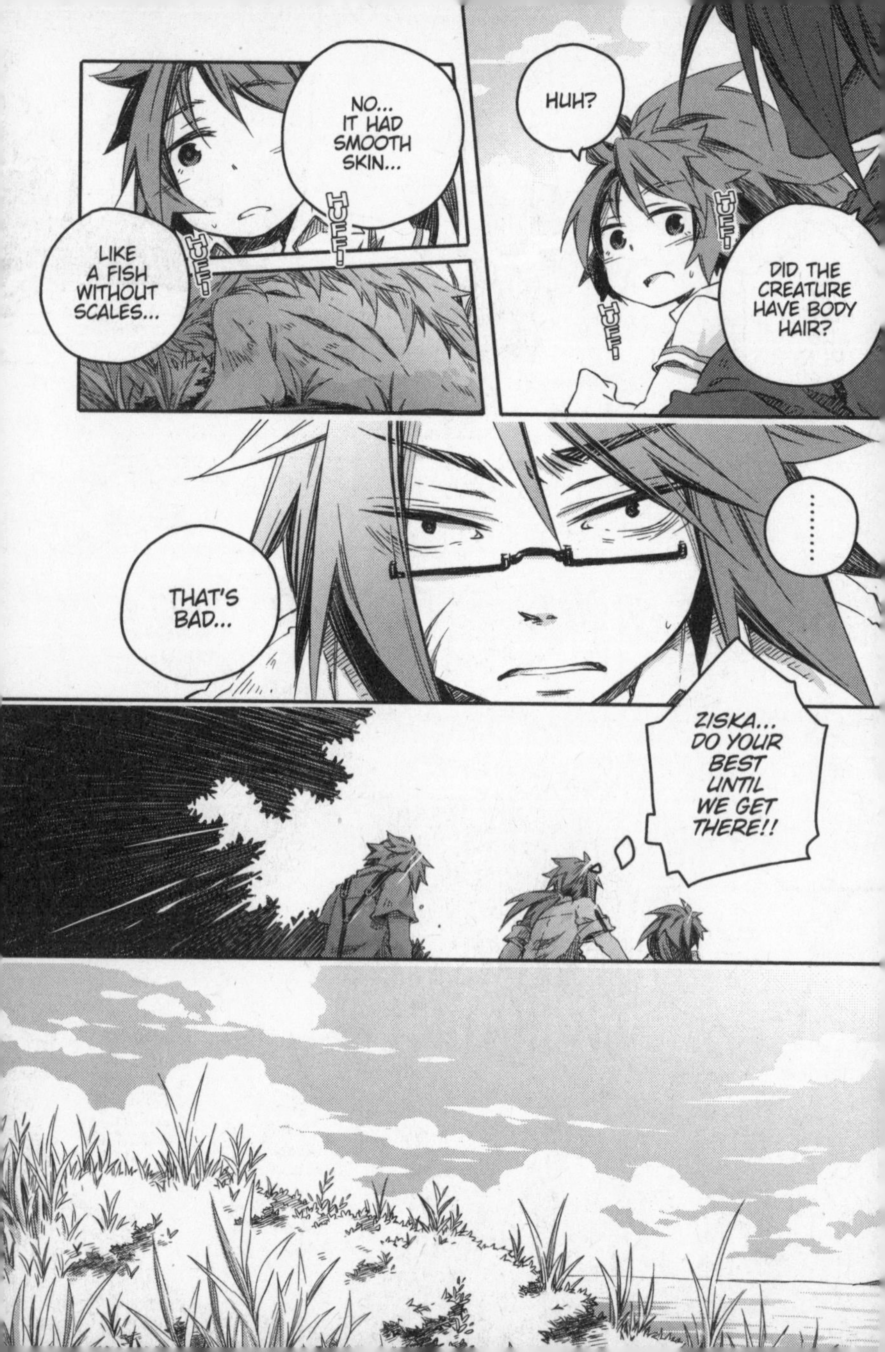
HUH?
HUFF!
HUFF!
DID THE CREATURE HAVE BODY HAIR?
NO... IT HAD SMOOTH SKIN...
HUFF!
HUFF!
LIKE A FISH WITHOUT SCALES...
......
THAT'S BAD...
ZISKA... DO YOUR BEST UNTIL WE GET THERE!!

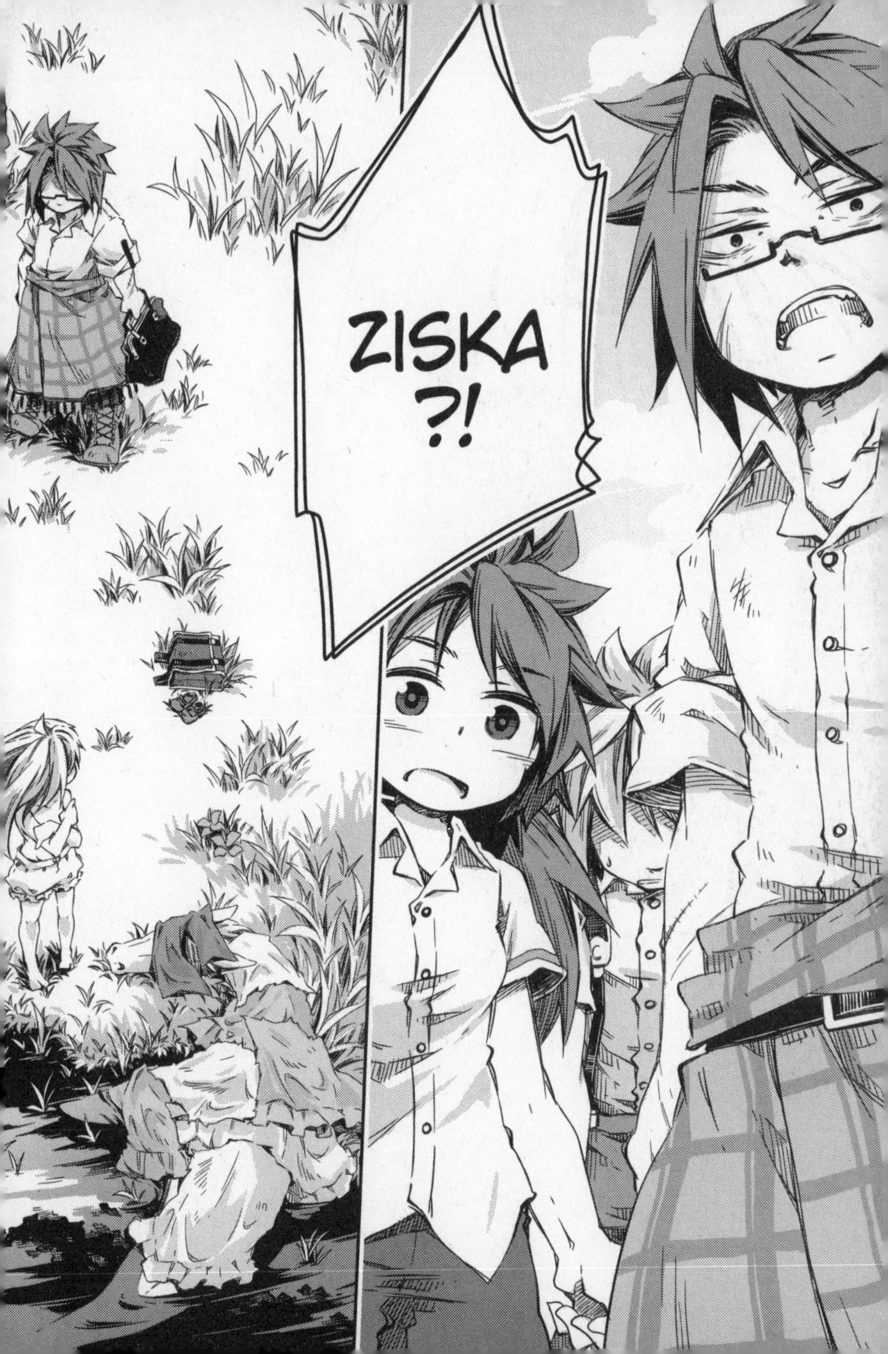
ZISKA ?!

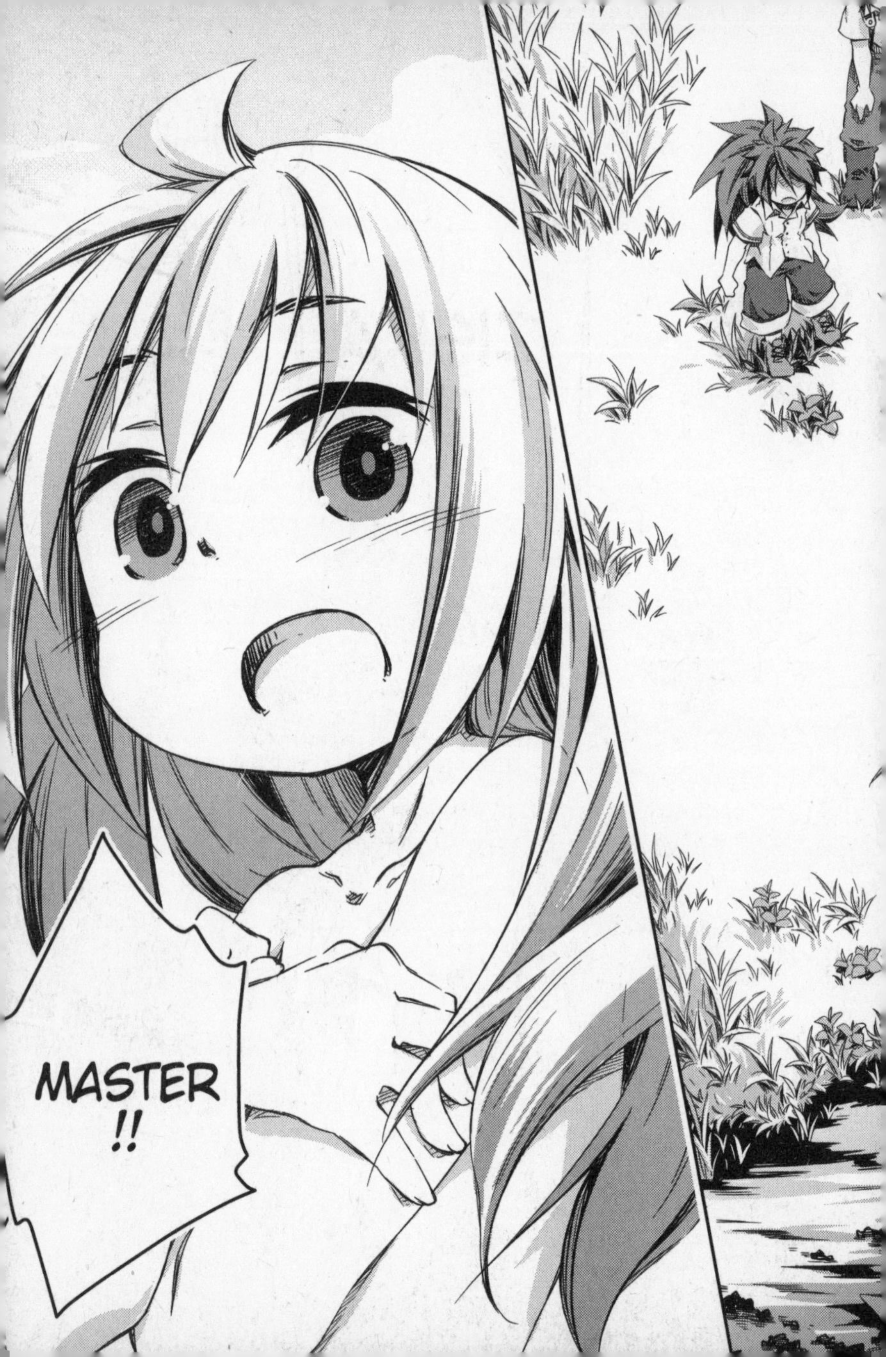
MASTER
!!

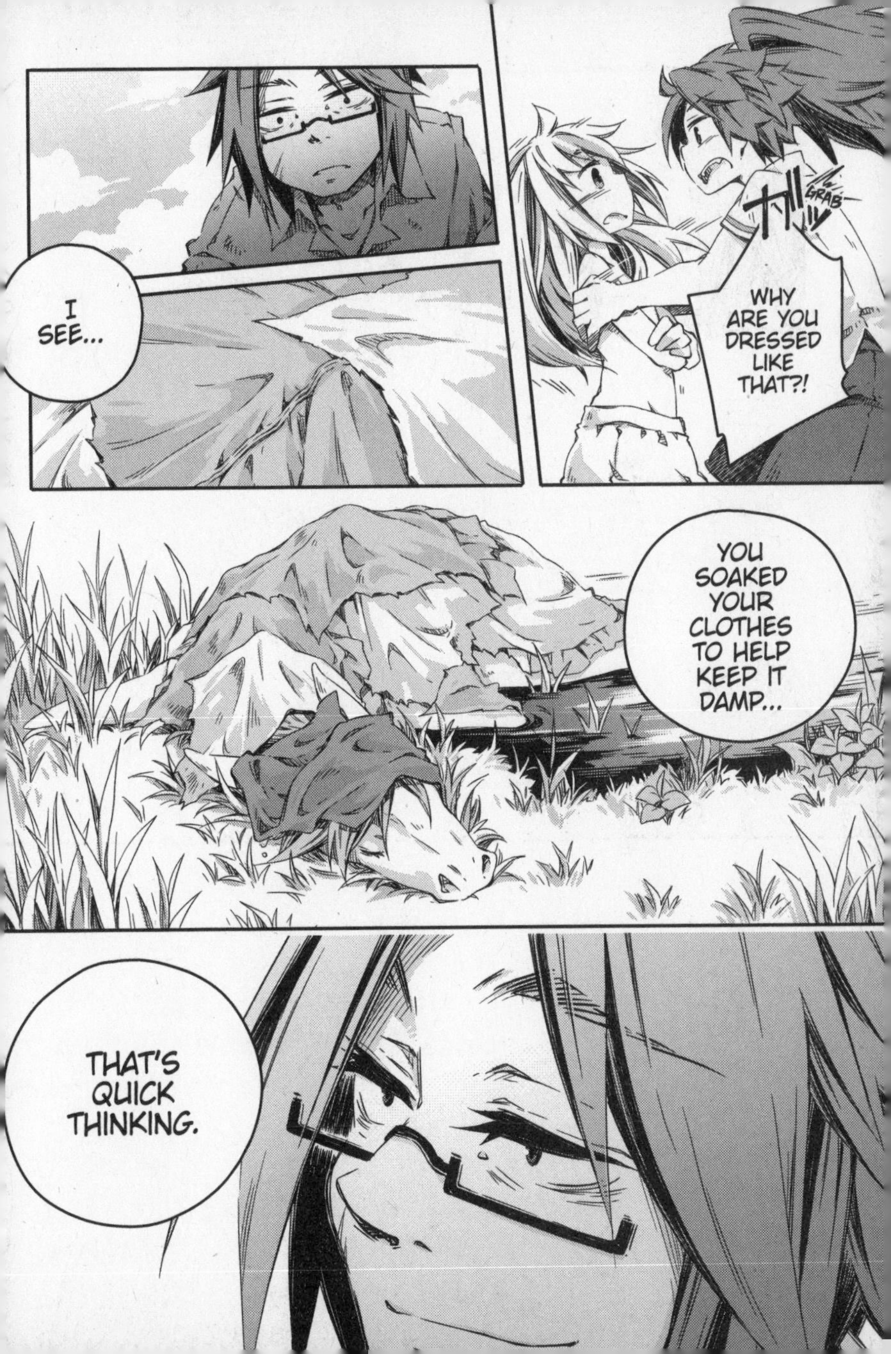
GRAB
WHY ARE YOU DRESSED LIKE THAT?!
I SEE...
YOU SOAKED YOUR CLOTHES TO HELP KEEP IT DAMP...
THAT'S QUICK THINKING.

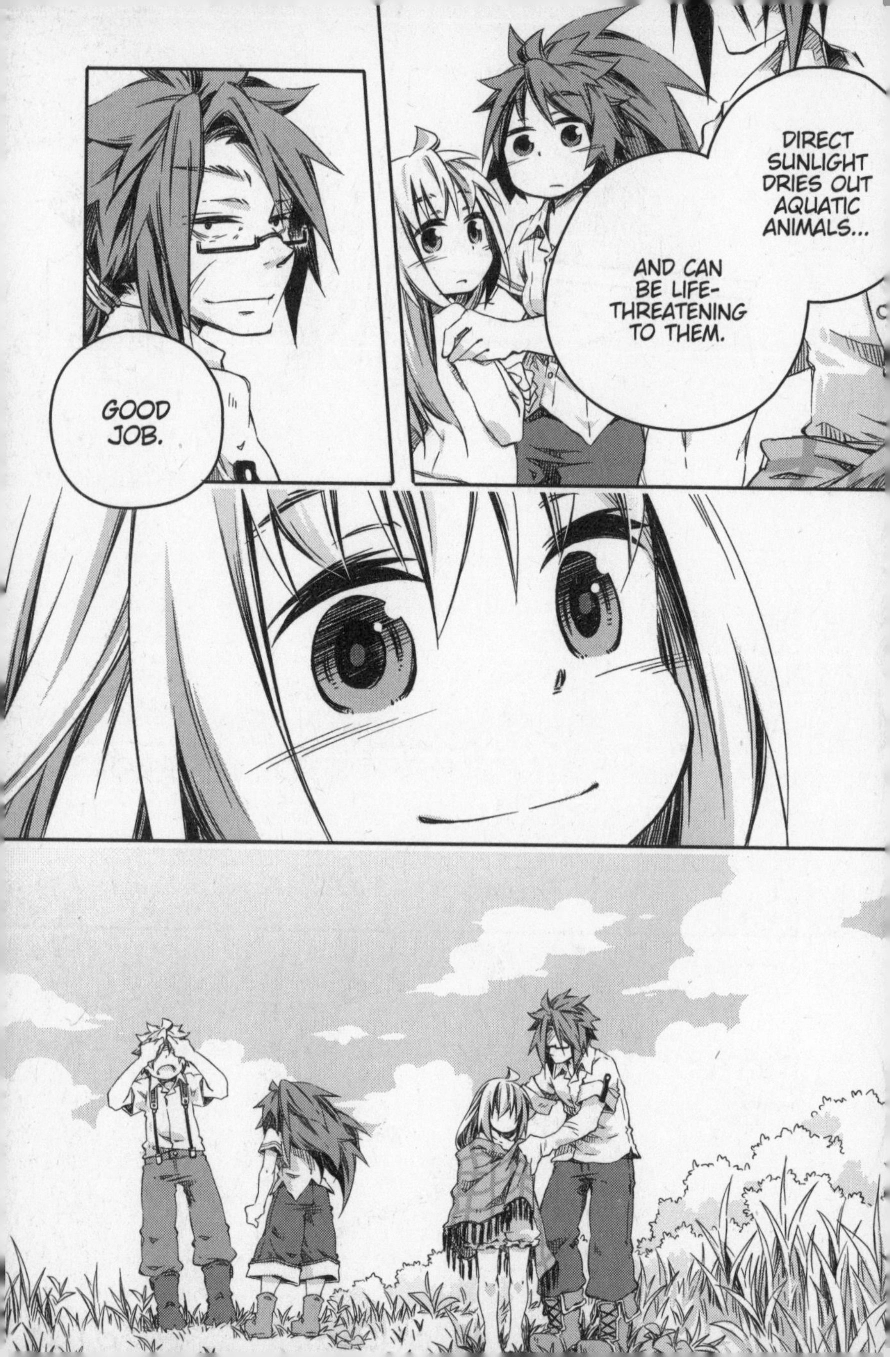
DIRECT SUNLIGHT DRIES OUT AQUATIC ANIMALS...
AND CAN BE LIFE-THREATENING TO THEM.
GOOD JOB.

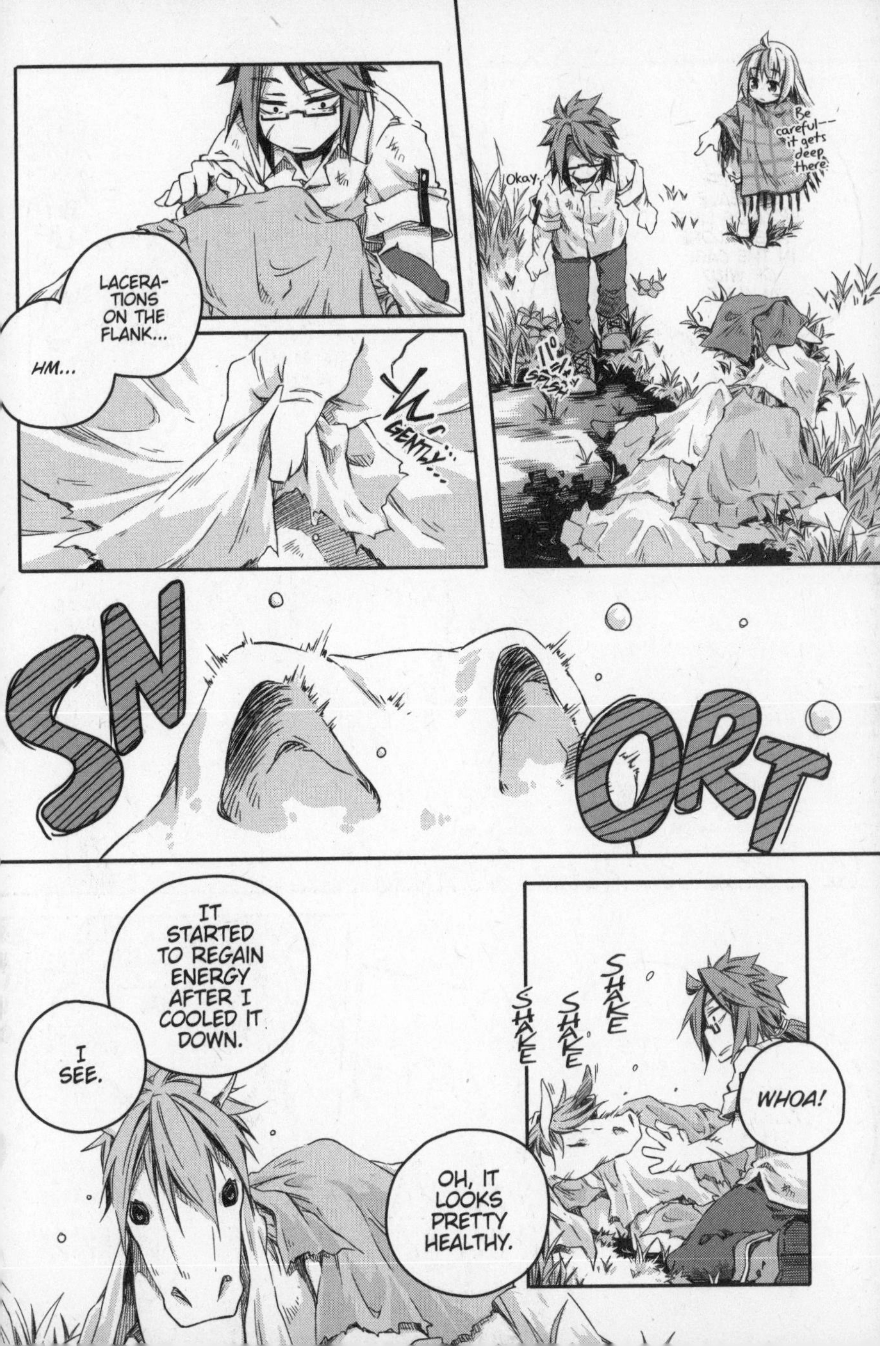
Be careful-- it gets deep there.
Okay.
SPLSH
LACERATIONS ON THE FLANK...
HM...
GENTLY...
SNORT
SHAKE SHAKE SHAKE
WHOA!
OH, IT LOOKS PRETTY HEALTHY.
IT STARTED TO REGAIN ENERGY AFTER I COOLED IT DOWN.
I SEE.

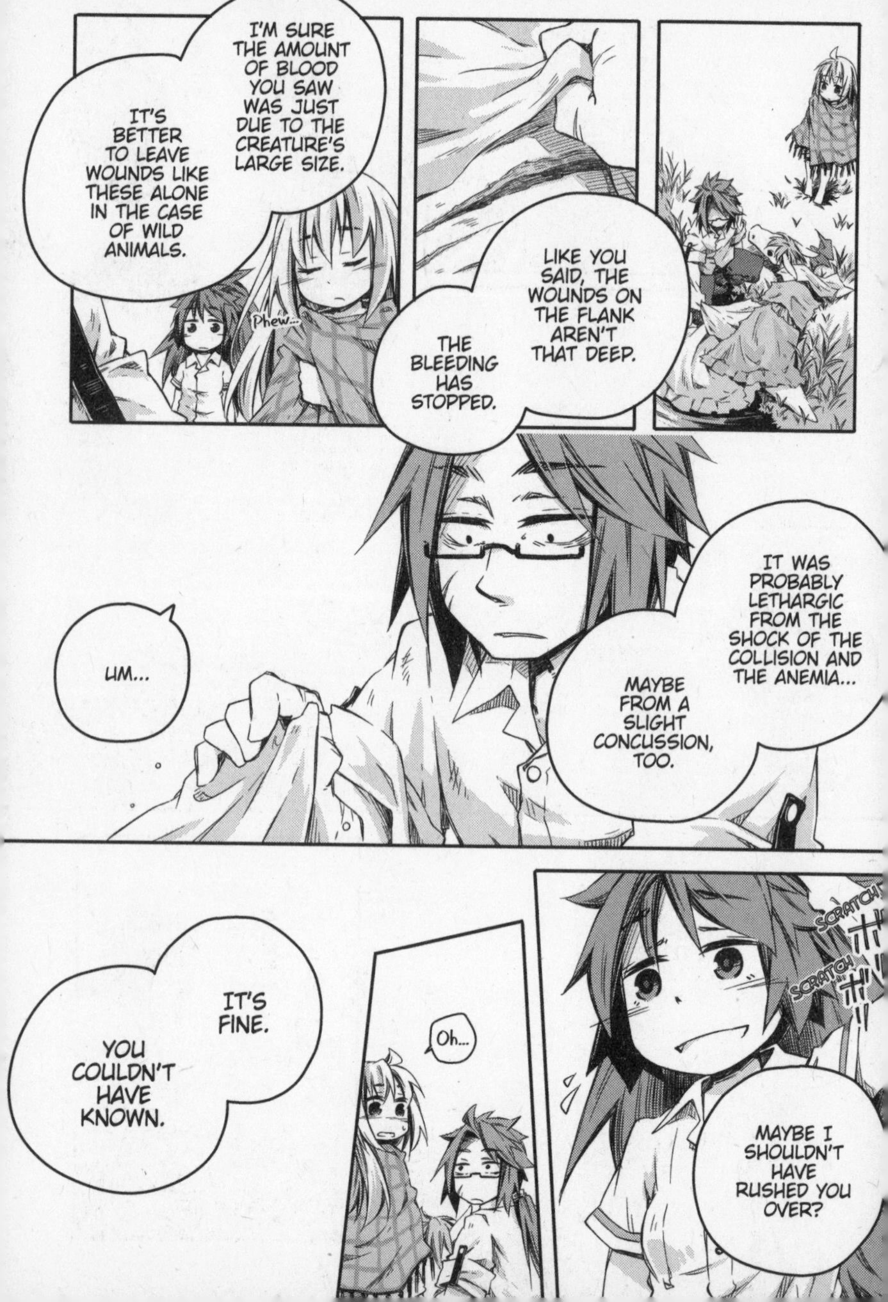

LIKE YOU SAID, THE WOUNDS ON THE FLANK AREN'T THAT DEEP.
THE BLEEDING HAS STOPPED.
I'M SURE THE AMOUNT OF BLOOD YOU SAW WAS JUST DUE TO THE CREATURE'S LARGE SIZE.
IT'S BETTER TO LEAVE WOUNDS LIKE THESE ALONE IN THE CASE OF WILD ANIMALS.
Phew...
IT WAS PROBABLY LETHARGIC FROM THE SHOCK OF THE COLLISION AND THE ANEMIA...
MAYBE FROM A SLIGHT CONCUSSION, TOO.
UM...
SCRATCH
SCRATCH
MAYBE I SHOULDN'T HAVE RUSHED YOU OVER?
Oh...
IT'S FINE.
YOU COULDN'T HAVE KNOWN.

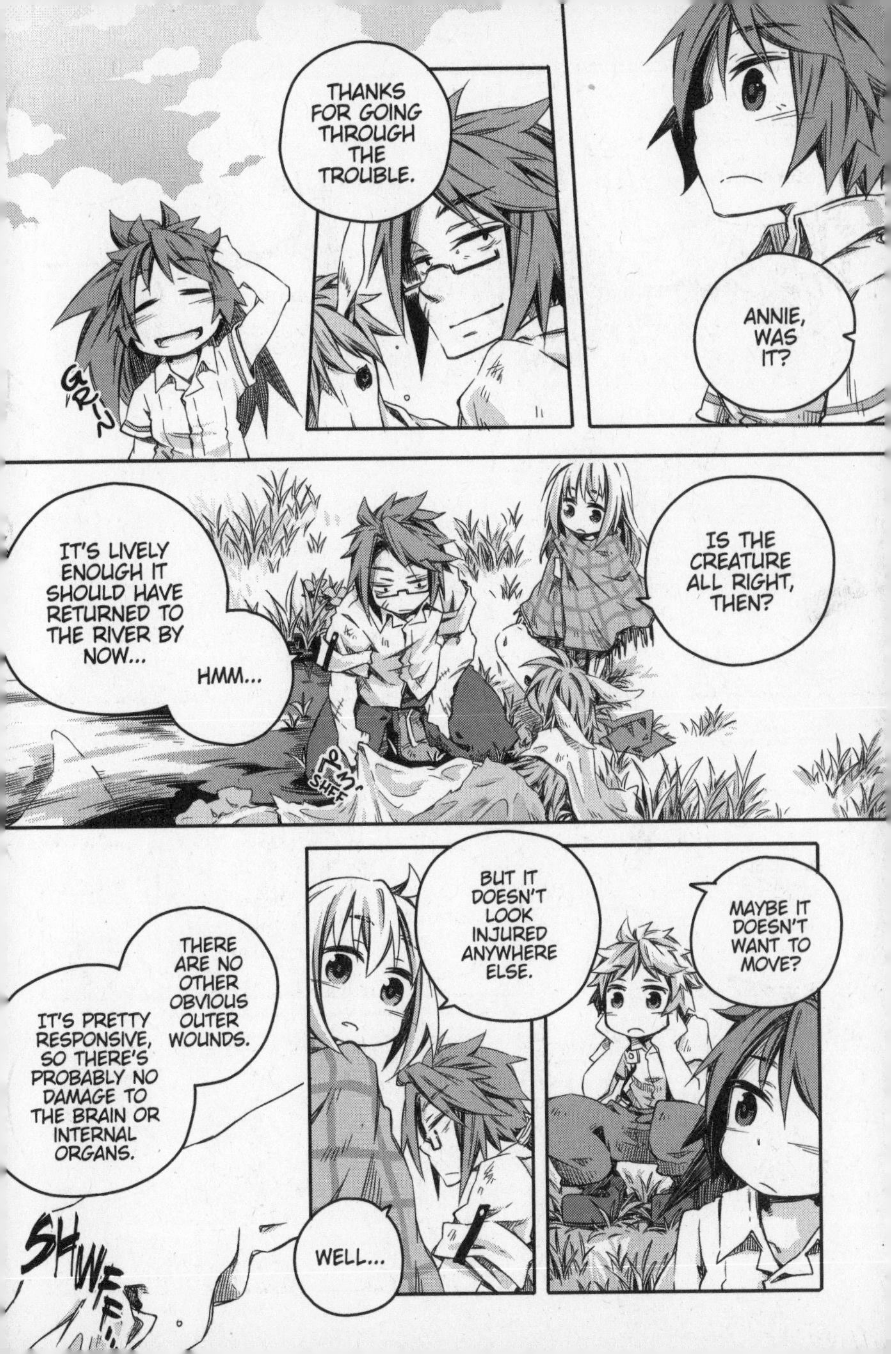
ANNIE, WAS IT?
THANKS FOR GOING THROUGH THE TROUBLE.
GRIN
IS THE CREATURE ALL RIGHT, THEN?
IT'S LIVELY ENOUGH IT SHOULD HAVE RETURNED TO THE RIVER BY NOW...
HMM...
SHFF
MAYBE IT DOESN'T WANT TO MOVE?
BUT IT DOESN'T LOOK INJURED ANYWHERE ELSE.
WELL...
THERE ARE NO OTHER OBVIOUS OUTER WOUNDS.
IT'S PRETTY RESPONSIVE, SO THERE'S PROBABLY NO DAMAGE TO THE BRAIN OR INTERNAL ORGANS.
SHWFF...

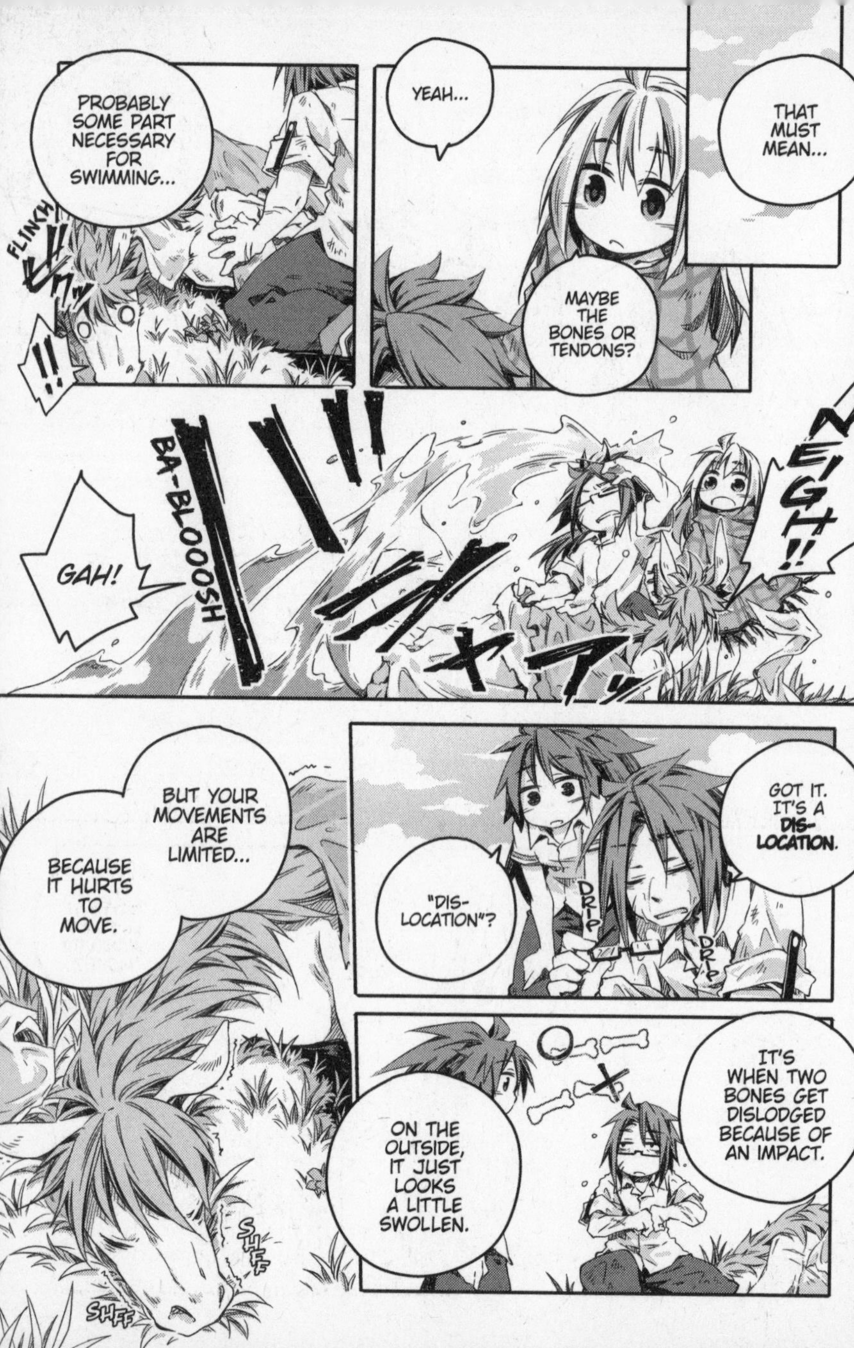
THAT MUST MEAN...
MAYBE THE BONES OR TENDONS?
YEAH...
PROBABLY SOME PART NECESSARY FOR SWIMMING...
FLINCH
!!
NEIGH!!
BA-BLOOOSH
GAH!
GOT IT. IT'S A **DISLOCATION**.
"DIS-LOCATION"?
DRIP
DRIP
IT'S WHEN TWO BONES GET DISLODGED BECAUSE OF AN IMPACT.
ON THE OUTSIDE, IT JUST LOOKS A LITTLE SWOLLEN.
BUT YOUR MOVEMENTS ARE LIMITED...
BECAUSE IT HURTS TO MOVE.
SHFF
SHFF

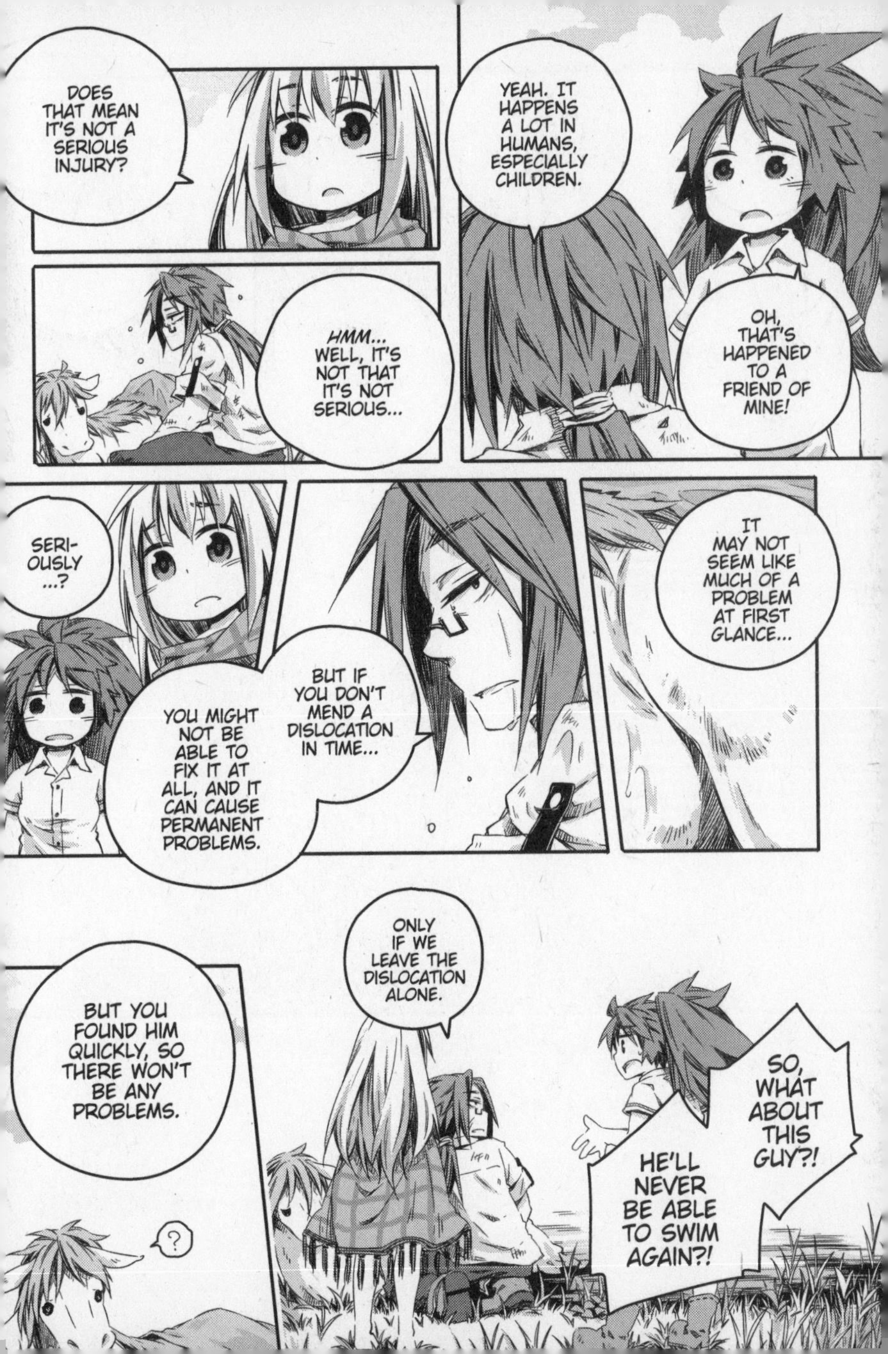
YEAH. IT HAPPENS A LOT IN HUMANS, ESPECIALLY CHILDREN.
OH, THAT'S HAPPENED TO A FRIEND OF MINE!
DOES THAT MEAN IT'S NOT A SERIOUS INJURY?
HMM... WELL, IT'S NOT THAT IT'S NOT SERIOUS...
IT MAY NOT SEEM LIKE MUCH OF A PROBLEM AT FIRST GLANCE...
BUT IF YOU DON'T MEND A DISLOCATION IN TIME...
YOU MIGHT NOT BE ABLE TO FIX IT AT ALL, AND IT CAN CAUSE PERMANENT PROBLEMS.
SERIOUSLY...?
SO, WHAT ABOUT THIS GUY?!
HE'LL NEVER BE ABLE TO SWIM AGAIN?!
ONLY IF WE LEAVE THE DISLOCATION ALONE.
BUT YOU FOUND HIM QUICKLY, SO THERE WON'T BE ANY PROBLEMS.
?

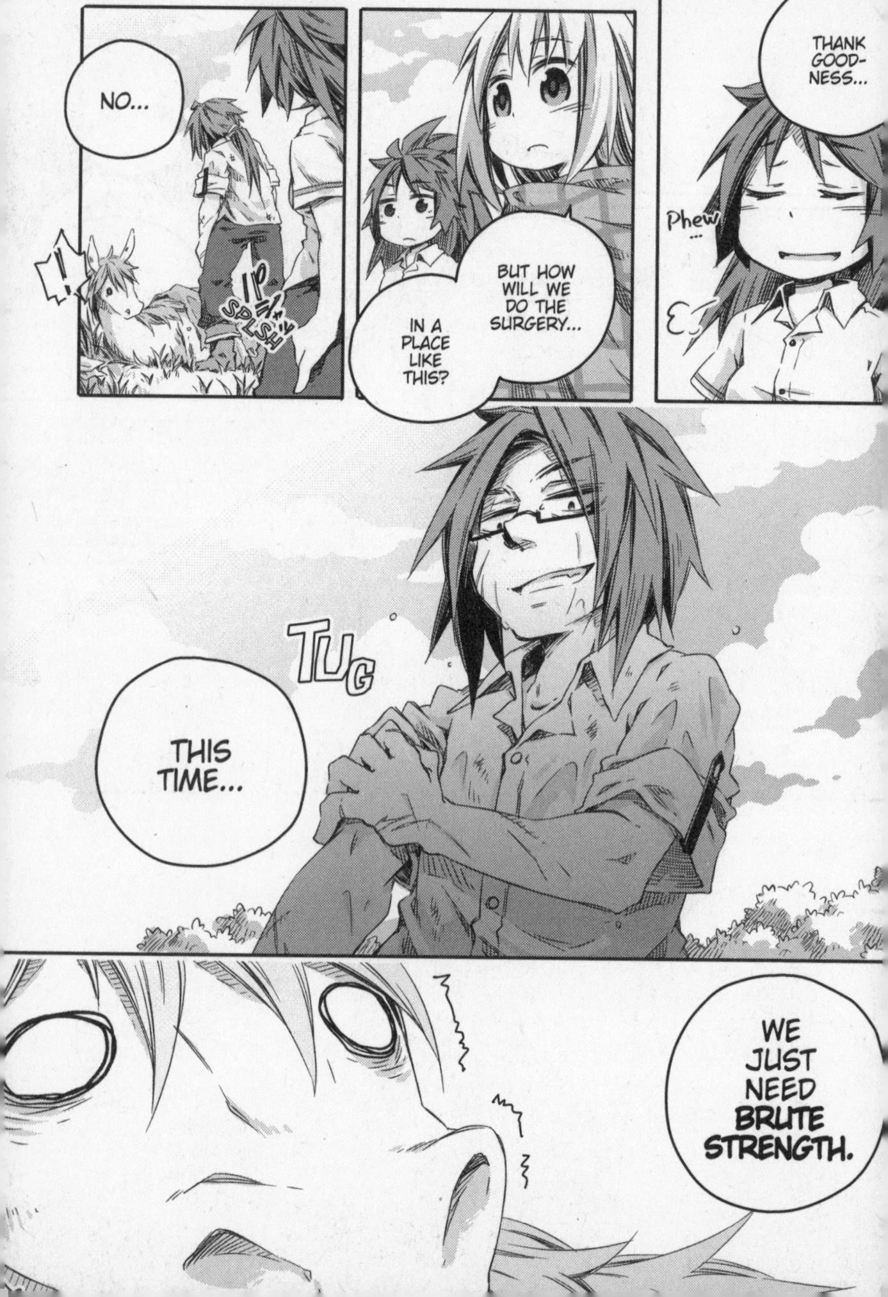
THANK GOODNESS...
Phew...
BUT HOW WILL WE DO THE SURGERY...
IN A PLACE LIKE THIS?
NO...
!
SPLSH
TUG
THIS TIME...
WE JUST NEED **BRUTE STRENGTH.**

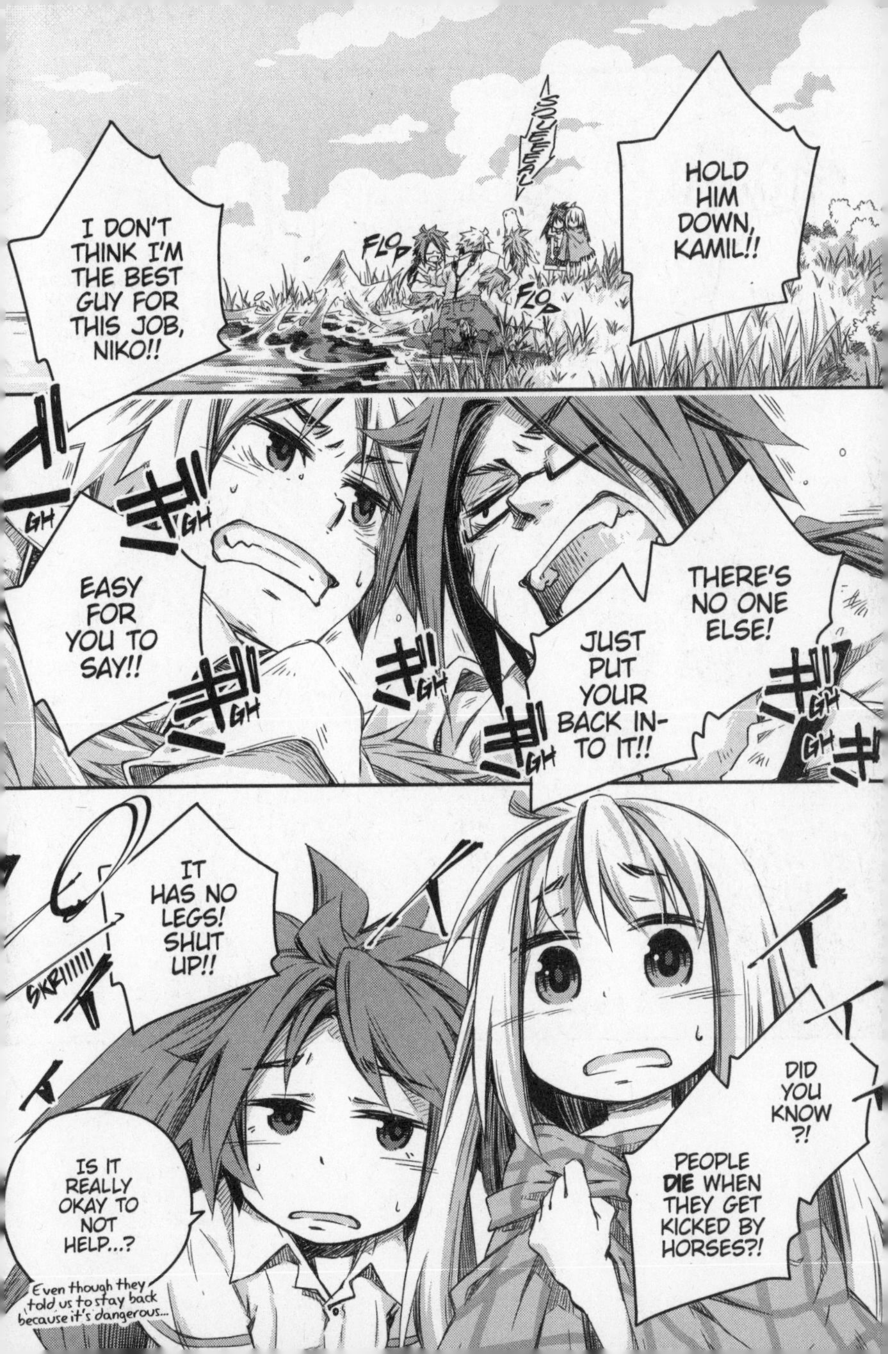
HOLD HIM DOWN, KAMIL!!
SQUEEEAL
FLOP
FLOP
I DON'T THINK I'M THE BEST GUY FOR THIS JOB, NIKO!!
THERE'S NO ONE ELSE!
GH
GH
JUST PUT YOUR BACK IN-TO IT!!
GH
GH
EASY FOR YOU TO SAY!!
GH
GH
GH
DID YOU KNOW?!
PEOPLE DIE WHEN THEY GET KICKED BY HORSES?!
IT HAS NO LEGS! SHUT UP!!
SKRIIIIII
IS IT REALLY OKAY TO NOT HELP...?
Even though they told us to stay back because it's dangerous...

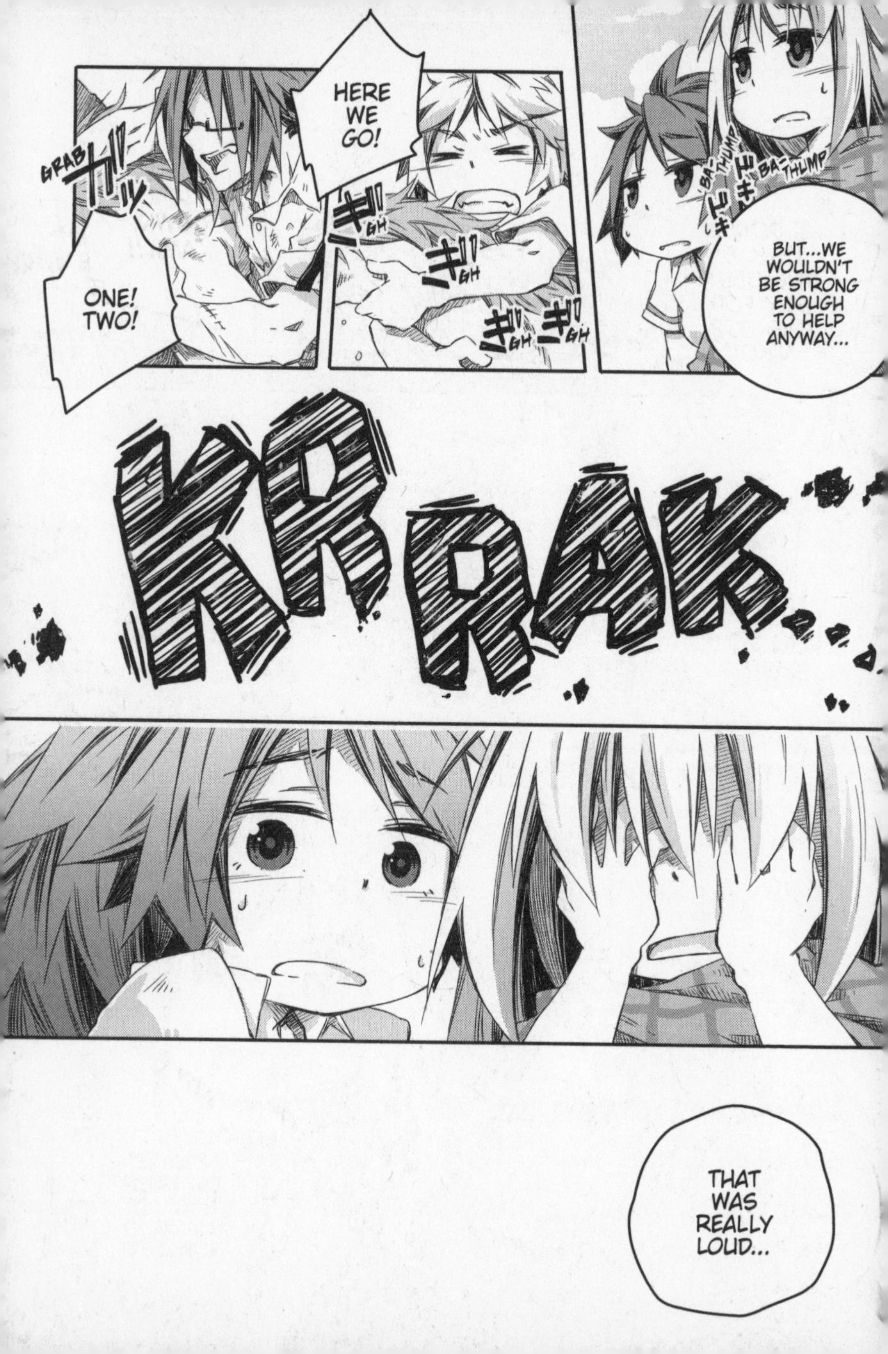
BA-THUMP BA-THUMP
BUT...WE WOULDN'T BE STRONG ENOUGH TO HELP ANYWAY...
HERE WE GO!
GH GH GH GH
GRAB
ONE! TWO!
KRRAK
THAT WAS REALLY LOUD...

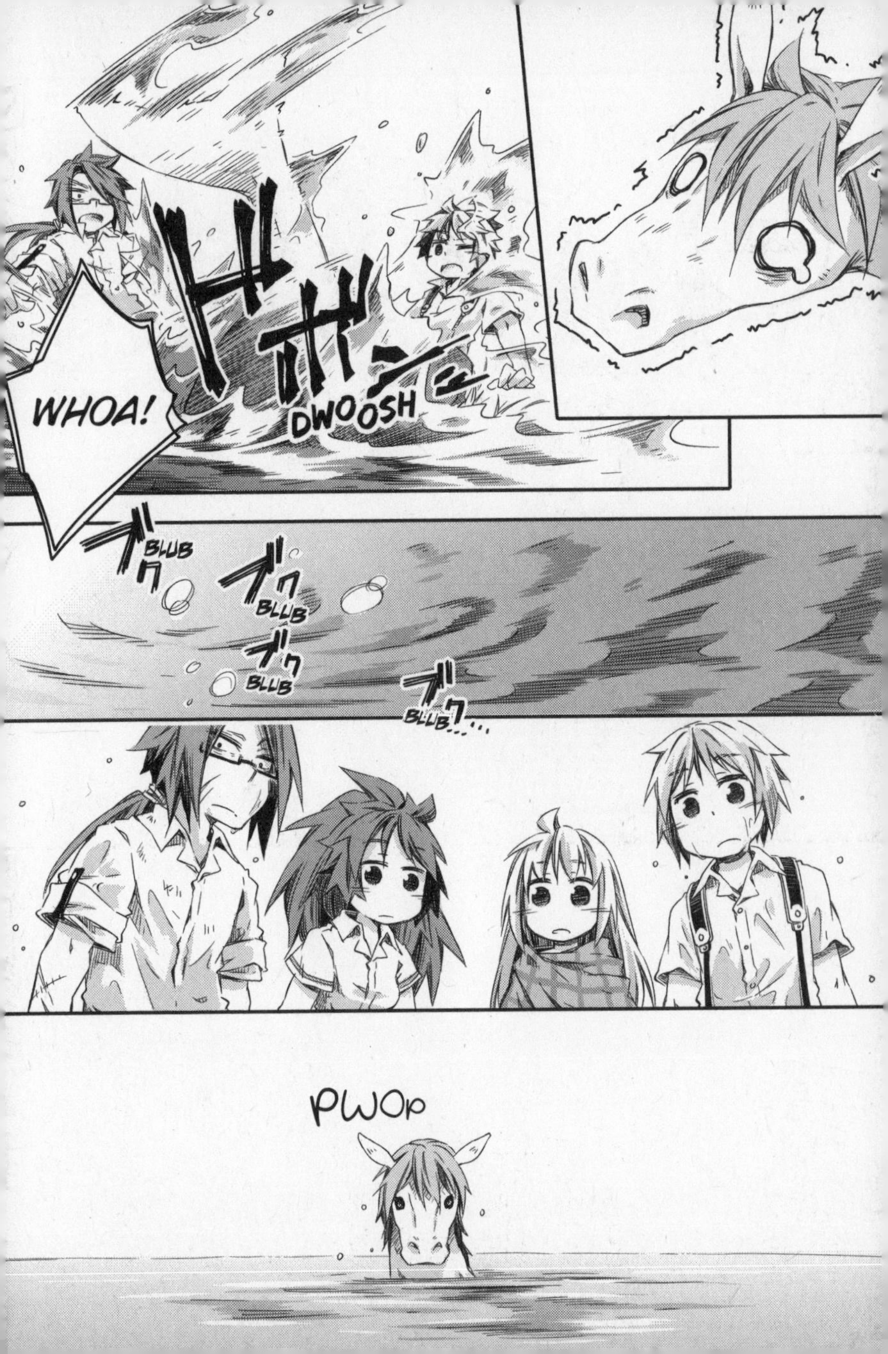
DWOOSH
WHOA!
BLUB
BLUB
BLUB
BLUB...
PWOP

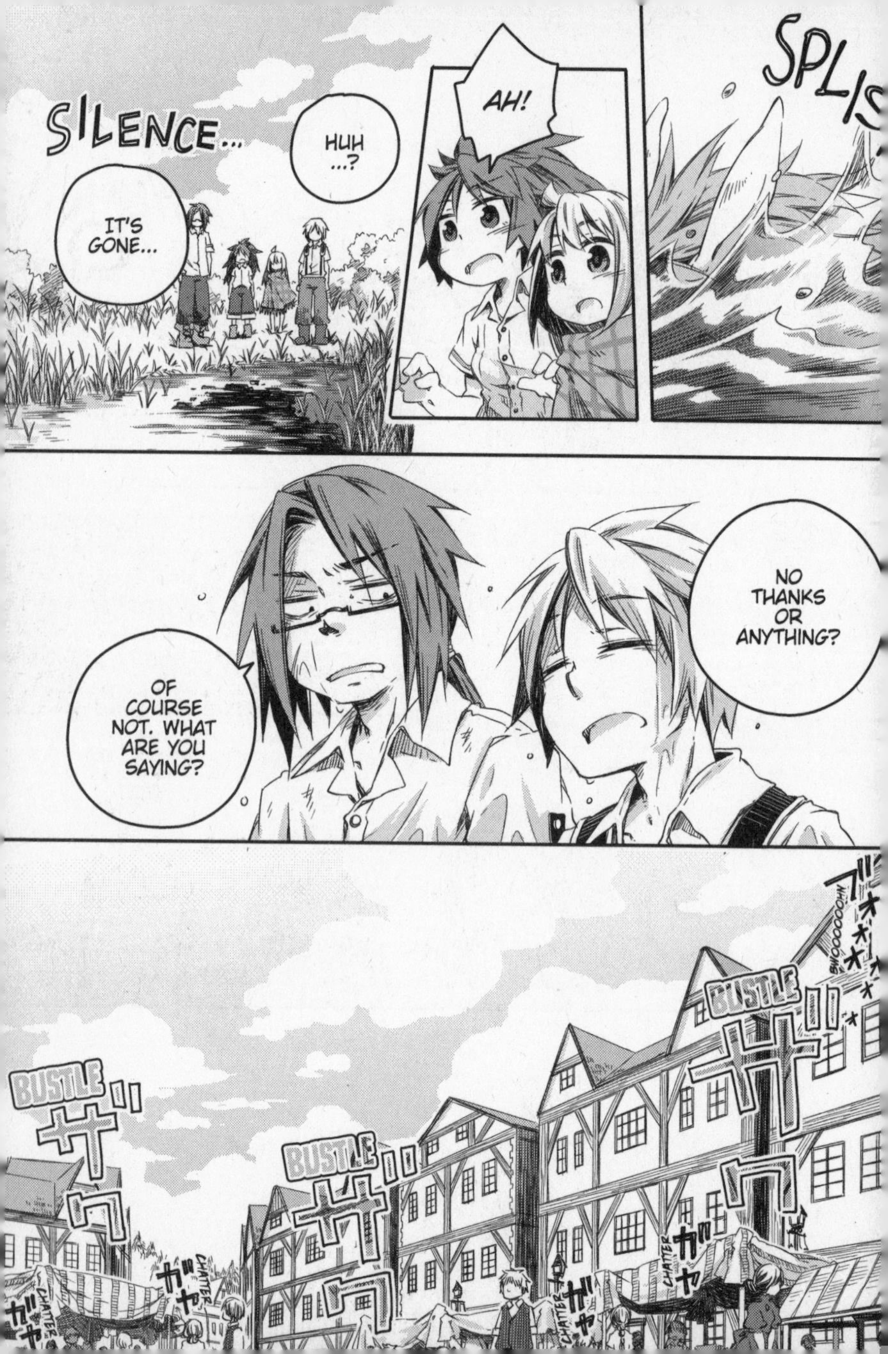
SPLIS
AH!
HUH ...?
SILENCE...
IT'S GONE...
NO THANKS OR ANYTHING?
OF COURSE NOT. WHAT ARE YOU SAYING?
BWOOOOOOHN
BUSTLE
CHATTER
BUSTLE
CHATTER
BUSTLE
CHATTER
CHATTER

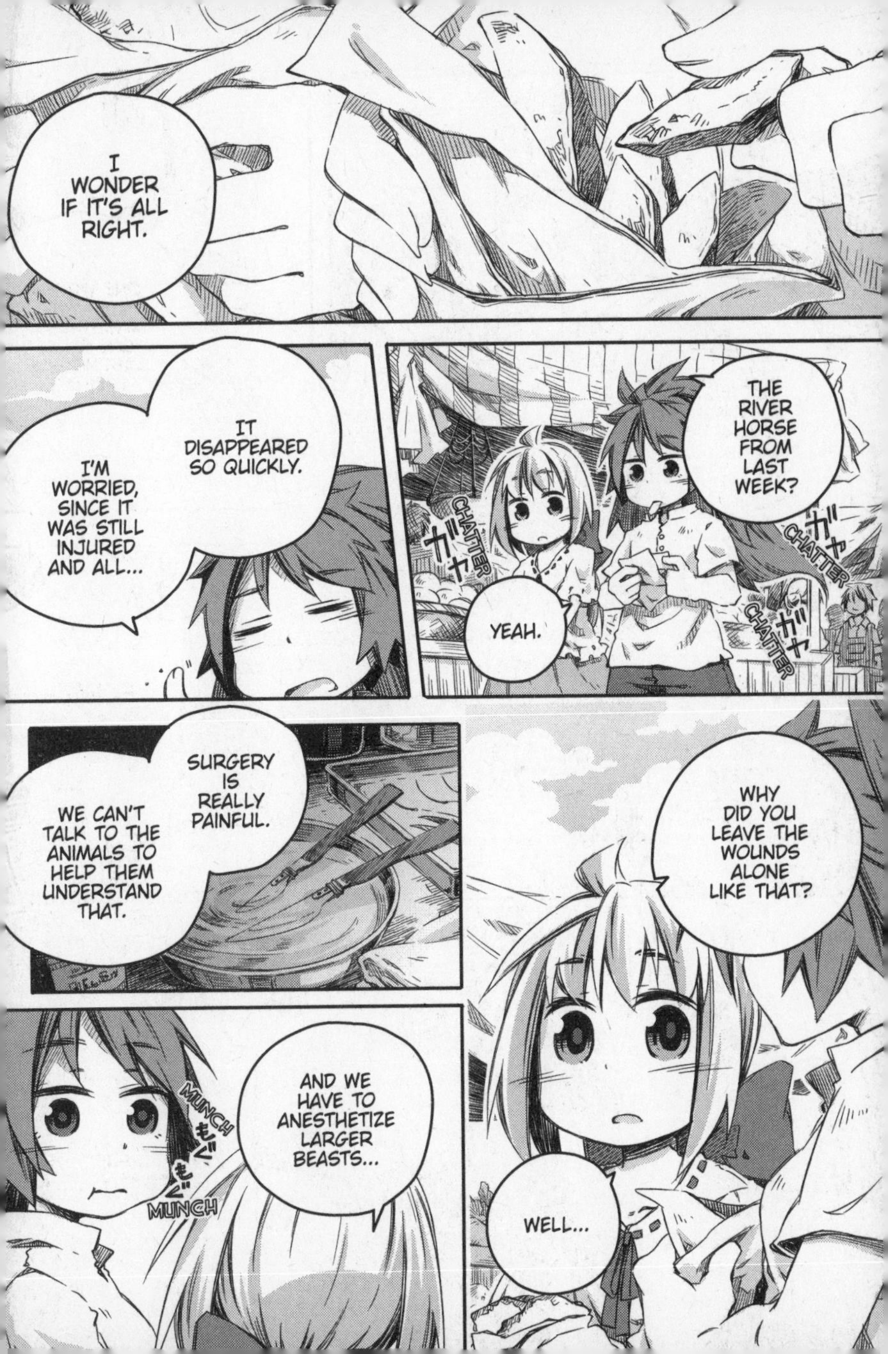

I WONDER IF IT'S ALL RIGHT.
THE RIVER HORSE FROM LAST WEEK?
ガヤ CHATTER
ガヤ CHATTER
ガヤ CHATTER
YEAH.
IT DISAPPEARED SO QUICKLY.
I'M WORRIED, SINCE IT WAS STILL INJURED AND ALL...
WHY DID YOU LEAVE THE WOUNDS ALONE LIKE THAT?
WELL...
SURGERY IS REALLY PAINFUL.
WE CAN'T TALK TO THE ANIMALS TO HELP THEM UNDERSTAND THAT.
AND WE HAVE TO ANESTHETIZE LARGER BEASTS...
もぐ MUNCH
もぐ MUNCH

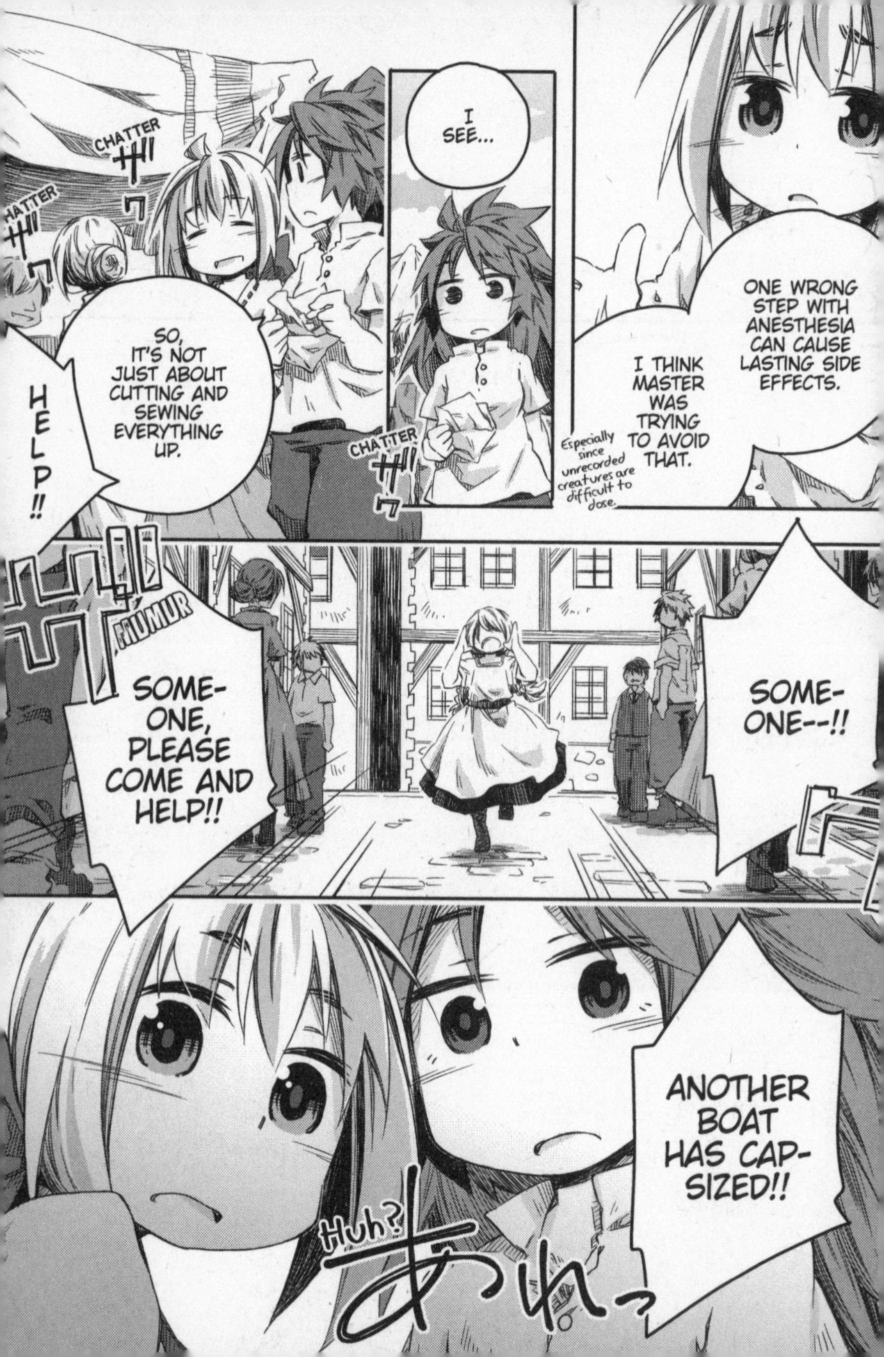

ONE WRONG STEP WITH ANESTHESIA CAN CAUSE LASTING SIDE EFFECTS.
I THINK MASTER WAS TRYING TO AVOID THAT.
Especially since unrecorded creatures are difficult to dose.
I SEE...
CHATTER
CHATTER
CHATTER
SO, IT'S NOT JUST ABOUT CUTTING AND SEWING EVERYTHING UP.
HELP!!
SOME-ONE--!!
MUMUR
SOME-ONE, PLEASE COME AND HELP!!
ANOTHER BOAT HAS CAP-SIZED!!
Huh?

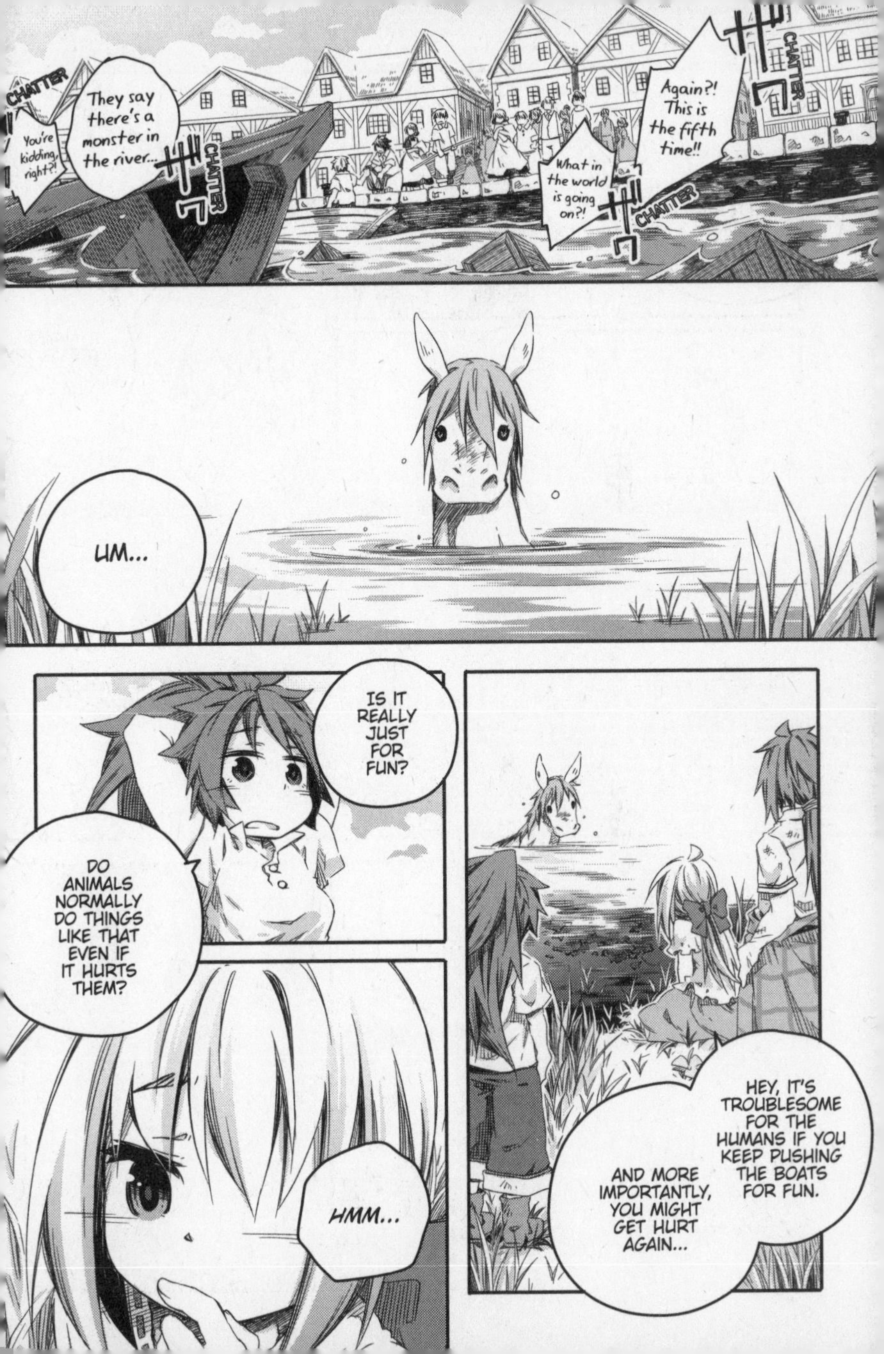
CHATTER
Again?! This is the fifth time!!
What in the world is going on?!
CHATTER
They say there's a monster in the river...
CHATTER
You're kidding, right?!
CHATTER
UM...
HEY, IT'S TROUBLESOME FOR THE HUMANS IF YOU KEEP PUSHING THE BOATS FOR FUN.
AND MORE IMPORTANTLY, YOU MIGHT GET HURT AGAIN...
IS IT REALLY JUST FOR FUN?
DO ANIMALS NORMALLY DO THINGS LIKE THAT EVEN IF IT HURTS THEM?
HMM...

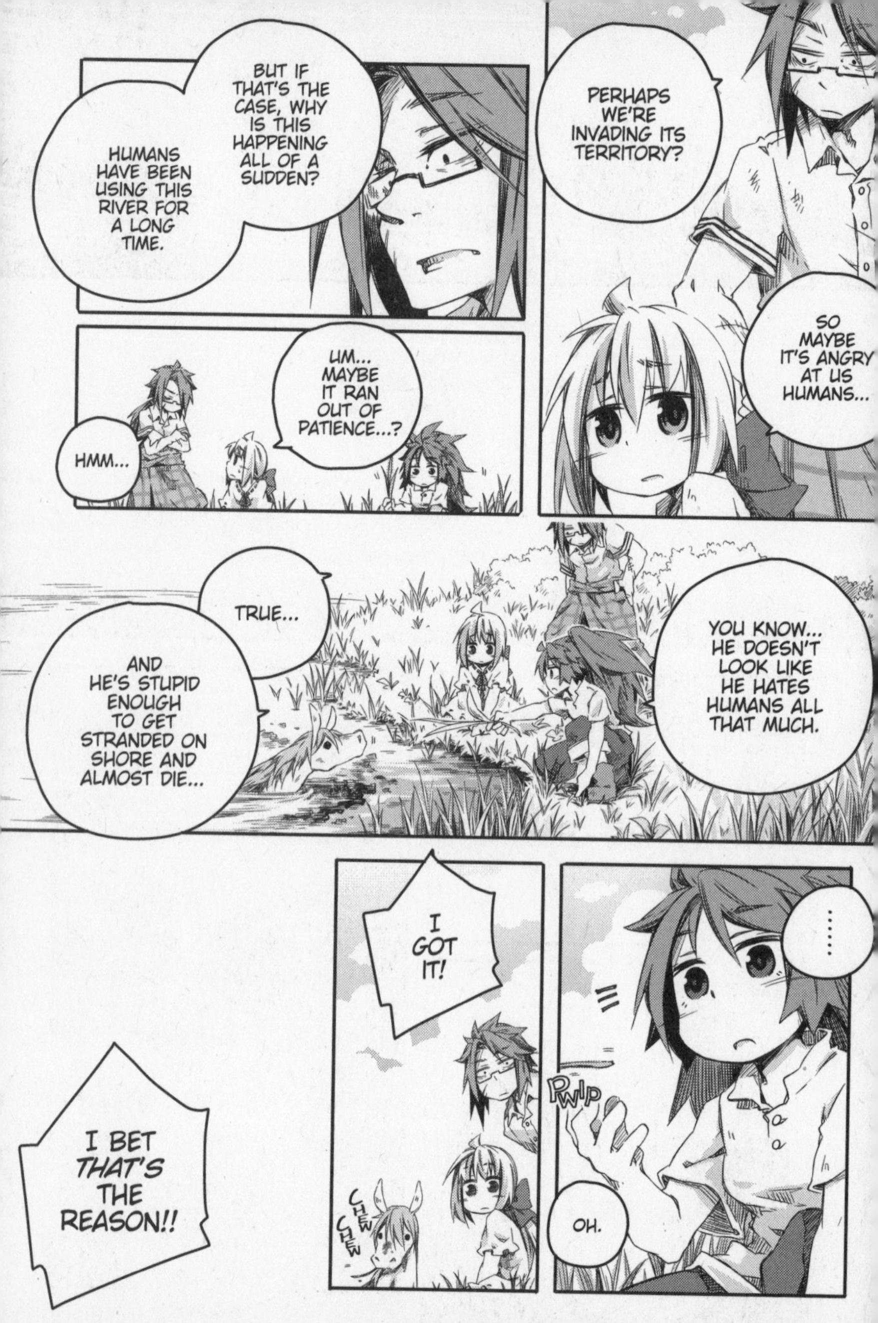
PERHAPS WE'RE INVADING ITS TERRITORY?
SO MAYBE IT'S ANGRY AT US HUMANS...
BUT IF THAT'S THE CASE, WHY IS THIS HAPPENING ALL OF A SUDDEN?
HUMANS HAVE BEEN USING THIS RIVER FOR A LONG TIME.
UM... MAYBE IT RAN OUT OF PATIENCE...?
HMM...
YOU KNOW... HE DOESN'T LOOK LIKE HE HATES HUMANS ALL THAT MUCH.
TRUE...
AND HE'S STUPID ENOUGH TO GET STRANDED ON SHORE AND ALMOST DIE...
......
PWIP
OH.
I GOT IT!
CHEW CHEW
I BET *THAT'S* THE REASON!!

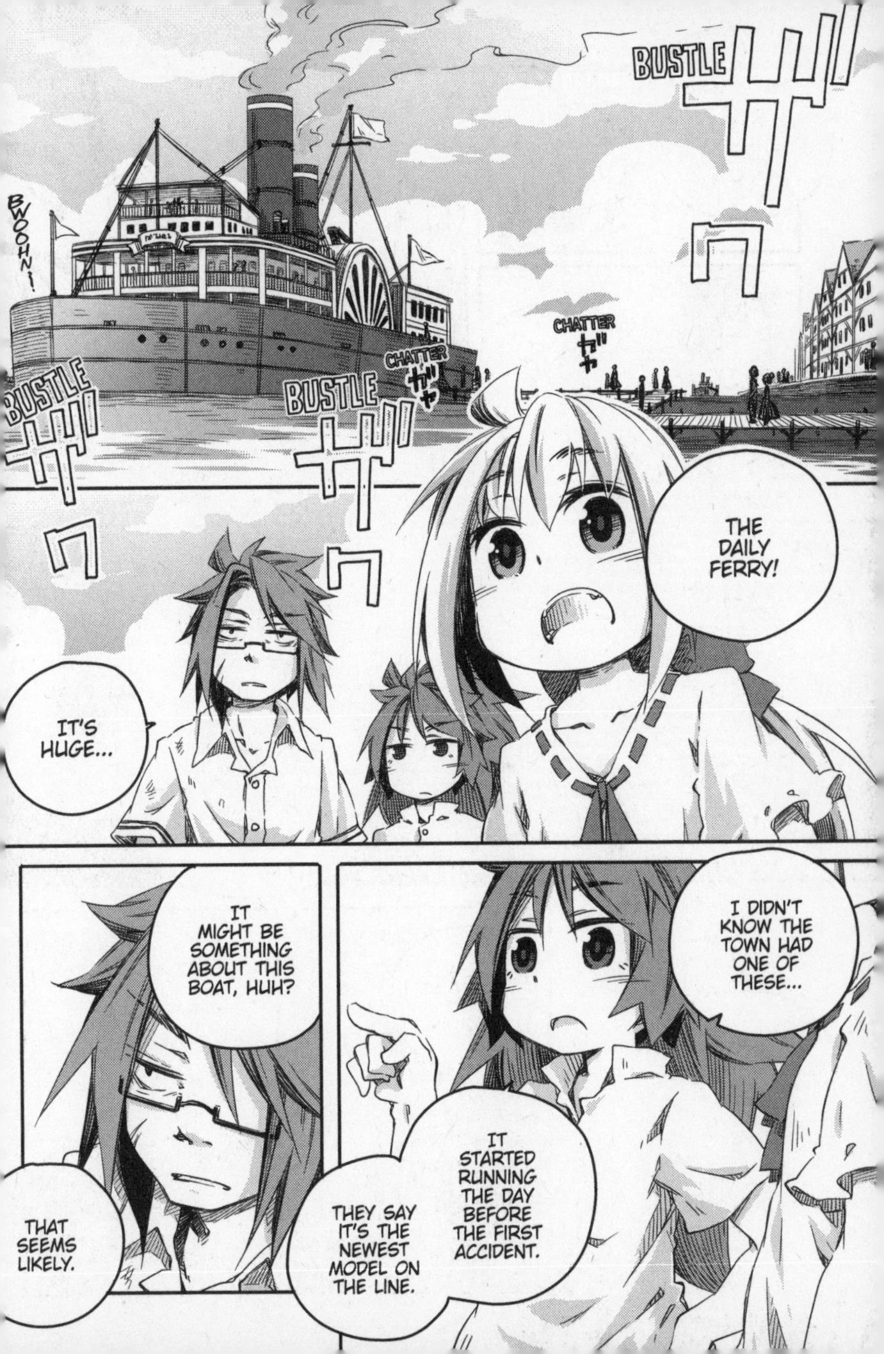
BUSTLE
CHATTER
CHATTER
BUSTLE
BWOOOHN!
BUSTLE
THE DAILY FERRY!
IT'S HUGE...
I DIDN'T KNOW THE TOWN HAD ONE OF THESE...
IT STARTED RUNNING THE DAY BEFORE THE FIRST ACCIDENT.
THEY SAY IT'S THE NEWEST MODEL ON THE LINE.
IT MIGHT BE SOMETHING ABOUT THIS BOAT, HUH?
THAT SEEMS LIKELY.

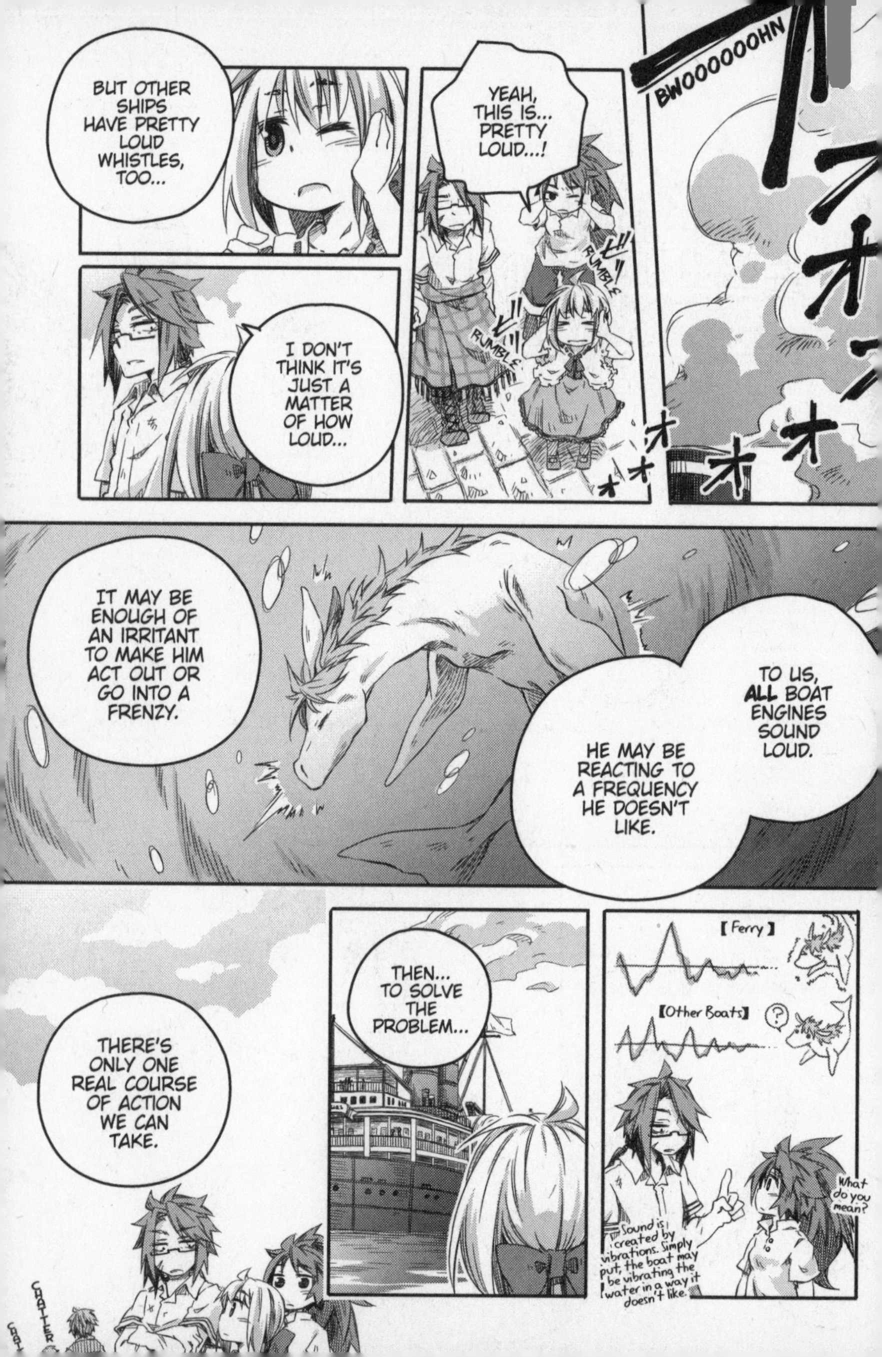
BWOOOOOOHN
YEAH, THIS IS... PRETTY LOUD...!
RUMBLE
RUMBLE
BUT OTHER SHIPS HAVE PRETTY LOUD WHISTLES, TOO...
I DON'T THINK IT'S JUST A MATTER OF HOW LOUD...
TO US, **ALL** BOAT ENGINES SOUND LOUD.
HE MAY BE REACTING TO A FREQUENCY HE DOESN'T LIKE.
IT MAY BE ENOUGH OF AN IRRITANT TO MAKE HIM ACT OUT OR GO INTO A FRENZY.
【Ferry】
【Other Boats】
What do you mean?
Sound is created by vibrations. Simply put, the boat may be vibrating the water in a way it doesn't like.
THEN... TO SOLVE THE PROBLEM...
THERE'S ONLY ONE REAL COURSE OF ACTION WE CAN TAKE.
CHAPTER

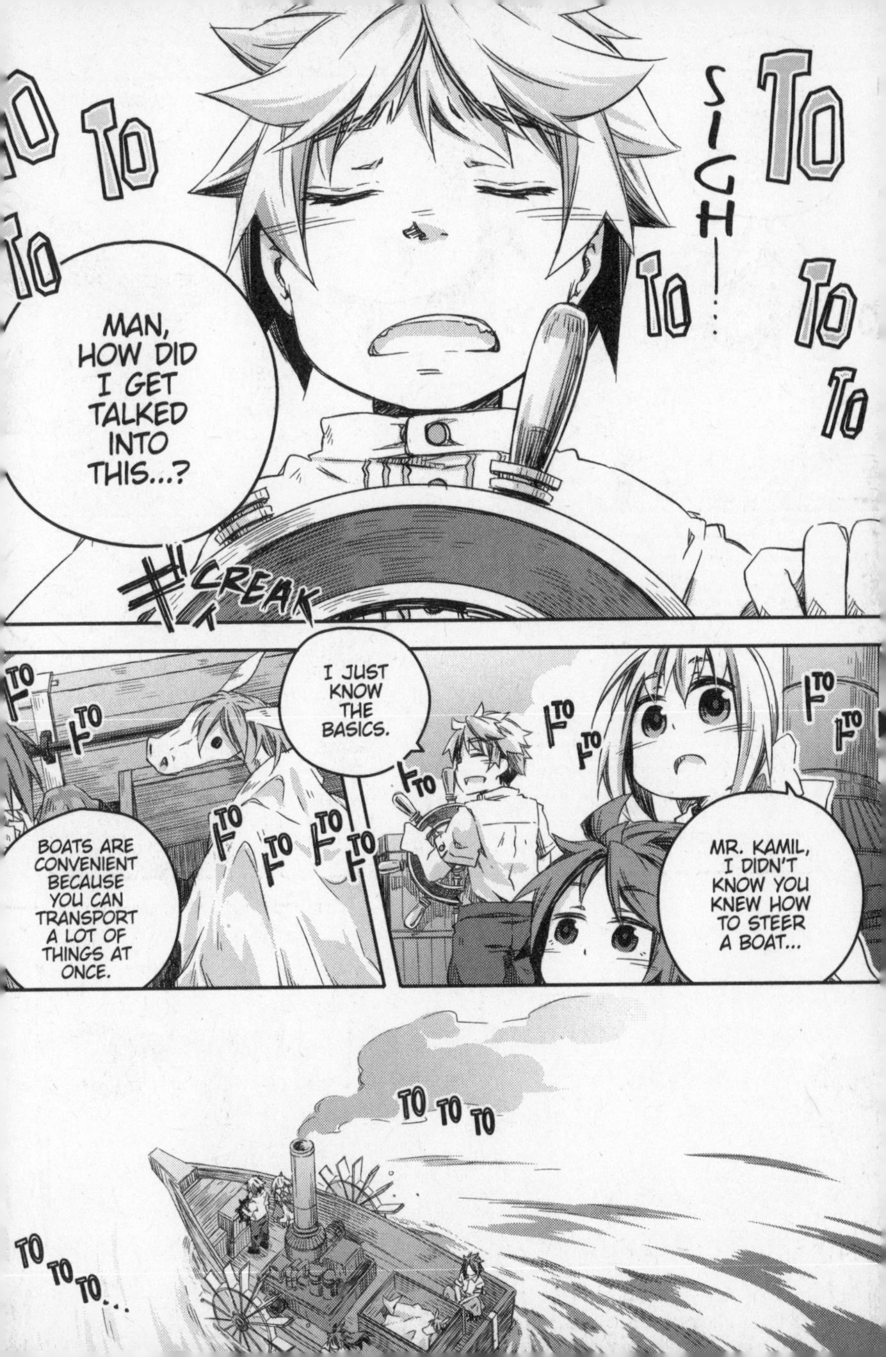
TO
SIGH...
TO TO TO
TO TO TO
MAN, HOW DID I GET TALKED INTO THIS...?
CREAK
トTO トTO トTO
MR. KAMIL, I DIDN'T KNOW YOU KNEW HOW TO STEER A BOAT...
I JUST KNOW THE BASICS.
トTO トTO トTO
トTO トTO
BOATS ARE CONVENIENT BECAUSE YOU CAN TRANSPORT A LOT OF THINGS AT ONCE.
TO TO TO
TO TO TO...

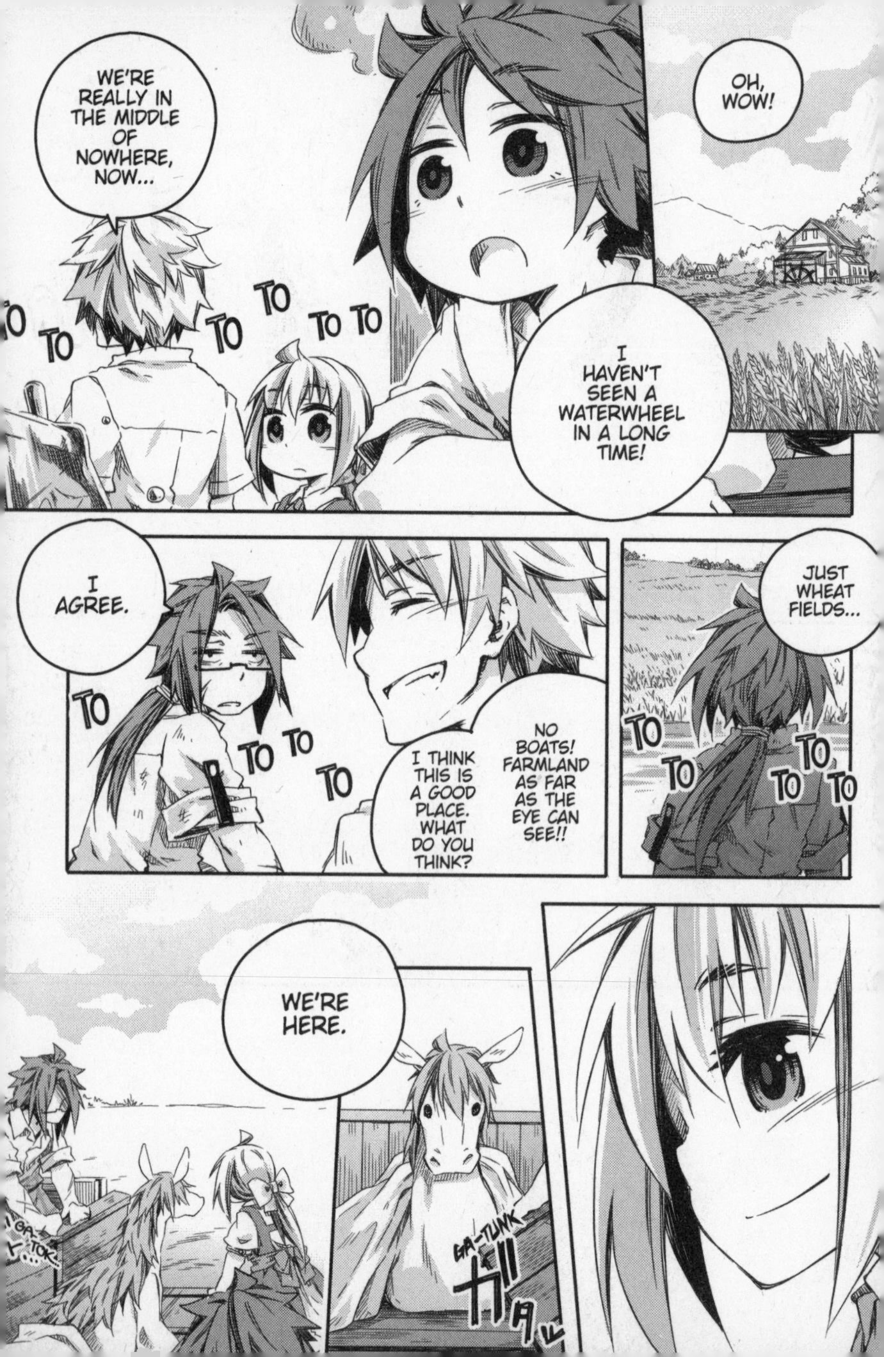
OH, WOW!
I HAVEN'T SEEN A WATERWHEEL IN A LONG TIME!
WE'RE REALLY IN THE MIDDLE OF NOWHERE, NOW...
TO TO TO TO TO
JUST WHEAT FIELDS...
TO TO TO TO TO
NO BOATS! FARMLAND AS FAR AS THE EYE CAN SEE!!
I THINK THIS IS A GOOD PLACE. WHAT DO YOU THINK?
I AGREE.
TO TO TO TO
WE'RE HERE.
GA-TUNK
GA-TOK...

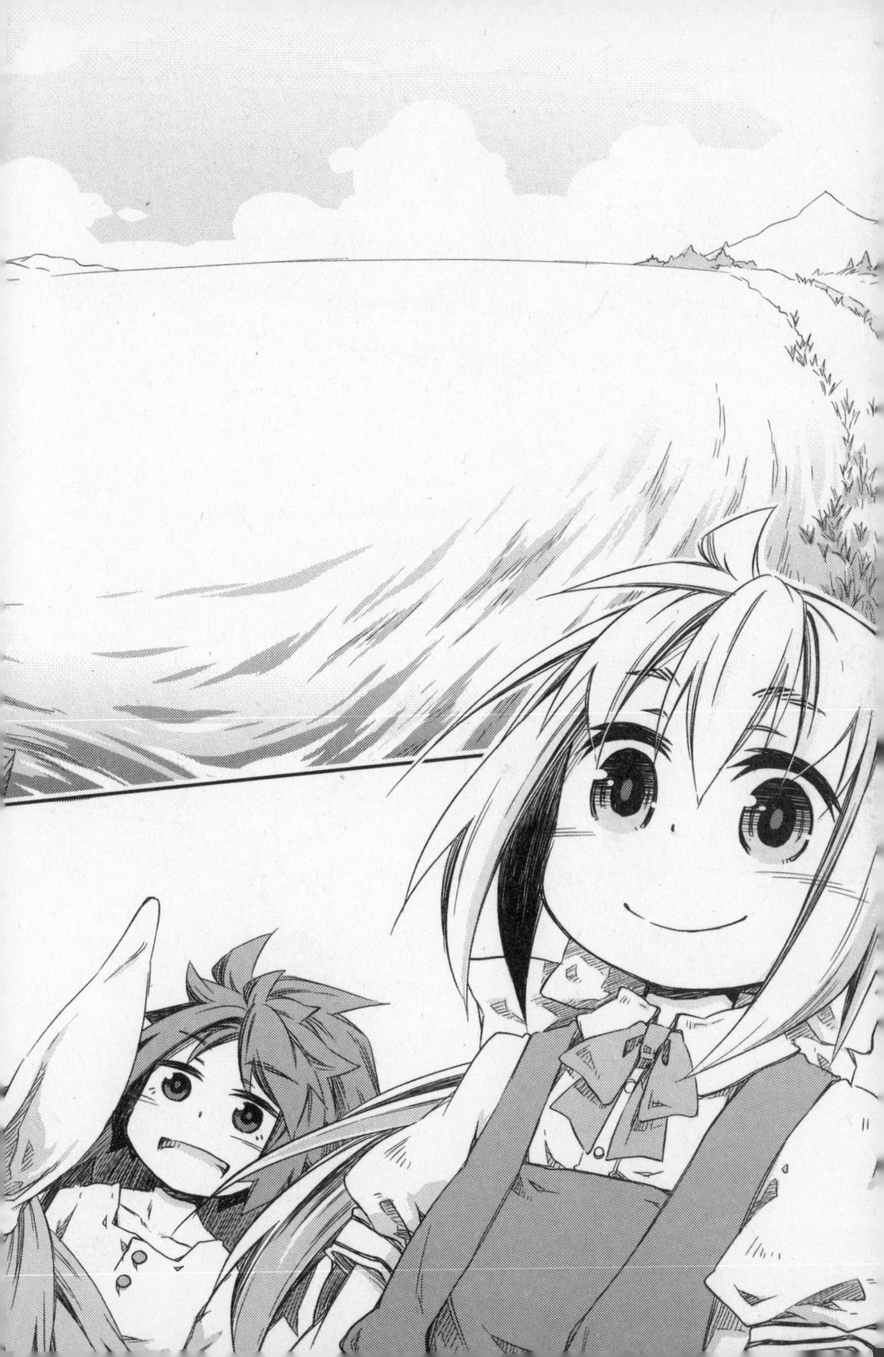

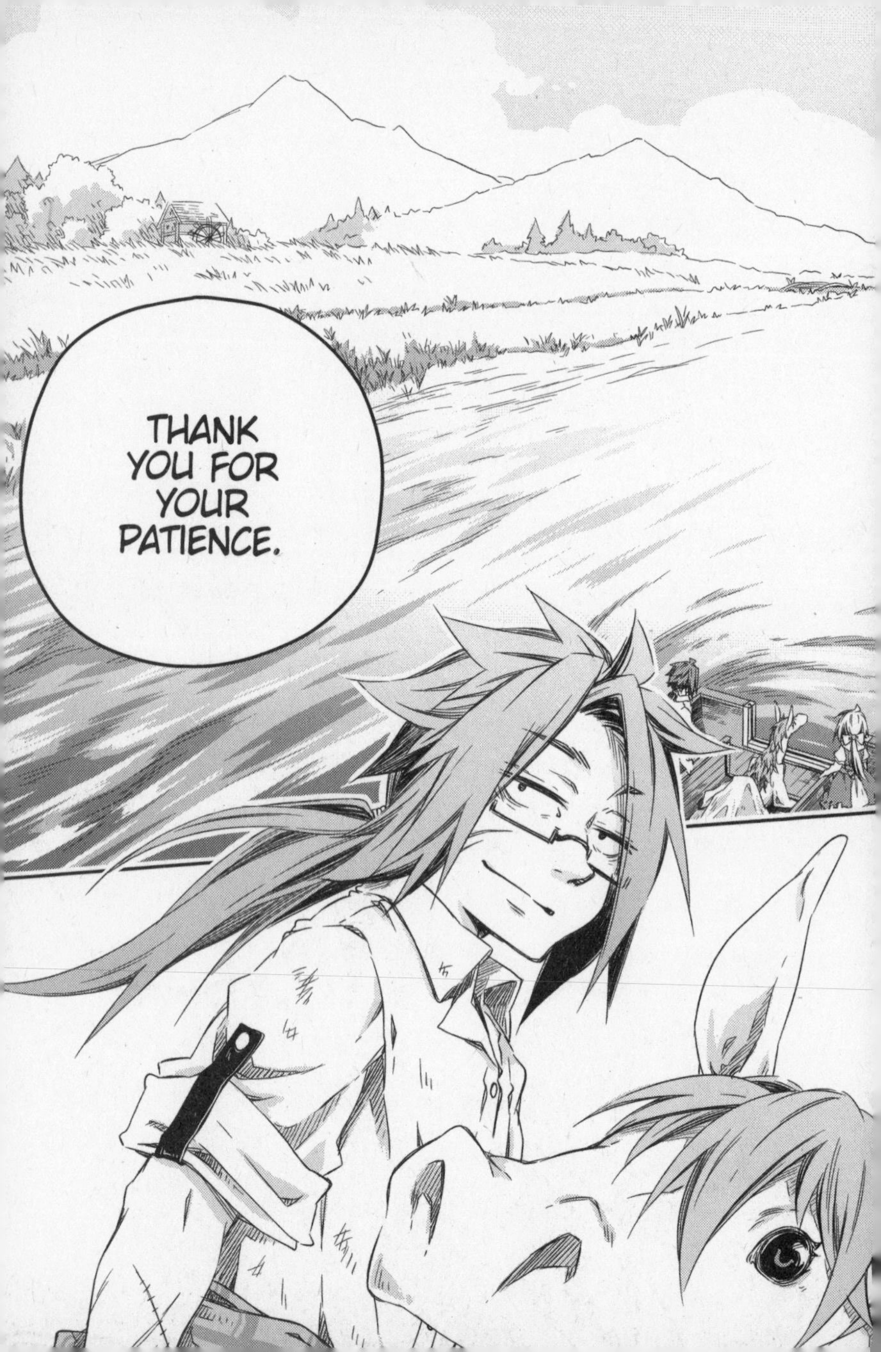
THANK YOU FOR YOUR PATIENCE.

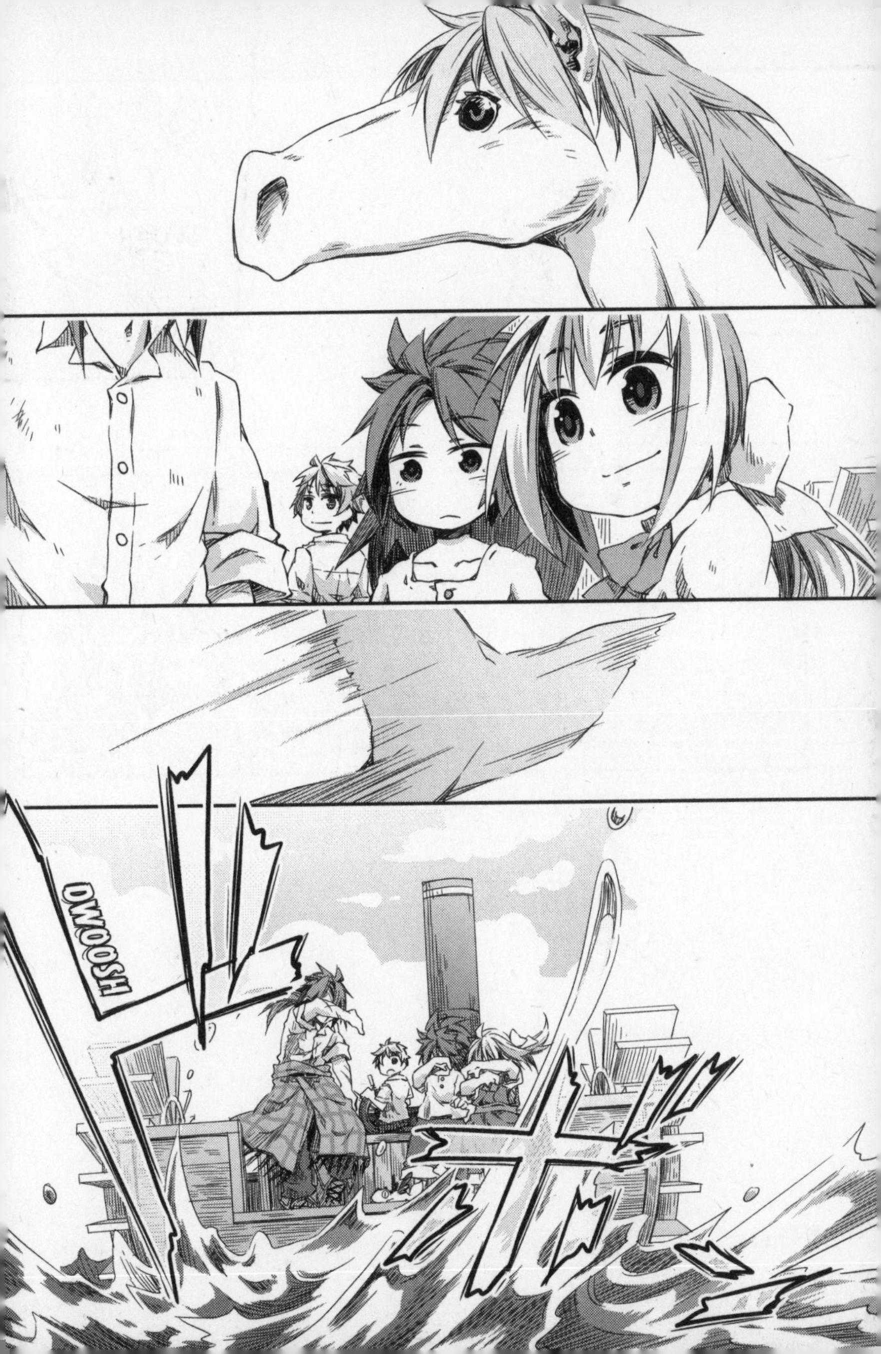
DWOOSH!

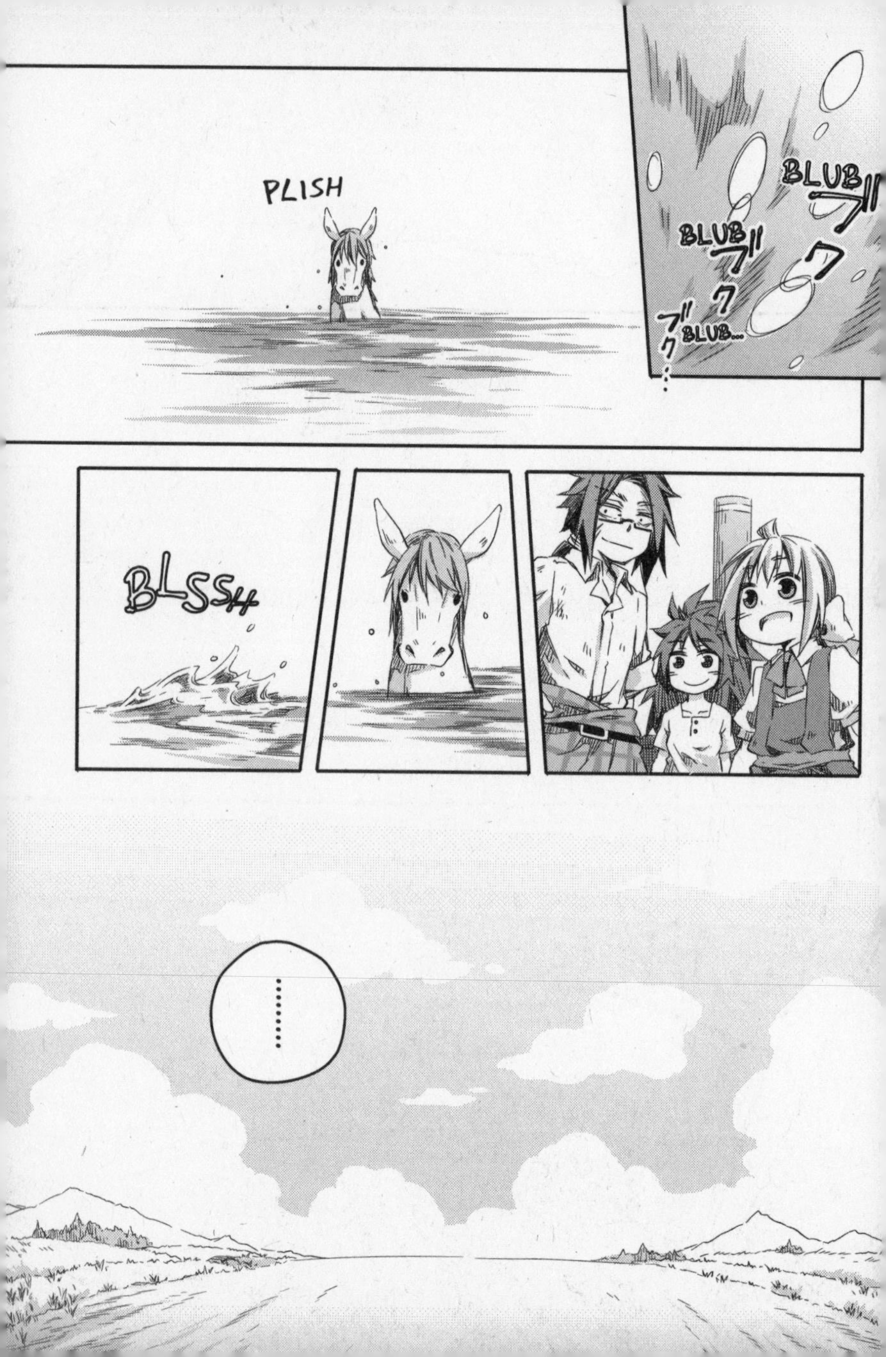
BLUB
ブク
BLUB
ブク
ブク…
BLUB...
PLISH
BLSSH
……

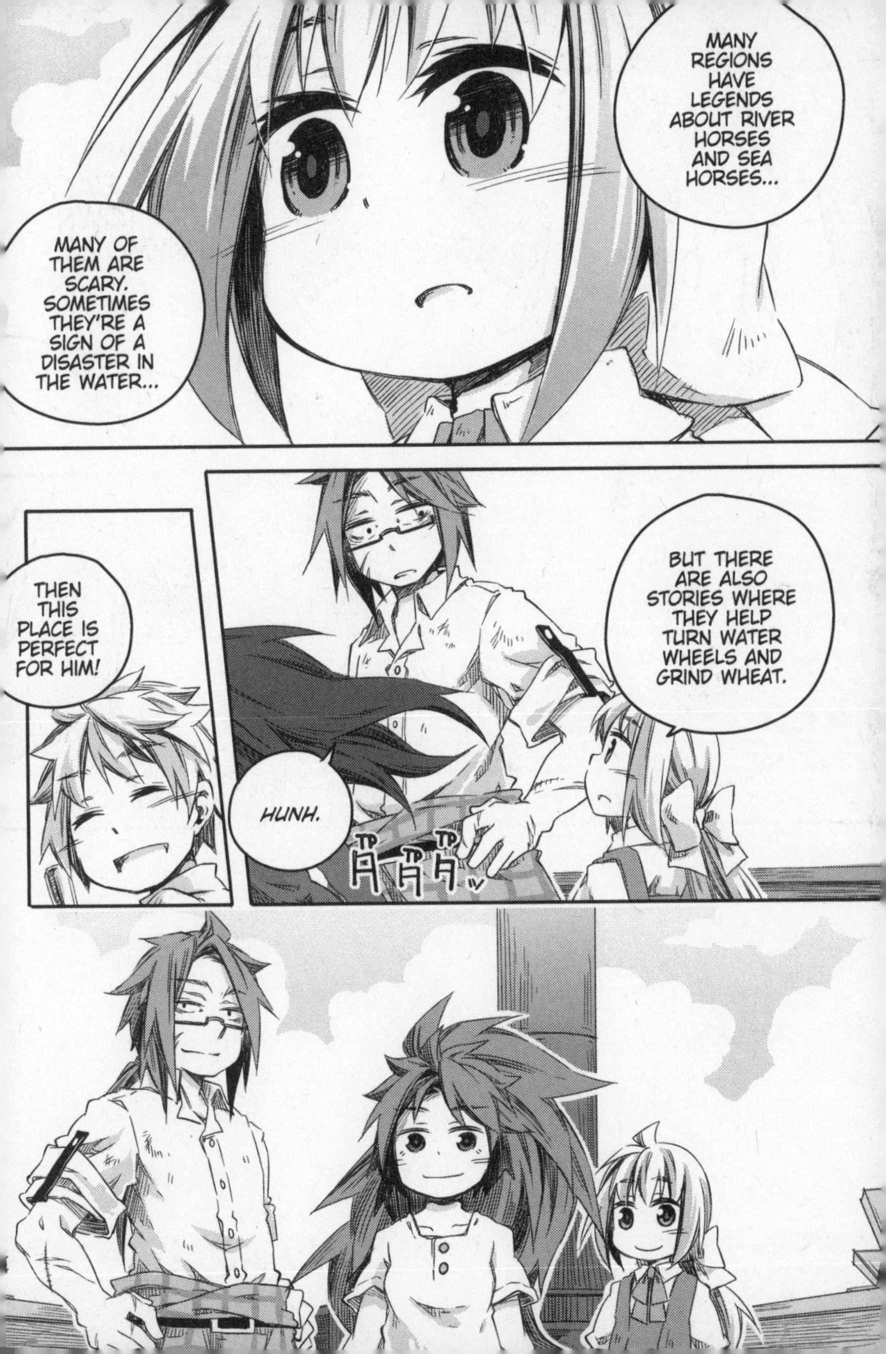
MANY REGIONS HAVE LEGENDS ABOUT RIVER HORSES AND SEA HORSES...
MANY OF THEM ARE SCARY. SOMETIMES THEY'RE A SIGN OF A DISASTER IN THE WATER...
BUT THERE ARE ALSO STORIES WHERE THEY HELP TURN WATER WHEELS AND GRIND WHEAT.
HUNH.
TP TP TP
THEN THIS PLACE IS PERFECT FOR HIM!

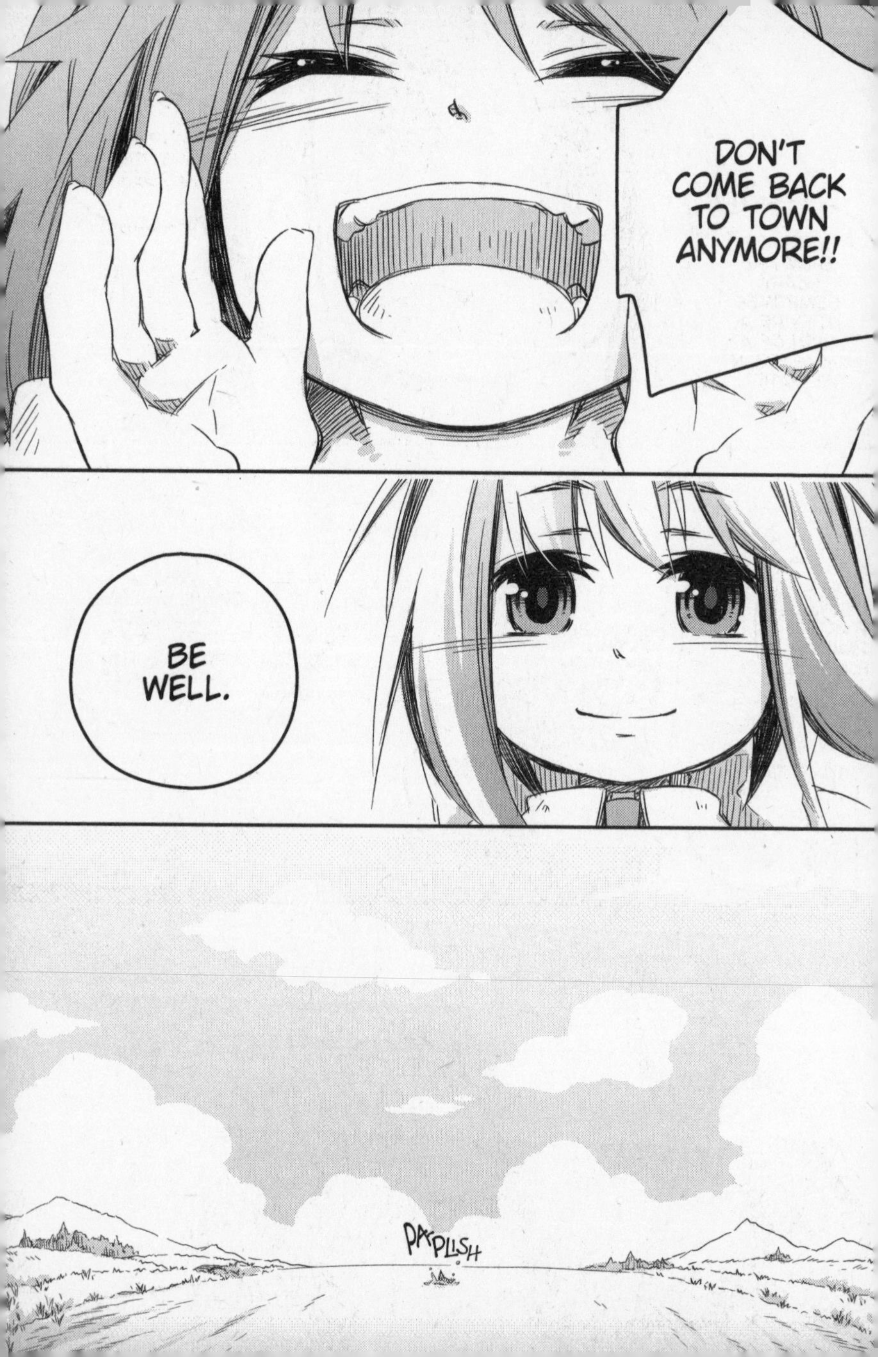
DON'T COME BACK TO TOWN ANYMORE!!
BE WELL.
PAPLISH

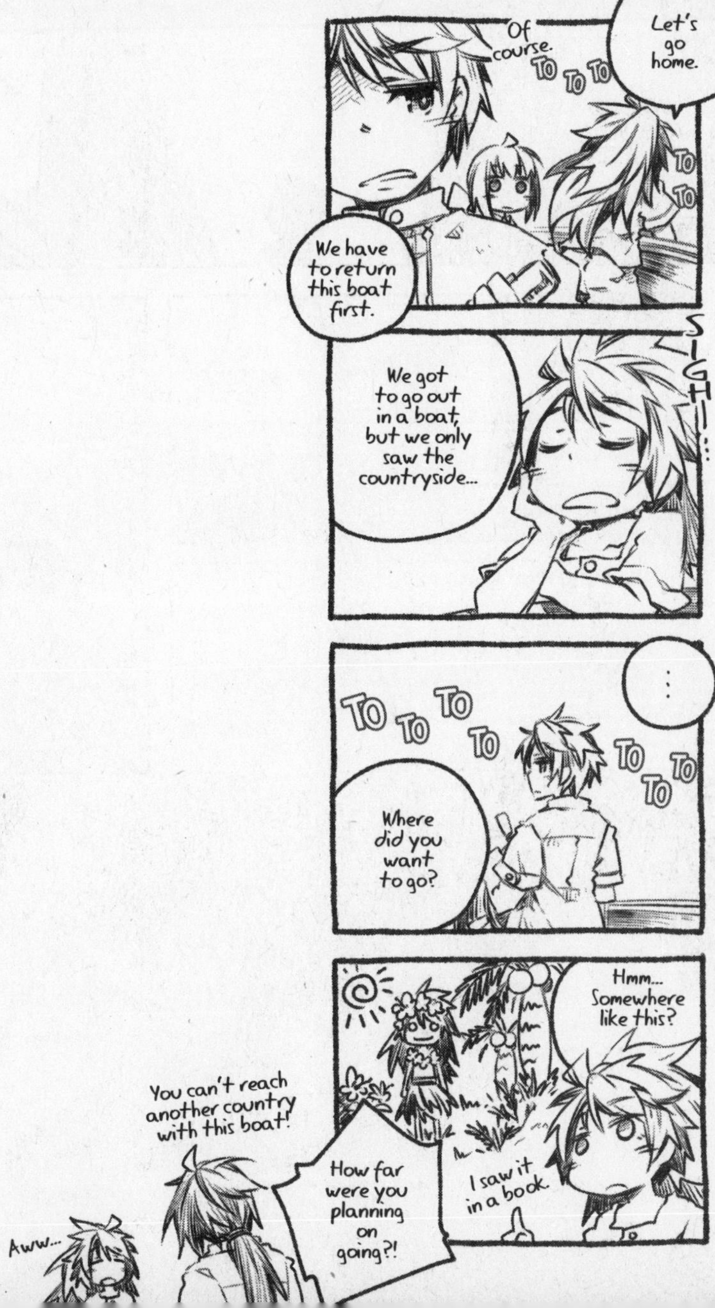
Let's go home.
Of course.
TO TO TO
TO TO
We have to return this boat first.
SIGH...
We got to go out in a boat, but we only saw the countryside...
...
TO TO TO TO TO TO TO TO
Where did you want to go?
Hmm... Somewhere like this?
I saw it in a book.
How far were you planning on going?!
You can't reach another country with this boat!
Aww...

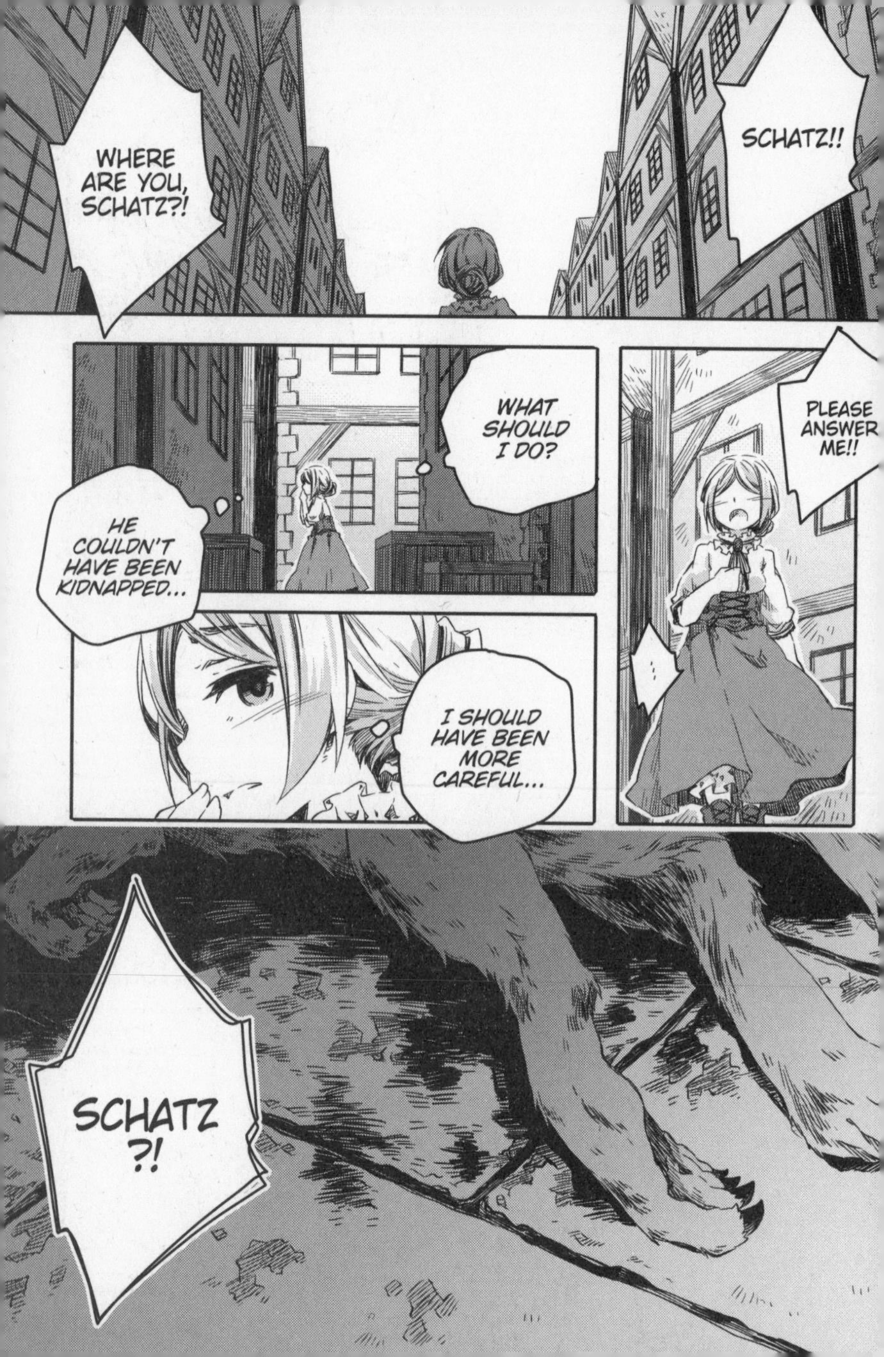
SCHATZ!!
WHERE ARE YOU, SCHATZ?!
PLEASE ANSWER ME!!
...
WHAT SHOULD I DO?
HE COULDN'T HAVE BEEN KIDNAPPED...
I SHOULD HAVE BEEN MORE CAREFUL...
SCHATZ ?!

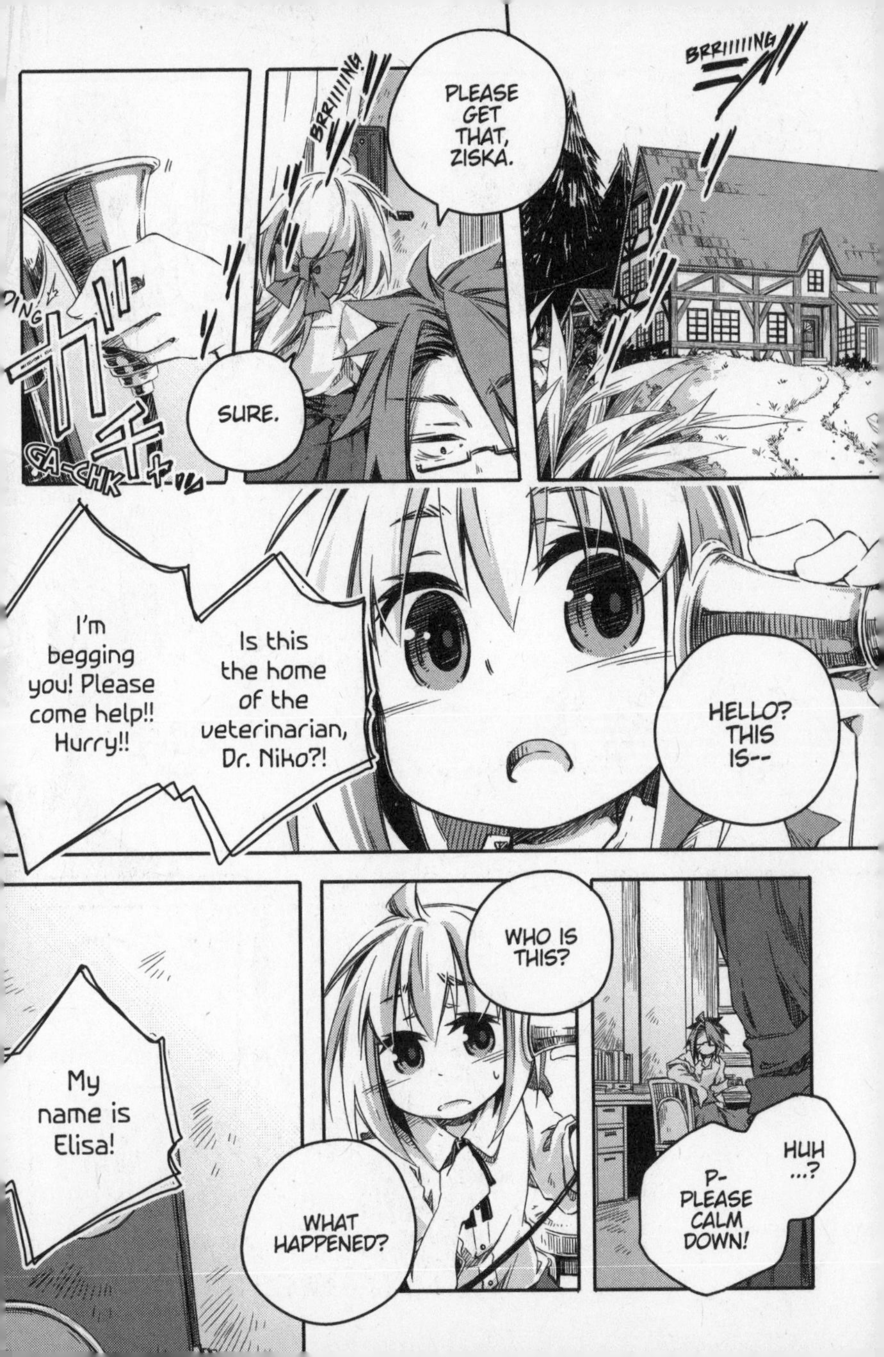
BRRIIIIING
PLEASE GET THAT, ZISKA.
BRRIIIIING
SURE.
DING
GA-CHK
HELLO? THIS IS--
Is this the home of the veterinarian, Dr. Niko?!
I'm begging you! Please come help!! Hurry!!
HUH ...?
P- PLEASE CALM DOWN!
WHO IS THIS?
WHAT HAPPENED?
My name is Elisa!

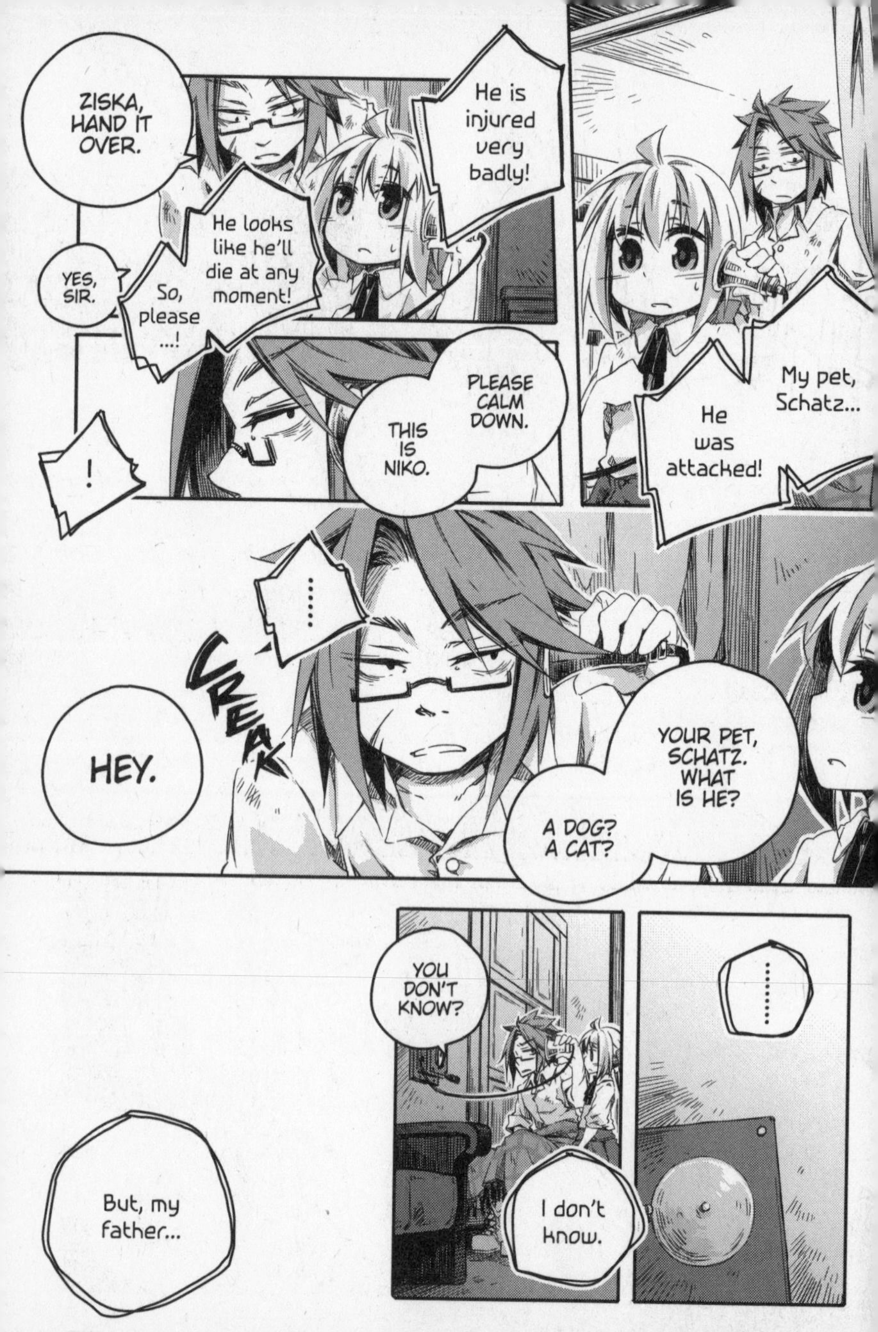
My pet, Schatz...
He was attacked!
He is injured very badly!
He looks like he'll die at any moment!
So, please ...!
ZISKA, HAND IT OVER.
YES, SIR.
PLEASE CALM DOWN.
THIS IS NIKO.
!
......
CREAK
HEY.
YOUR PET, SCHATZ. WHAT IS HE?
A DOG? A CAT?
....
I don't know.
YOU DON'T KNOW?
But, my father...

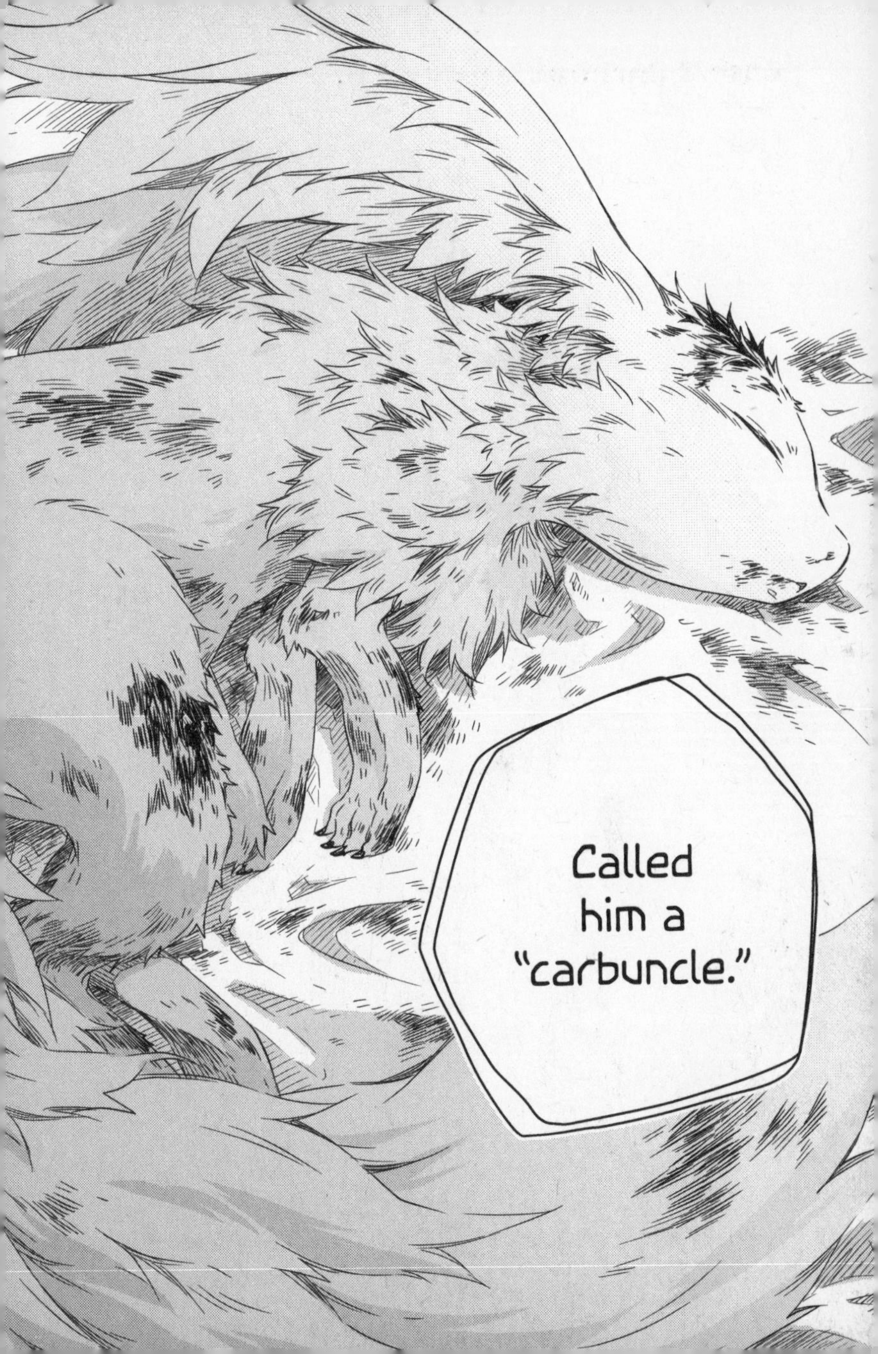
Called him a "carbuncle."

[Case 7: Carbuncle (Part 1)]

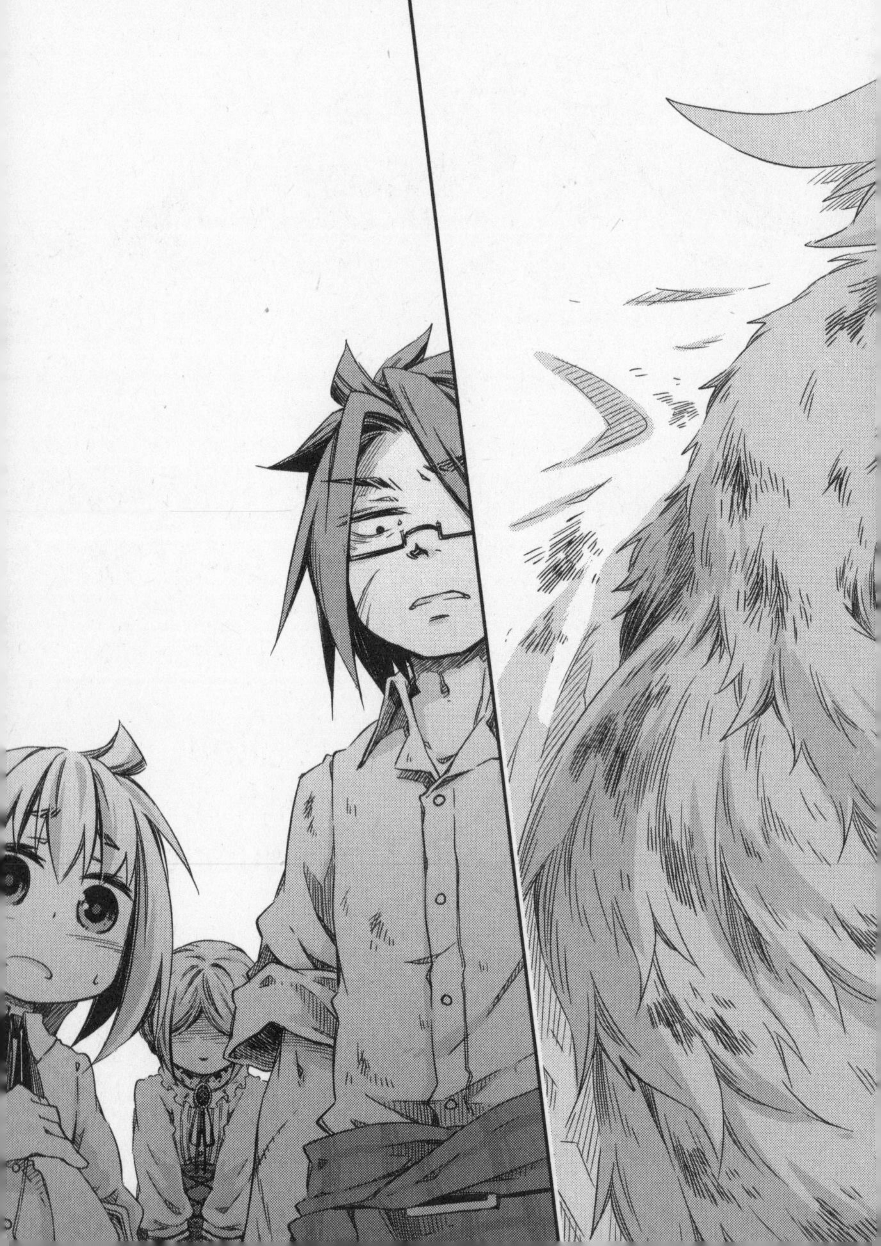

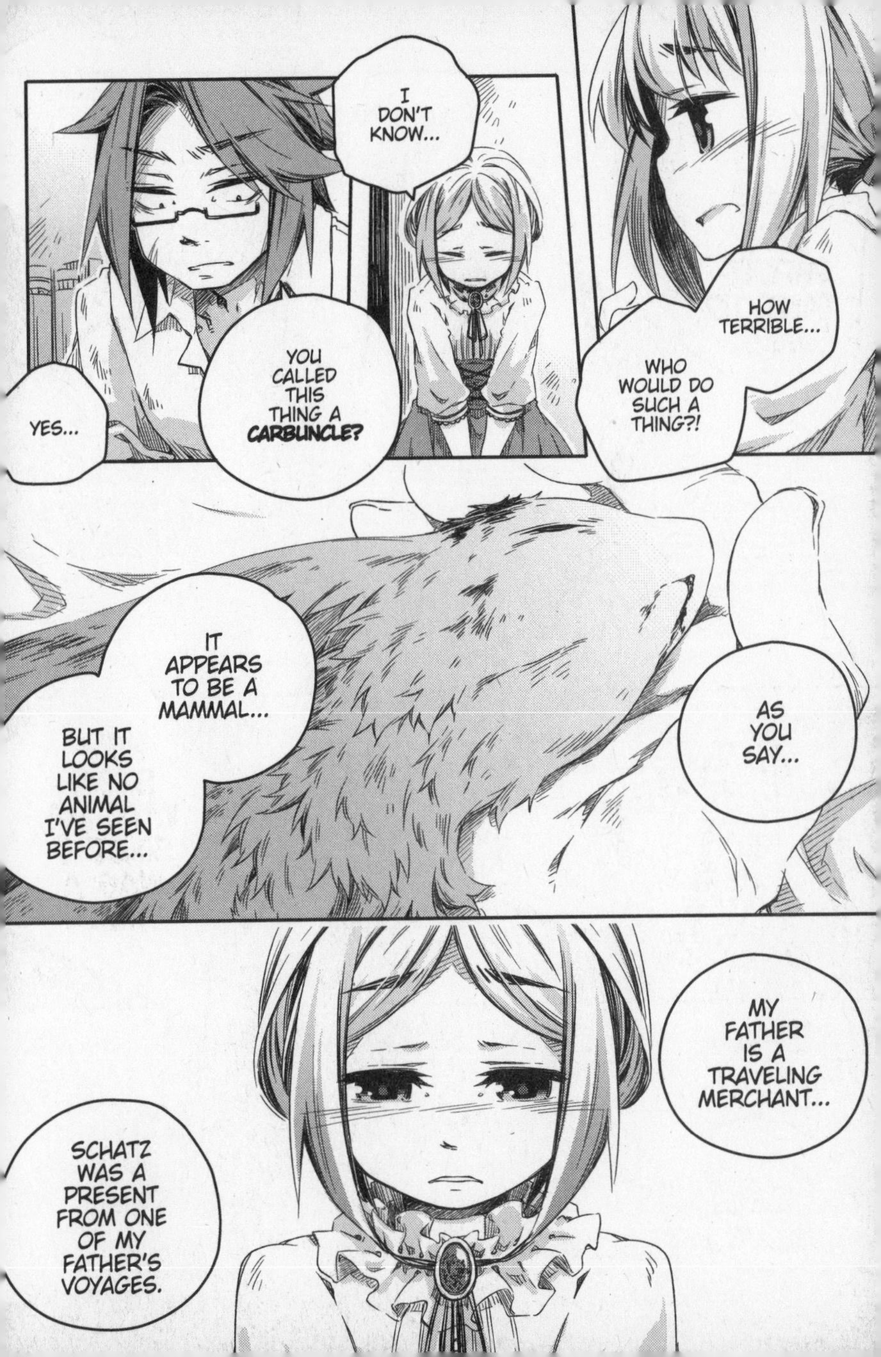
HOW TERRIBLE...
WHO WOULD DO SUCH A THING?!
I DON'T KNOW...
YOU CALLED THIS THING A **CARBUNCLE?**
YES...
AS YOU SAY...
IT APPEARS TO BE A MAMMAL...
BUT IT LOOKS LIKE NO ANIMAL I'VE SEEN BEFORE...
MY FATHER IS A TRAVELING MERCHANT...
SCHATZ WAS A PRESENT FROM ONE OF MY FATHER'S VOYAGES.

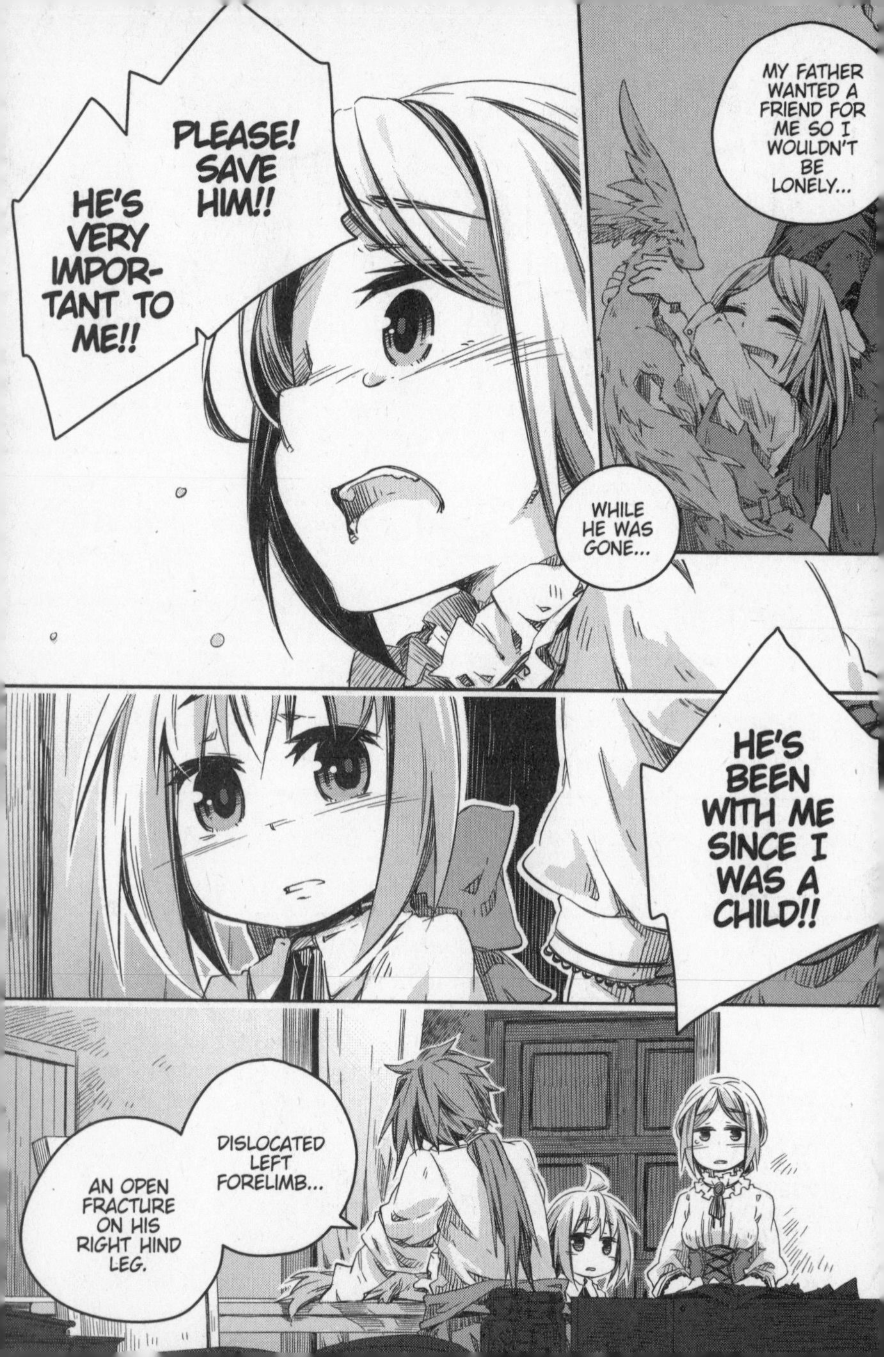
MY FATHER WANTED A FRIEND FOR ME SO I WOULDN'T BE LONELY...
WHILE HE WAS GONE...
PLEASE! SAVE HIM!!
HE'S VERY IMPOR-TANT TO ME!!
HE'S BEEN WITH ME SINCE I WAS A CHILD!!
DISLOCATED LEFT FORELIMB...
AN OPEN FRACTURE ON HIS RIGHT HIND LEG.

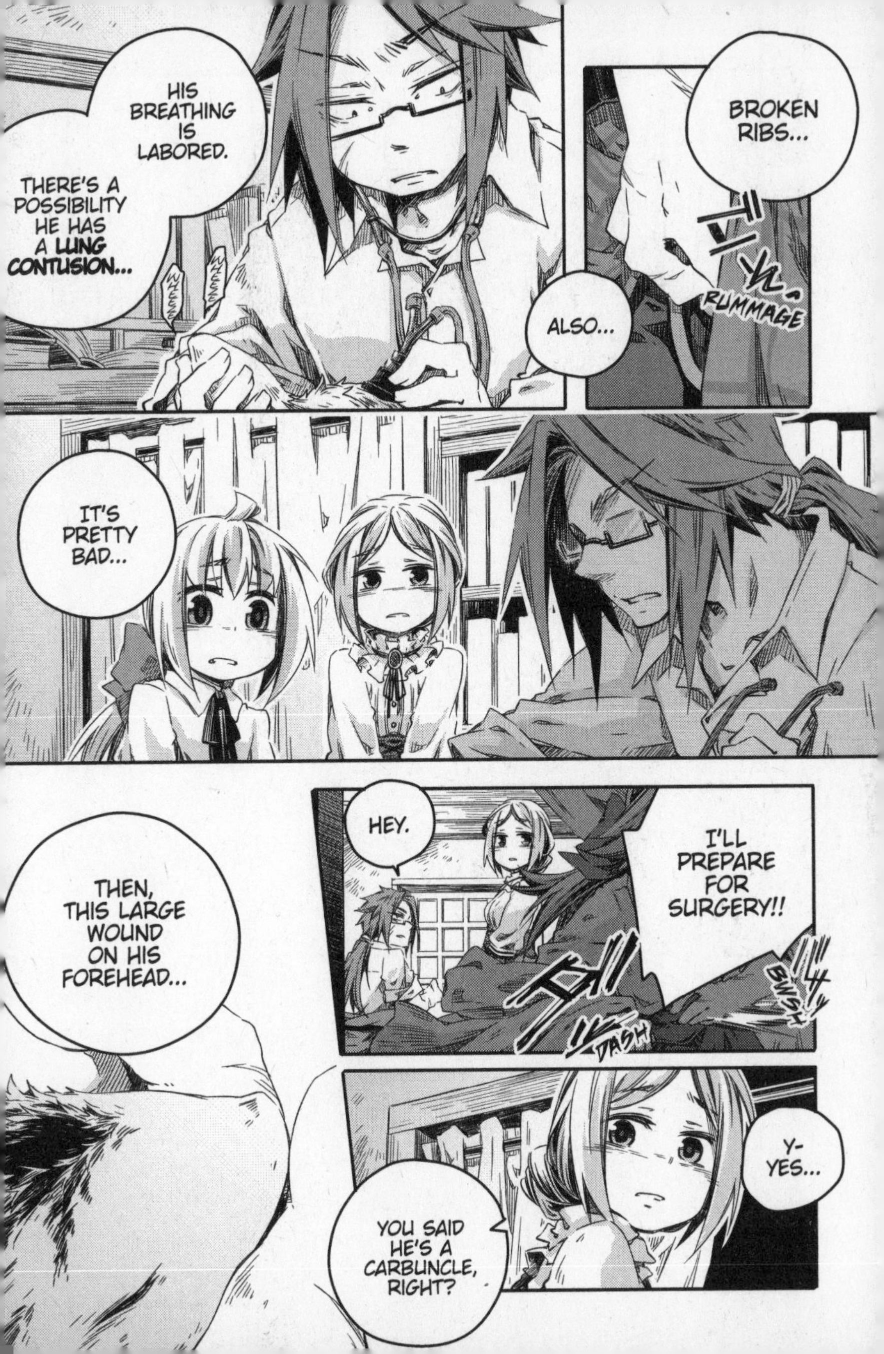

BROKEN RIBS...
RUMMAGE
ALSO...
HIS BREATHING IS LABORED.
THERE'S A POSSIBILITY HE HAS A **LUNG CONTUSION...**
WHEEZE
IT'S PRETTY BAD...
HEY.
I'LL PREPARE FOR SURGERY!!
BUSH
DASH
THEN, THIS LARGE WOUND ON HIS FOREHEAD...
Y-YES...
YOU SAID HE'S A CARBUNCLE, RIGHT?

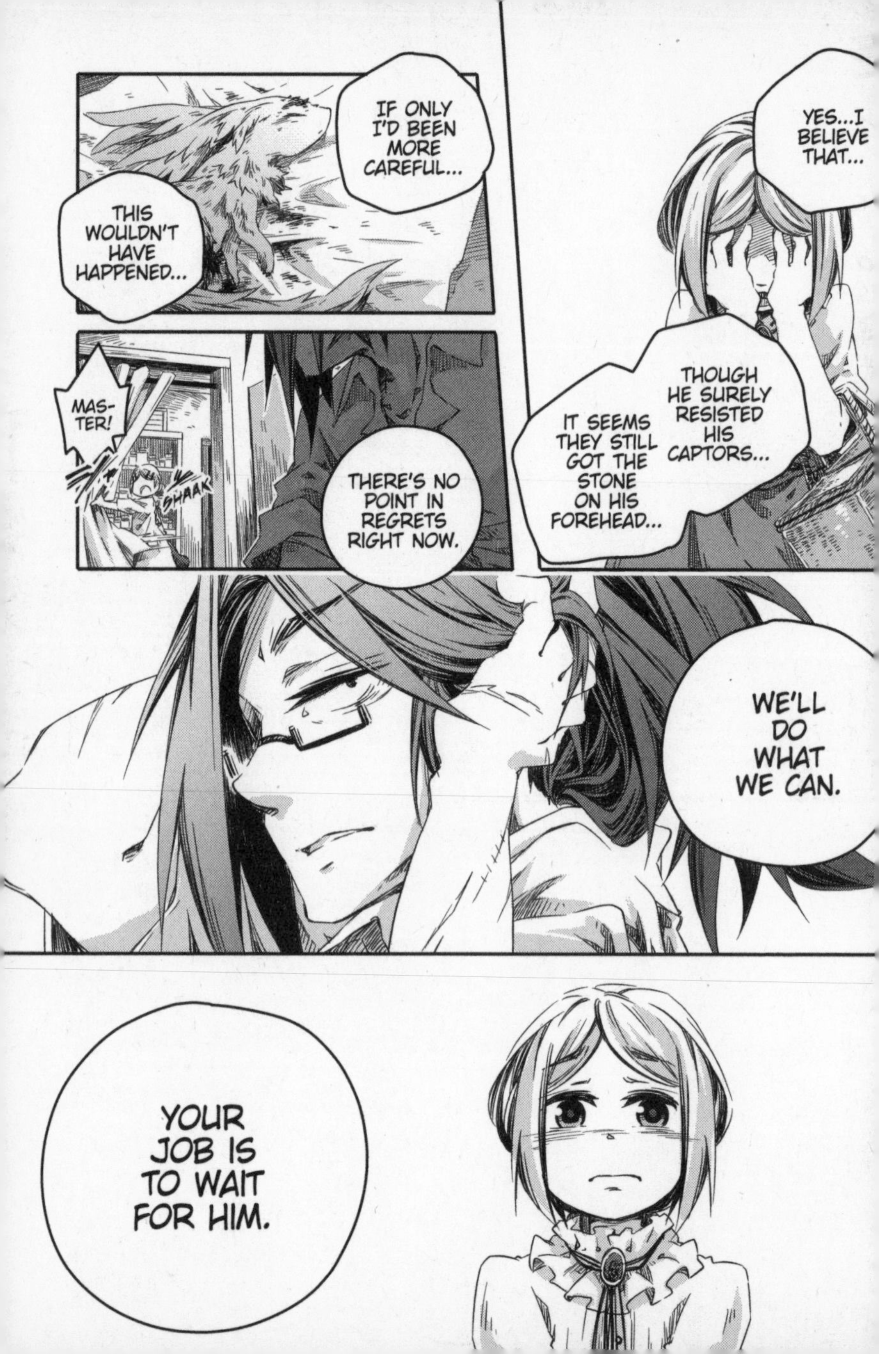
YES...I BELIEVE THAT...
THOUGH HE SURELY RESISTED HIS CAPTORS...
IT SEEMS THEY STILL GOT THE STONE ON HIS FOREHEAD...
IF ONLY I'D BEEN MORE CAREFUL...
THIS WOULDN'T HAVE HAPPENED...
THERE'S NO POINT IN REGRETS RIGHT NOW.
SHAAK
MAS-TER!
WE'LL DO WHAT WE CAN.
YOUR JOB IS TO WAIT FOR HIM.

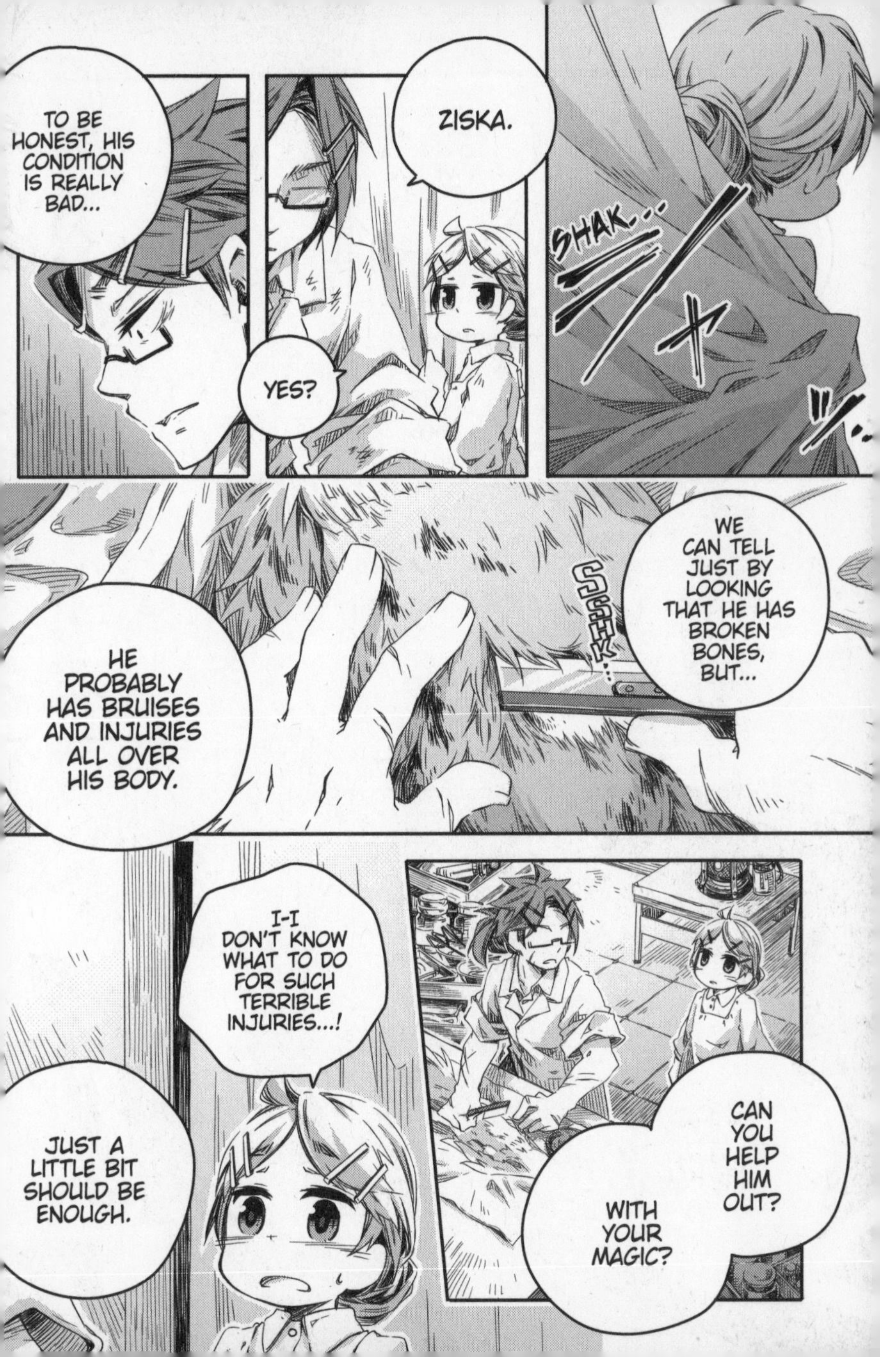
SHAK...
ZISKA.
YES?
TO BE HONEST, HIS CONDITION IS REALLY BAD...
WE CAN TELL JUST BY LOOKING THAT HE HAS BROKEN BONES, BUT...
SSHK...
HE PROBABLY HAS BRUISES AND INJURIES ALL OVER HIS BODY.
CAN YOU HELP HIM OUT?
WITH YOUR MAGIC?
I-I DON'T KNOW WHAT TO DO FOR SUCH TERRIBLE INJURIES...!
JUST A LITTLE BIT SHOULD BE ENOUGH.

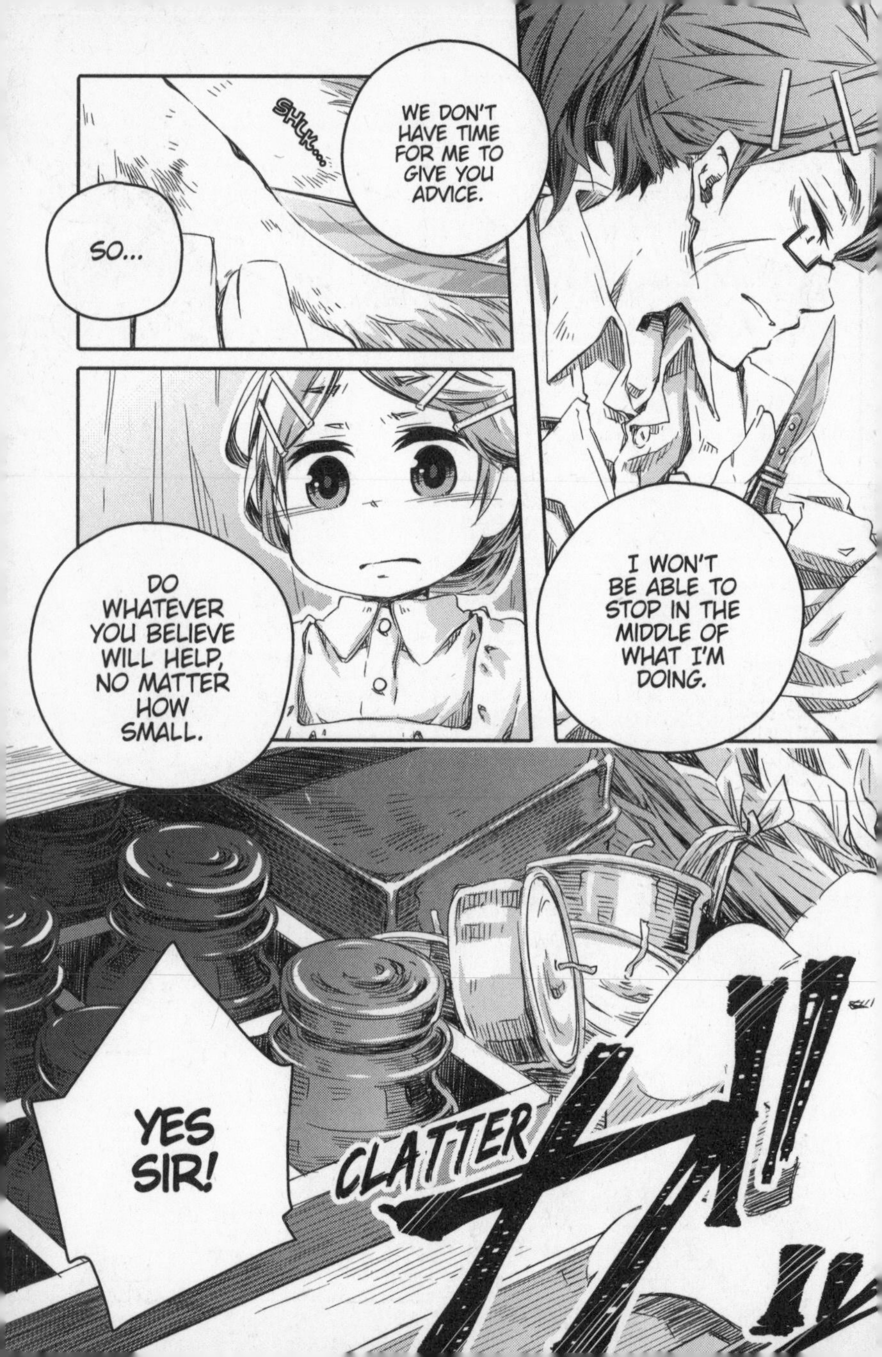
WE DON'T HAVE TIME FOR ME TO GIVE YOU ADVICE.
I WON'T BE ABLE TO STOP IN THE MIDDLE OF WHAT I'M DOING.
SHLK...
SO...
DO WHATEVER YOU BELIEVE WILL HELP, NO MATTER HOW SMALL.
CLATTER
YES SIR!

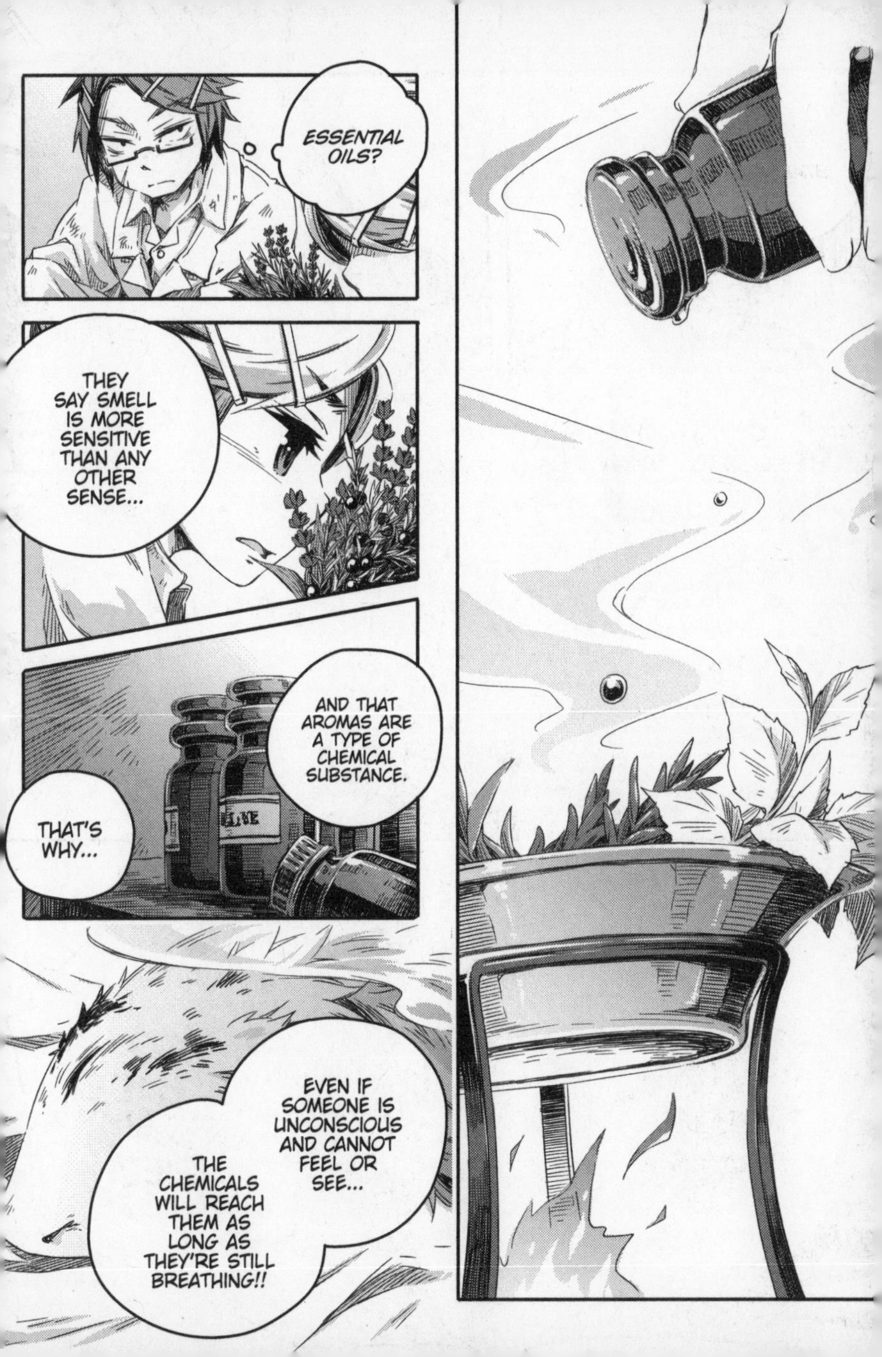
ESSENTIAL OILS?
THEY SAY SMELL IS MORE SENSITIVE THAN ANY OTHER SENSE...
AND THAT AROMAS ARE A TYPE OF CHEMICAL SUBSTANCE.
THAT'S WHY...
EVEN IF SOMEONE IS UNCONSCIOUS AND CANNOT FEEL OR SEE...
THE CHEMICALS WILL REACH THEM AS LONG AS THEY'RE STILL BREATHING!!

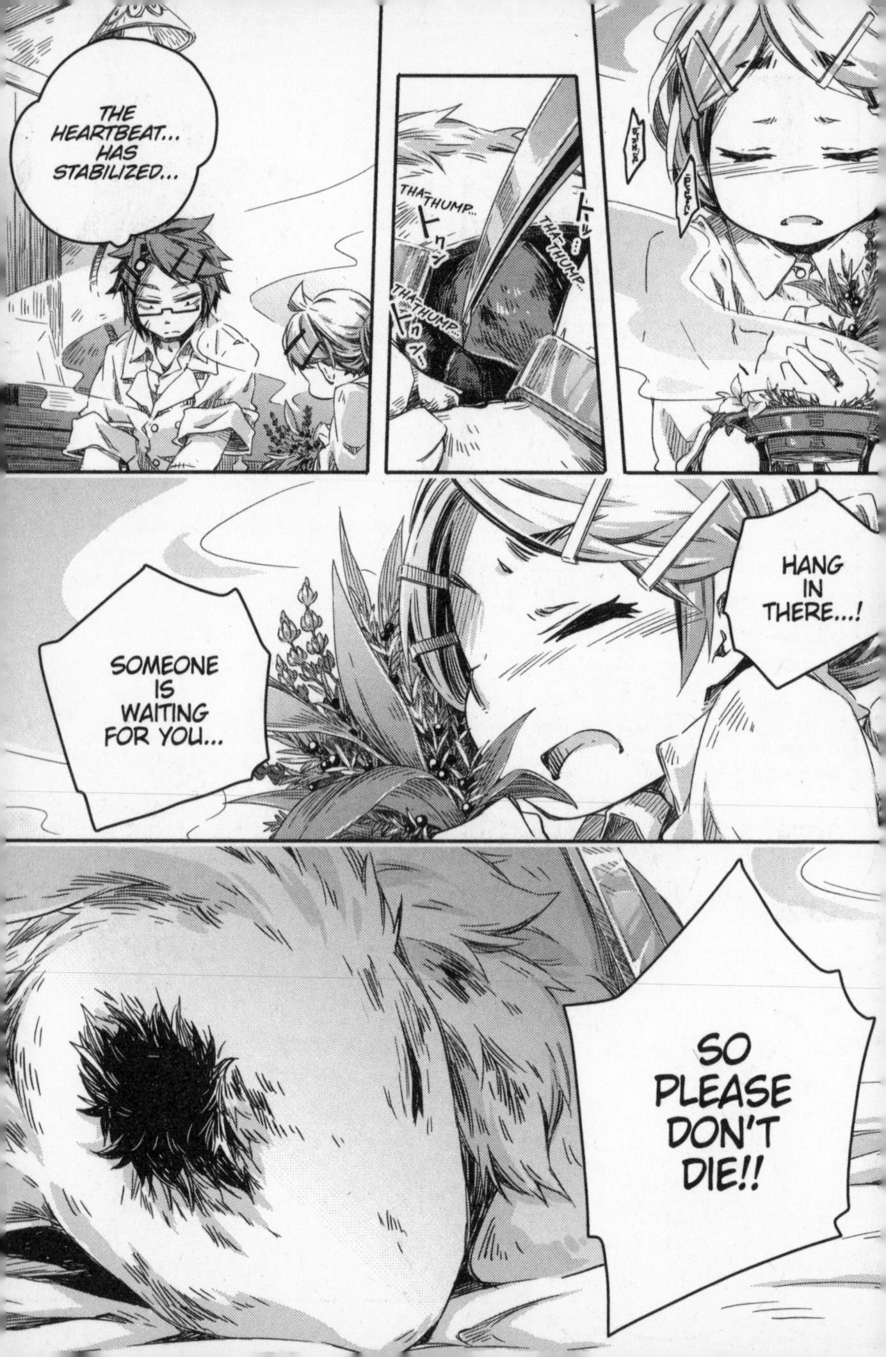

THA-THUMP...
THA-THUMP...
THA-THUMP...
THE HEARTBEAT... HAS STABILIZED...
HANG IN THERE...!
SOMEONE IS WAITING FOR YOU...
SO PLEASE DON'T DIE!!

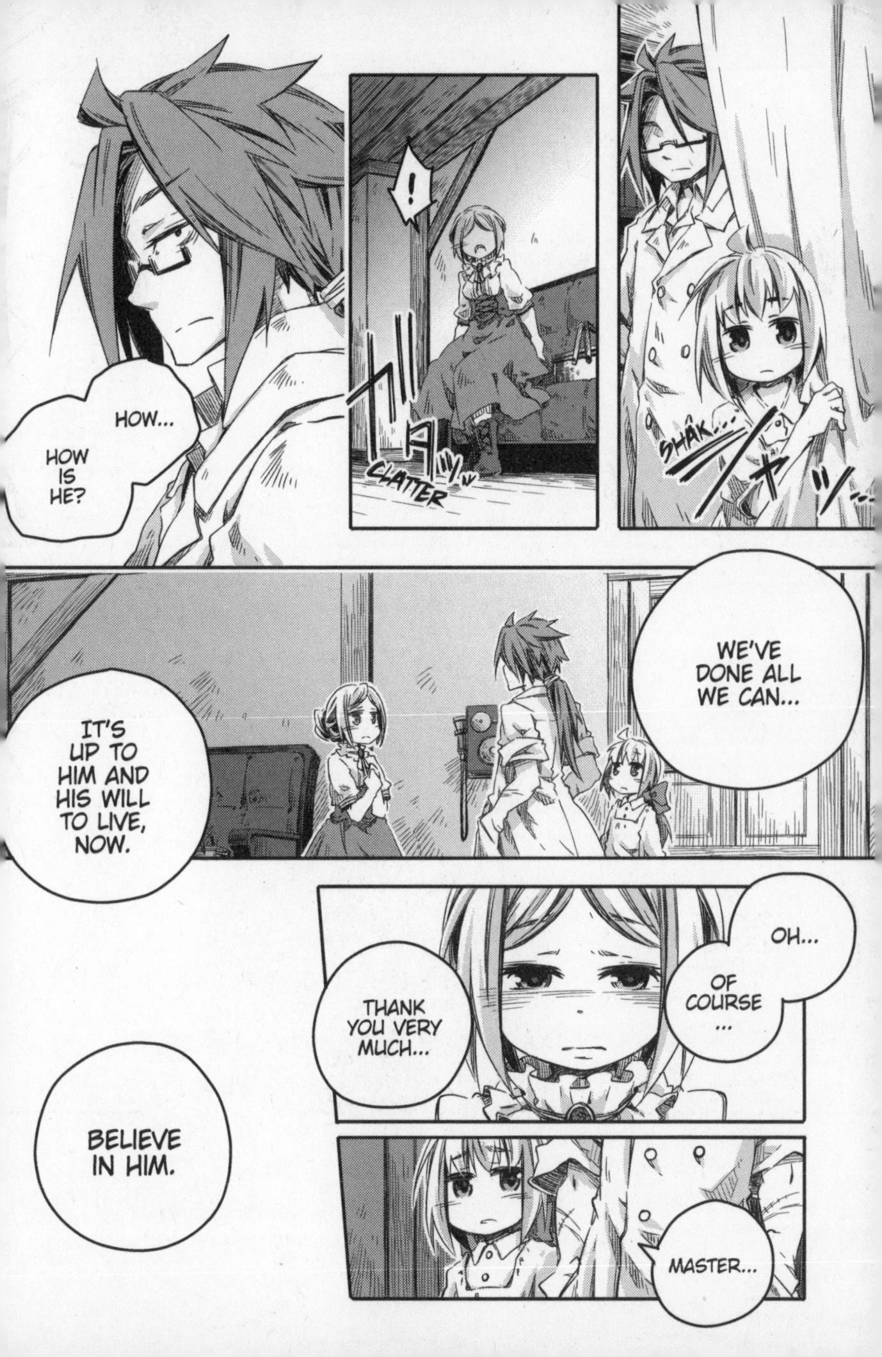
SHAK...
!
CLATTER
HOW...
HOW IS HE?
WE'VE DONE ALL WE CAN...
IT'S UP TO HIM AND HIS WILL TO LIVE, NOW.
OH...
OF COURSE...
THANK YOU VERY MUCH...
MASTER...
BELIEVE IN HIM.

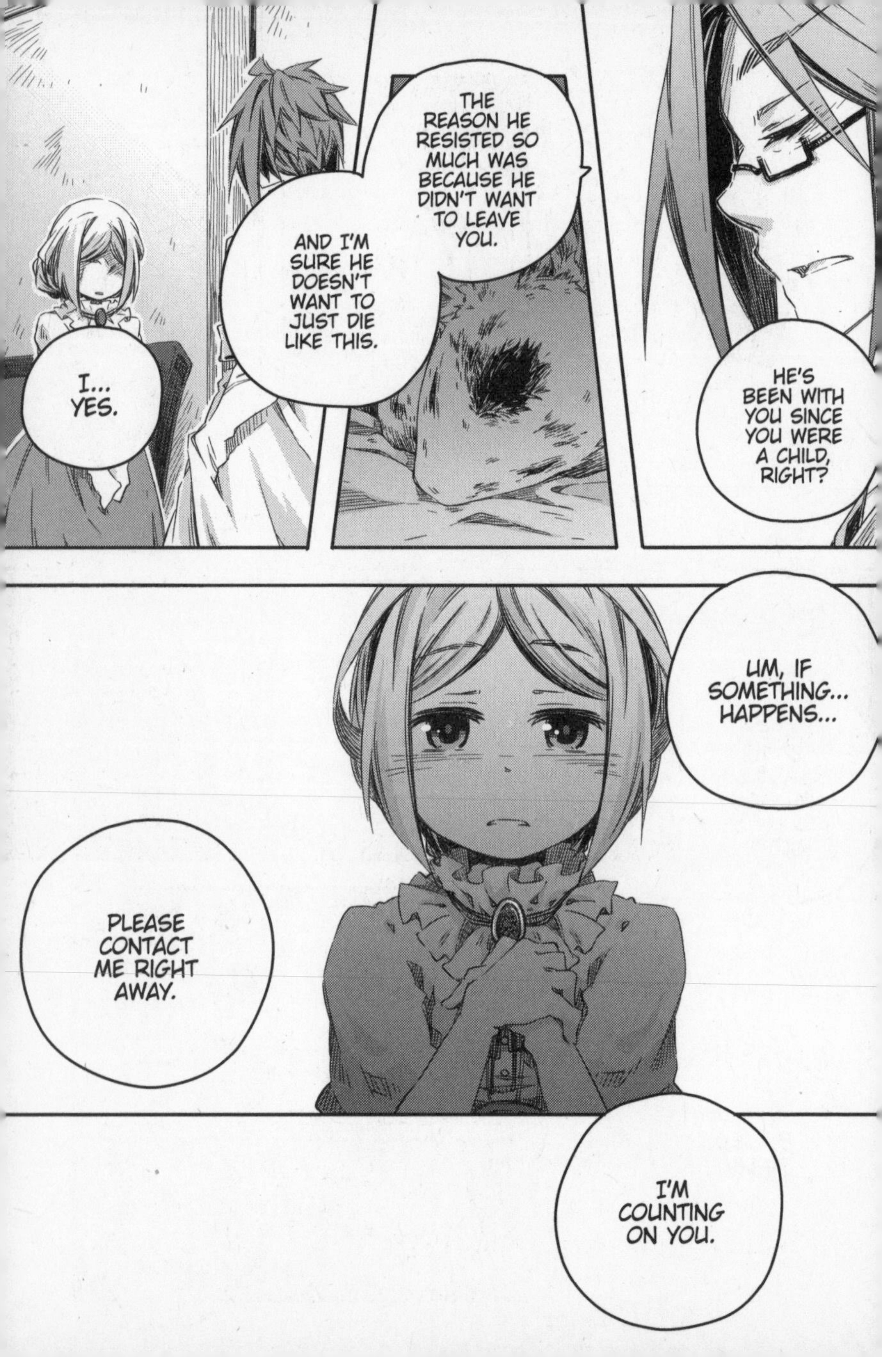
HE'S BEEN WITH YOU SINCE YOU WERE A CHILD, RIGHT?
THE REASON HE RESISTED SO MUCH WAS BECAUSE HE DIDN'T WANT TO LEAVE YOU.
AND I'M SURE HE DOESN'T WANT TO JUST DIE LIKE THIS.
I... YES.
UM, IF SOMETHING... HAPPENS...
PLEASE CONTACT ME RIGHT AWAY.
I'M COUNTING ON YOU.

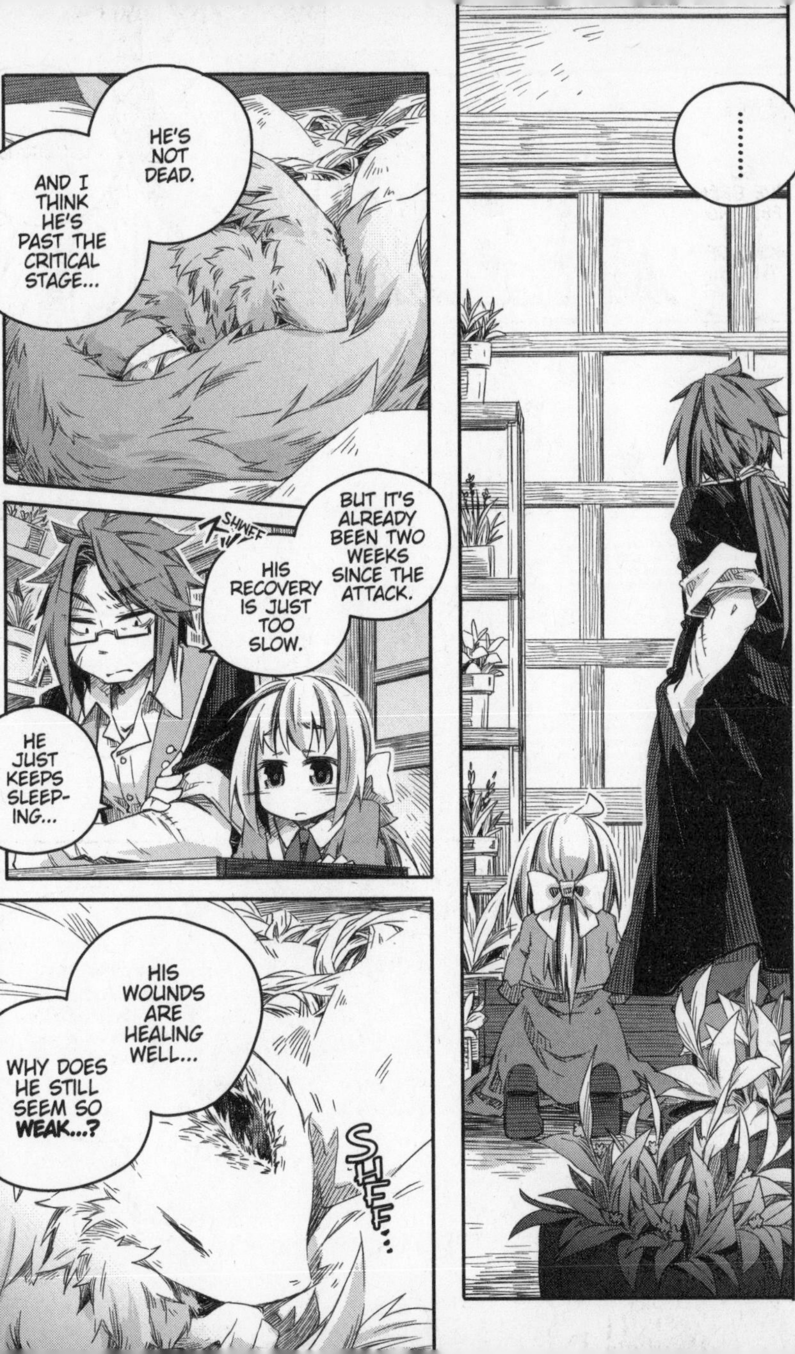
......
HE'S NOT DEAD.
AND I THINK HE'S PAST THE CRITICAL STAGE...
SHWFF
BUT IT'S ALREADY BEEN TWO WEEKS SINCE THE ATTACK.
HIS RECOVERY IS JUST TOO SLOW.
HE JUST KEEPS SLEEP-ING...
HIS WOUNDS ARE HEALING WELL...
WHY DOES HE STILL SEEM SO **WEAK...?**
SHFF...

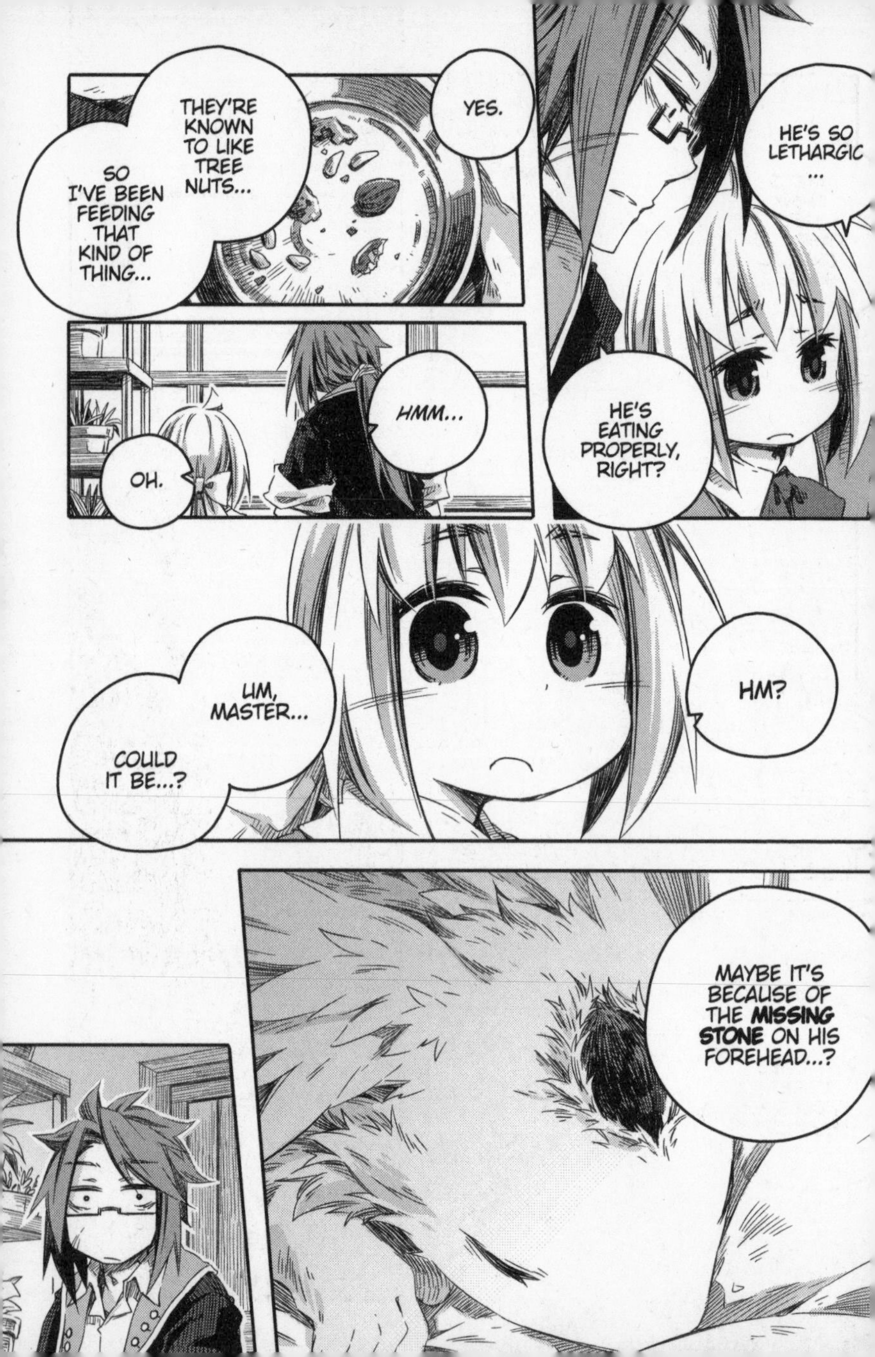
HE'S SO LETHARGIC...
HE'S EATING PROPERLY, RIGHT?
YES.
THEY'RE KNOWN TO LIKE TREE NUTS...
SO I'VE BEEN FEEDING THAT KIND OF THING...
HMM...
OH.
HM?
UM, MASTER...
COULD IT BE...?
MAYBE IT'S BECAUSE OF THE **MISSING STONE** ON HIS FOREHEAD...?

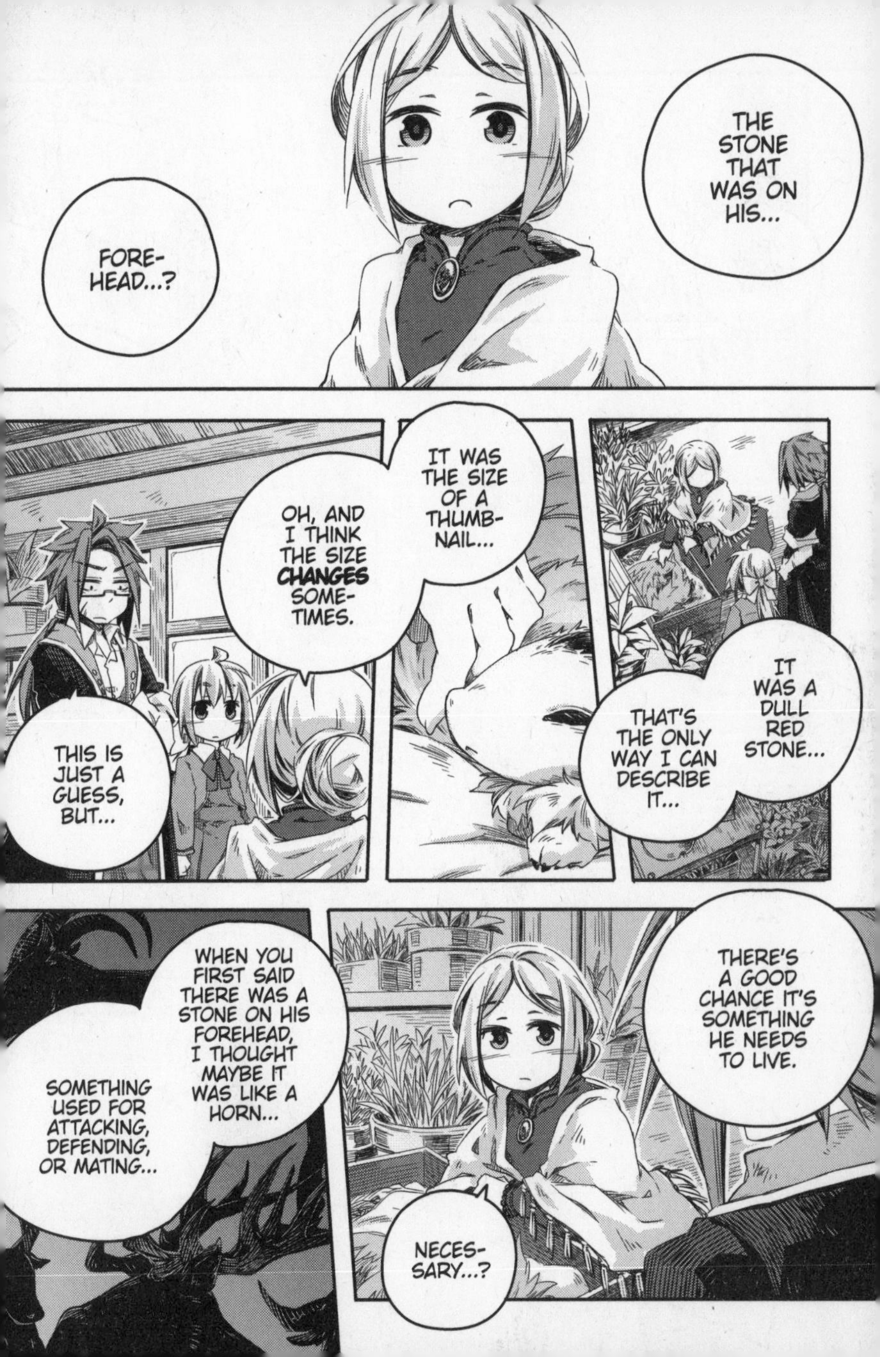
THE STONE THAT WAS ON HIS...
FORE-HEAD...?
IT WAS A DULL RED STONE...
THAT'S THE ONLY WAY I CAN DESCRIBE IT...
IT WAS THE SIZE OF A THUMB-NAIL...
OH, AND I THINK THE SIZE **CHANGES** SOME-TIMES.
THIS IS JUST A GUESS, BUT...
THERE'S A GOOD CHANCE IT'S SOMETHING HE NEEDS TO LIVE.
NECES-SARY...?
WHEN YOU FIRST SAID THERE WAS A STONE ON HIS FOREHEAD, I THOUGHT MAYBE IT WAS LIKE A HORN...
SOMETHING USED FOR ATTACKING, DEFENDING, OR MATING...

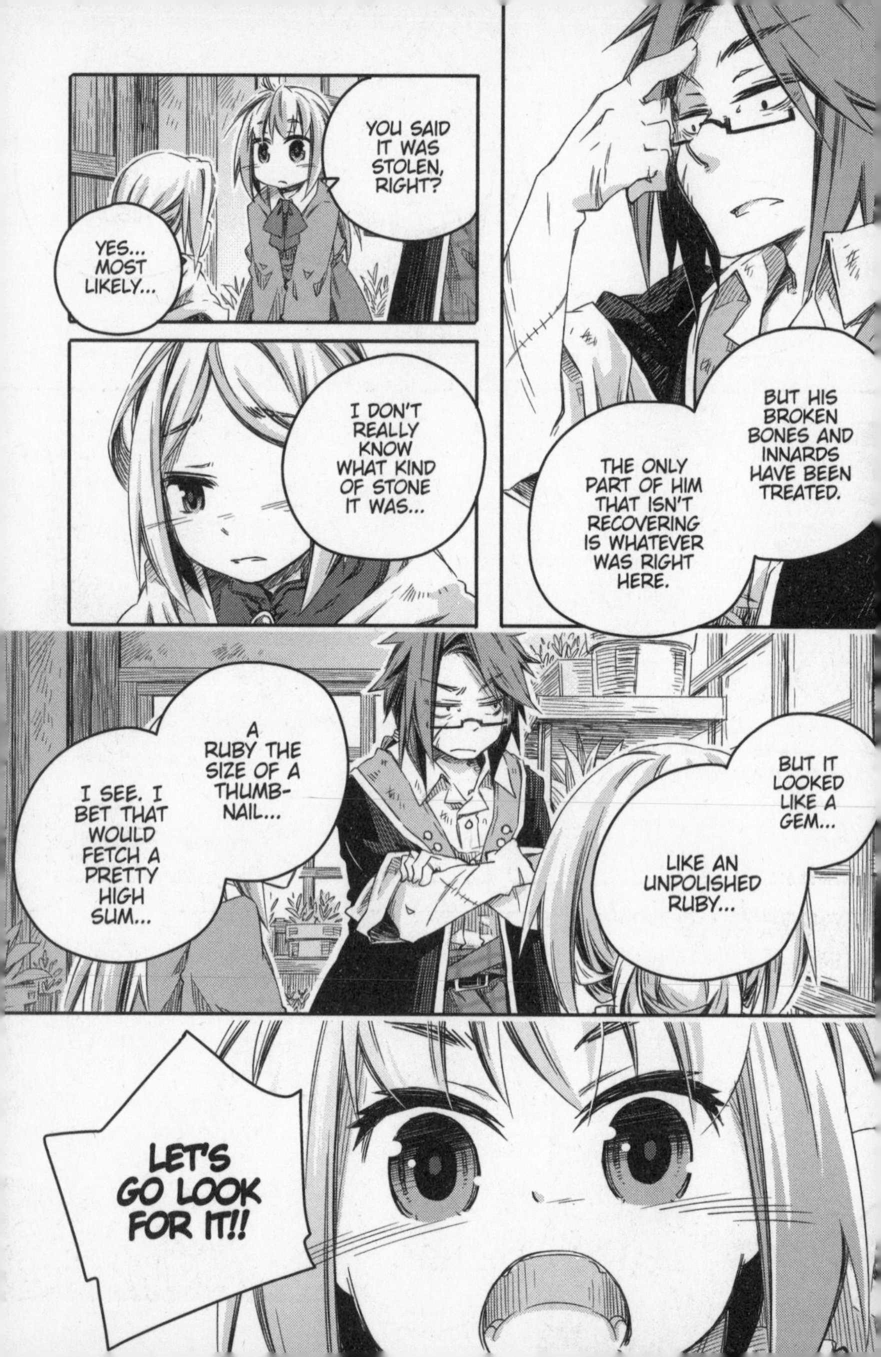
BUT HIS BROKEN BONES AND INNARDS HAVE BEEN TREATED.
THE ONLY PART OF HIM THAT ISN'T RECOVERING IS WHATEVER WAS RIGHT HERE.
YOU SAID IT WAS STOLEN, RIGHT?
YES... MOST LIKELY...
I DON'T REALLY KNOW WHAT KIND OF STONE IT WAS...
BUT IT LOOKED LIKE A GEM...
LIKE AN UNPOLISHED RUBY...
A RUBY THE SIZE OF A THUMB-NAIL...
I SEE. I BET THAT WOULD FETCH A PRETTY HIGH SUM...
LET'S GO LOOK FOR IT!!

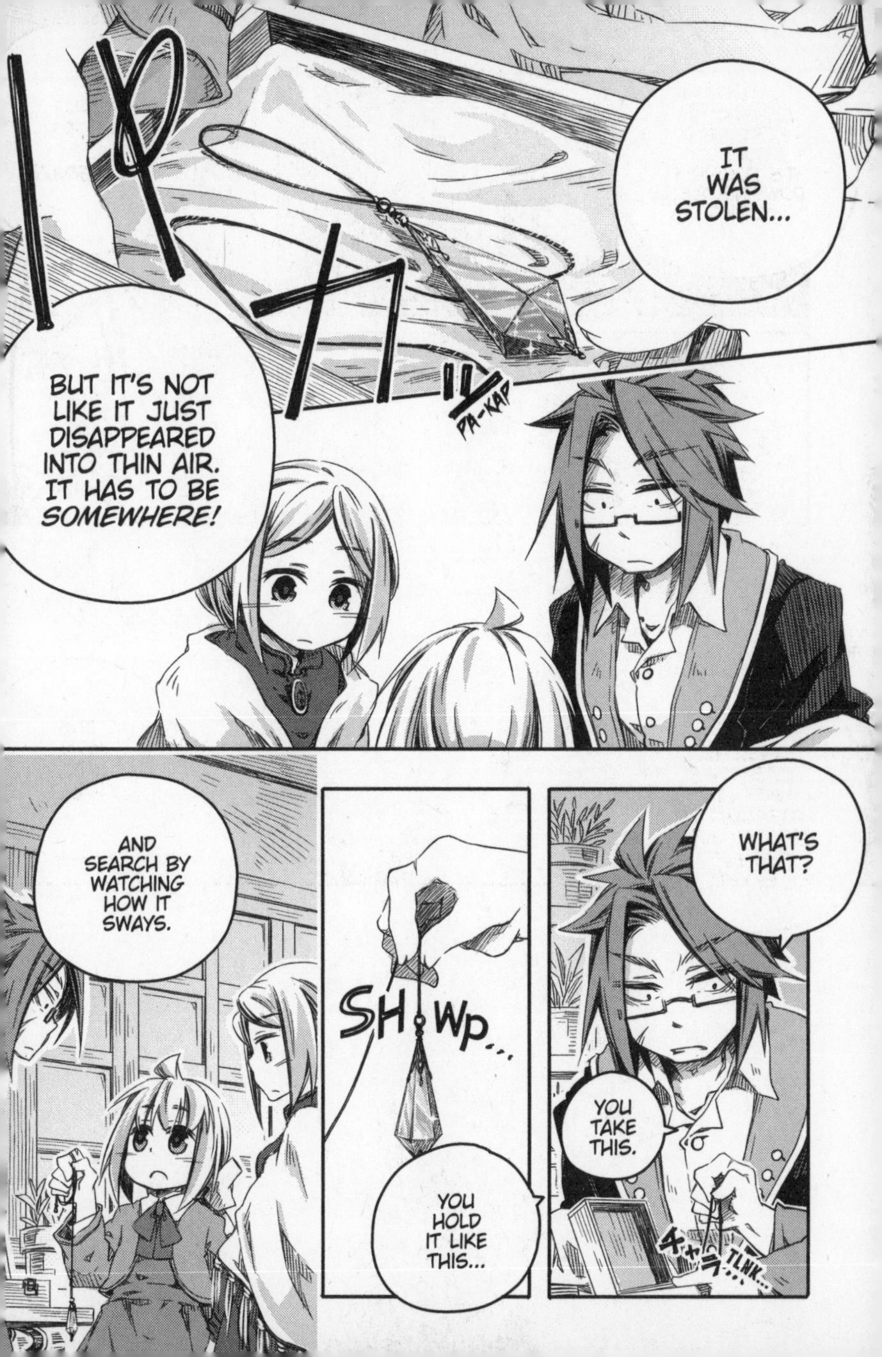
IT WAS STOLEN...
BUT IT'S NOT LIKE IT JUST DISAPPEARED INTO THIN AIR. IT HAS TO BE *SOMEWHERE!*
PA-KAP
WHAT'S THAT?
YOU TAKE THIS.
チャラ
TLNK...
SHWp...
YOU HOLD IT LIKE THIS...
AND SEARCH BY WATCHING HOW IT SWAYS.

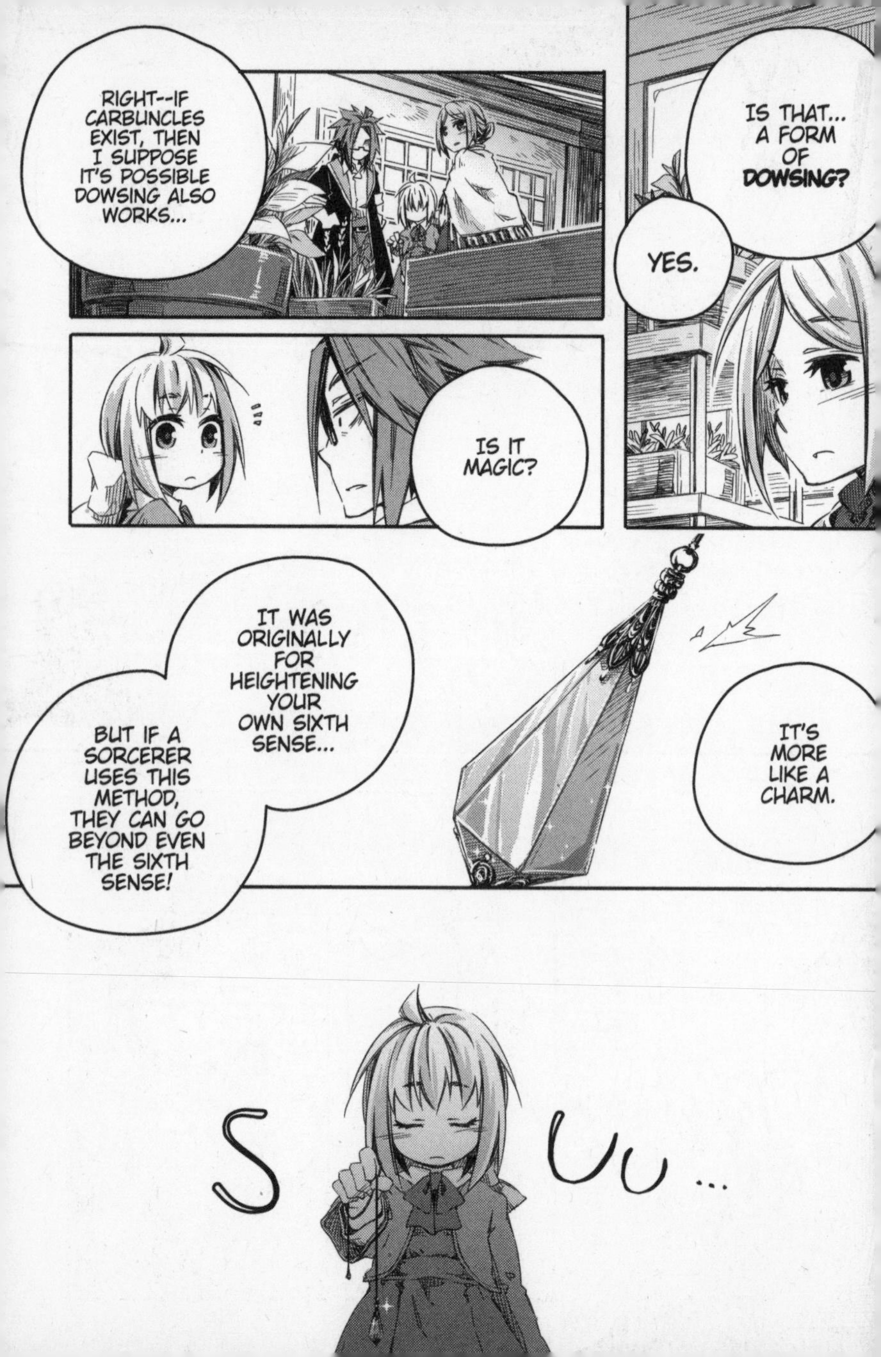
IS THAT... A FORM OF DOWSING?
YES.
RIGHT--IF CARBUNCLES EXIST, THEN I SUPPOSE IT'S POSSIBLE DOWSING ALSO WORKS...
IS IT MAGIC?
IT'S MORE LIKE A CHARM.
IT WAS ORIGINALLY FOR HEIGHTENING YOUR OWN SIXTH SENSE...
BUT IF A SORCERER USES THIS METHOD, THEY CAN GO BEYOND EVEN THE SIXTH SENSE!
SUU...

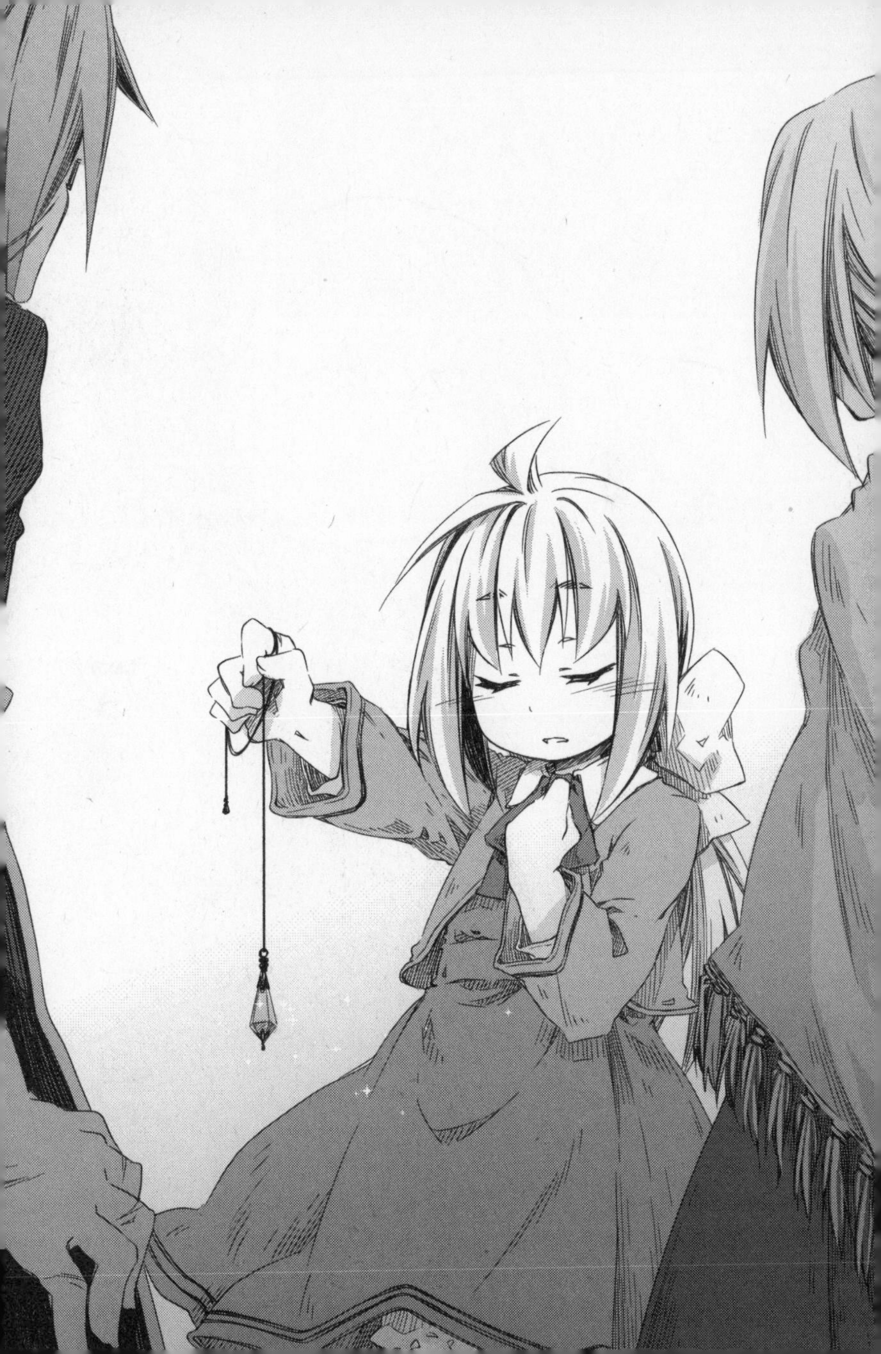

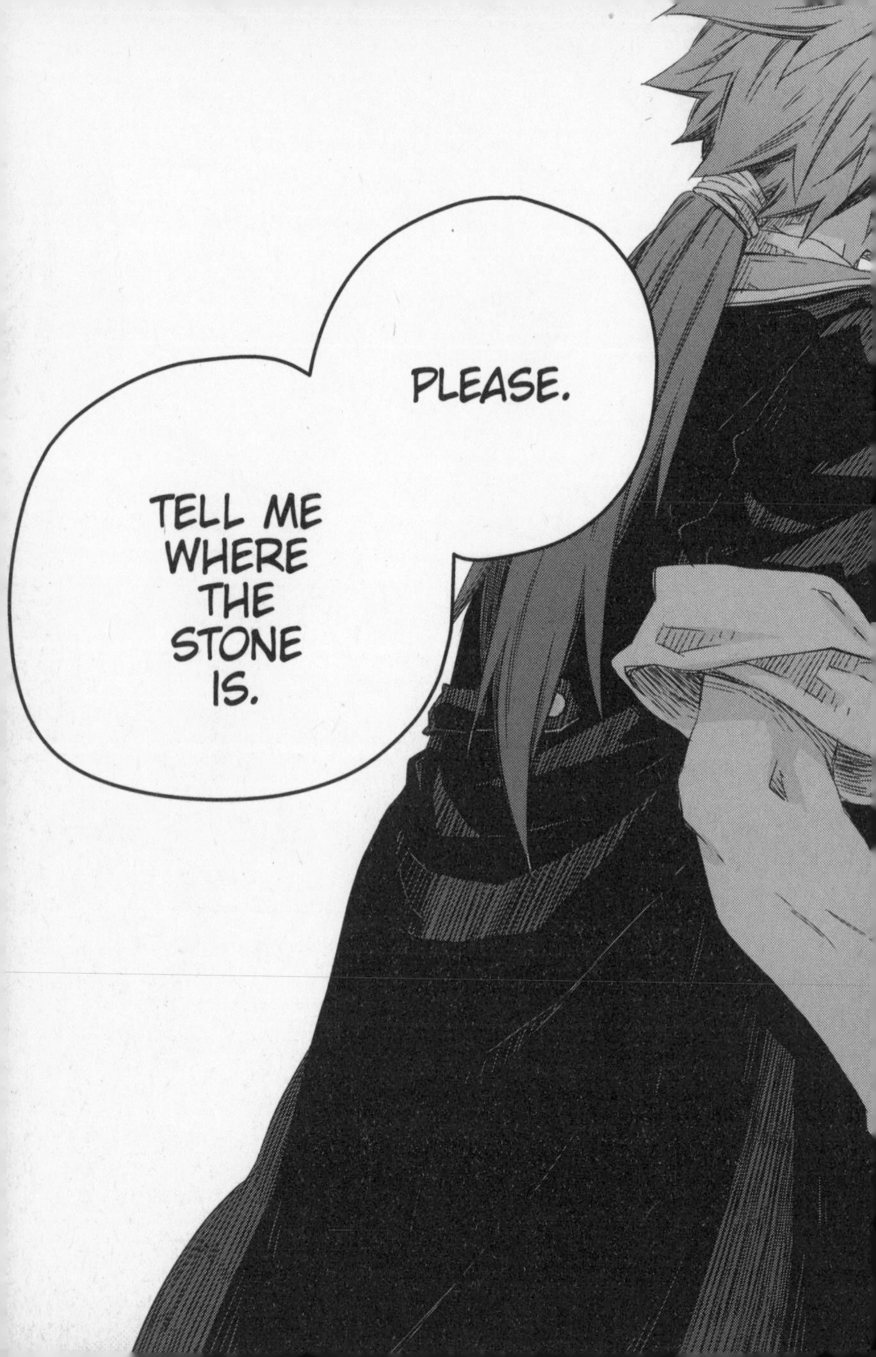
PLEASE.
TELL ME WHERE THE STONE IS.

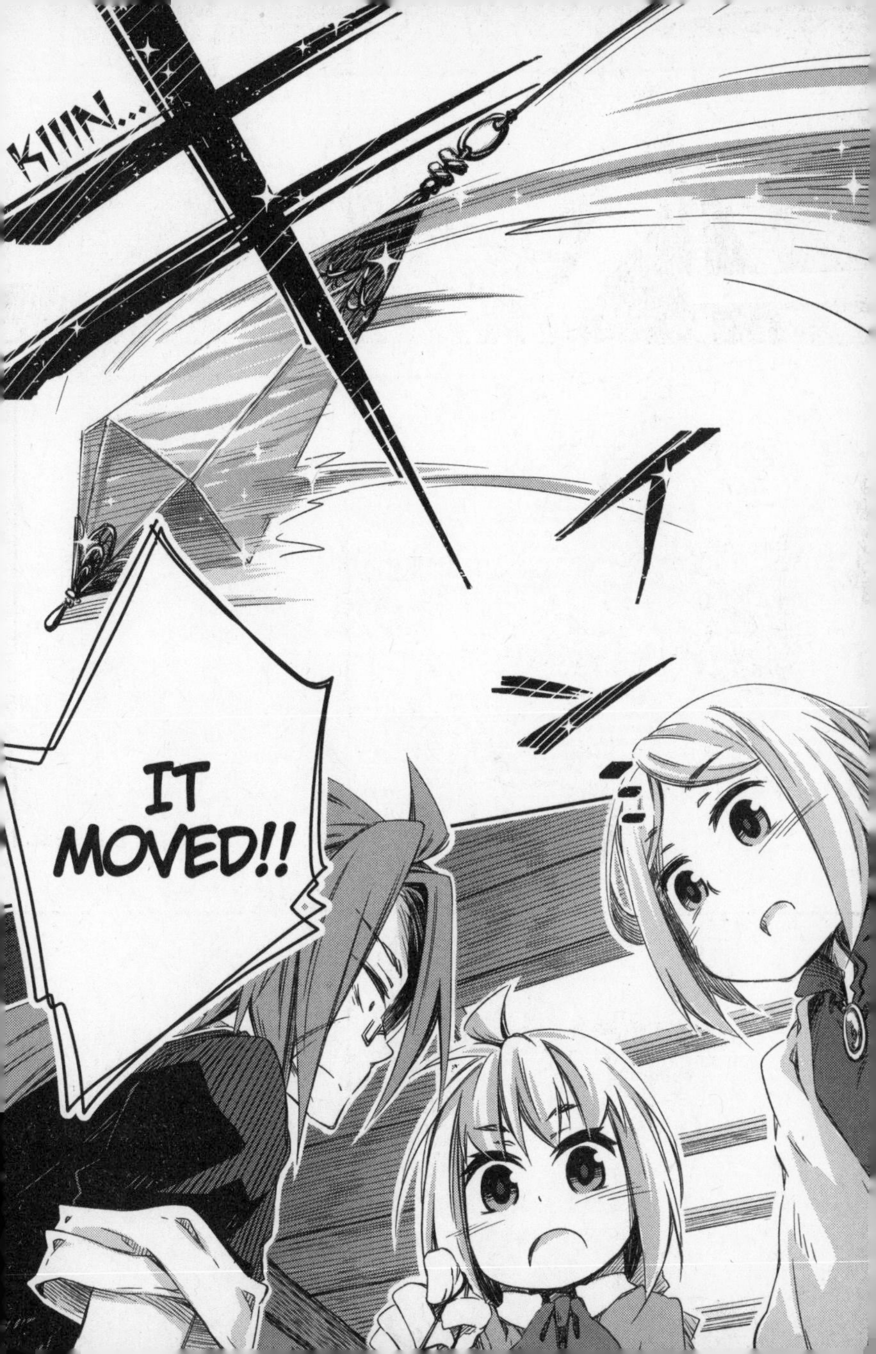
KIIIN...
IT MOVED!!

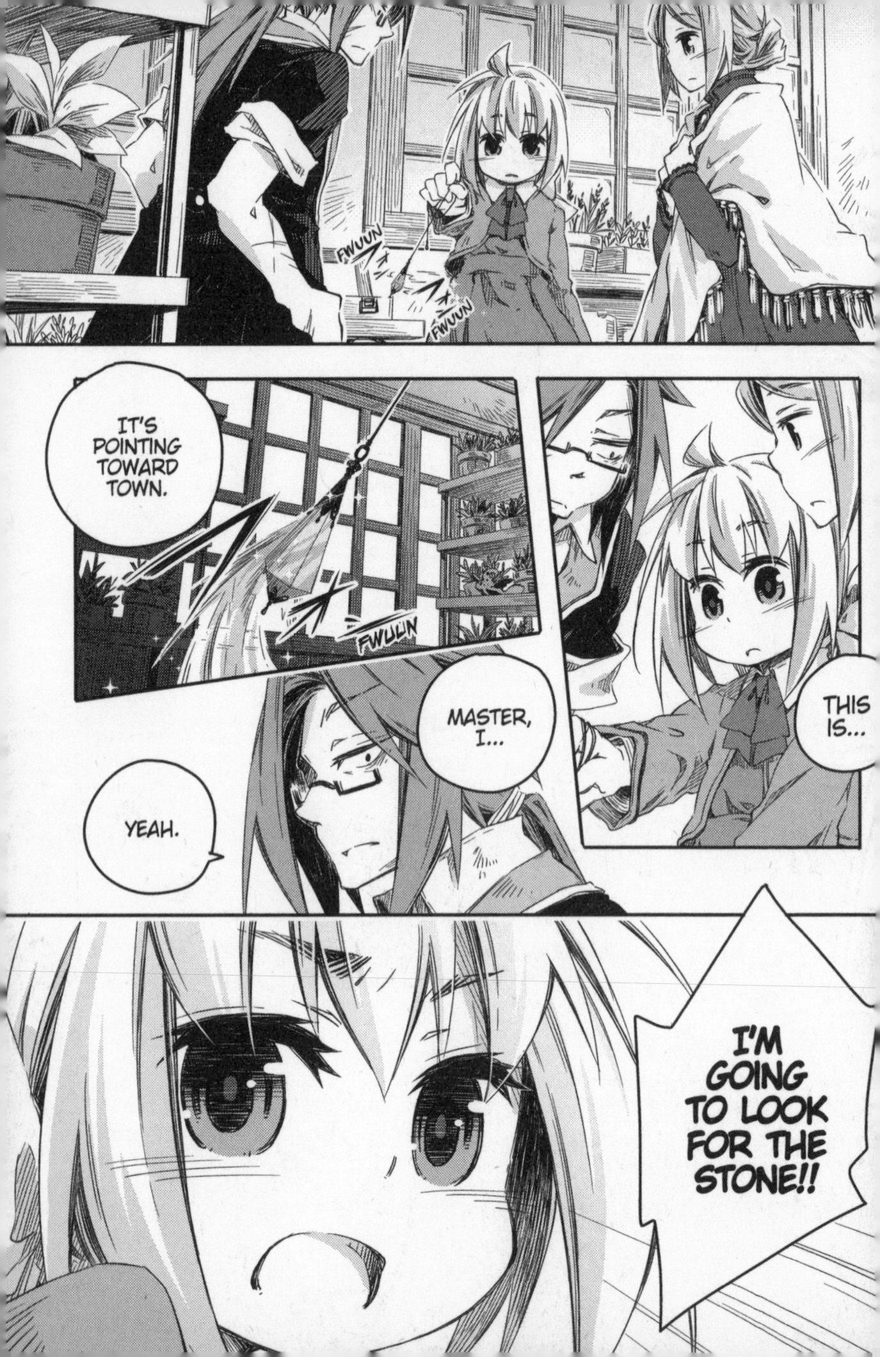
FWUUN
FWUUN
THIS IS...
IT'S POINTING TOWARD TOWN.
FWUUN
MASTER, I...
YEAH.
I'M GOING TO LOOK FOR THE STONE!!

There is a puk hiding
in every chapter!

Try to find them all.

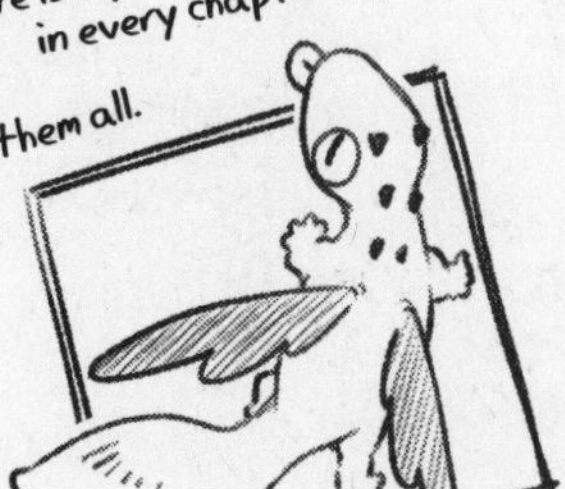

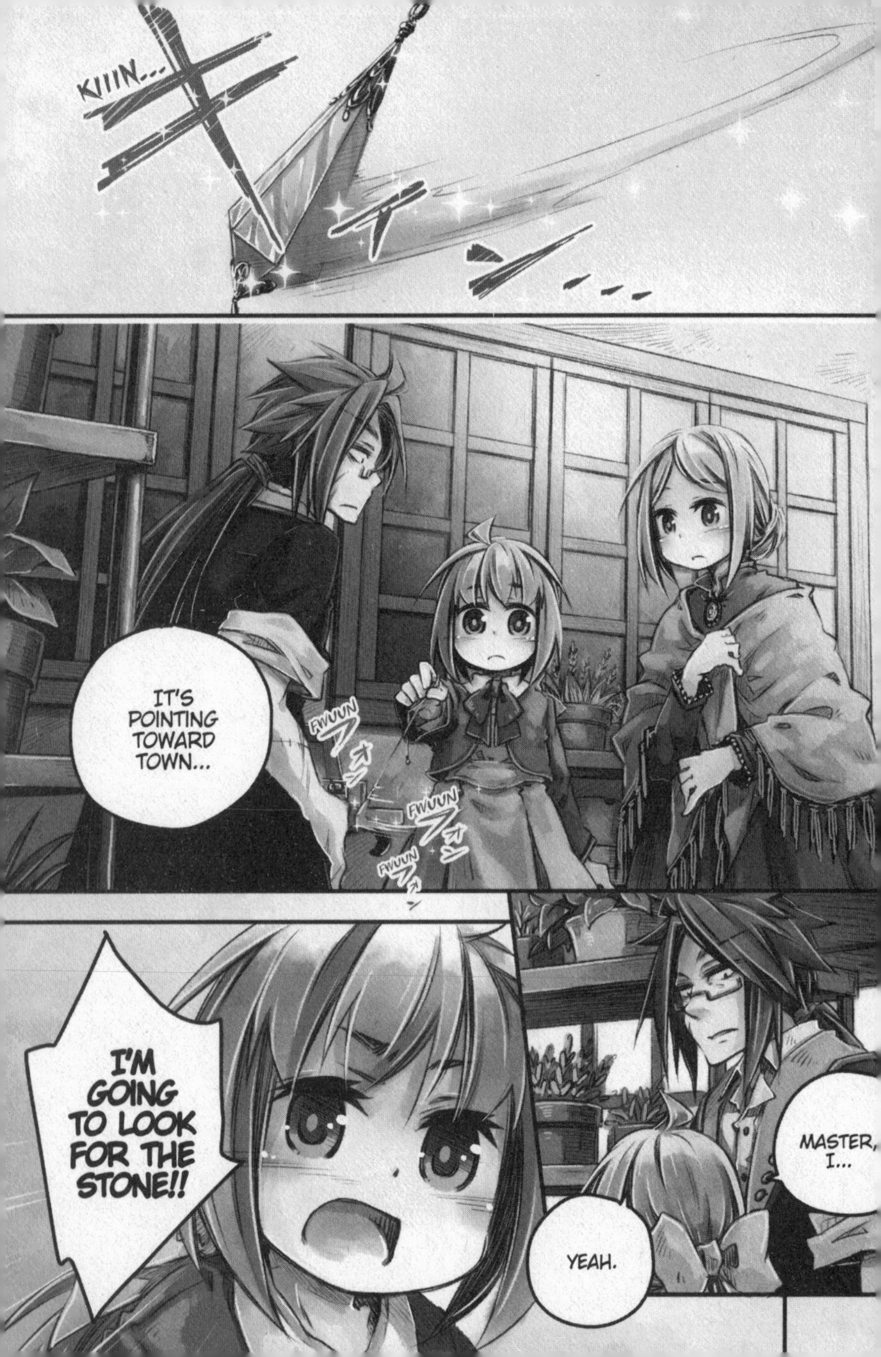
KIIIN...
IT'S POINTING TOWARD TOWN...
FWUUN
FWUUN
FWUUN
MASTER, I...
YEAH.
I'M GOING TO LOOK FOR THE STONE!!

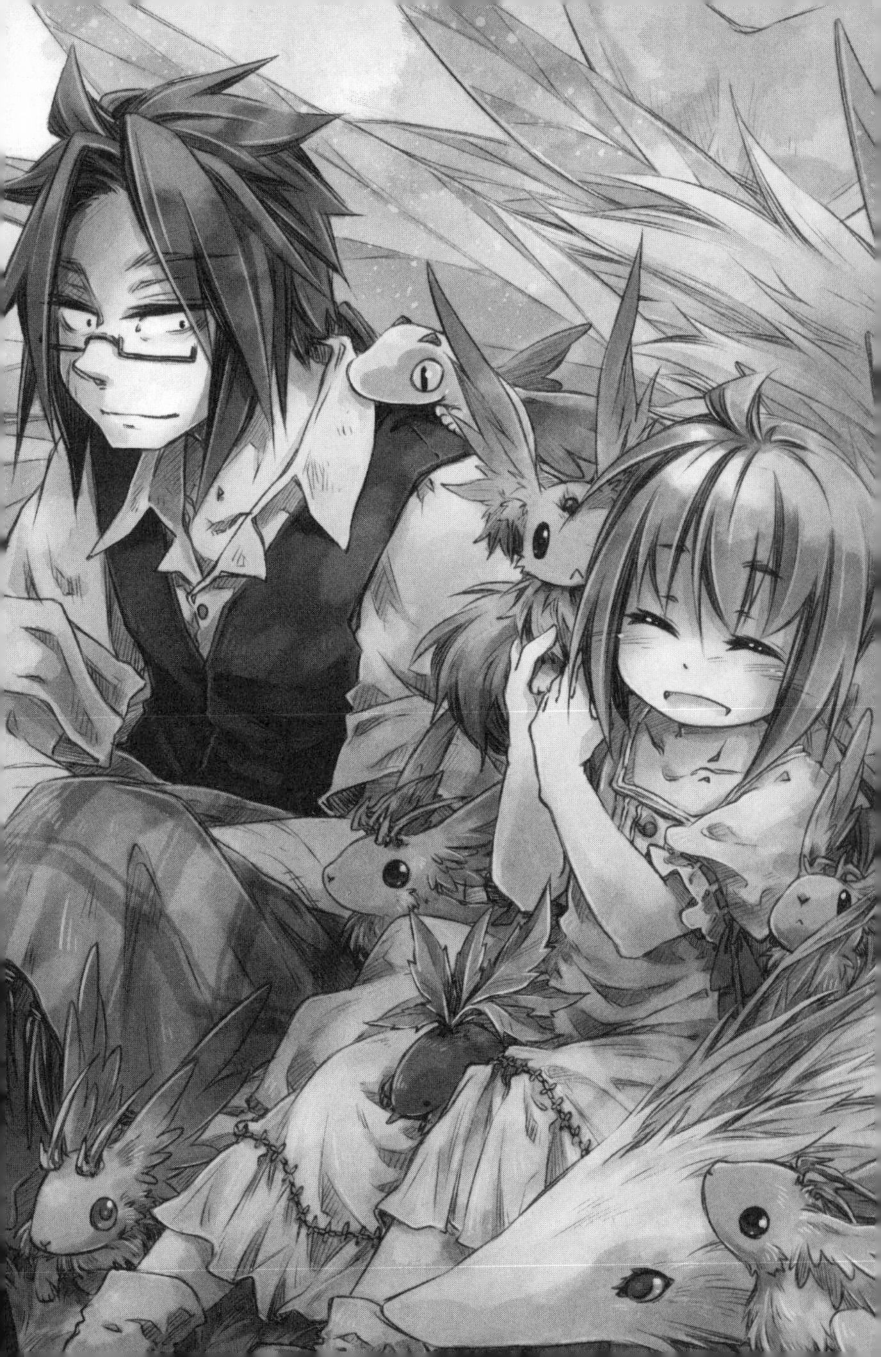

[Case 8: Carbuncle (Part 2)]

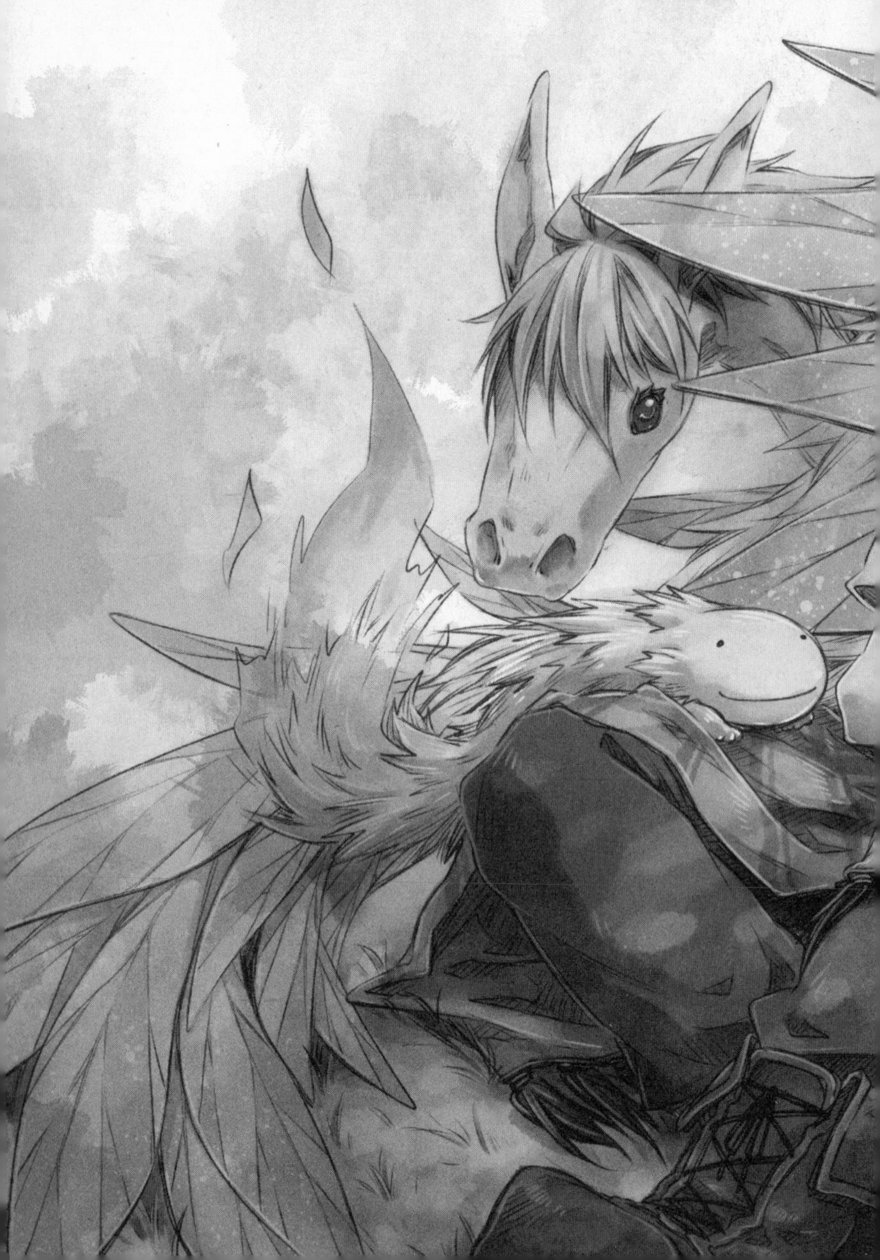

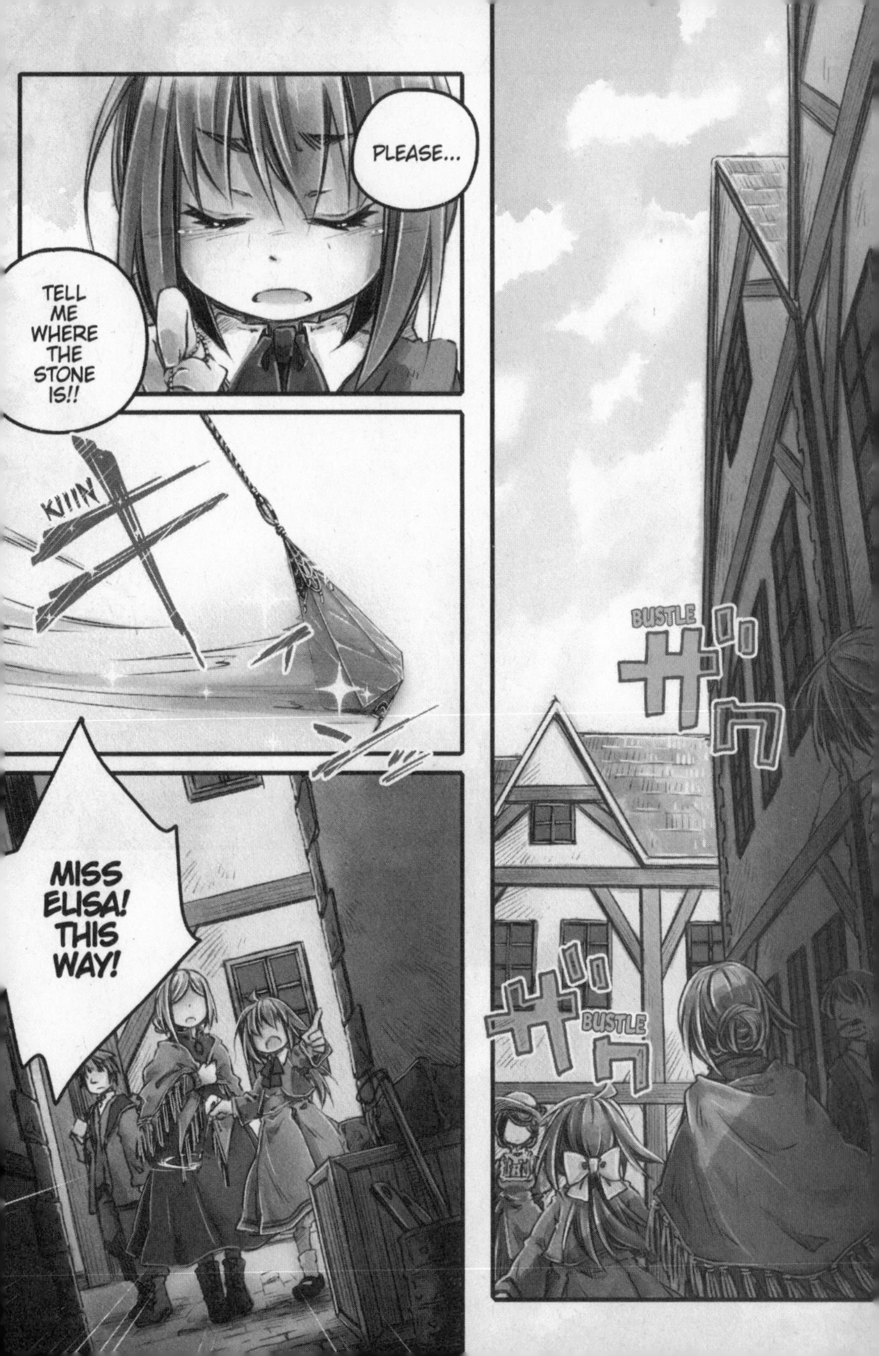
BUSTLE
BUSTLE
PLEASE...
TELL ME WHERE THE STONE IS!!
KIIIN
MISS ELISA! THIS WAY!

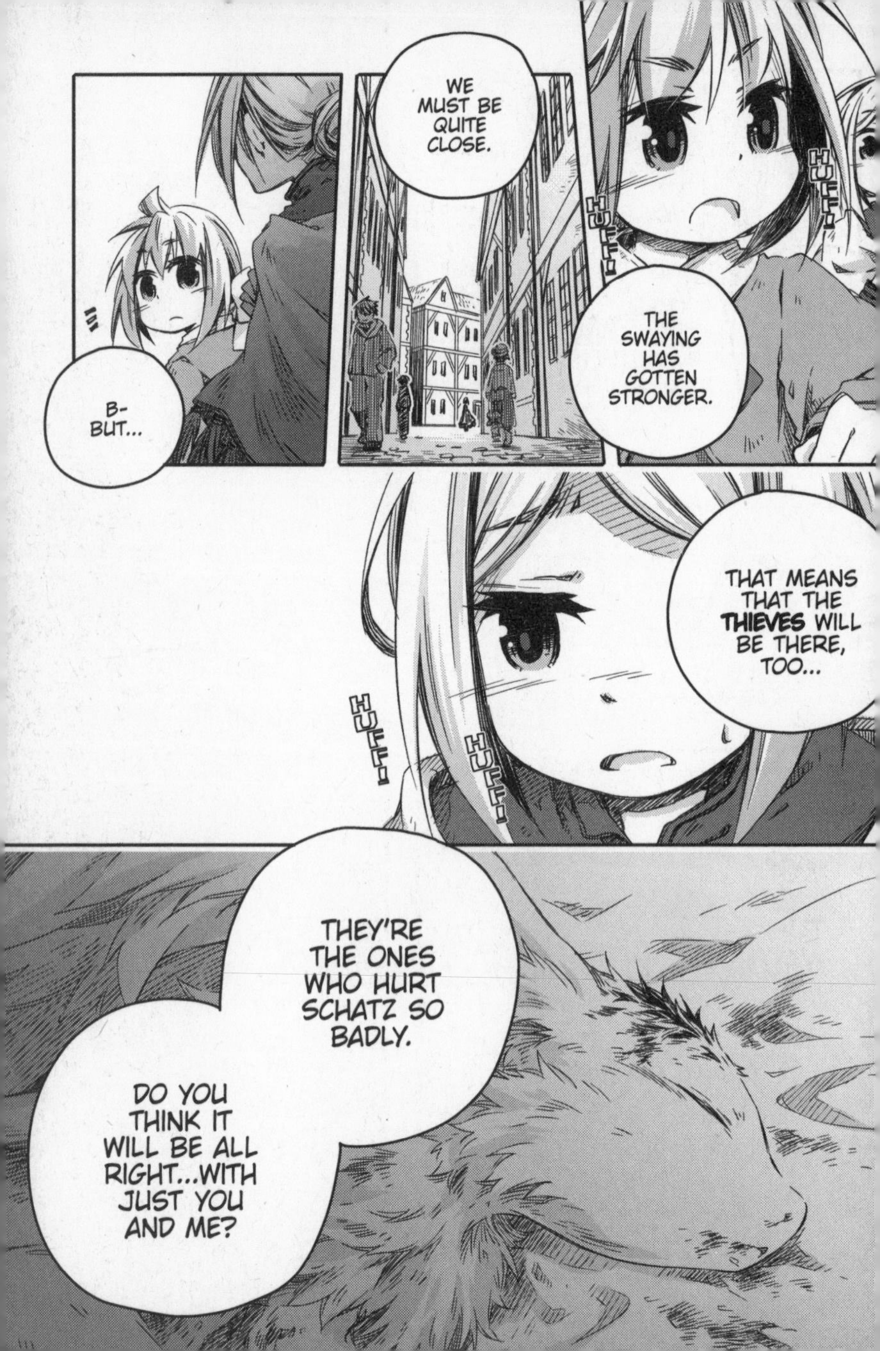
HUFF HUFF
THE SWAYING HAS GOTTEN STRONGER.
WE MUST BE QUITE CLOSE.
B-BUT...
THAT MEANS THAT THE THIEVES WILL BE THERE, TOO...
HUFF HUFF
THEY'RE THE ONES WHO HURT SCHATZ SO BADLY.
DO YOU THINK IT WILL BE ALL RIGHT...WITH JUST YOU AND ME?

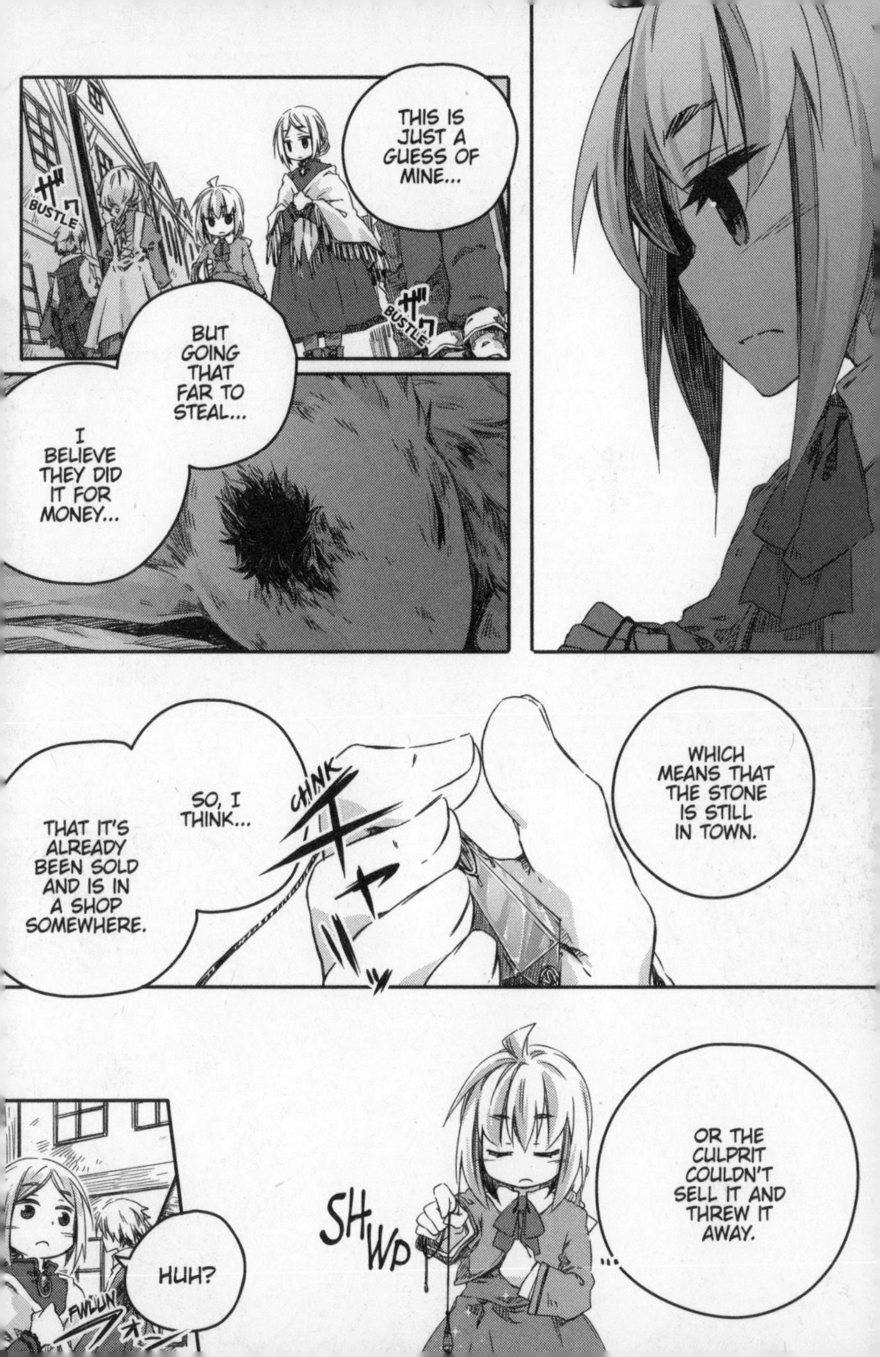
THIS IS JUST A GUESS OF MINE...
BUSTLE
BUSTLE
BUT GOING THAT FAR TO STEAL...
I BELIEVE THEY DID IT FOR MONEY...
WHICH MEANS THAT THE STONE IS STILL IN TOWN.
CHINK
SO, I THINK...
THAT IT'S ALREADY BEEN SOLD AND IS IN A SHOP SOMEWHERE.
OR THE CULPRIT COULDN'T SELL IT AND THREW IT AWAY.
...
SHWP
HUH?
FWUUN

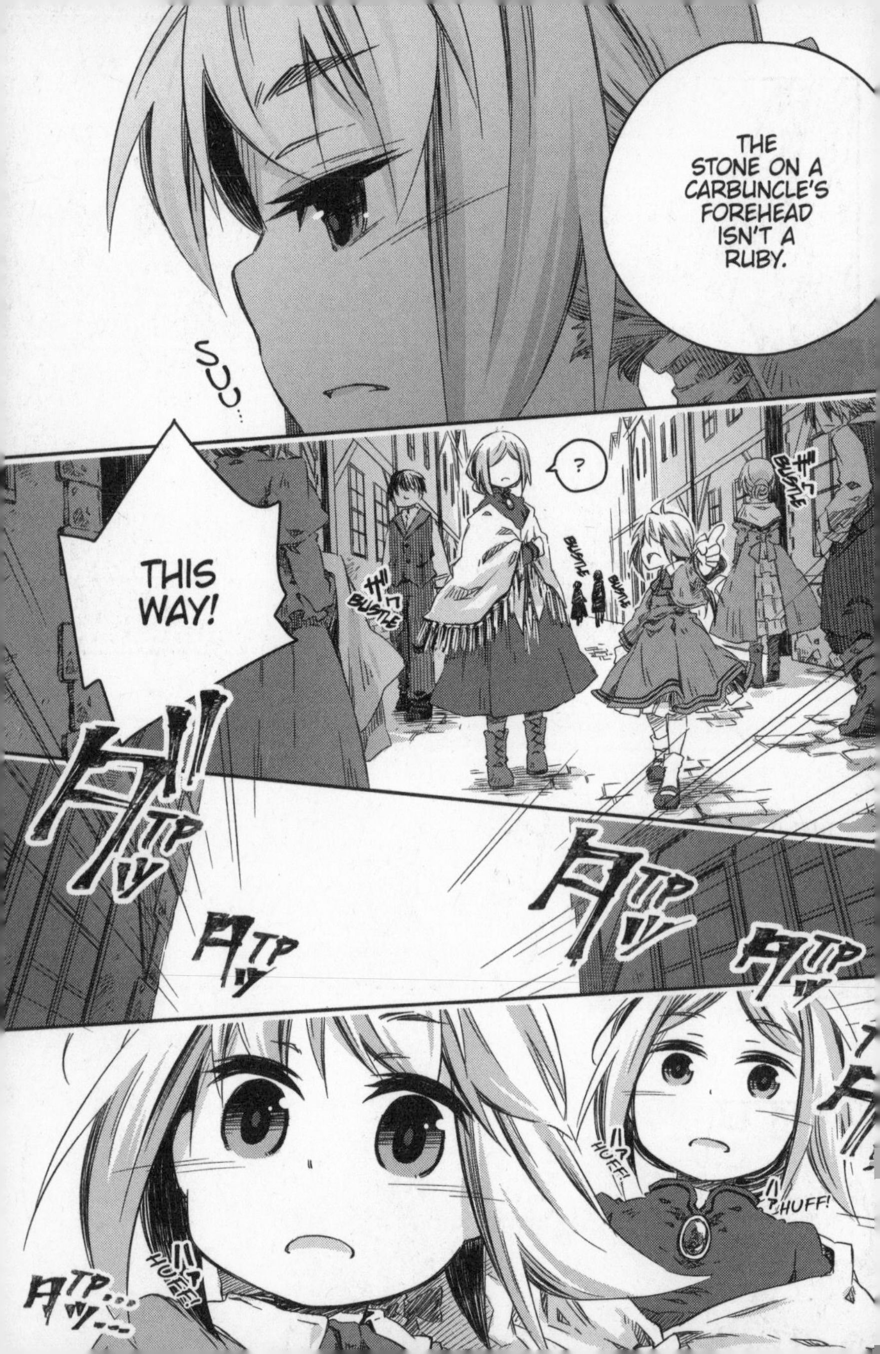

THE STONE ON A CARBUNCLE'S FOREHEAD ISN'T A RUBY.
SUU...
BUSTLE
?
BUSTLE
BUSTLE
BUSTLE
THIS WAY!
TP
TP
TP
TP
HUFF!
HUFF!
HUFF!
TP...

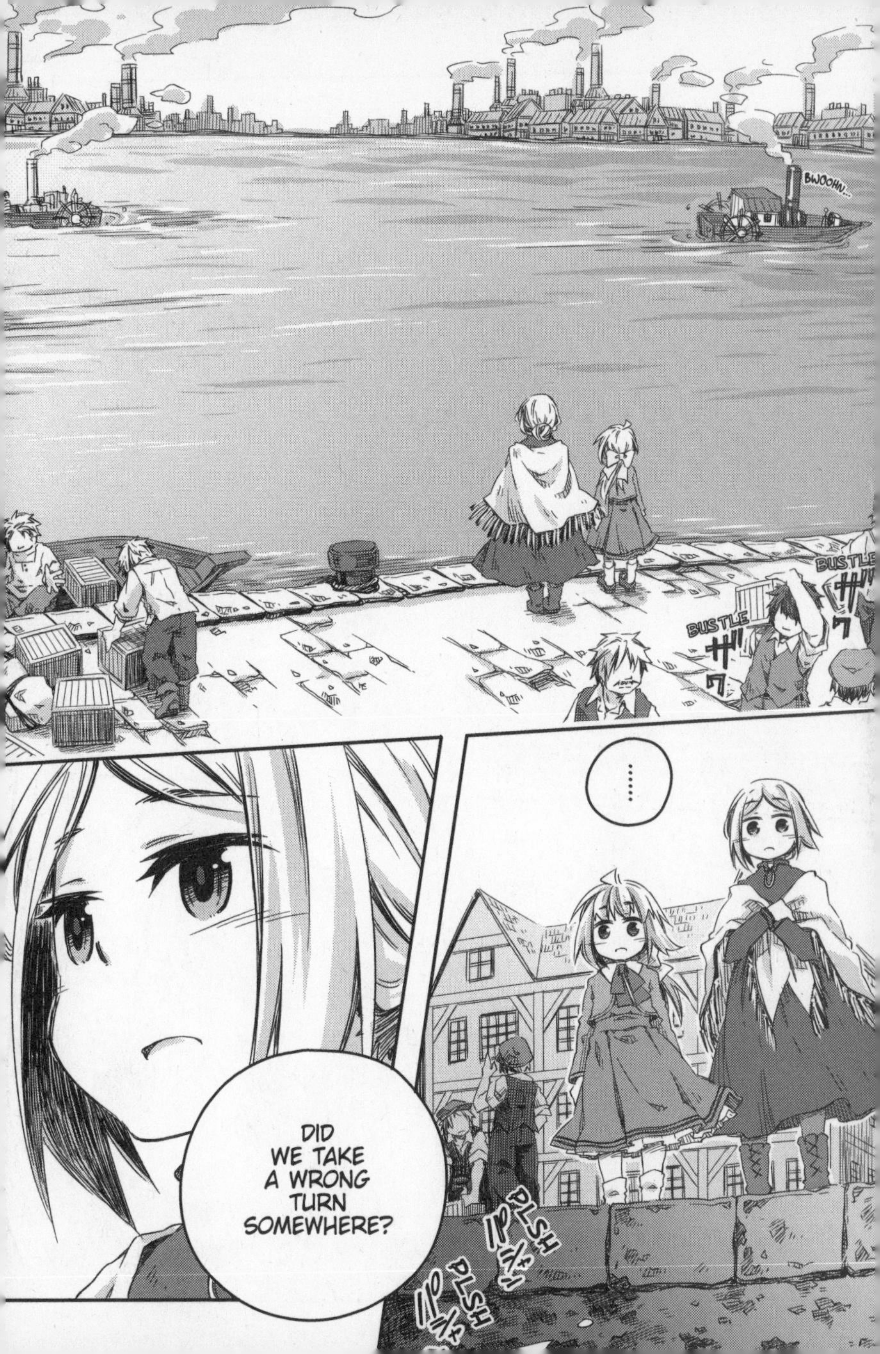
BWOOHN...
BUSTLE ザッ
BUSTLE ザッ
......
PLSH パシャ
PLSH パシャ
DID WE TAKE A WRONG TURN SOMEWHERE?

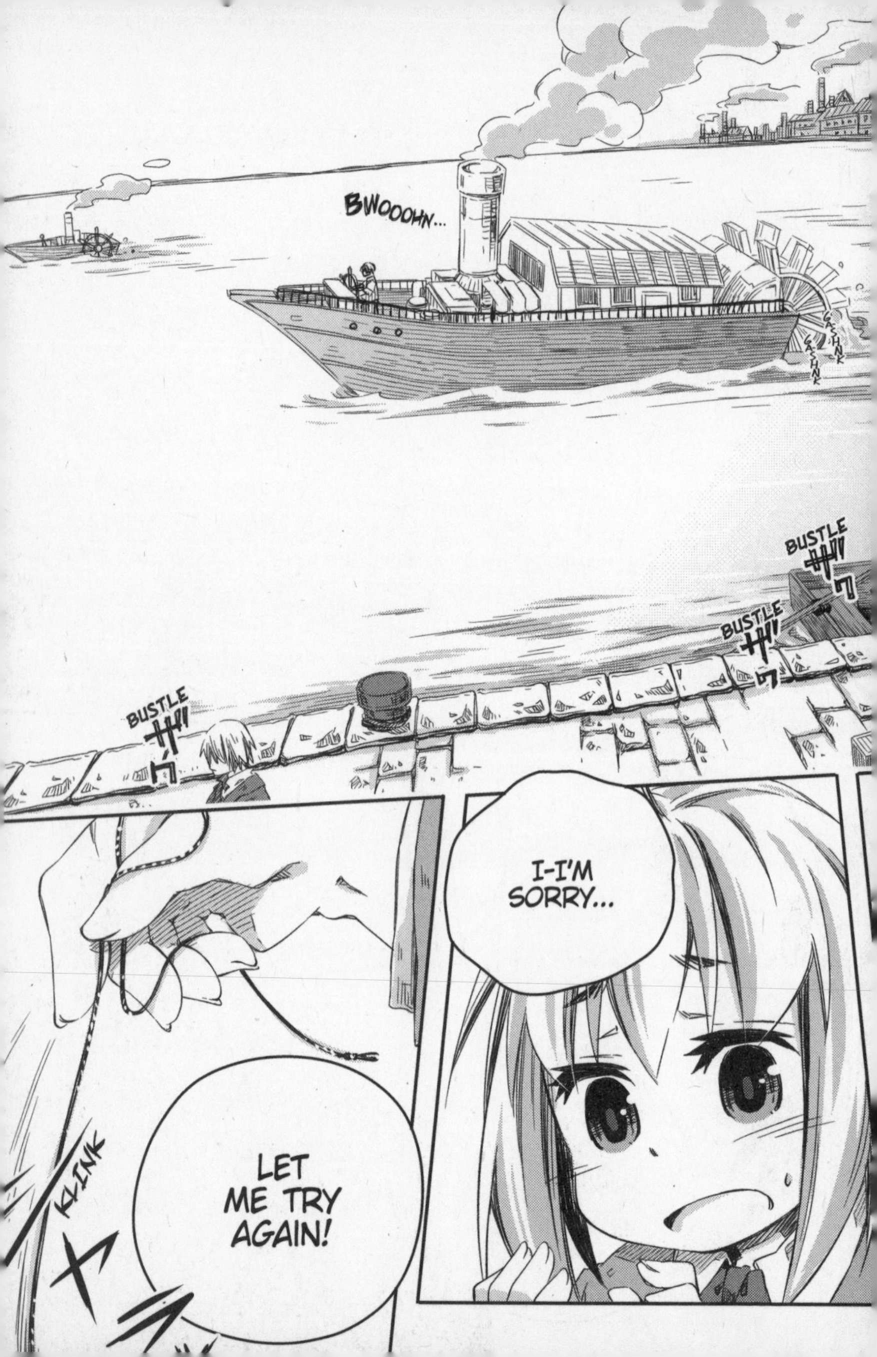
BWOOOHN...
GASHNK
GASHNK
BUSTLE
BUSTLE
BUSTLE
I-I'M SORRY...
LET ME TRY AGAIN!
KLINK

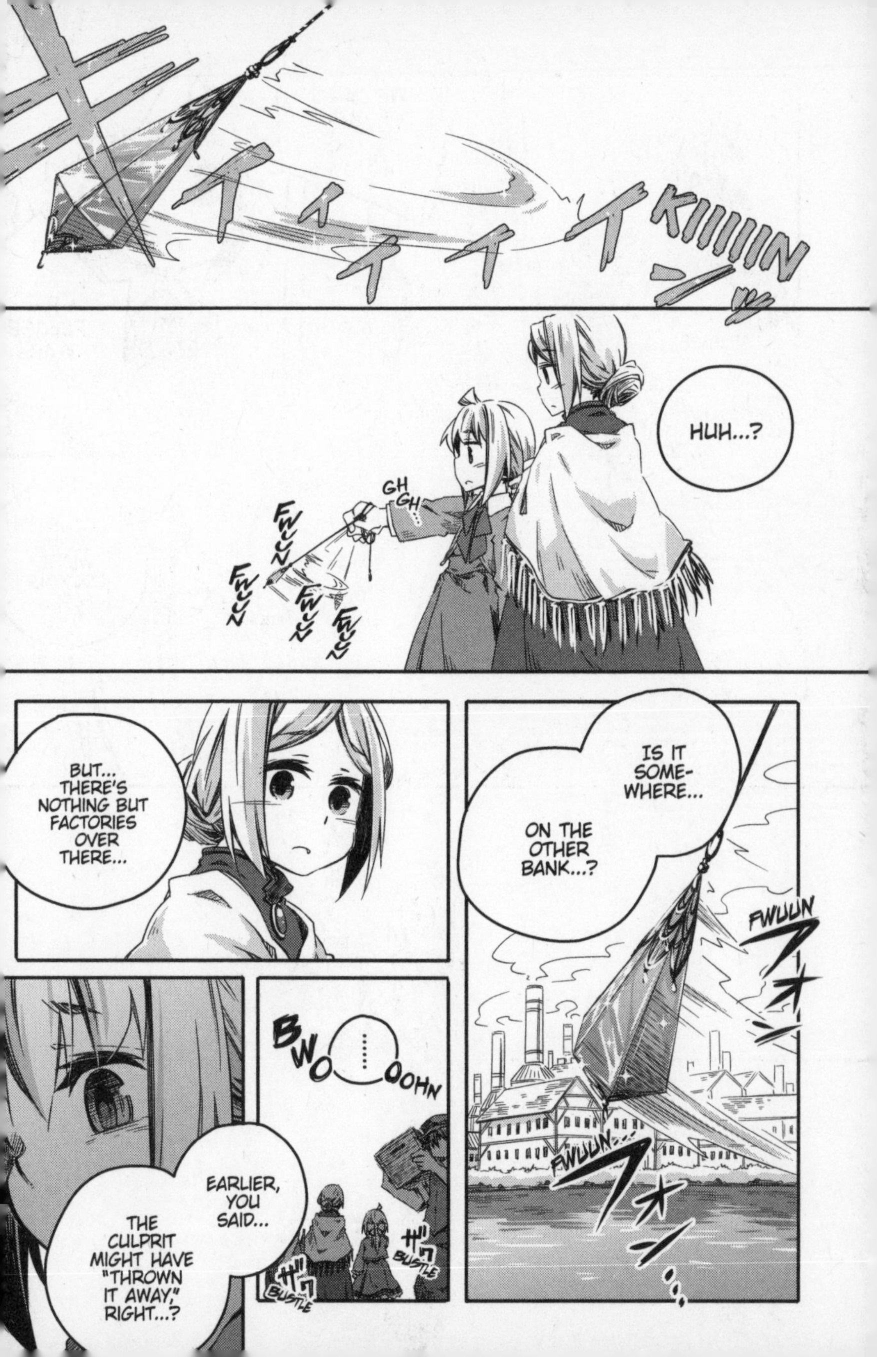
KIIIIIN
HUH...?
GH GH...
FWUUN
FWUUN
FWUUN
FWUUN
IS IT SOMEWHERE...
ON THE OTHER BANK...?
FWUUN
FWUUN...
BUT... THERE'S NOTHING BUT FACTORIES OVER THERE...
BWO
......
OOHN
BUSTLE
BUSTLE
EARLIER, YOU SAID...
THE CULPRIT MIGHT HAVE "THROWN IT AWAY," RIGHT...?

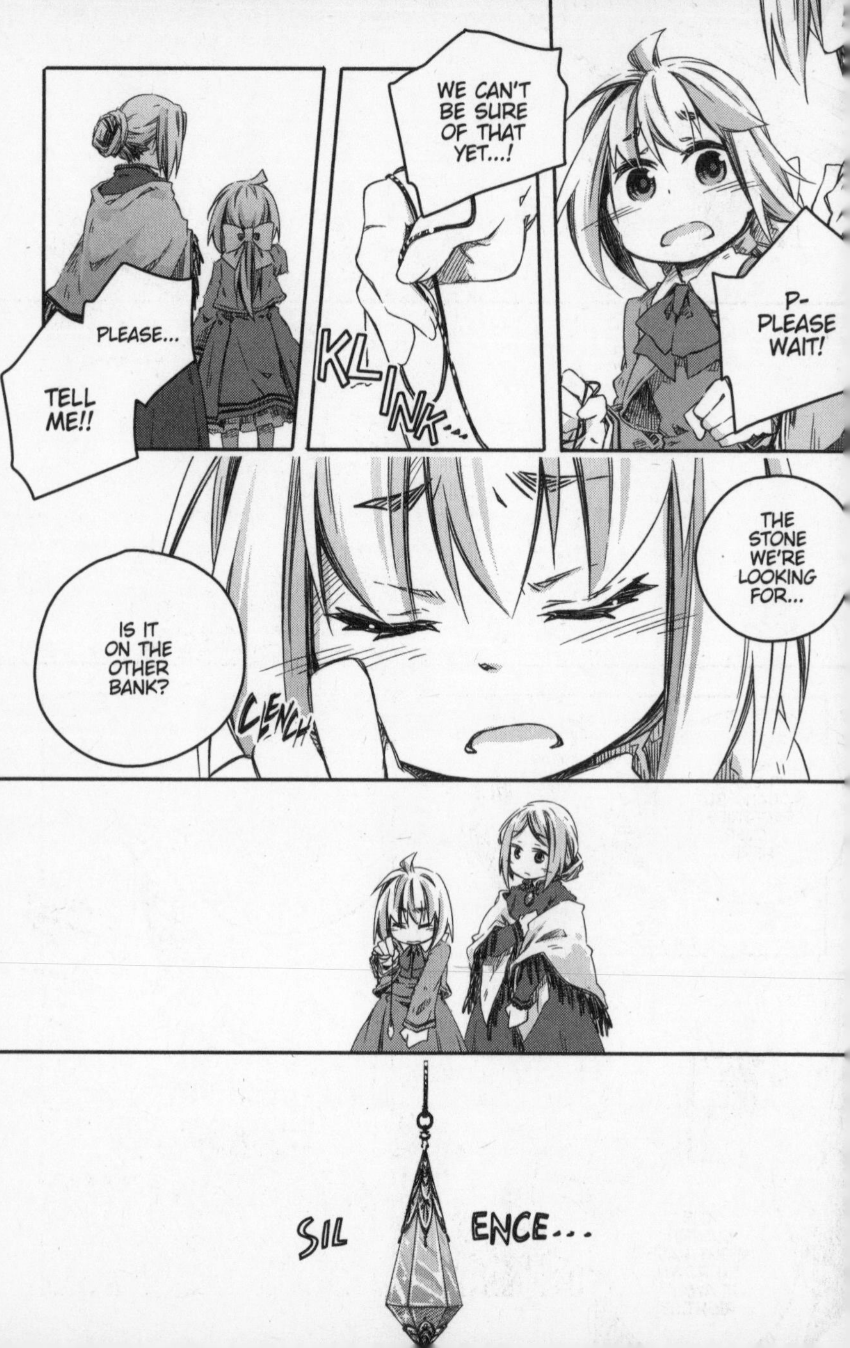
P- PLEASE WAIT!
WE CAN'T BE SURE OF THAT YET...!
KLINK...
PLEASE...
TELL ME!!
THE STONE WE'RE LOOKING FOR...
IS IT ON THE OTHER BANK?
CLENCH
SILENCE...

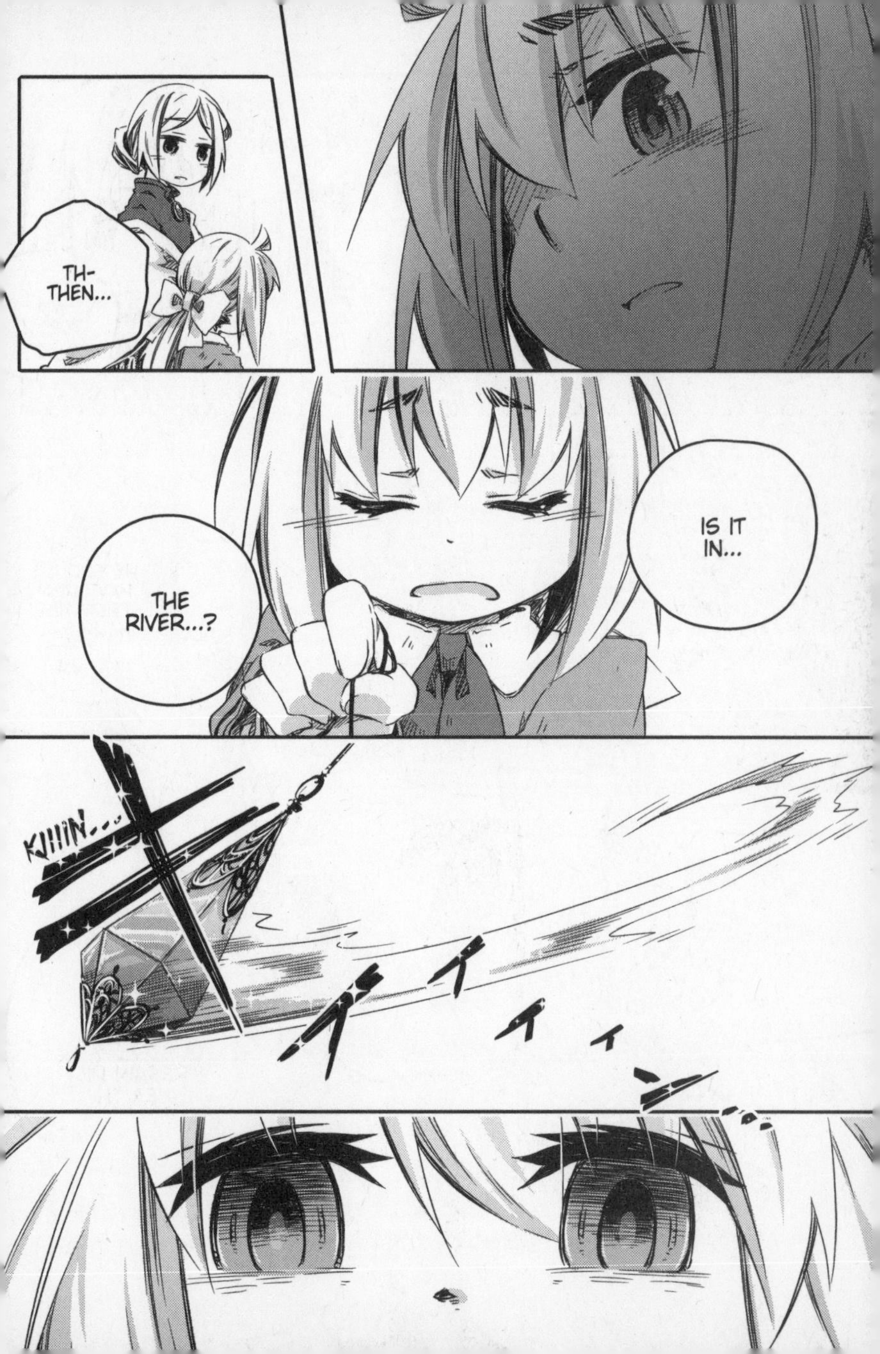
TH-
THEN...
IS IT IN...
THE RIVER...?
KIIIIN...

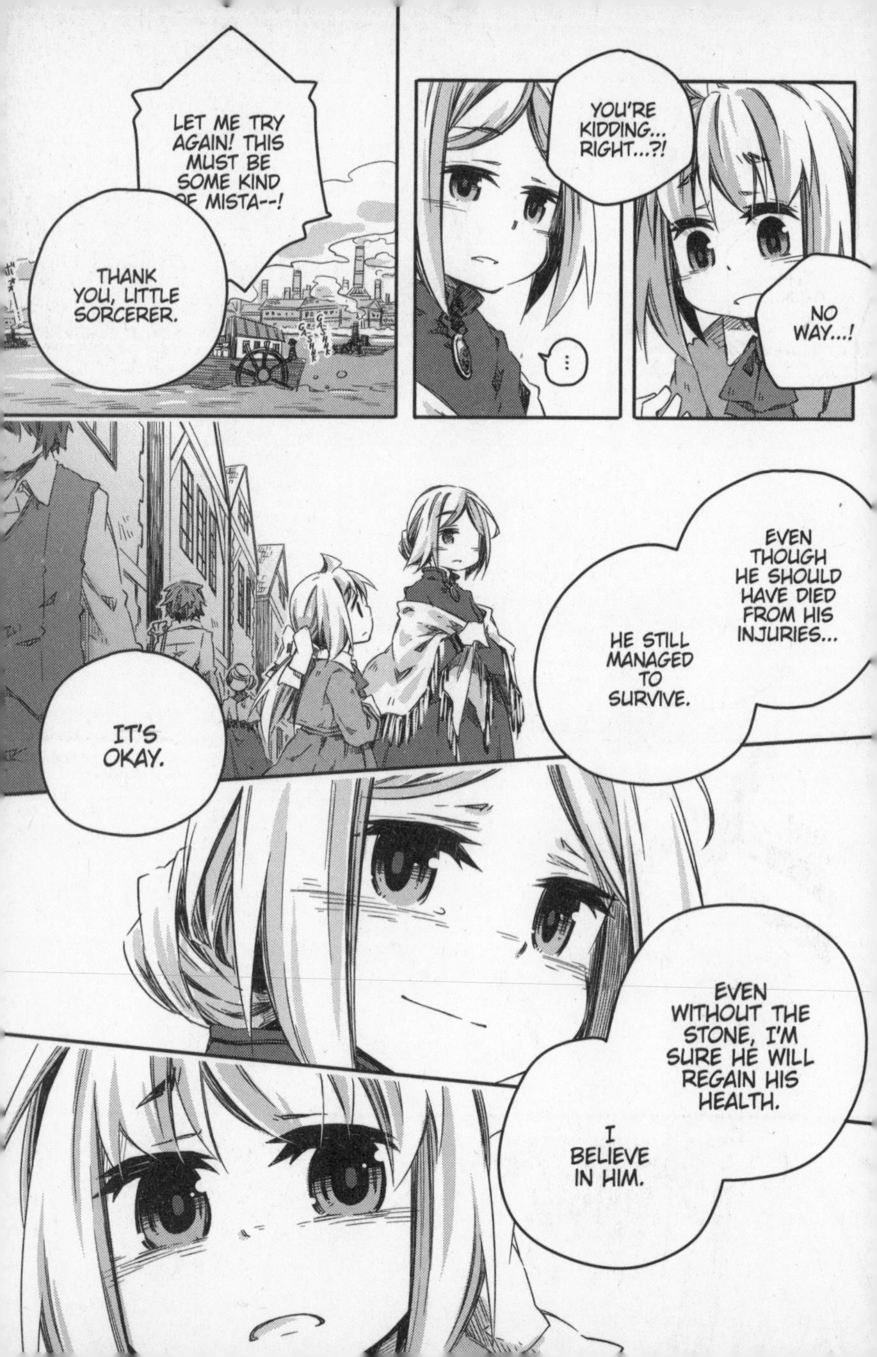

YOU'RE KIDDING... RIGHT...?!
NO WAY...!
...
LET ME TRY AGAIN! THIS MUST BE SOME KIND OF MISTA--!
THANK YOU, LITTLE SORCERER.
EVEN THOUGH HE SHOULD HAVE DIED FROM HIS INJURIES...
HE STILL MANAGED TO SURVIVE.
IT'S OKAY.
EVEN WITHOUT THE STONE, I'M SURE HE WILL REGAIN HIS HEALTH.
I BELIEVE IN HIM.

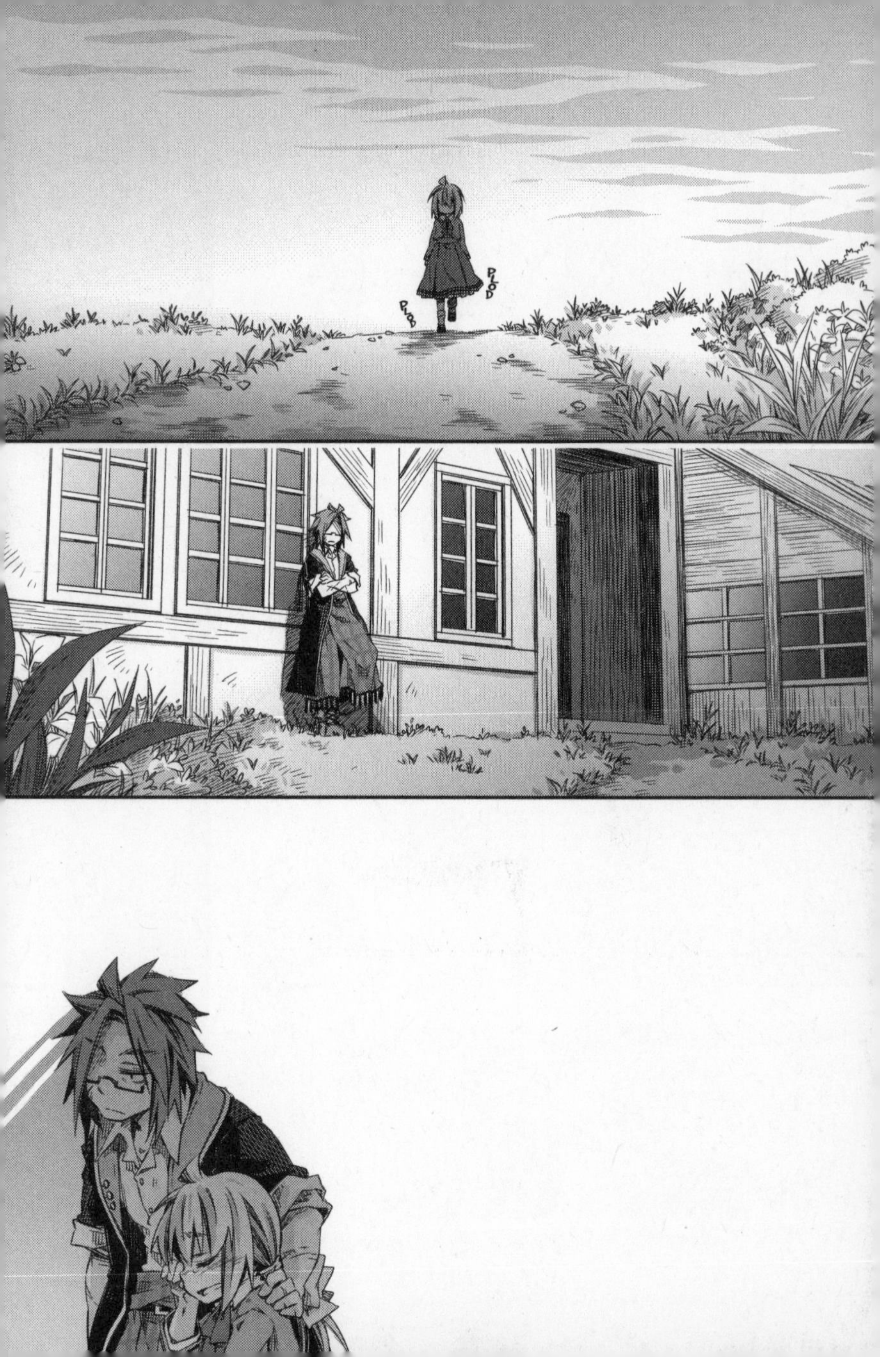
PLOD
PLOD

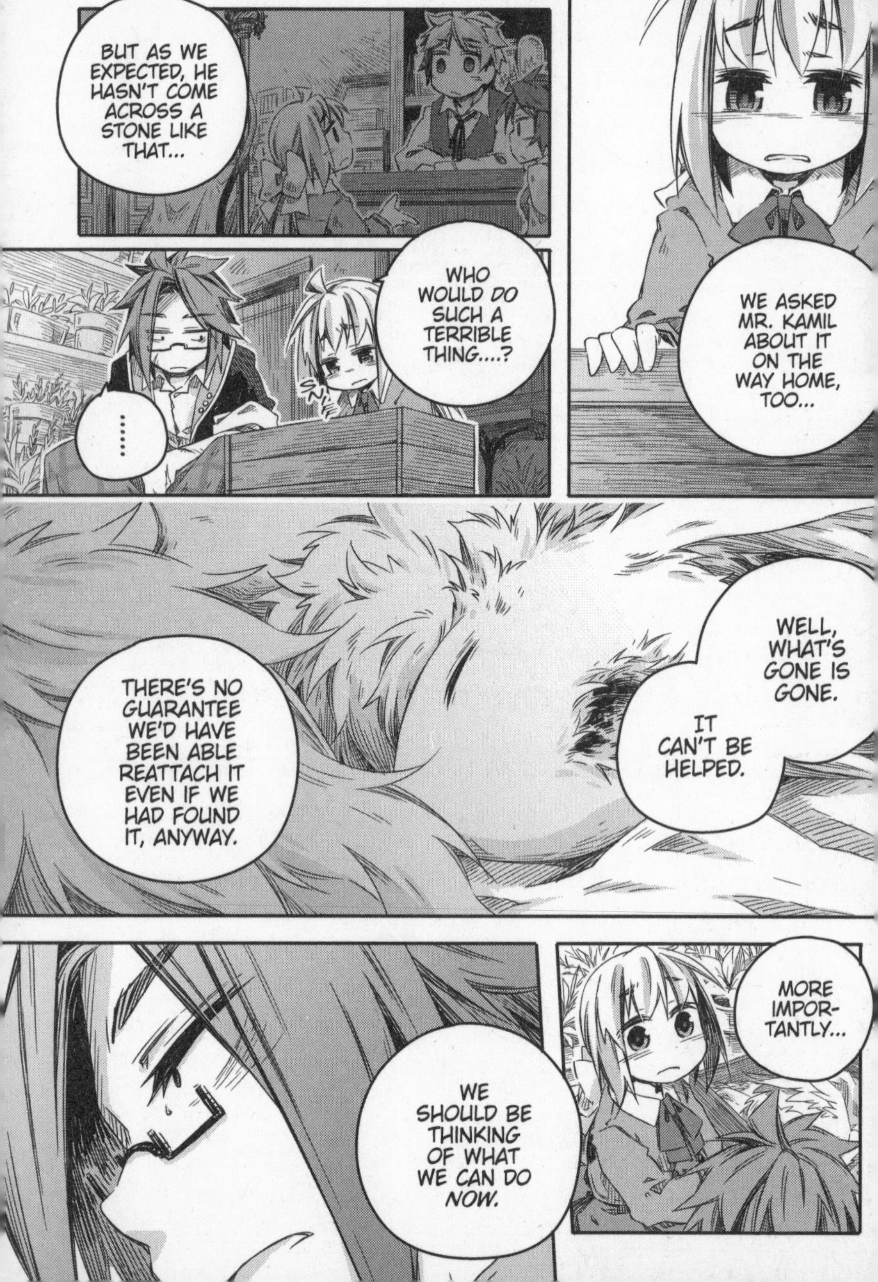
WE ASKED MR. KAMIL ABOUT IT ON THE WAY HOME, TOO...
BUT AS WE EXPECTED, HE HASN'T COME ACROSS A STONE LIKE THAT...
WHO WOULD *DO* SUCH A TERRIBLE THING....?
......
WELL, WHAT'S GONE IS GONE.
IT CAN'T BE HELPED.
THERE'S NO GUARANTEE WE'D HAVE BEEN ABLE REATTACH IT EVEN IF WE HAD FOUND IT, ANYWAY.
MORE IMPOR-TANTLY...
WE SHOULD BE THINKING OF WHAT WE CAN DO *NOW.*

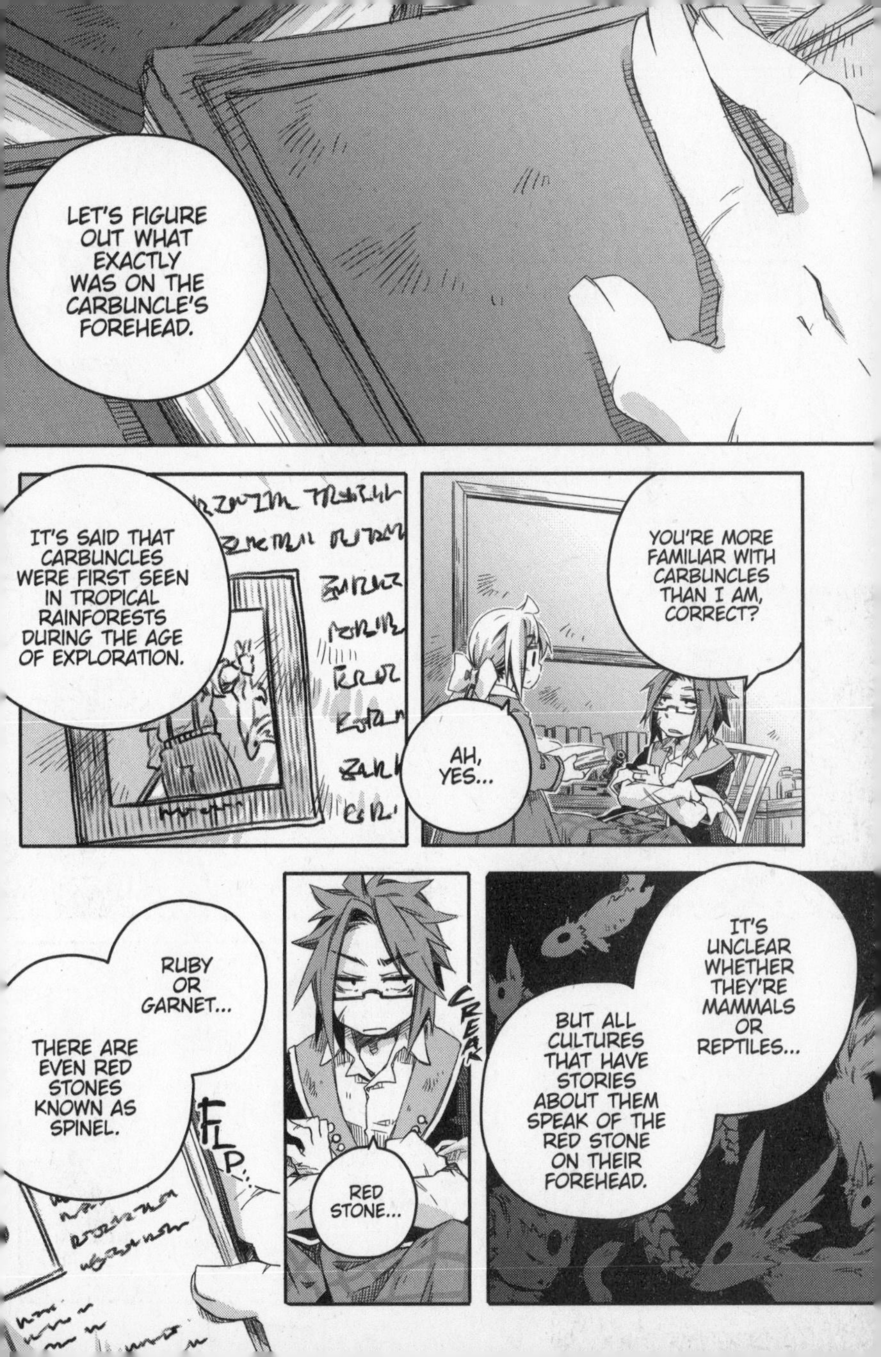
LET'S FIGURE OUT WHAT EXACTLY WAS ON THE CARBUNCLE'S FOREHEAD.
YOU'RE MORE FAMILIAR WITH CARBUNCLES THAN I AM, CORRECT?
AH, YES...
IT'S SAID THAT CARBUNCLES WERE FIRST SEEN IN TROPICAL RAINFORESTS DURING THE AGE OF EXPLORATION.
IT'S UNCLEAR WHETHER THEY'RE MAMMALS OR REPTILES...
BUT ALL CULTURES THAT HAVE STORIES ABOUT THEM SPEAK OF THE RED STONE ON THEIR FOREHEAD.
CREAK
RED STONE...
RUBY OR GARNET...
THERE ARE EVEN RED STONES KNOWN AS SPINEL.
FLIP...

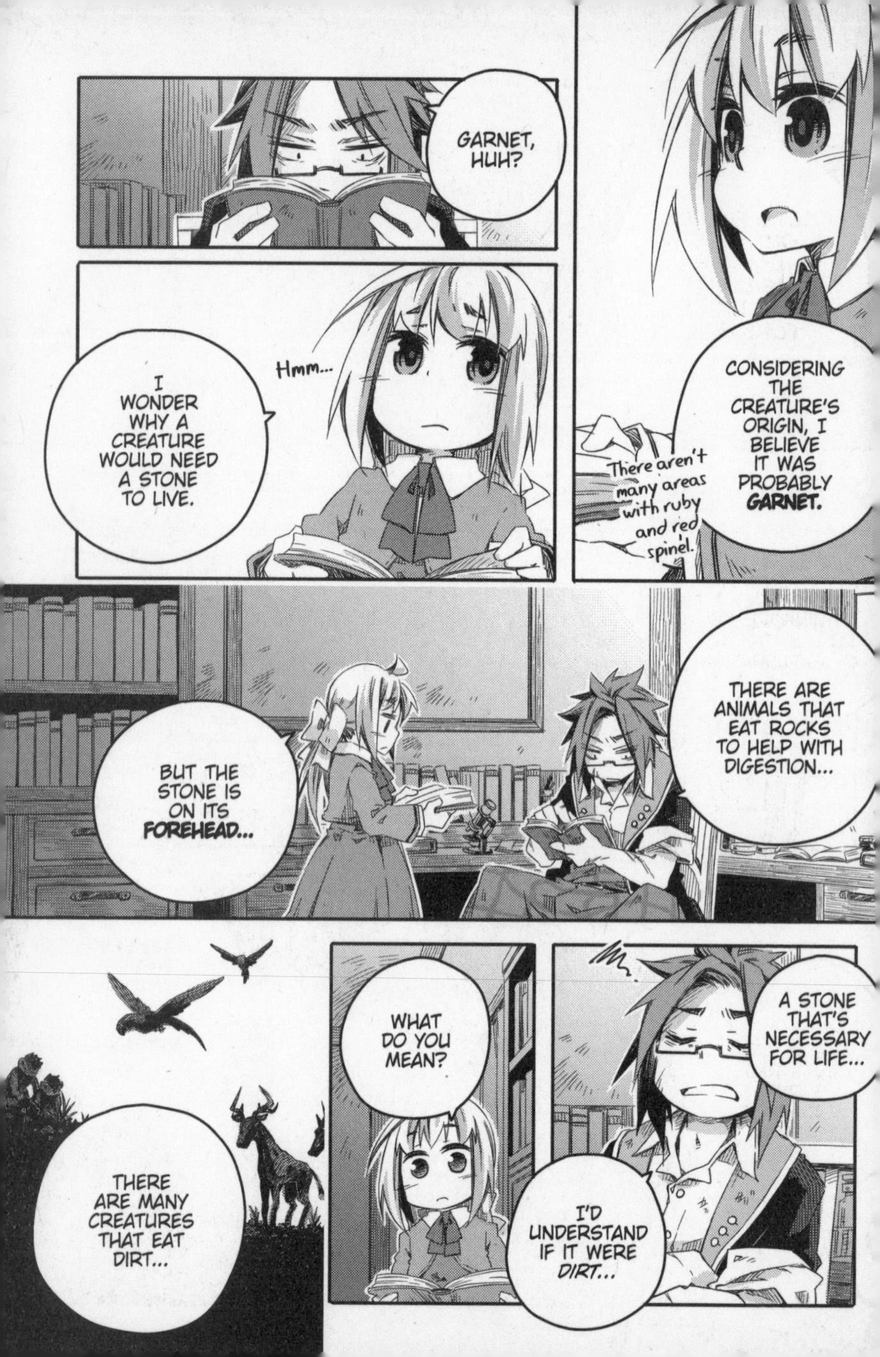
CONSIDERING THE CREATURE'S ORIGIN, I BELIEVE IT WAS PROBABLY GARNET.
There aren't many areas with ruby and red spinel.
GARNET, HUH?
Hmm...
I WONDER WHY A CREATURE WOULD NEED A STONE TO LIVE.
THERE ARE ANIMALS THAT EAT ROCKS TO HELP WITH DIGESTION...
BUT THE STONE IS ON ITS FOREHEAD...
A STONE THAT'S NECESSARY FOR LIFE...
I'D UNDERSTAND IF IT WERE DIRT...
WHAT DO YOU MEAN?
THERE ARE MANY CREATURES THAT EAT DIRT...

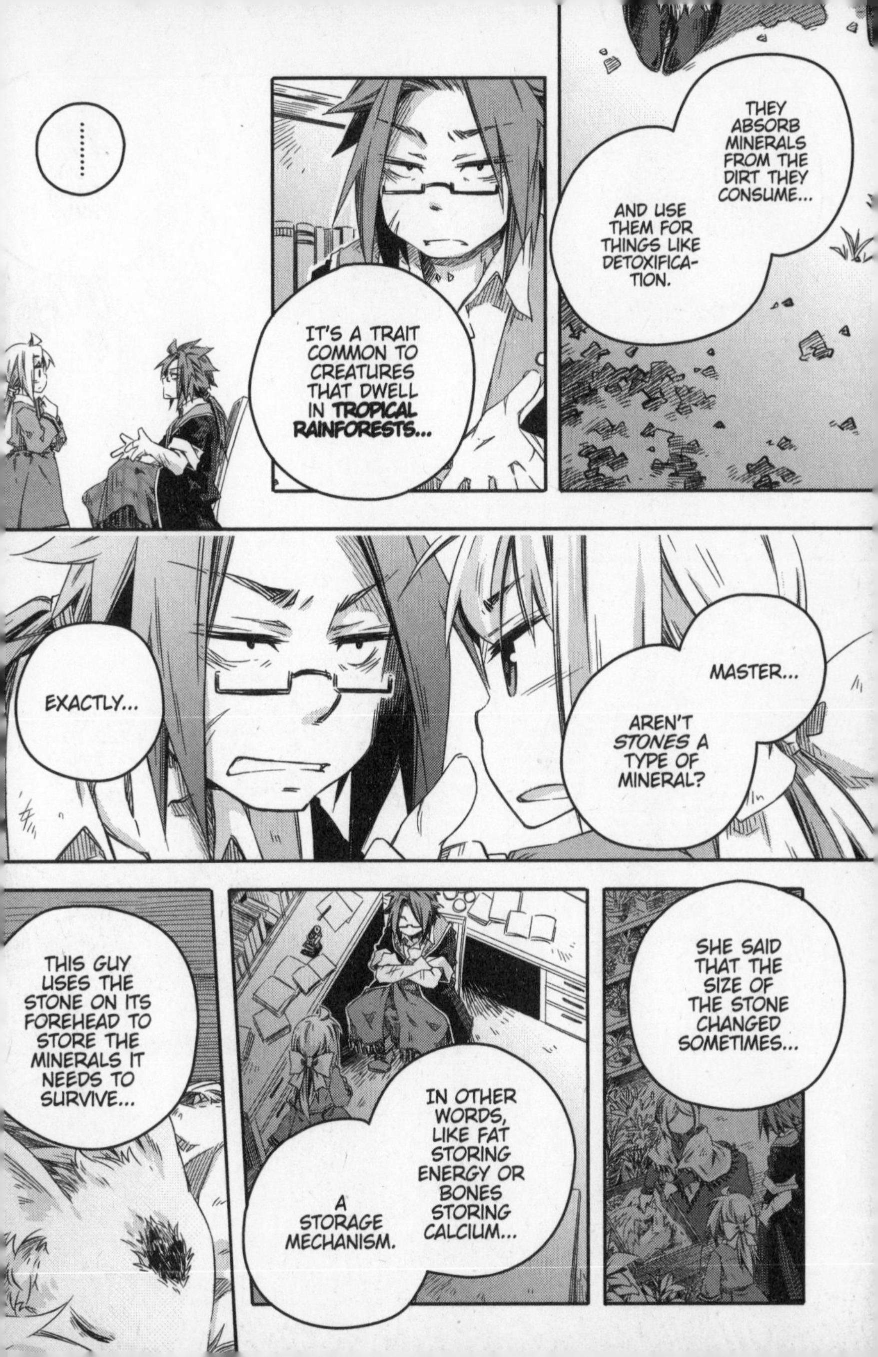
THEY ABSORB MINERALS FROM THE DIRT THEY CONSUME...
AND USE THEM FOR THINGS LIKE DETOXIFICA- TION.
IT'S A TRAIT COMMON TO CREATURES THAT DWELL IN **TROPICAL RAINFORESTS...**
......
MASTER...
AREN'T *STONES* A TYPE OF MINERAL?
EXACTLY...
SHE SAID THAT THE SIZE OF THE STONE CHANGED SOMETIMES...
IN OTHER WORDS, LIKE FAT STORING ENERGY OR BONES STORING CALCIUM...
A STORAGE MECHANISM.
THIS GUY USES THE STONE ON ITS FOREHEAD TO STORE THE MINERALS IT NEEDS TO SURVIVE...

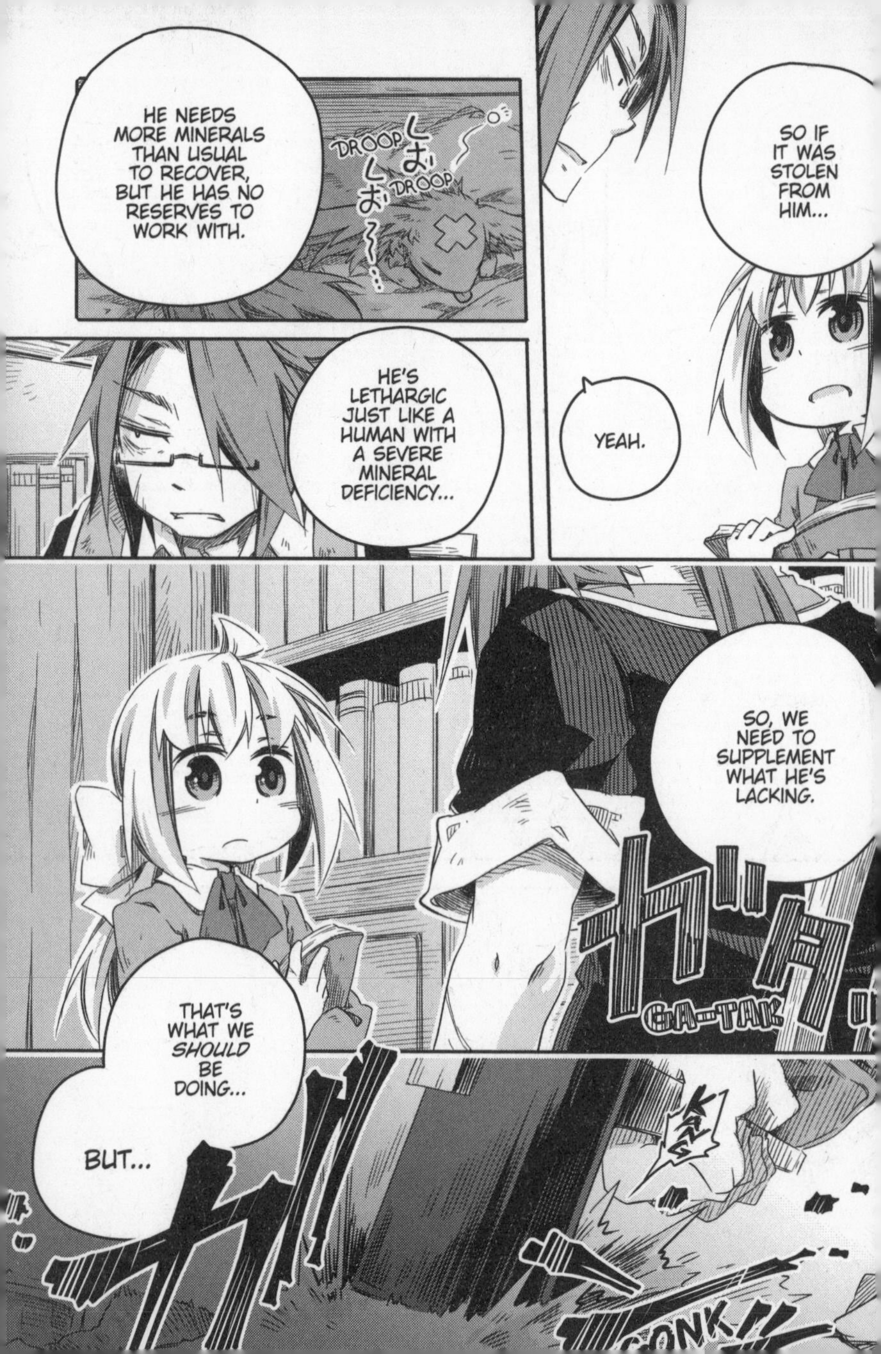
SO IF IT WAS STOLEN FROM HIM...
YEAH.
HE NEEDS MORE MINERALS THAN USUAL TO RECOVER, BUT HE HAS NO RESERVES TO WORK WITH.
DROOP DROOP
HE'S LETHARGIC JUST LIKE A HUMAN WITH A SEVERE MINERAL DEFICIENCY...
SO, WE NEED TO SUPPLEMENT WHAT HE'S LACKING.
GA-TAK
THAT'S WHAT WE *SHOULD* BE DOING...
KANG
BUT...
GONK!!

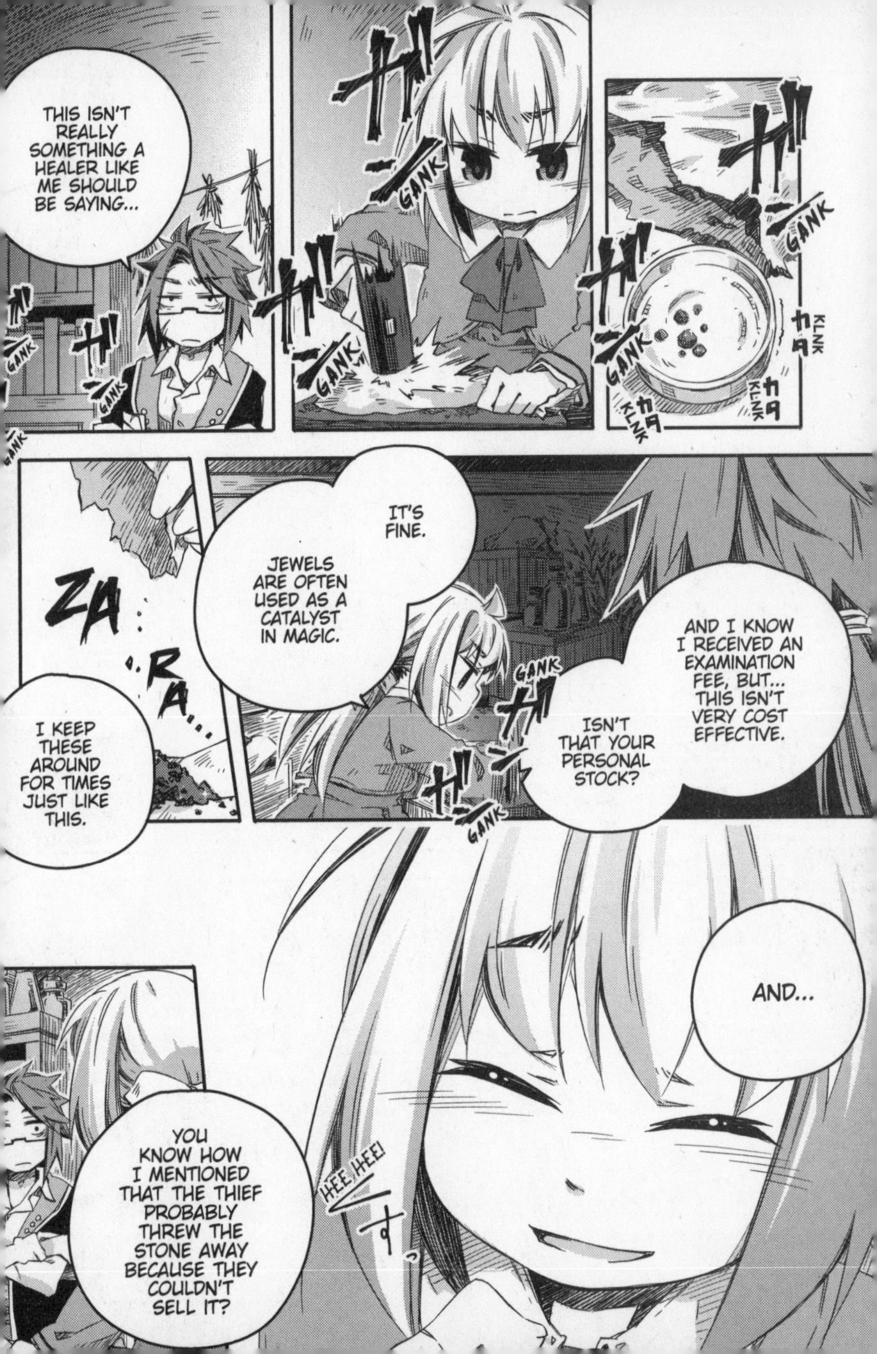
GANK
KLNK
KLNK
KLNK
GANK
GANK
GANK
THIS ISN'T REALLY SOMETHING A HEALER LIKE ME SHOULD BE SAYING...
GANK
GANK
GANK
AND I KNOW I RECEIVED AN EXAMINATION FEE, BUT... THIS ISN'T VERY COST EFFECTIVE.
ISN'T THAT YOUR PERSONAL STOCK?
GANK
GANK
IT'S FINE.
JEWELS ARE OFTEN USED AS A CATALYST IN MAGIC.
ZA... RA...
I KEEP THESE AROUND FOR TIMES JUST LIKE THIS.
AND...
HEE HEE!
YOU KNOW HOW I MENTIONED THAT THE THIEF PROBABLY THREW THE STONE AWAY BECAUSE THEY COULDN'T SELL IT?

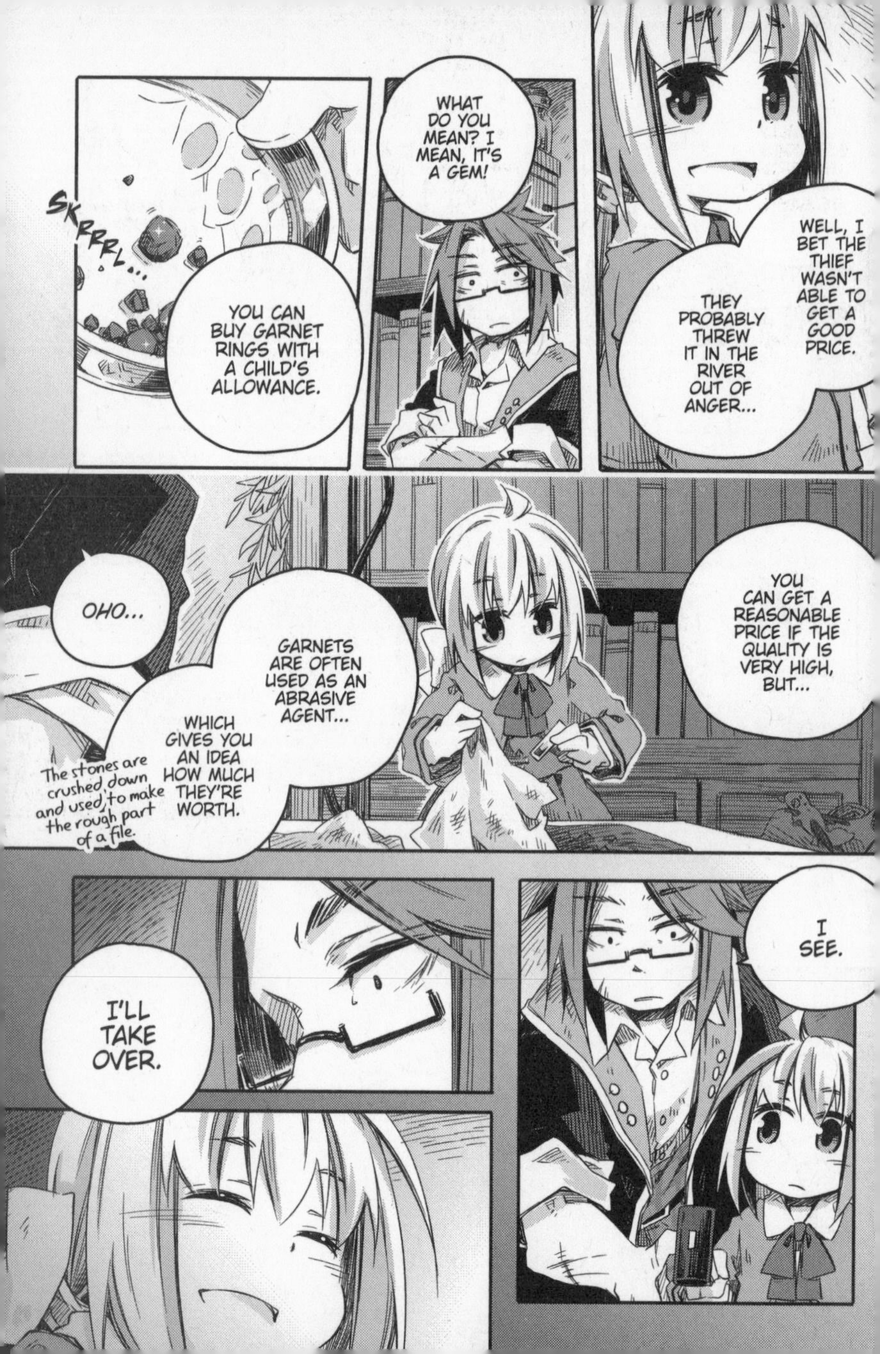
WELL, I BET THE THIEF WASN'T ABLE TO GET A GOOD PRICE.
THEY PROBABLY THREW IT IN THE RIVER OUT OF ANGER...
WHAT DO YOU MEAN? I MEAN, IT'S A GEM!
SKRRRL...
YOU CAN BUY GARNET RINGS WITH A CHILD'S ALLOWANCE.
YOU CAN GET A REASONABLE PRICE IF THE QUALITY IS VERY HIGH, BUT...
GARNETS ARE OFTEN USED AS AN ABRASIVE AGENT...
WHICH GIVES YOU AN IDEA HOW MUCH THEY'RE WORTH.
The stones are crushed down and used to make the rough part of a file.
OHO...
I SEE.
I'LL TAKE OVER.

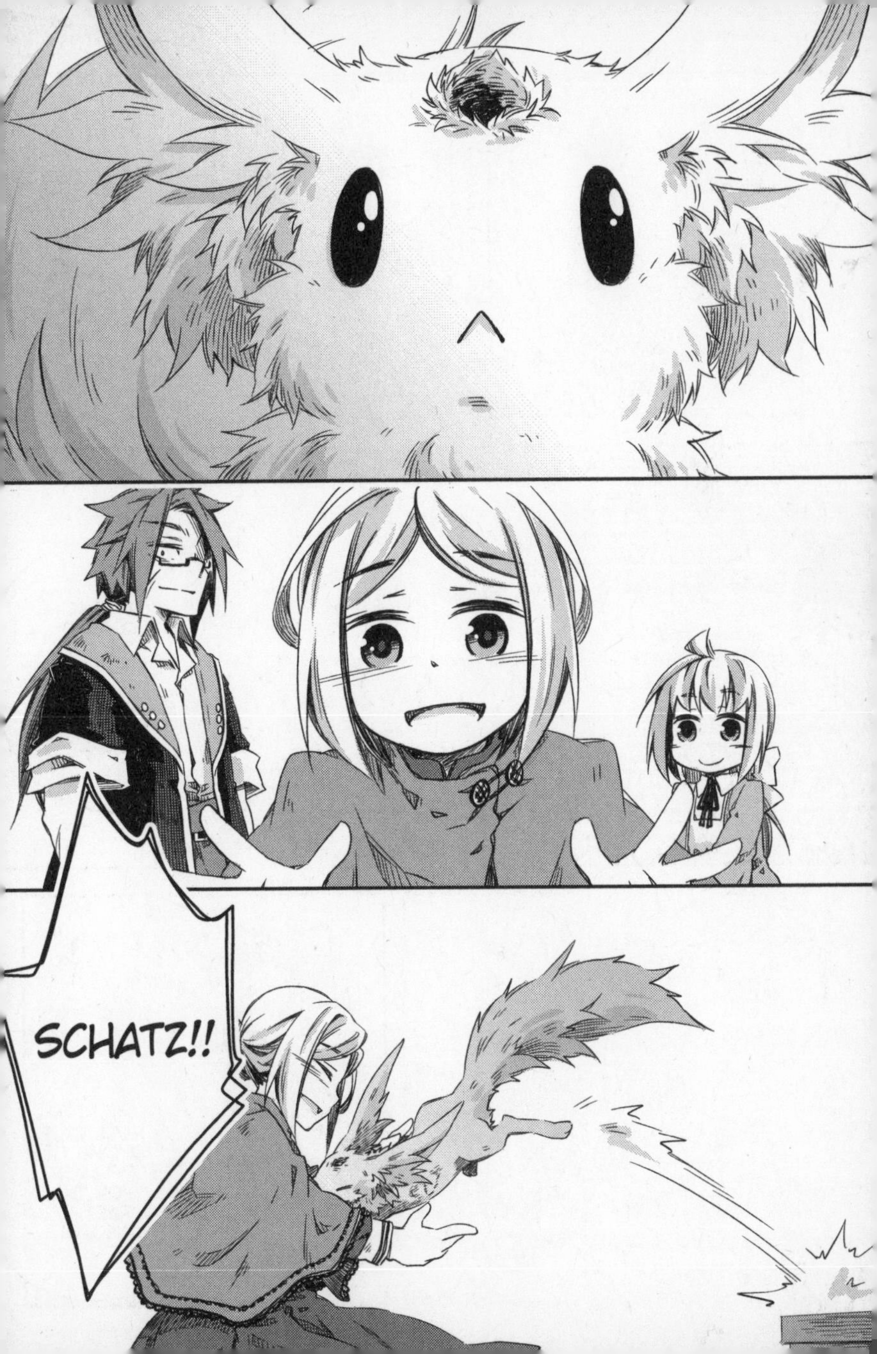
SCHATZ!!

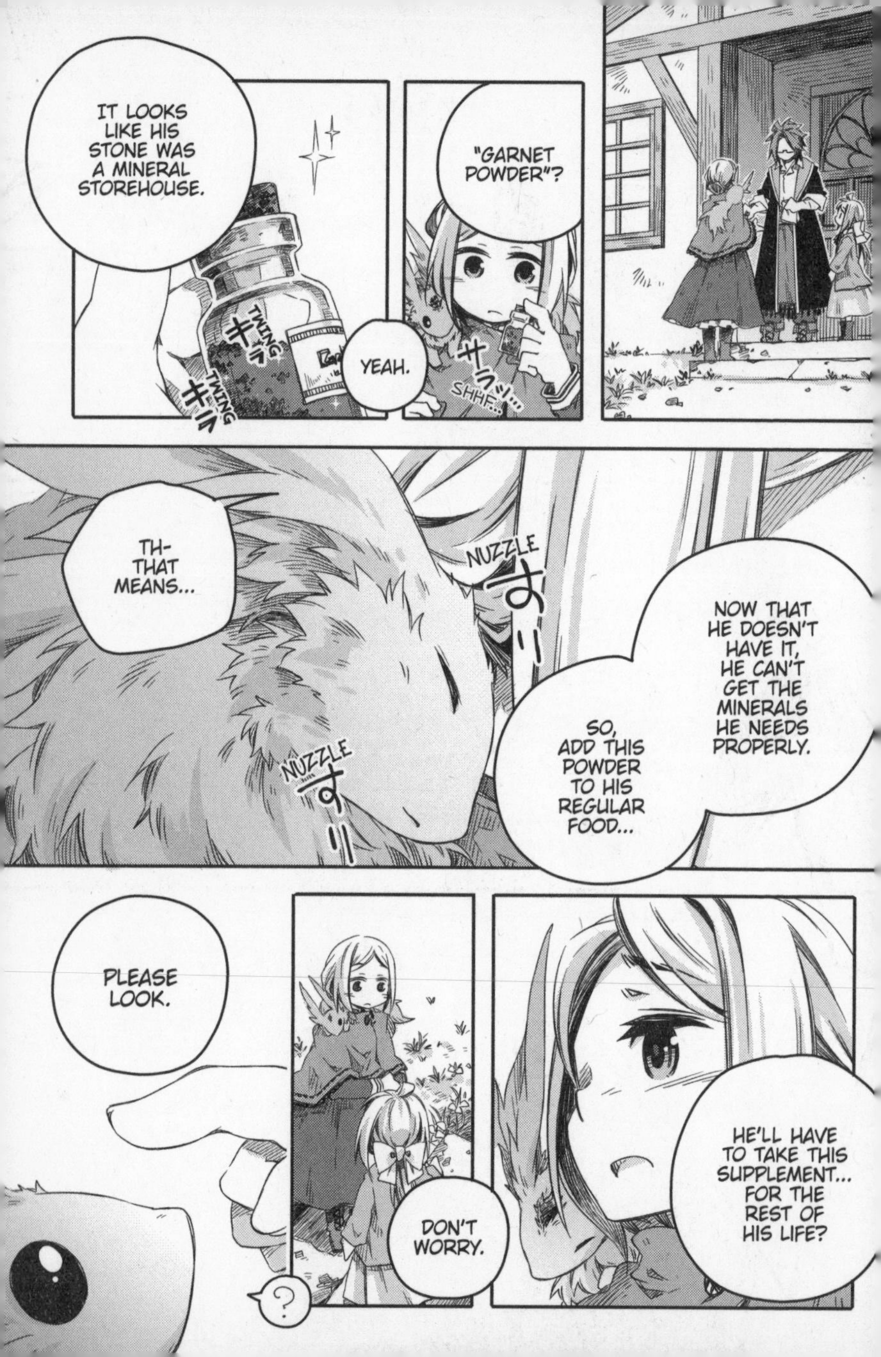

"GARNET POWDER"?
サラッ…
SHHF...
YEAH.
IT LOOKS LIKE HIS STONE WAS A MINERAL STOREHOUSE.
キラ
TWING
キラ
TWING
NOW THAT HE DOESN'T HAVE IT, HE CAN'T GET THE MINERALS HE NEEDS PROPERLY.
SO, ADD THIS POWDER TO HIS REGULAR FOOD...
NUZZLE
すり
TH- THAT MEANS...
NUZZLE
すり
HE'LL HAVE TO TAKE THIS SUPPLEMENT... FOR THE REST OF HIS LIFE?
DON'T WORRY.
PLEASE LOOK.
?

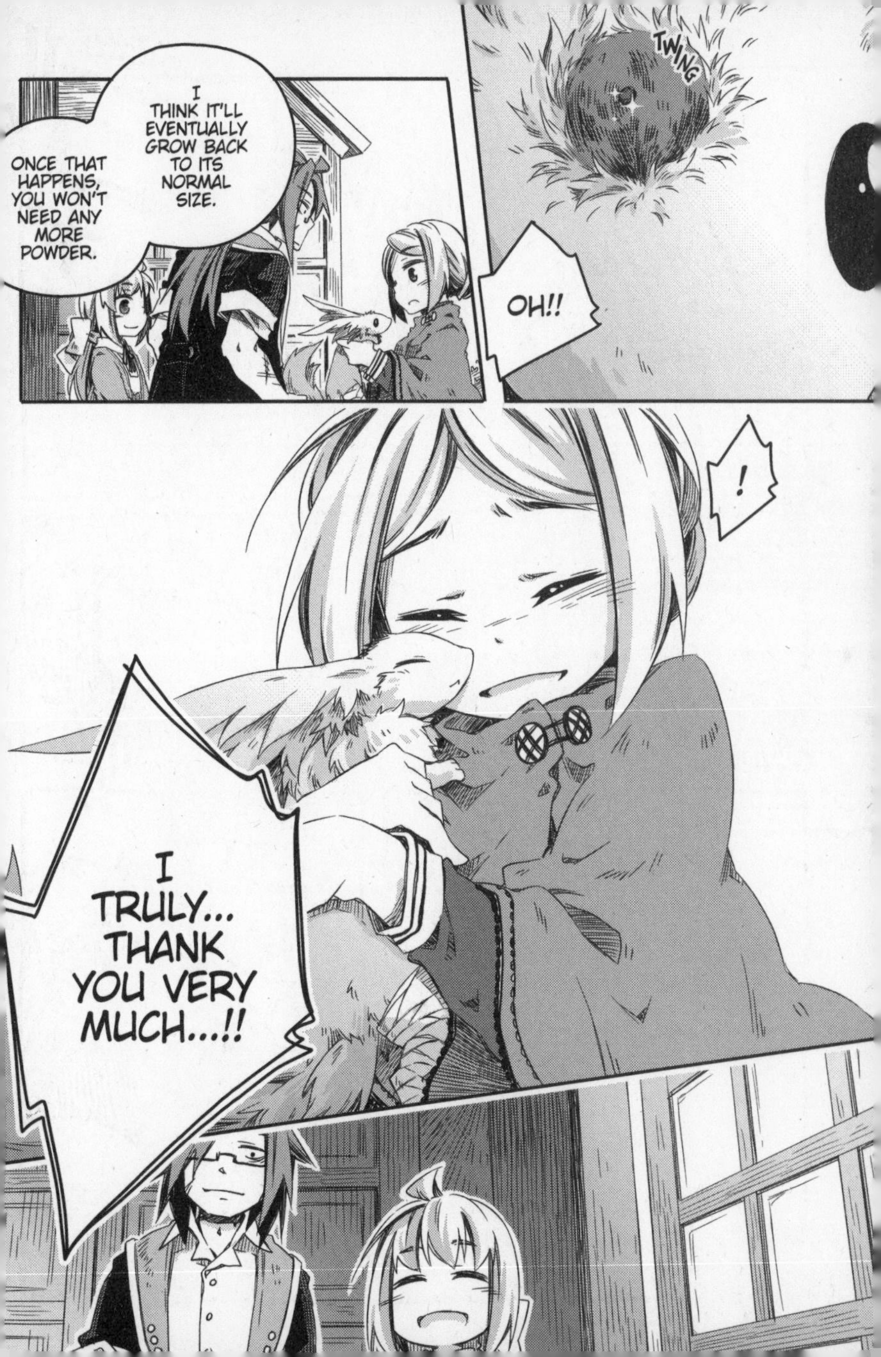
TWING
OH!!
I THINK IT'LL EVENTUALLY GROW BACK TO ITS NORMAL SIZE.
ONCE THAT HAPPENS, YOU WON'T NEED ANY MORE POWDER.
!
I TRULY... THANK YOU VERY MUCH...!!

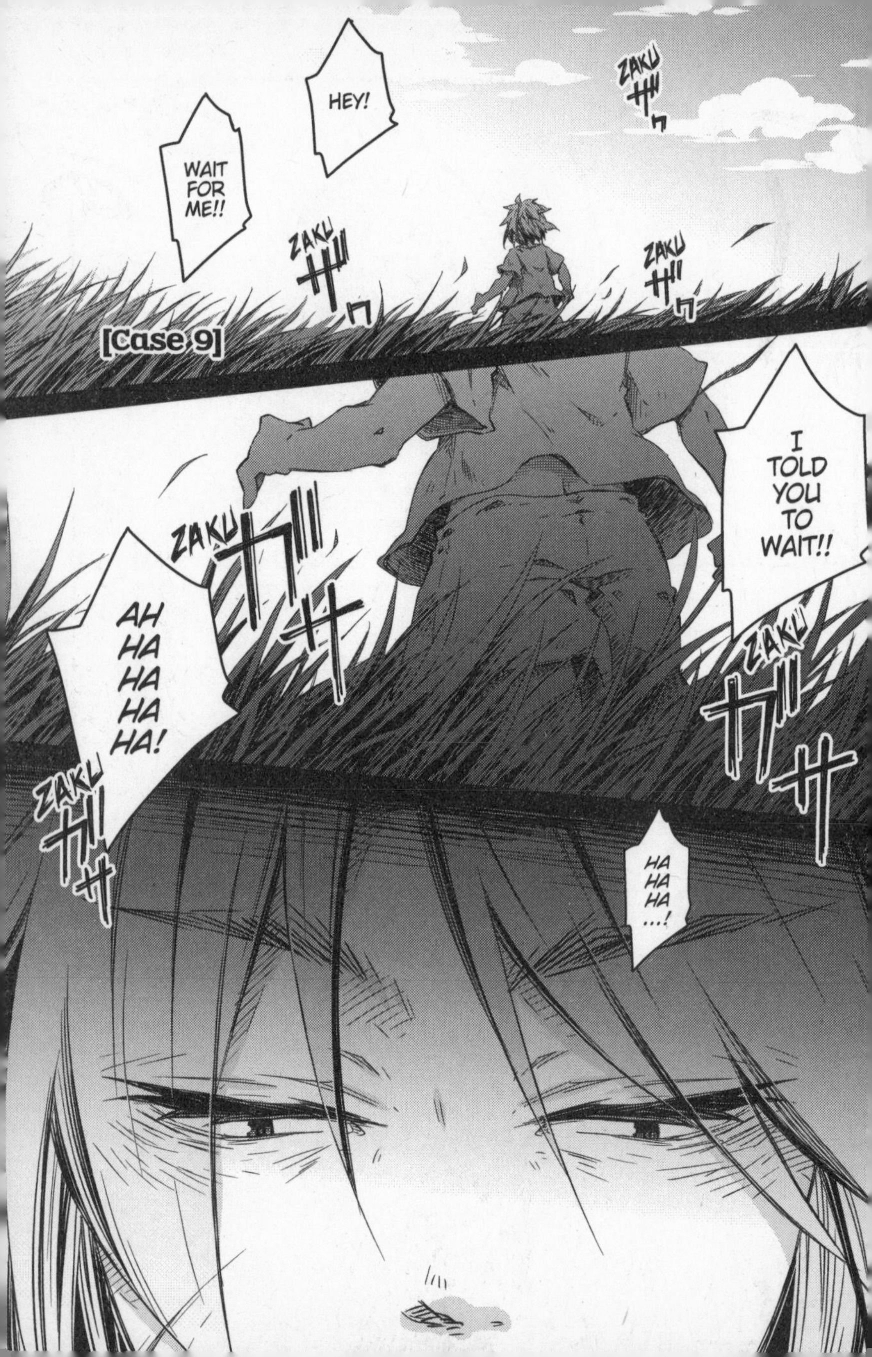
ZAKU
HEY!
WAIT FOR ME!!
ZAKU
ZAKU
[Case 9]
I TOLD YOU TO WAIT!!
ZAKU
ZAKU
AH HA HA HA HA HA!
ZAKU
HA HA HA ...!

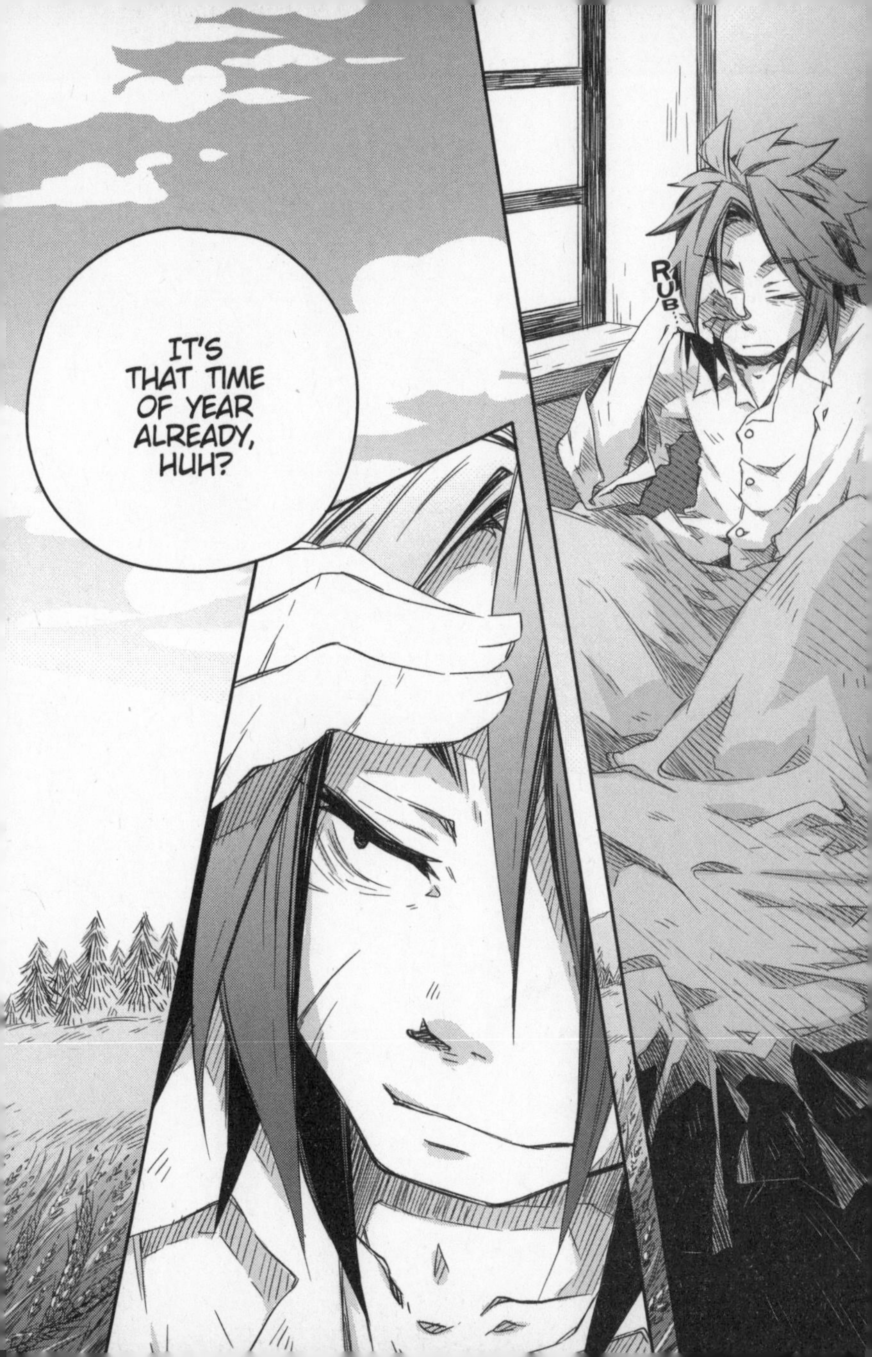
RUB...
IT'S THAT TIME OF YEAR ALREADY, HUH?

[Case 9: Progress and Selection]

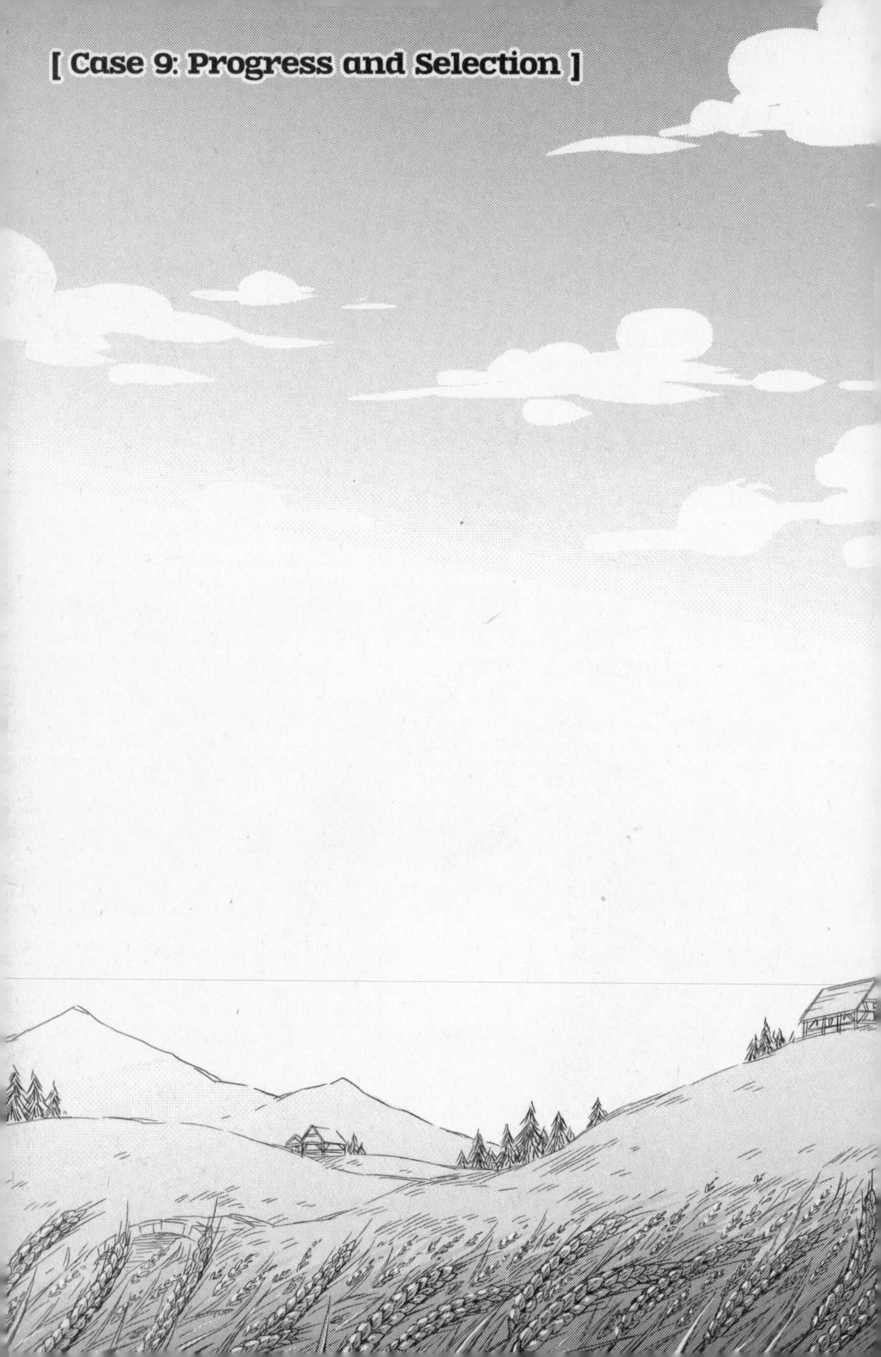

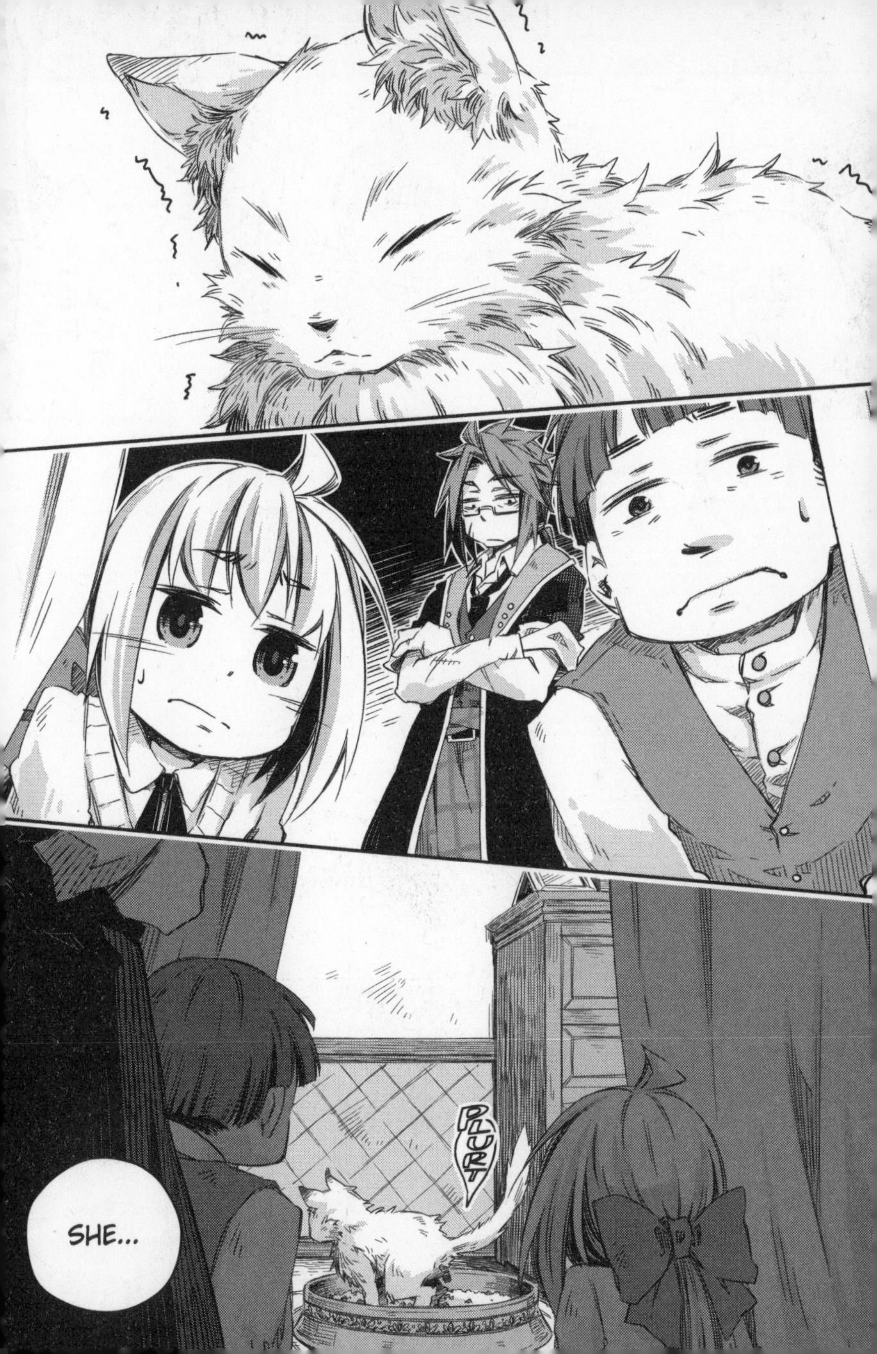
PLURT
SHE...

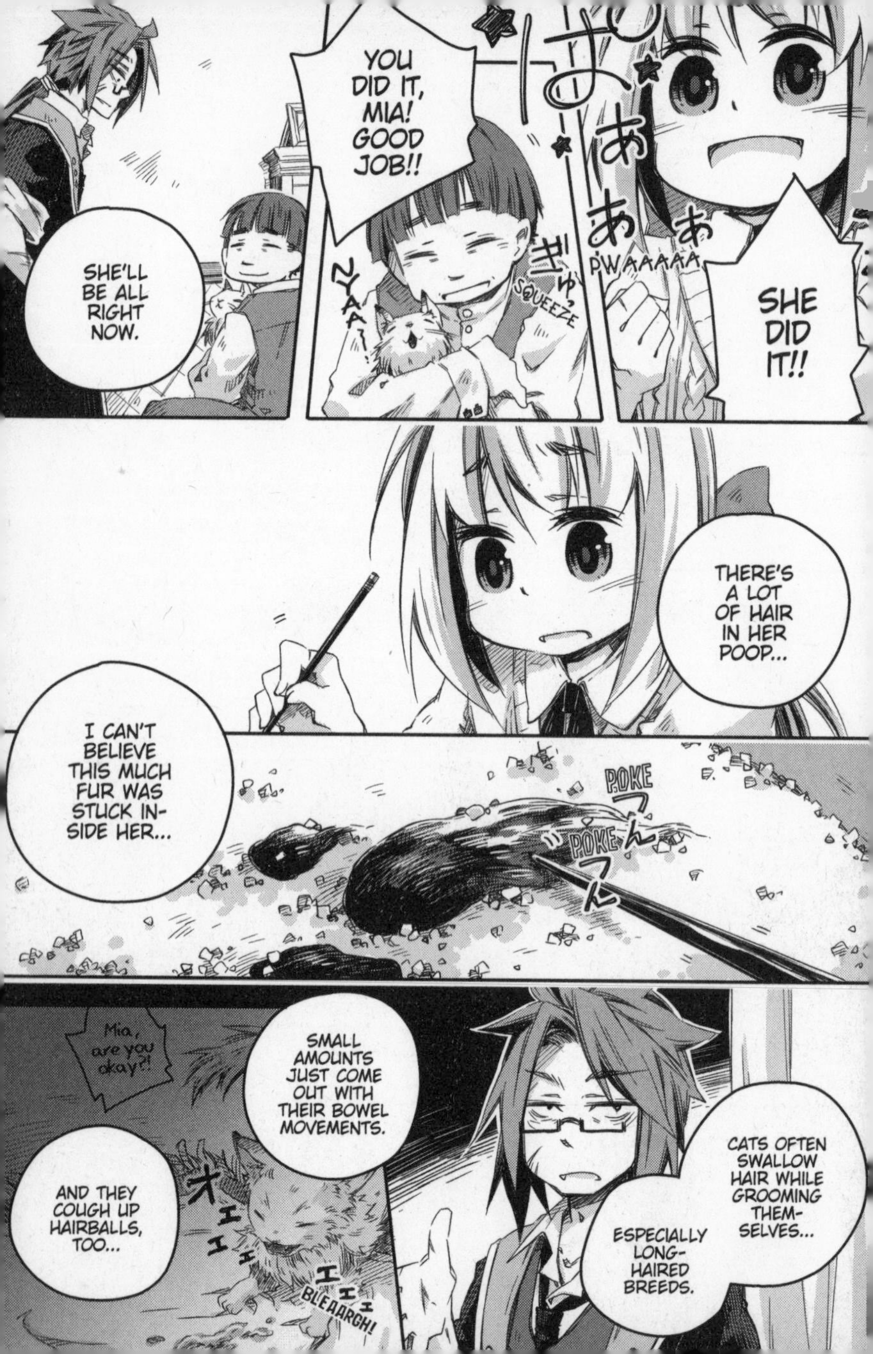
ぱあああ
PWAAAAA
SHE DID IT!!
YOU DID IT, MIA! GOOD JOB!!
ぎゅっ
SQUEEZE
NYAA
SHE'LL BE ALL RIGHT NOW.
THERE'S A LOT OF HAIR IN HER POOP...
I CAN'T BELIEVE THIS MUCH FUR WAS STUCK IN-SIDE HER...
POKE つん
POKE つん
CATS OFTEN SWALLOW HAIR WHILE GROOMING THEM-SELVES...
ESPECIALLY LONG-HAIRED BREEDS.
SMALL AMOUNTS JUST COME OUT WITH THEIR BOWEL MOVEMENTS.
AND THEY COUGH UP HAIRBALLS, TOO...
Mia, are you okay?!
BLEAARGH!

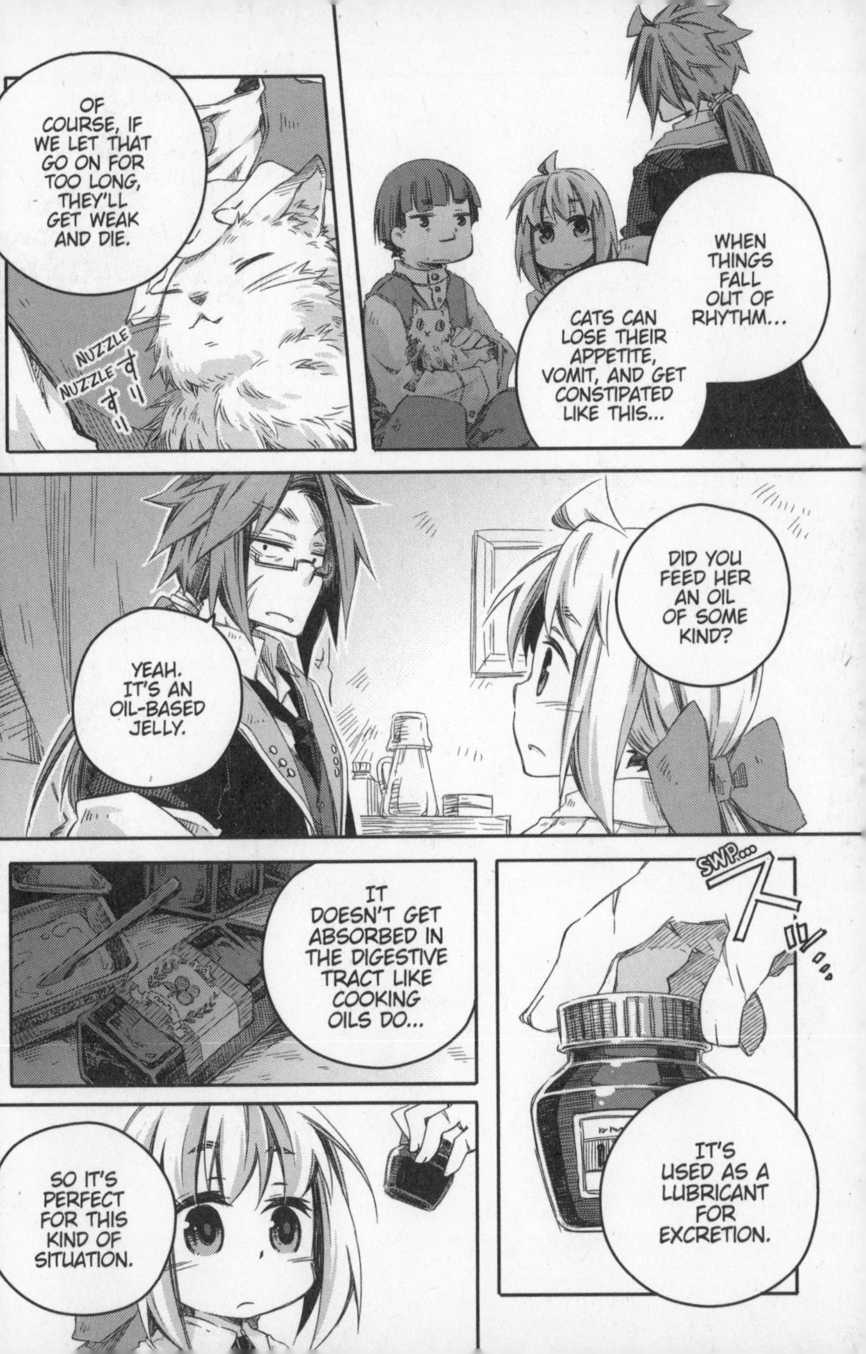
WHEN THINGS FALL OUT OF RHYTHM...
CATS CAN LOSE THEIR APPETITE, VOMIT, AND GET CONSTIPATED LIKE THIS...
OF COURSE, IF WE LET THAT GO ON FOR TOO LONG, THEY'LL GET WEAK AND DIE.
NUZZLE NUZZLE
すりすり
DID YOU FEED HER AN OIL OF SOME KIND?
YEAH. IT'S AN OIL-BASED JELLY.
SWP...
IT'S USED AS A LUBRICANT FOR EXCRETION.
IT DOESN'T GET ABSORBED IN THE DIGESTIVE TRACT LIKE COOKING OILS DO...
SO IT'S PERFECT FOR THIS KIND OF SITUATION.

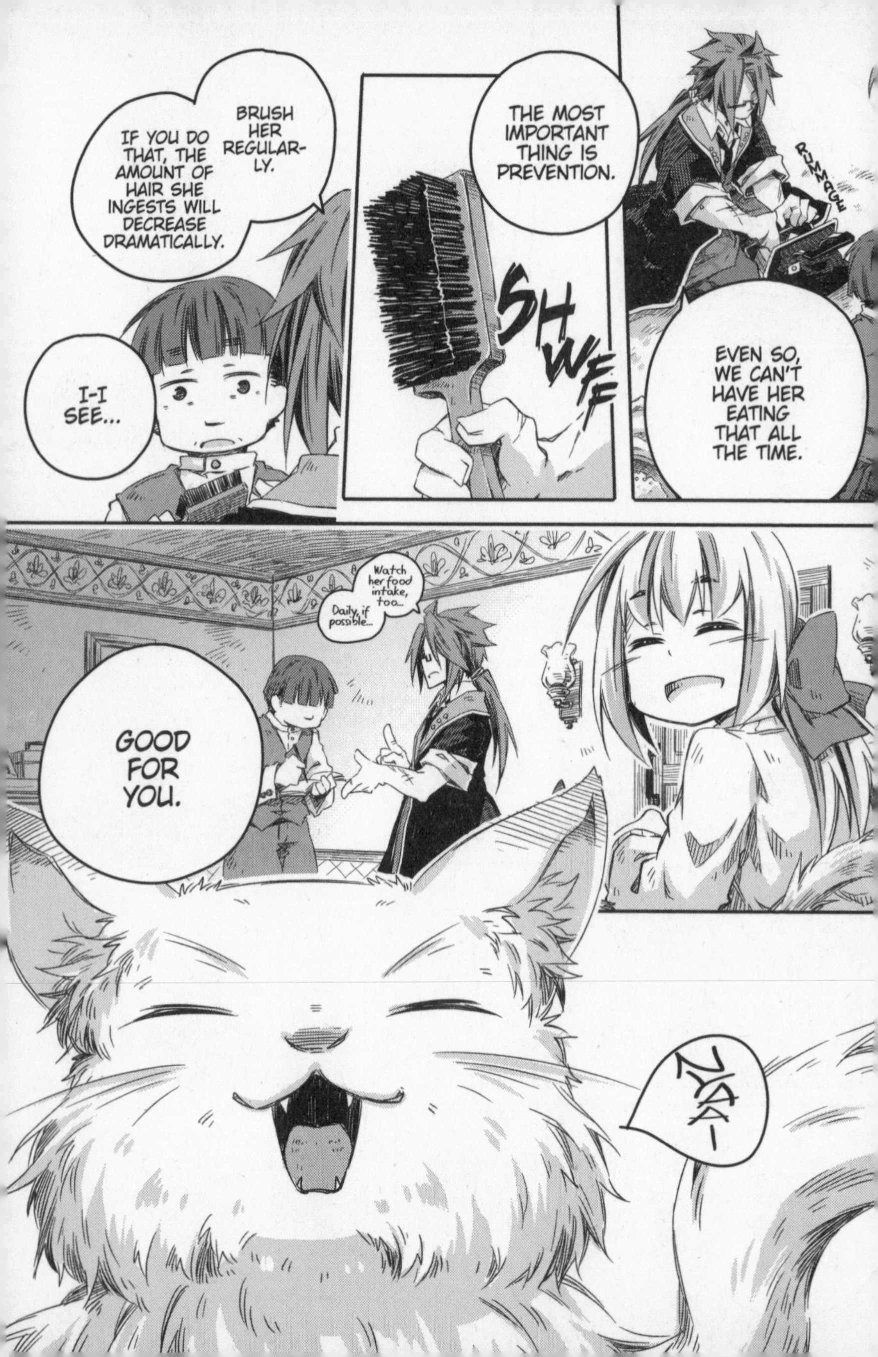
RUMMAGE
EVEN SO, WE CAN'T HAVE HER EATING THAT ALL THE TIME.
THE MOST IMPORTANT THING IS PREVENTION.
SHWFF
BRUSH HER REGULAR-LY.
IF YOU DO THAT, THE AMOUNT OF HAIR SHE INGESTS WILL DECREASE DRAMATICALLY.
I-I SEE...
Watch her food intake, too...
Daily, if possible...
GOOD FOR YOU.
NYAA-

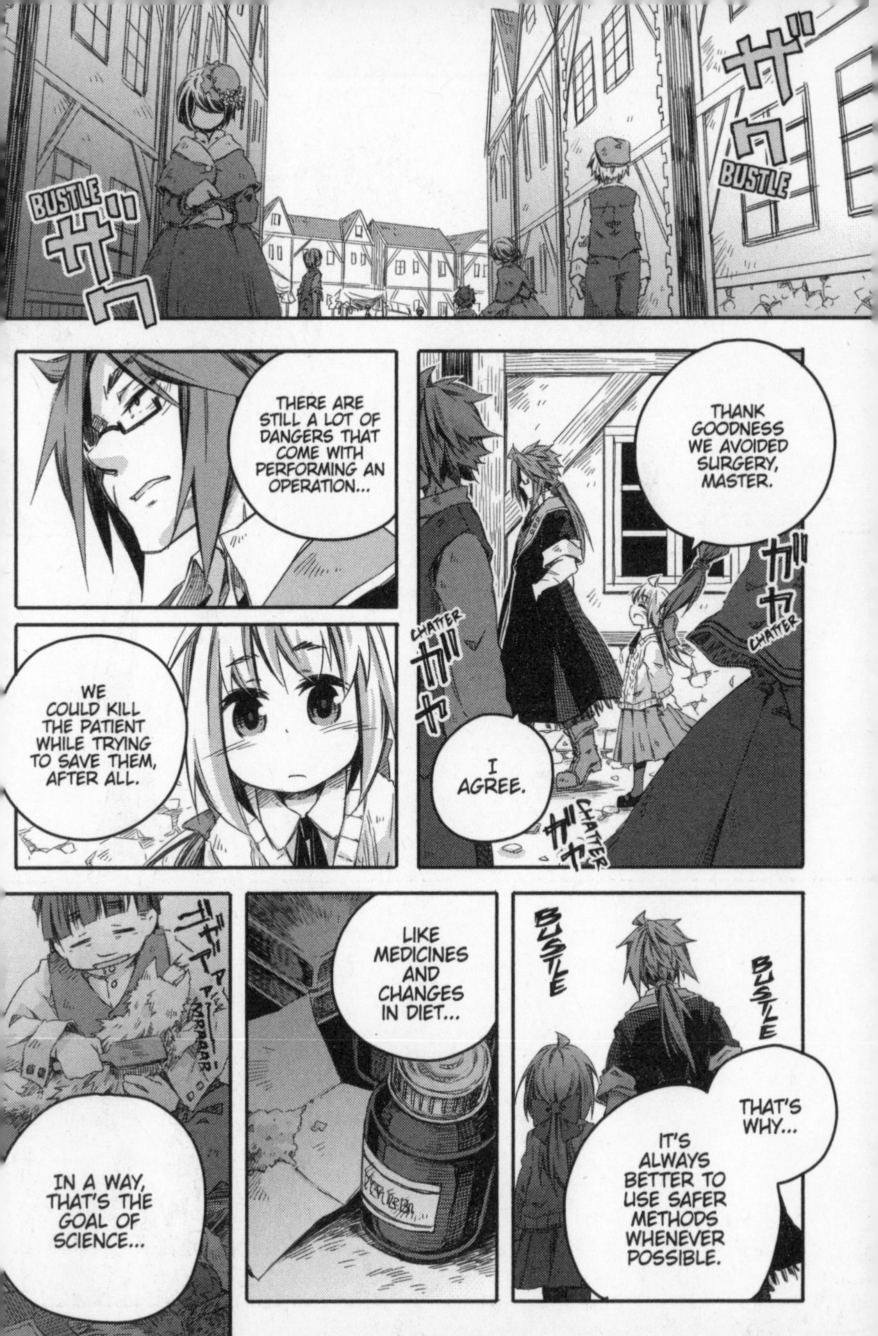

ザワ
BUSTLE
BUSTLE
ザワ
THANK GOODNESS WE AVOIDED SURGERY, MASTER.
がや
CHATTER
CHATTER
がや
I AGREE.
CHATTER
がや
THERE ARE STILL A LOT OF DANGERS THAT COME WITH PERFORMING AN OPERATION...
WE COULD KILL THE PATIENT WHILE TRYING TO SAVE THEM, AFTER ALL.
BUSTLE
BUSTLE
THAT'S WHY...
IT'S ALWAYS BETTER TO USE SAFER METHODS WHENEVER POSSIBLE.
LIKE MEDICINES AND CHANGES IN DIET...
IN A WAY, THAT'S THE GOAL OF SCIENCE...

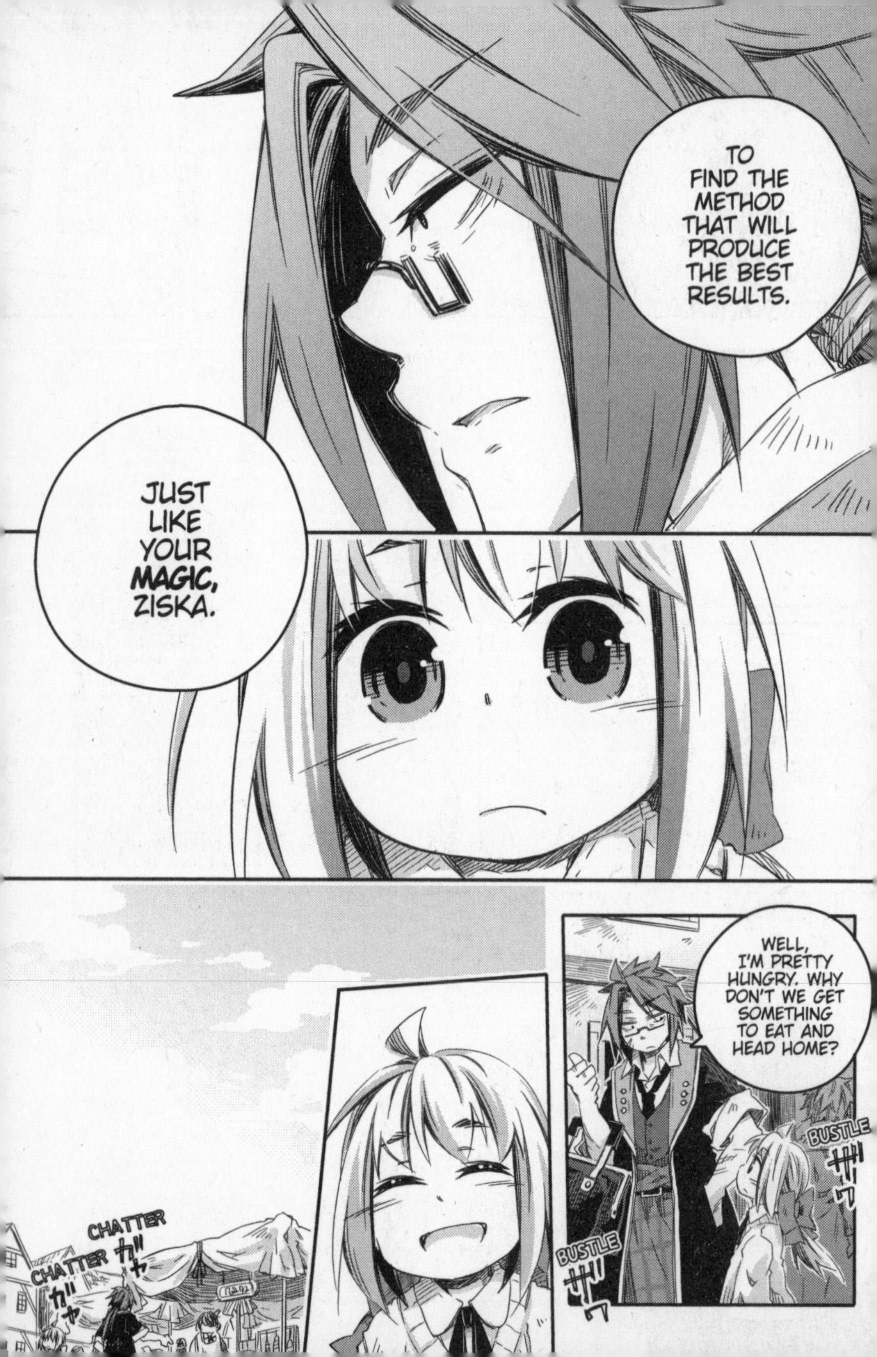
TO FIND THE METHOD THAT WILL PRODUCE THE BEST RESULTS.
JUST LIKE YOUR MAGIC, ZISKA.
WELL, I'M PRETTY HUNGRY. WHY DON'T WE GET SOMETHING TO EAT AND HEAD HOME?
BUSTLE
BUSTLE
CHATTER
CHATTER

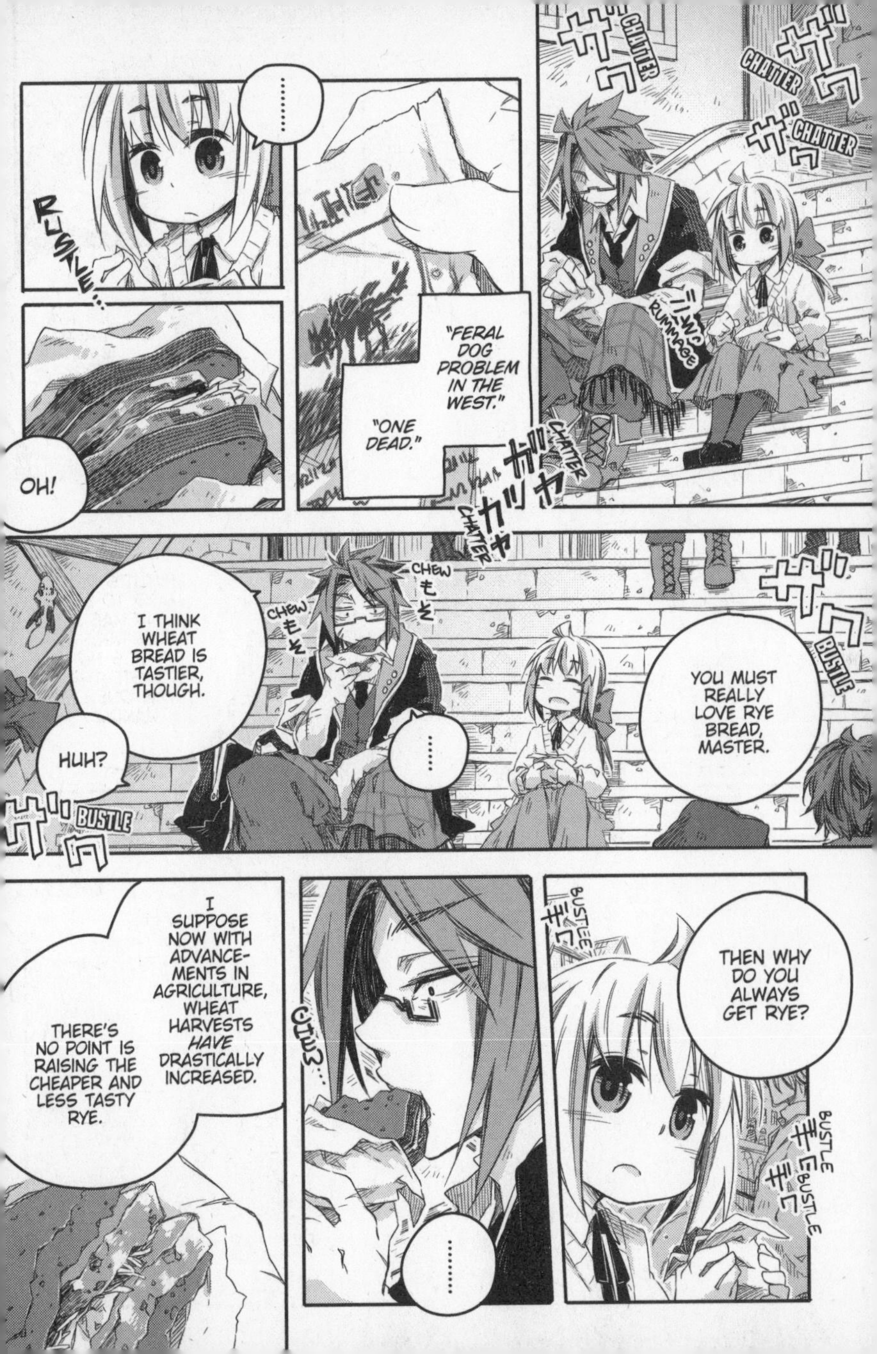
CHATTER
CHATTER
CHATTER
RUMMAGE
CHATTER
CHATTER
"FERAL DOG PROBLEM IN THE WEST."
"ONE DEAD."
......
RUSTLE...
OH!
BUSTLE
YOU MUST REALLY LOVE RYE BREAD, MASTER.
CHEW
CHEW
......
I THINK WHEAT BREAD IS TASTIER, THOUGH.
HUH?
BUSTLE
BUSTLE
THEN WHY DO YOU ALWAYS GET RYE?
BUSTLE
BUSTLE
CHEW...
......
I SUPPOSE NOW WITH ADVANCEMENTS IN AGRICULTURE, WHEAT HARVESTS *HAVE* DRASTICALLY INCREASED.
THERE'S NO POINT IS RAISING THE CHEAPER AND LESS TASTY RYE.

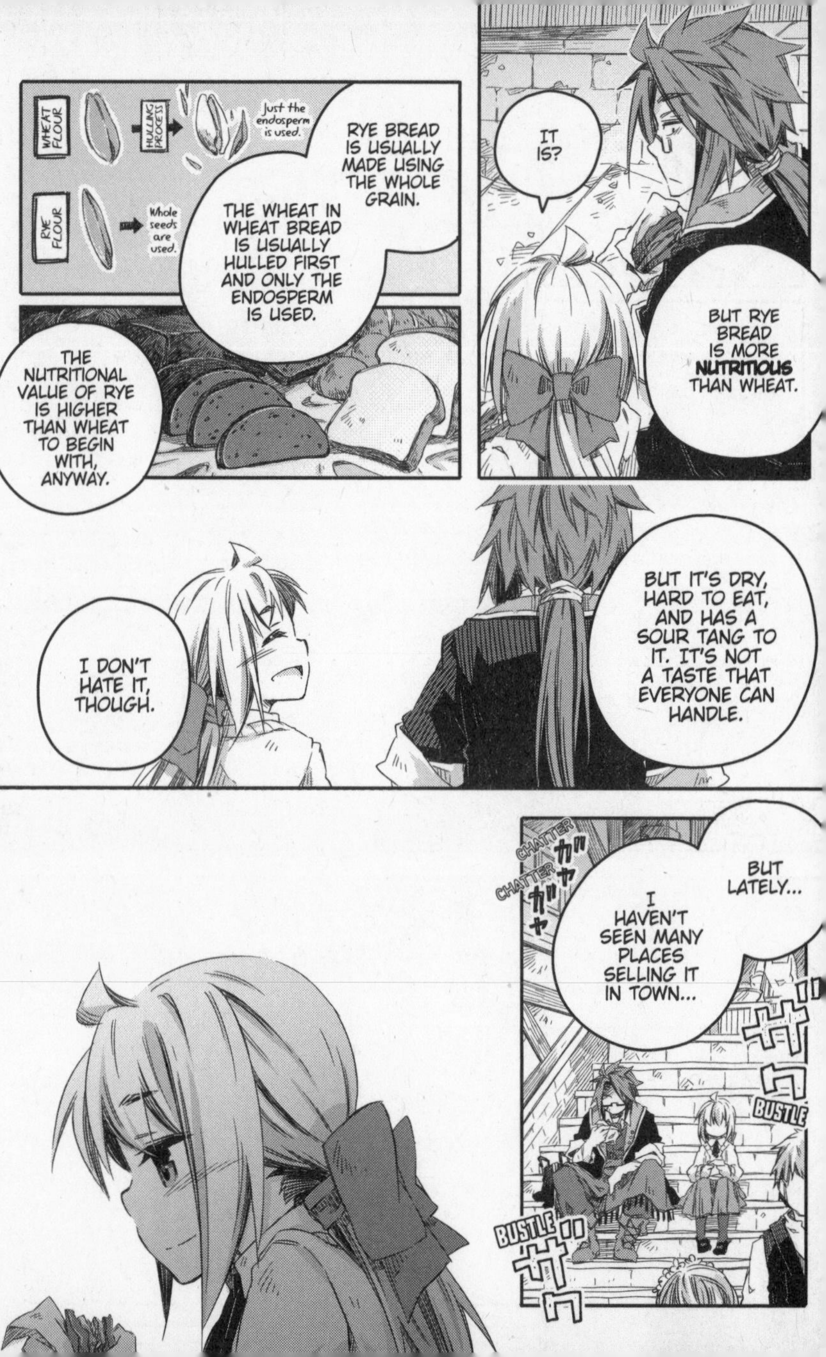
BUT RYE BREAD IS MORE **NUTRITIOUS** THAN WHEAT.
IT IS?
WHEAT FLOUR
HULLING PROCESS
Just the endosperm is used.
RYE FLOUR
Whole seeds are used.
RYE BREAD IS USUALLY MADE USING THE WHOLE GRAIN.
THE WHEAT IN WHEAT BREAD IS USUALLY HULLED FIRST AND ONLY THE ENDOSPERM IS USED.
THE NUTRITIONAL VALUE OF RYE IS HIGHER THAN WHEAT TO BEGIN WITH, ANYWAY.
BUT IT'S DRY, HARD TO EAT, AND HAS A SOUR TANG TO IT. IT'S NOT A TASTE THAT EVERYONE CAN HANDLE.
I DON'T HATE IT, THOUGH.
BUT LATELY... I HAVEN'T SEEN MANY PLACES SELLING IT IN TOWN...
CHATTER CHATTER
BUSTLE
BUSTLE

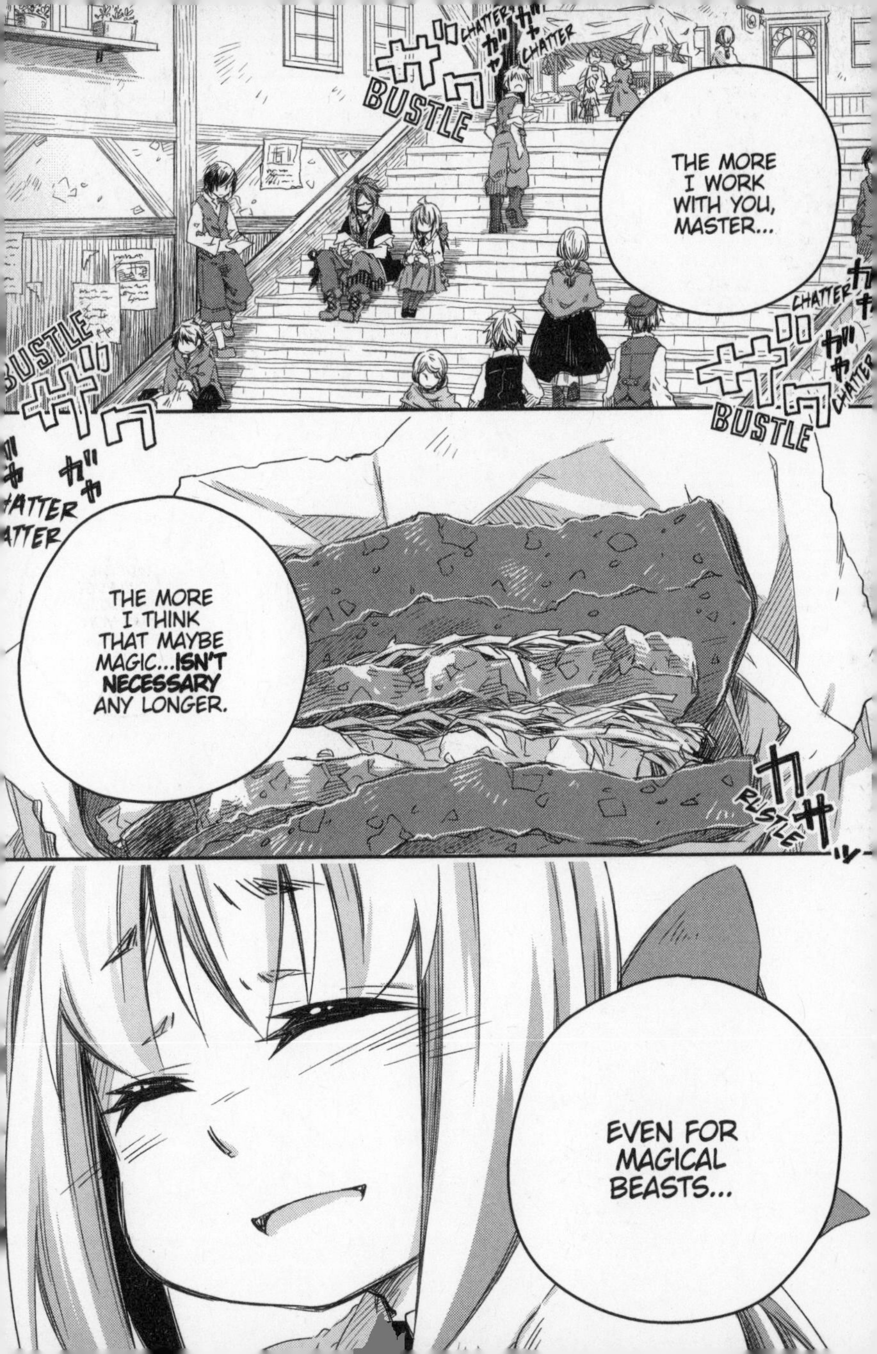
THE MORE I WORK WITH YOU, MASTER...
CHATTER
CHATTER
BUSTLE
CHATTER
CHATTER
BUSTLE
BUSTLE
CHATTER
CHATTER
THE MORE I THINK THAT MAYBE MAGIC...ISN'T NECESSARY ANY LONGER.
RUSTLE
EVEN FOR MAGICAL BEASTS...

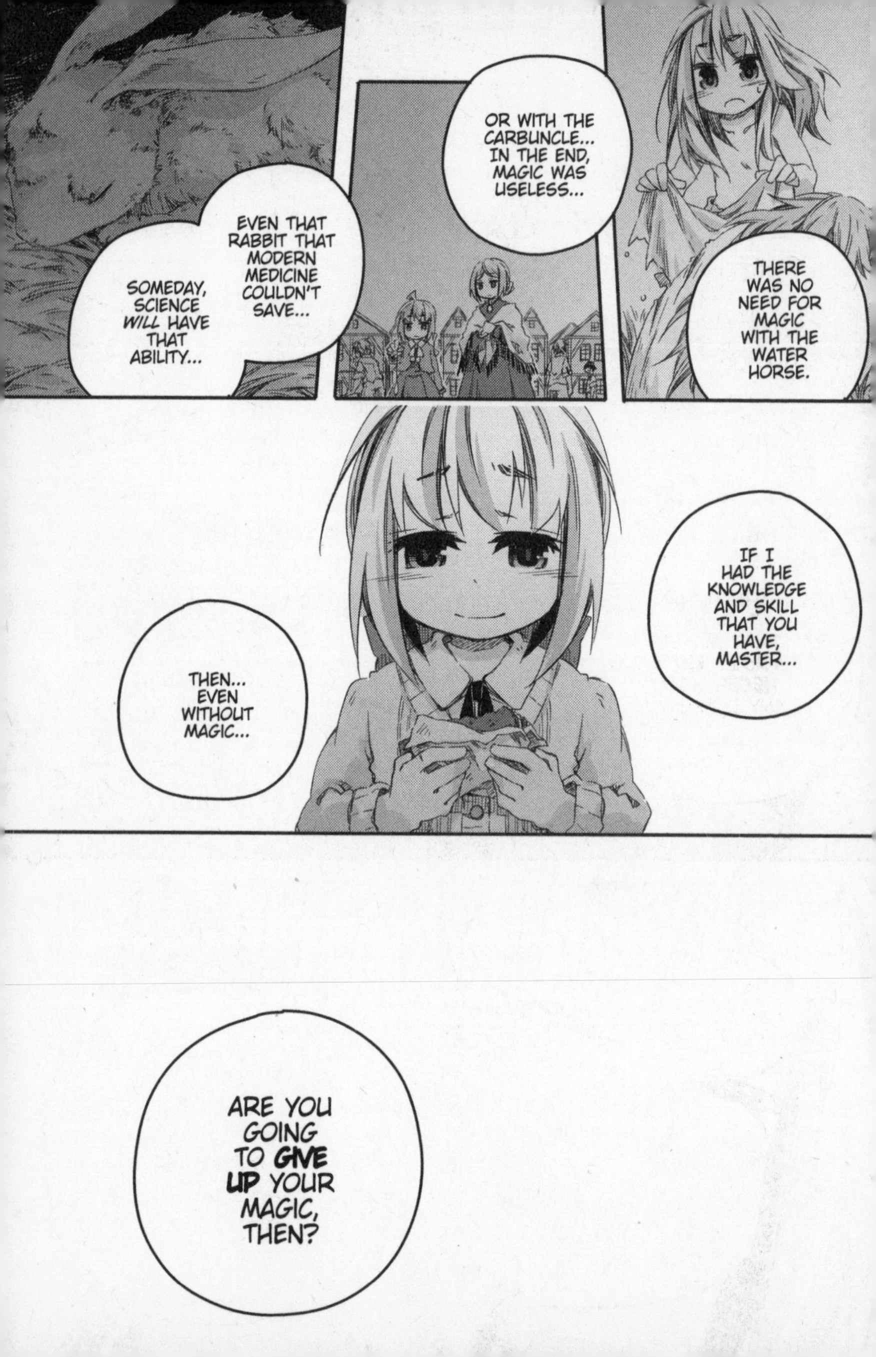
THERE WAS NO NEED FOR MAGIC WITH THE WATER HORSE.
OR WITH THE CARBUNCLE... IN THE END, MAGIC WAS USELESS...
EVEN THAT RABBIT THAT MODERN MEDICINE COULDN'T SAVE...
SOMEDAY, SCIENCE *WILL* HAVE THAT ABILITY...
IF I HAD THE KNOWLEDGE AND SKILL THAT YOU HAVE, MASTER...
THEN... EVEN WITHOUT MAGIC...
ARE YOU GOING TO **GIVE UP** YOUR MAGIC, THEN?

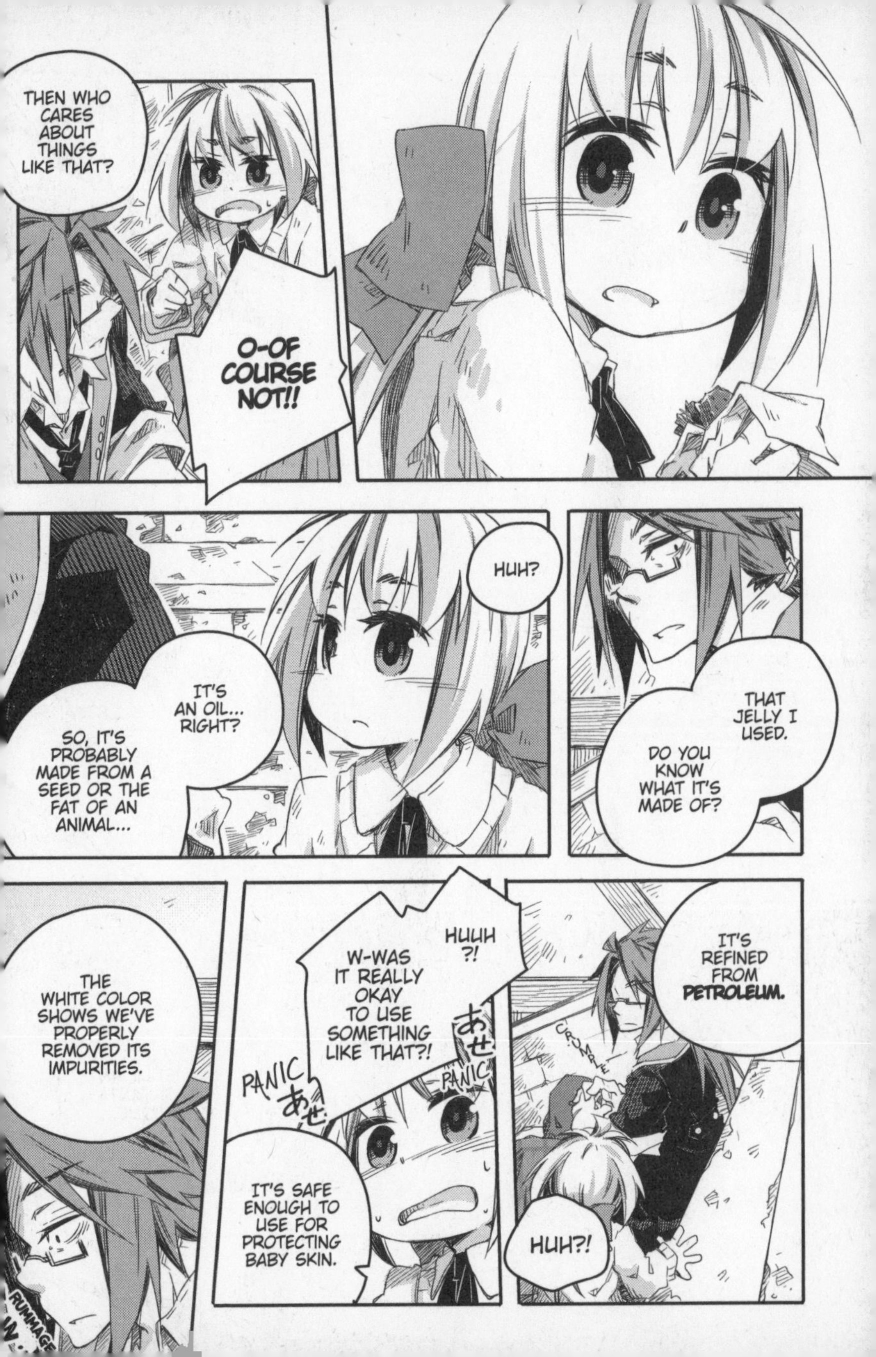
O-OF COURSE NOT!!
THEN WHO CARES ABOUT THINGS LIKE THAT?
THAT JELLY I USED.
DO YOU KNOW WHAT IT'S MADE OF?
HUH?
IT'S AN OIL... RIGHT?
SO, IT'S PROBABLY MADE FROM A SEED OR THE FAT OF AN ANIMAL...
IT'S REFINED FROM **PETROLEUM.**
CRUMPLE
HUH?!
HUUH ?!
W-WAS IT REALLY OKAY TO USE SOMETHING LIKE THAT?!
あせ PANIC
PANIC あせ
IT'S SAFE ENOUGH TO USE FOR PROTECTING BABY SKIN.
THE WHITE COLOR SHOWS WE'VE PROPERLY REMOVED ITS IMPURITIES.
RUMMAGE

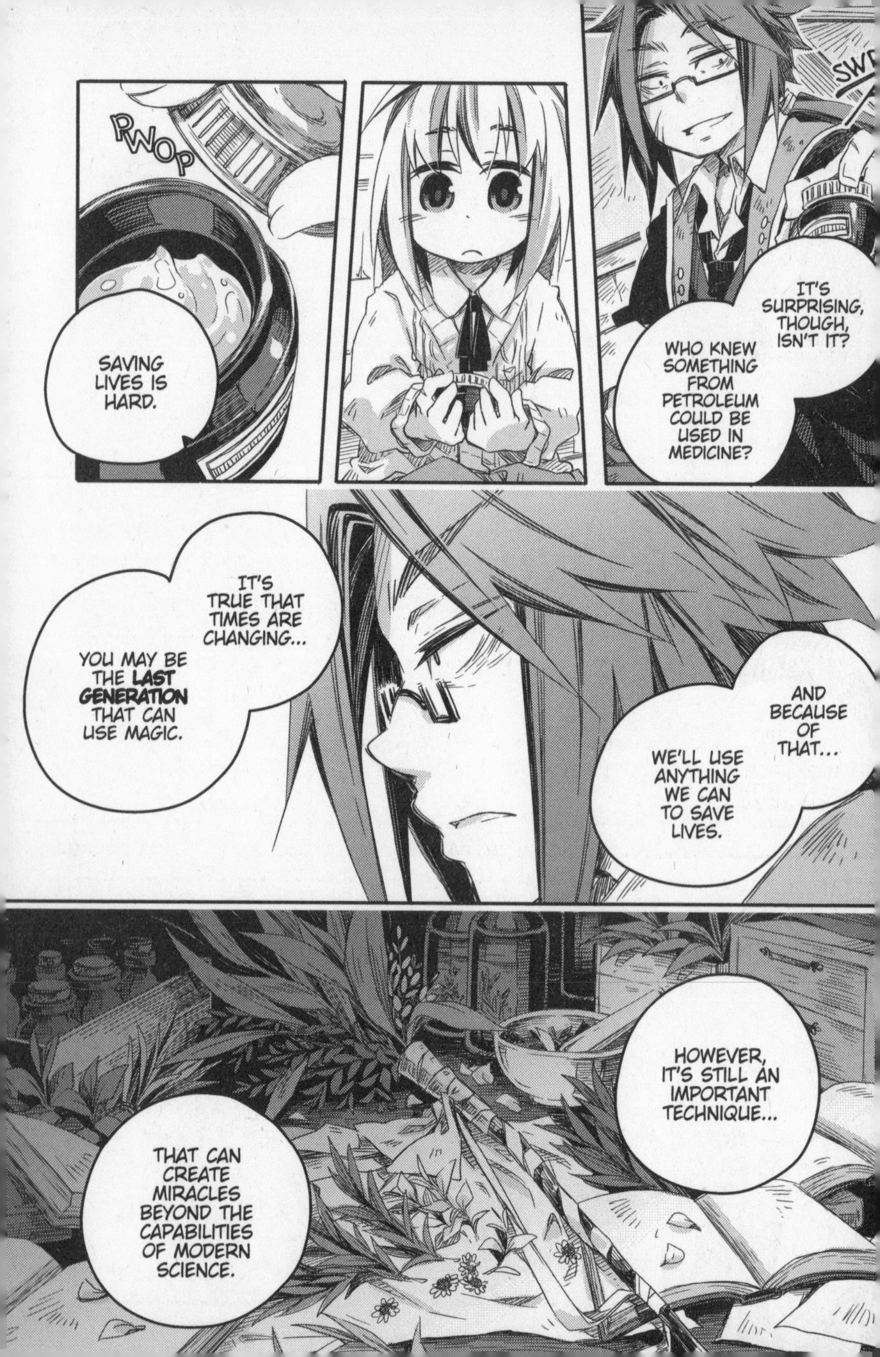
IT'S SURPRISING, THOUGH, ISN'T IT?
WHO KNEW SOMETHING FROM PETROLEUM COULD BE USED IN MEDICINE?
PWOP
SAVING LIVES IS HARD.
AND BECAUSE OF THAT...
WE'LL USE ANYTHING WE CAN TO SAVE LIVES.
IT'S TRUE THAT TIMES ARE CHANGING...
YOU MAY BE THE **LAST GENERATION** THAT CAN USE MAGIC.
HOWEVER, IT'S STILL AN IMPORTANT TECHNIQUE...
THAT CAN CREATE MIRACLES BEYOND THE CAPABILITIES OF MODERN SCIENCE.

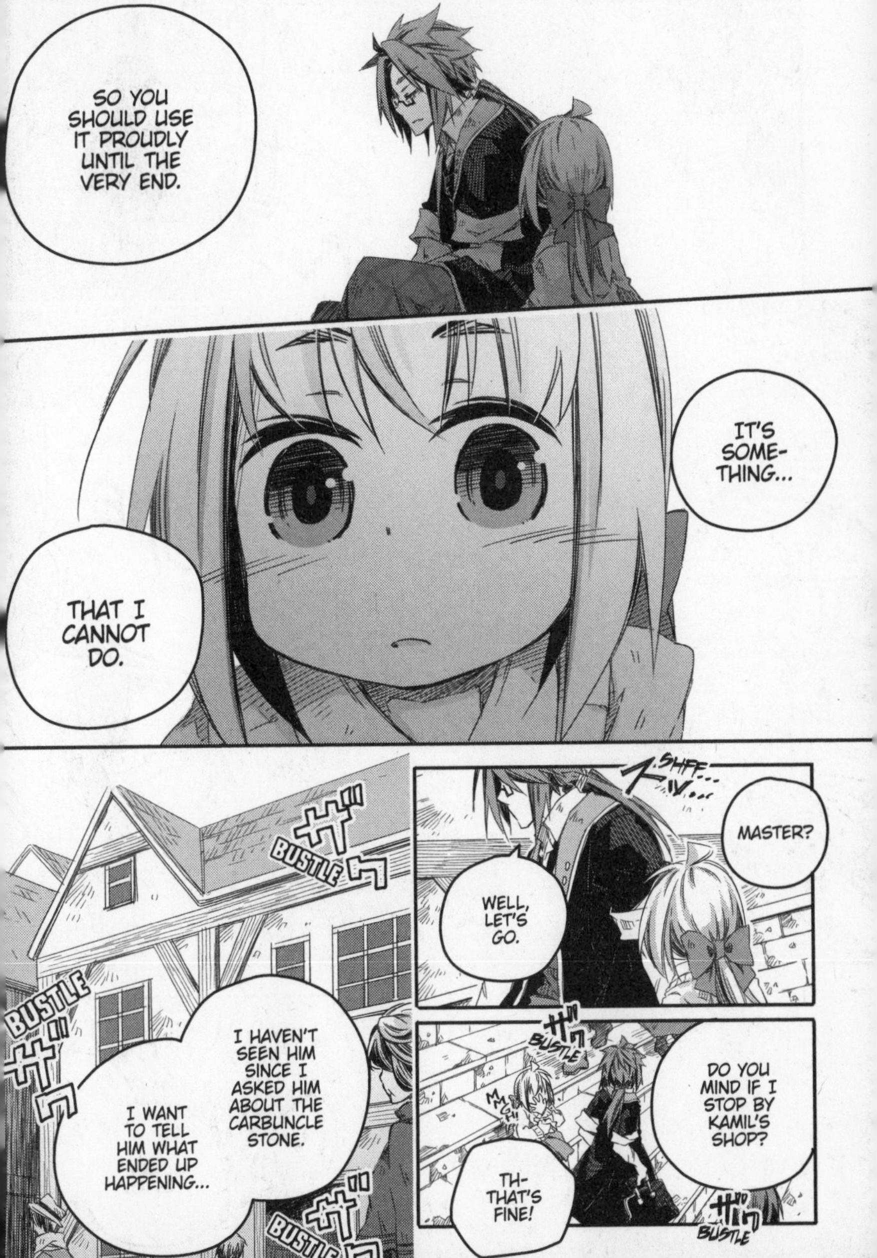
SO YOU SHOULD USE IT PROUDLY UNTIL THE VERY END.
IT'S SOME-THING...
THAT I CANNOT DO.
SHFF...
MASTER?
WELL, LET'S GO.
BUSTLE
DO YOU MIND IF I STOP BY KAMIL'S SHOP?
MNGH!!
TH-THAT'S FINE!
BUSTLE
BUSTLE
I HAVEN'T SEEN HIM SINCE I ASKED HIM ABOUT THE CARBUNCLE STONE.
I WANT TO TELL HIM WHAT ENDED UP HAPPENING...
BUSTLE
BUSTLE

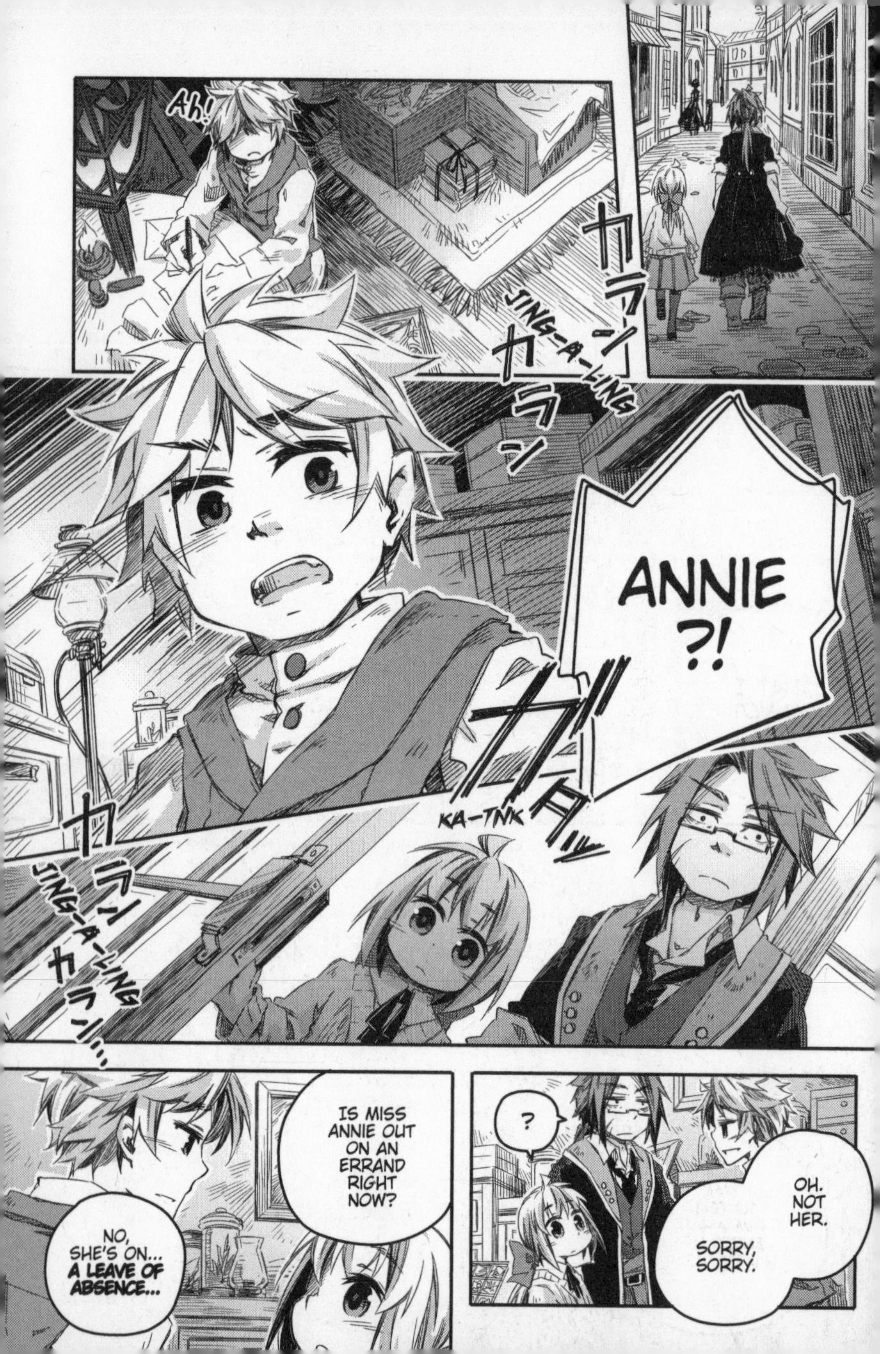
Ah!
カラーン カラン
JING-A-LING
ANNIE ?!
ガタッ
KA-TNK
カラン カラン…
JING-A-LING
?
OH. NOT HER.
SORRY, SORRY.
IS MISS ANNIE OUT ON AN ERRAND RIGHT NOW?
NO, SHE'S ON... **A LEAVE OF ABSENCE...**

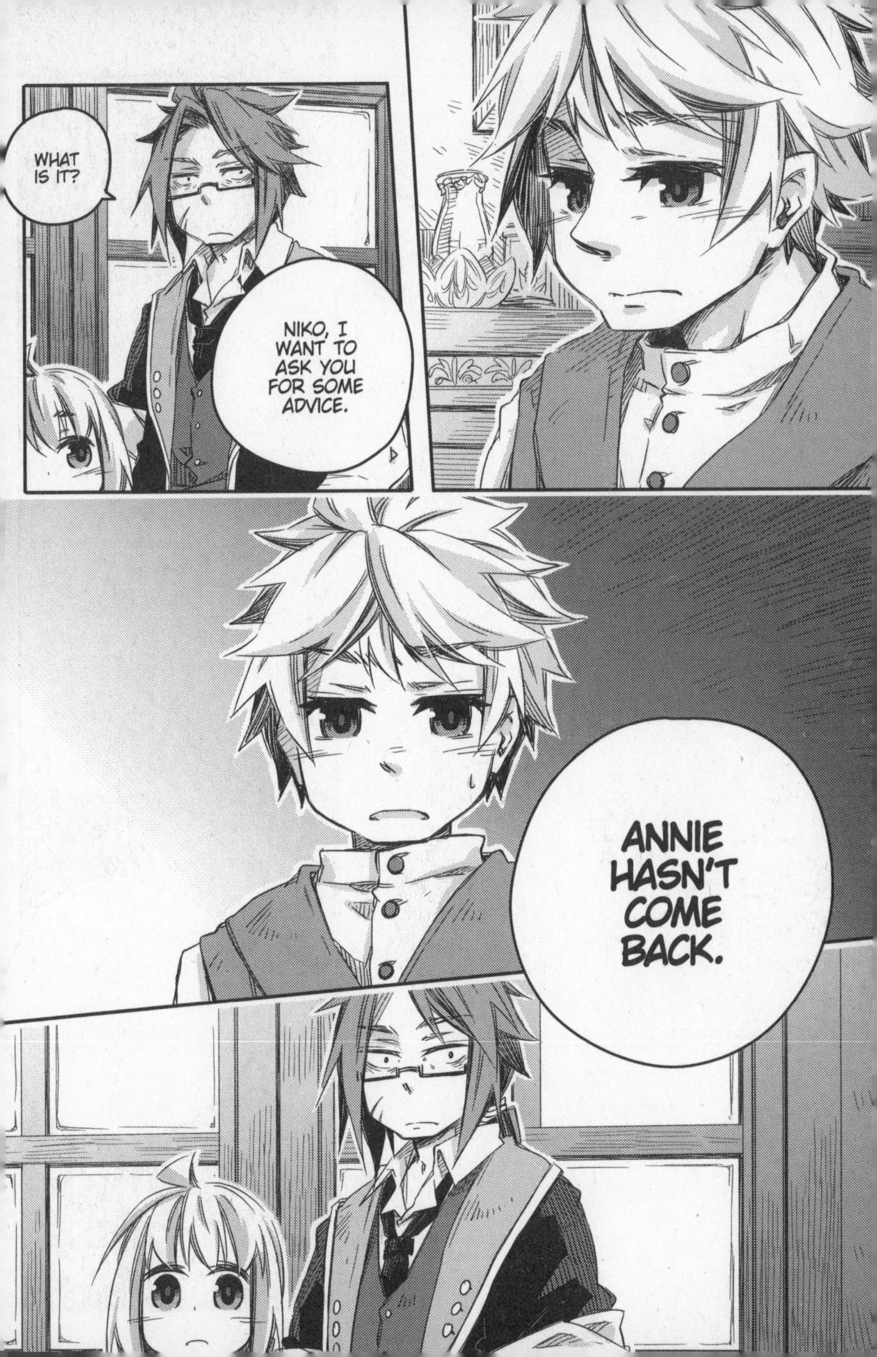
NIKO, I WANT TO ASK YOU FOR SOME ADVICE.
WHAT IS IT?
ANNIE HASN'T COME BACK.

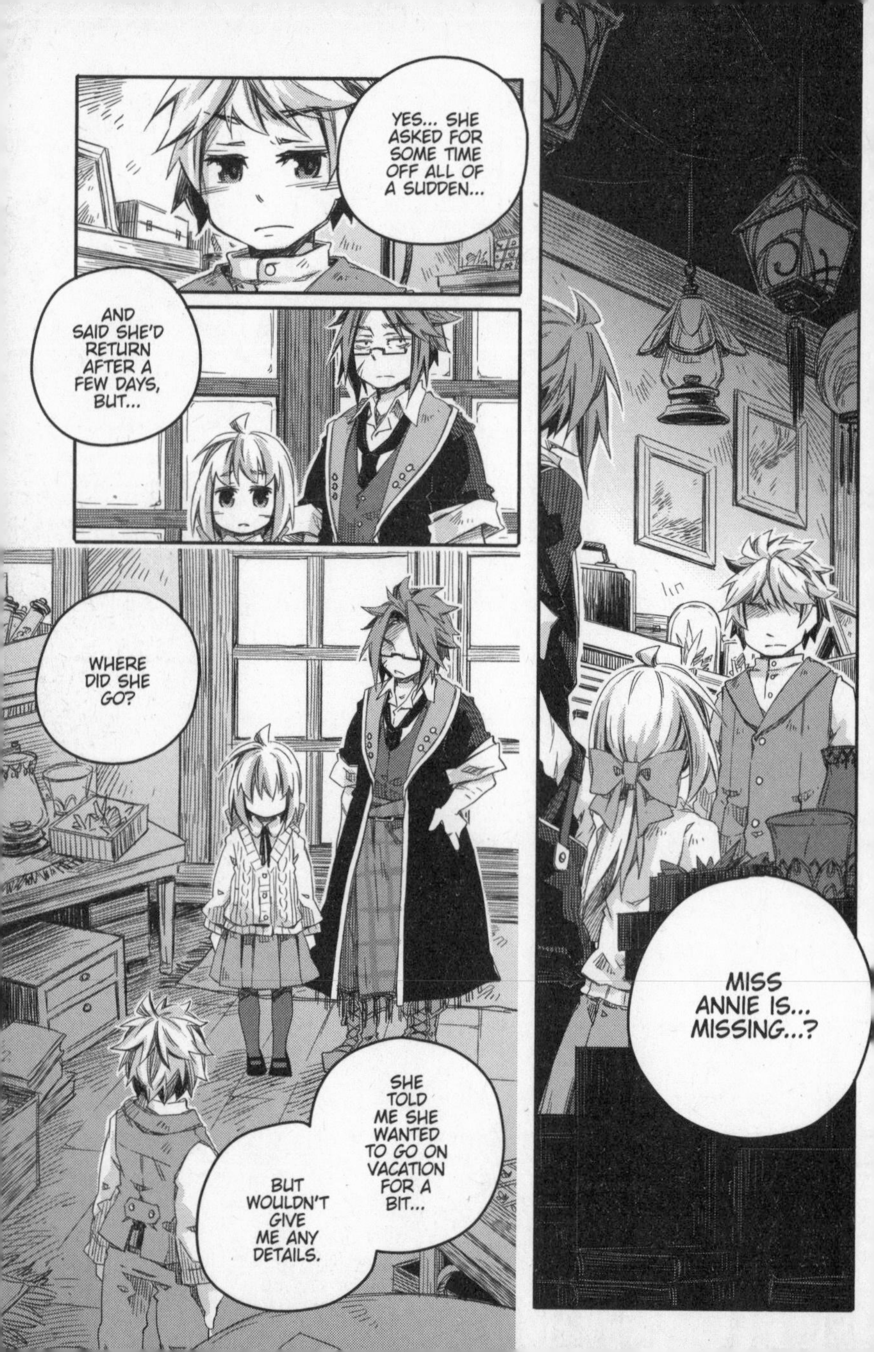
MISS ANNIE IS... MISSING...?
YES... SHE ASKED FOR SOME TIME OFF ALL OF A SUDDEN...
AND SAID SHE'D RETURN AFTER A FEW DAYS, BUT...
WHERE DID SHE GO?
SHE TOLD ME SHE WANTED TO GO ON VACATION FOR A BIT...
BUT WOULDN'T GIVE ME ANY DETAILS.

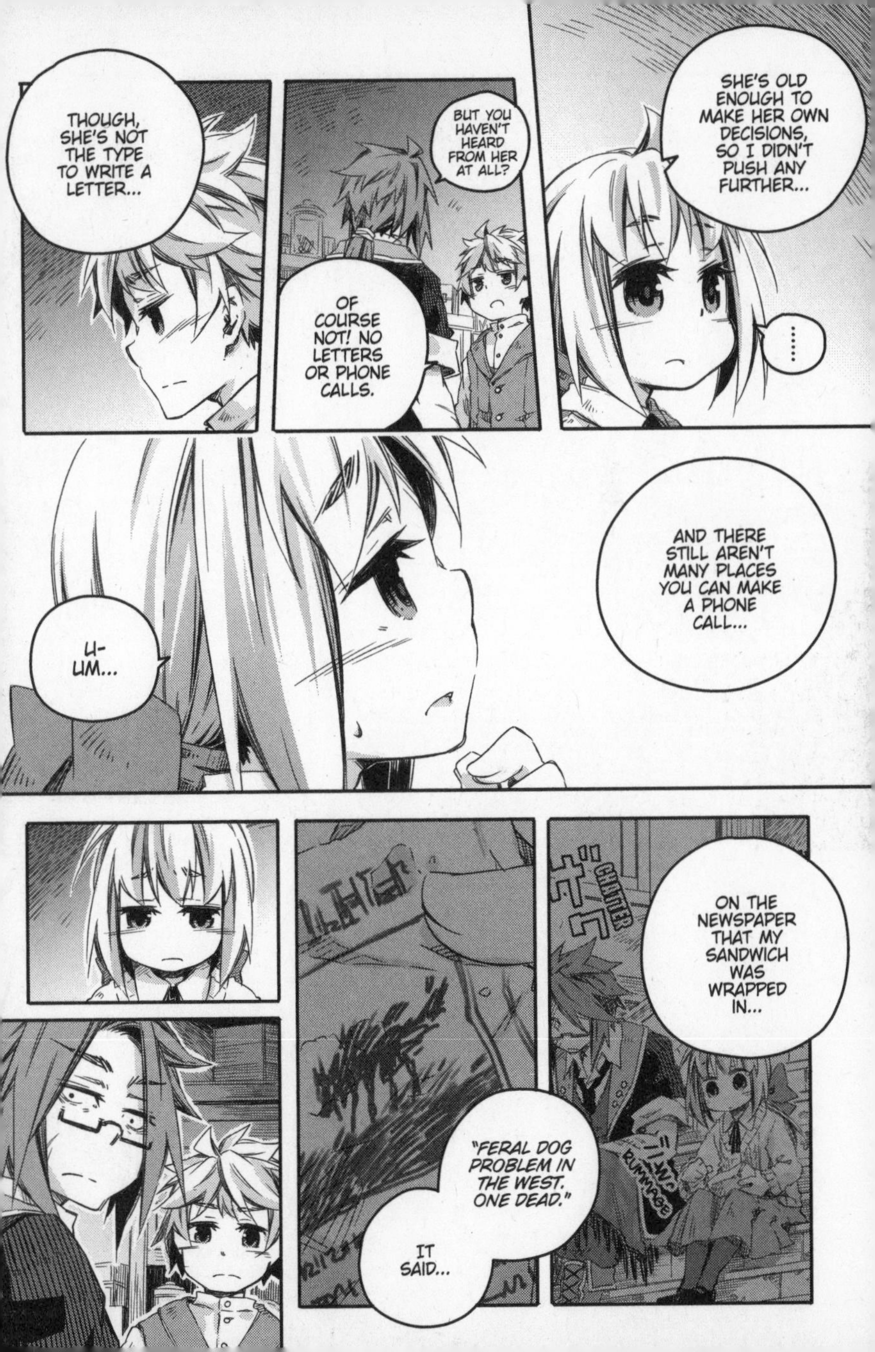
SHE'S OLD ENOUGH TO MAKE HER OWN DECISIONS, SO I DIDN'T PUSH ANY FURTHER...
......
BUT YOU HAVEN'T HEARD FROM HER AT ALL?
OF COURSE NOT! NO LETTERS OR PHONE CALLS.
THOUGH, SHE'S NOT THE TYPE TO WRITE A LETTER...
AND THERE STILL AREN'T MANY PLACES YOU CAN MAKE A PHONE CALL...
U-UM...
ON THE NEWSPAPER THAT MY SANDWICH WAS WRAPPED IN...
RUMMAGE
"FERAL DOG PROBLEM IN THE WEST. ONE DEAD."
IT SAID...

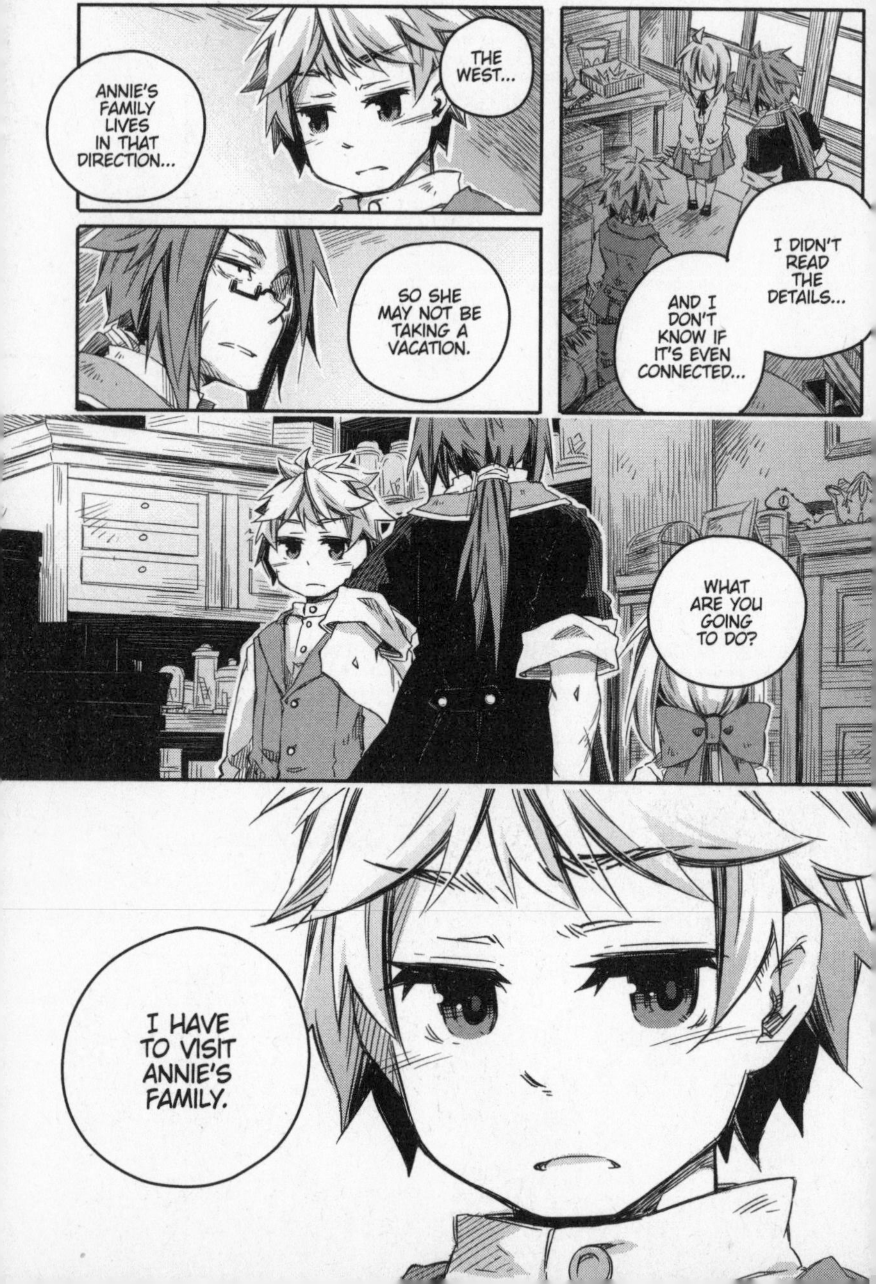
I DIDN'T READ THE DETAILS...
AND I DON'T KNOW IF IT'S EVEN CONNECTED...
THE WEST...
ANNIE'S FAMILY LIVES IN THAT DIRECTION...
SO SHE MAY NOT BE TAKING A VACATION.
WHAT ARE YOU GOING TO DO?
I HAVE TO VISIT ANNIE'S FAMILY.

[Case 10: Corroded Horn]

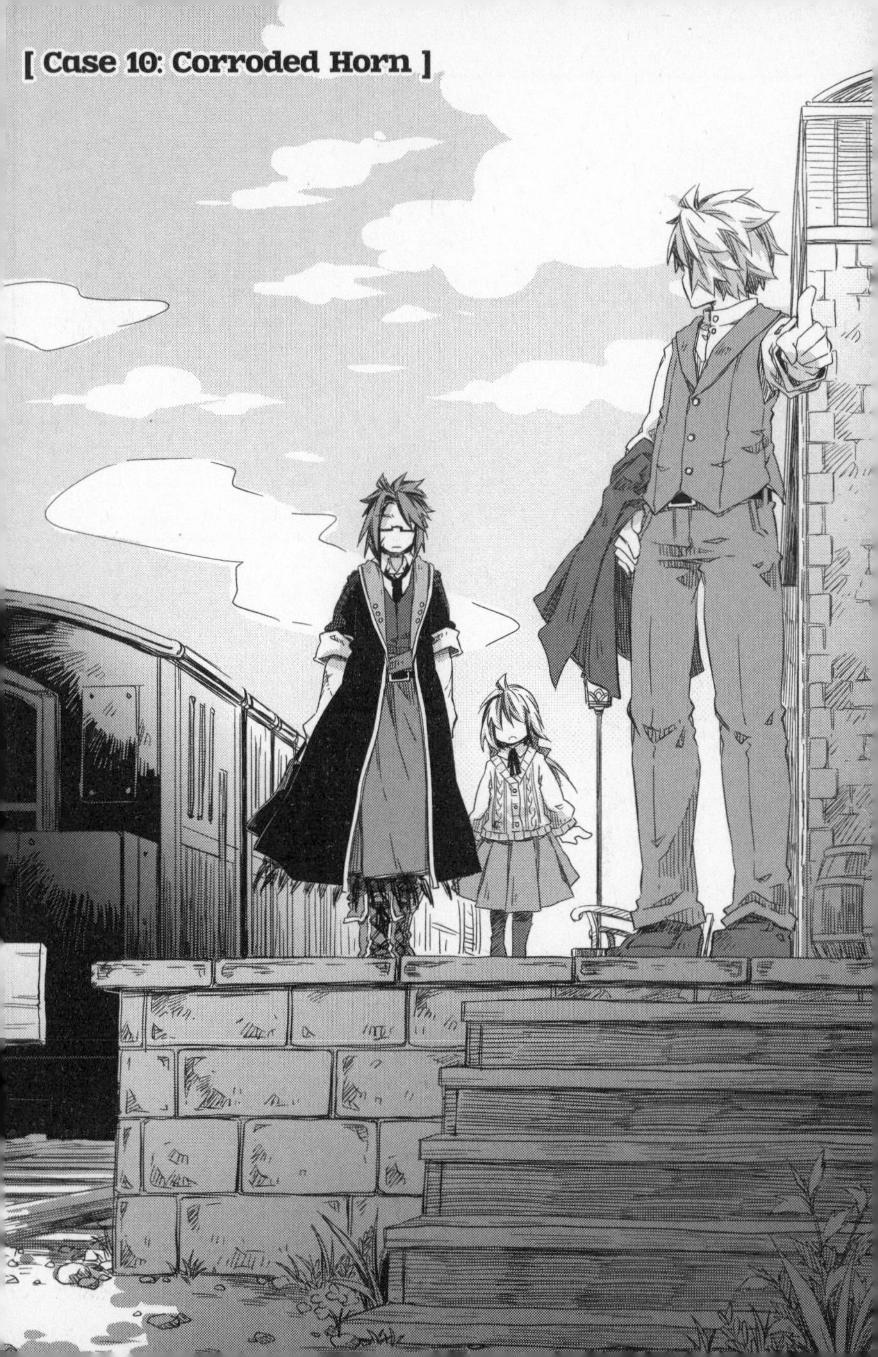

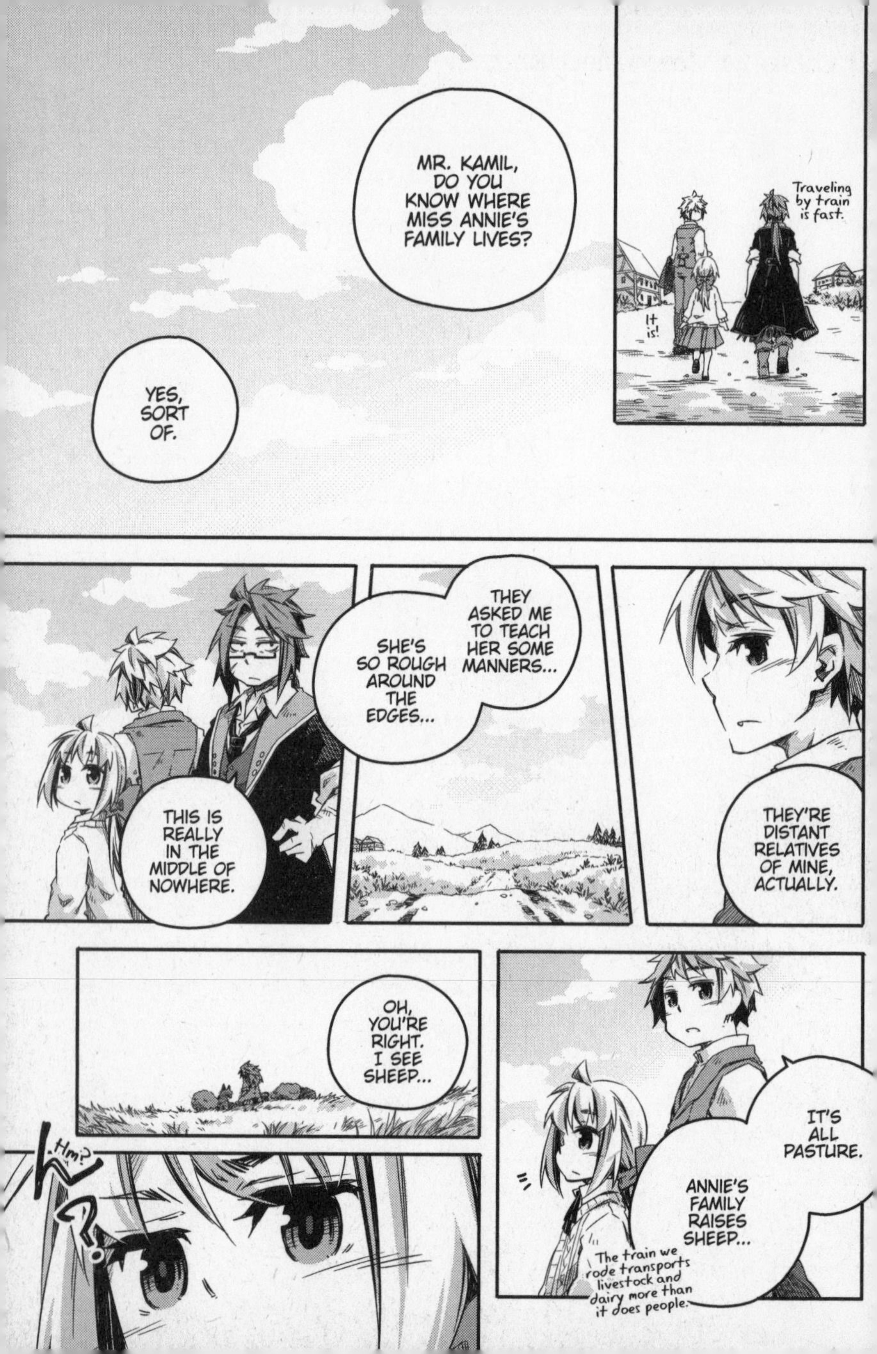
Traveling by train is fast.
It is!
MR. KAMIL, DO YOU KNOW WHERE MISS ANNIE'S FAMILY LIVES?
YES, SORT OF.
THEY'RE DISTANT RELATIVES OF MINE, ACTUALLY.
THEY ASKED ME TO TEACH HER SOME MANNERS...
SHE'S SO ROUGH AROUND THE EDGES...
THIS IS REALLY IN THE MIDDLE OF NOWHERE.
IT'S ALL PASTURE.
ANNIE'S FAMILY RAISES SHEEP...
The train we rode transports livestock and dairy more than it does people.
OH, YOU'RE RIGHT. I SEE SHEEP...
Hm?

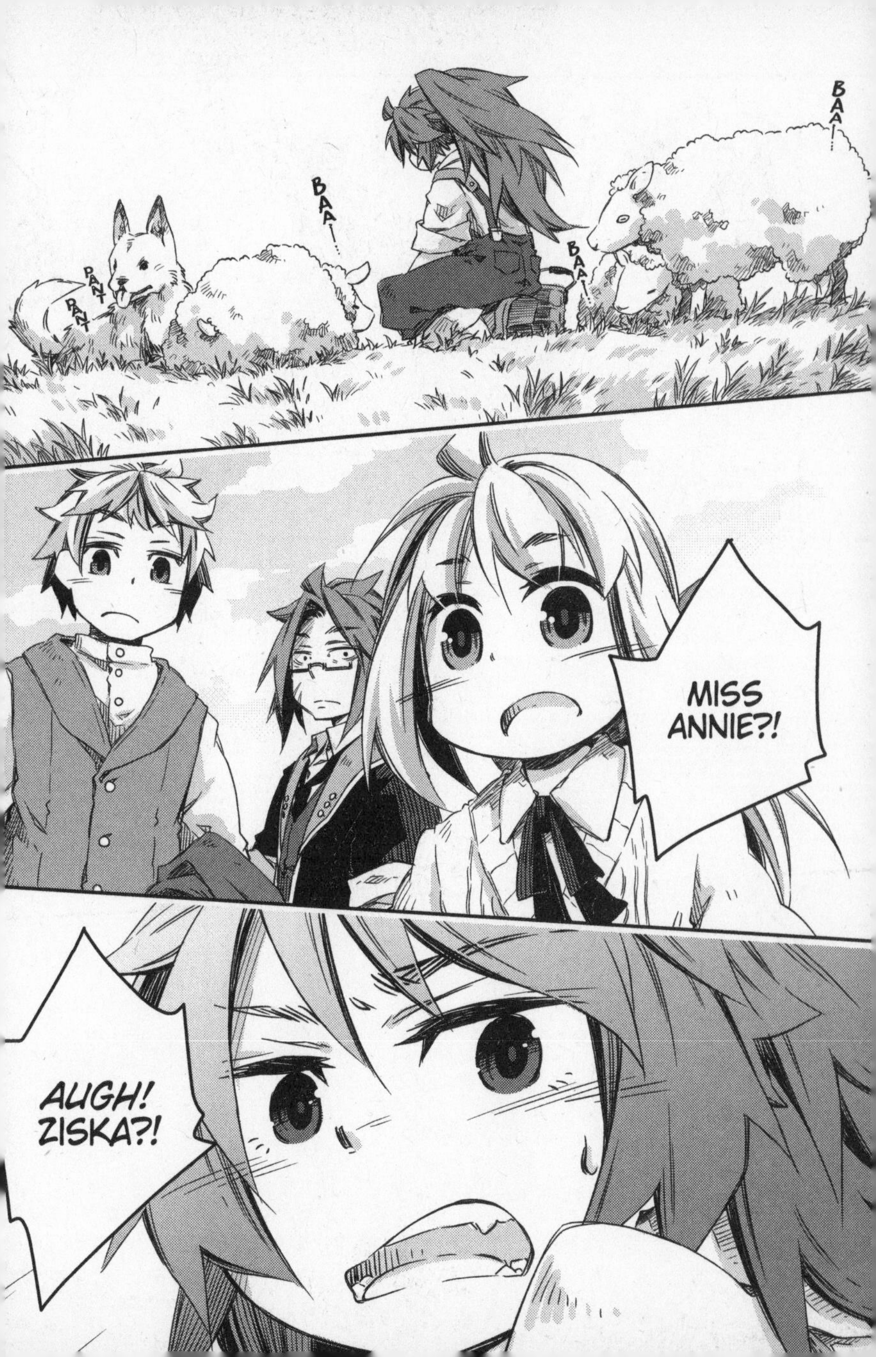
BAA...
BAA...
BAA...
PANT PANT
MISS ANNIE?!
AUGH! ZISKA?!

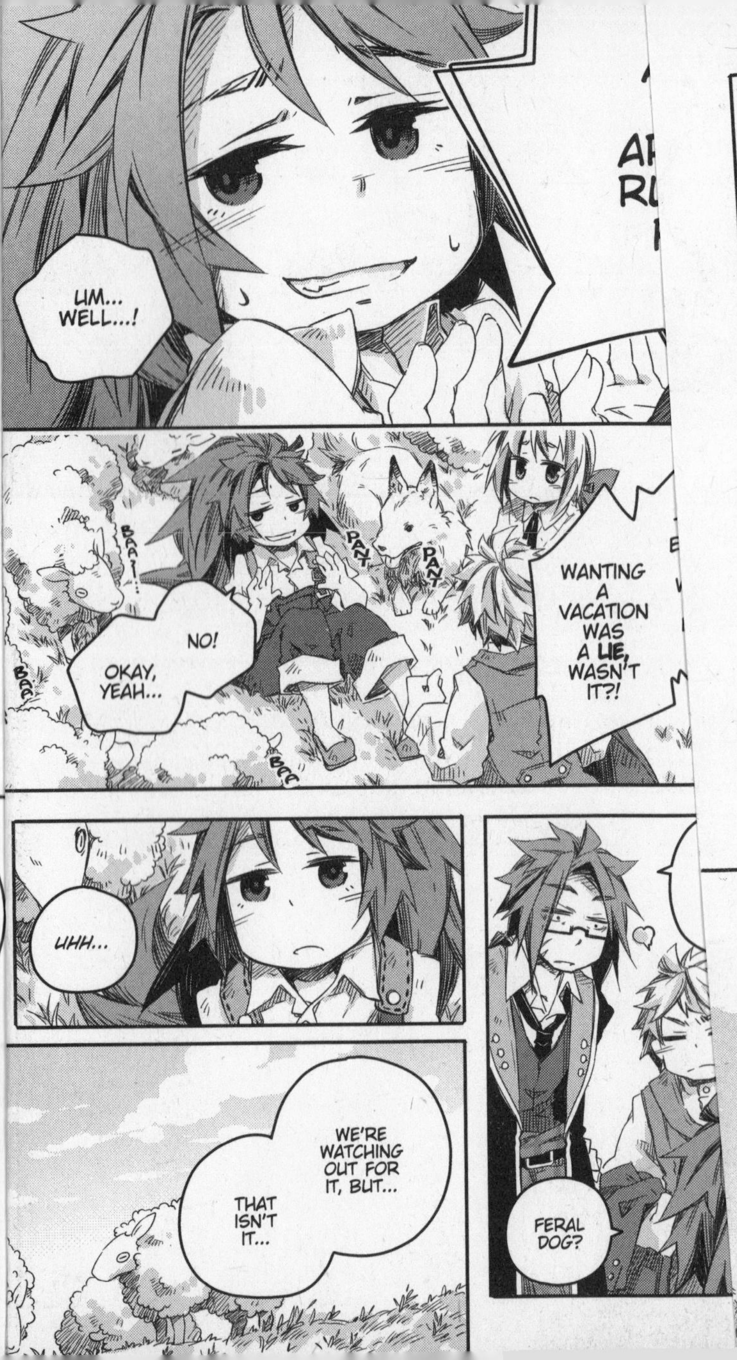
UM... WELL...!
WANTING A VACATION WAS A LIE, WASN'T IT?!
NO!
OKAY, YEAH...
PANT PANT
BAA!...
BAA
BAA
FERAL DOG?
UHH...
WE'RE WATCHING OUT FOR IT, BUT...
THAT ISN'T IT...

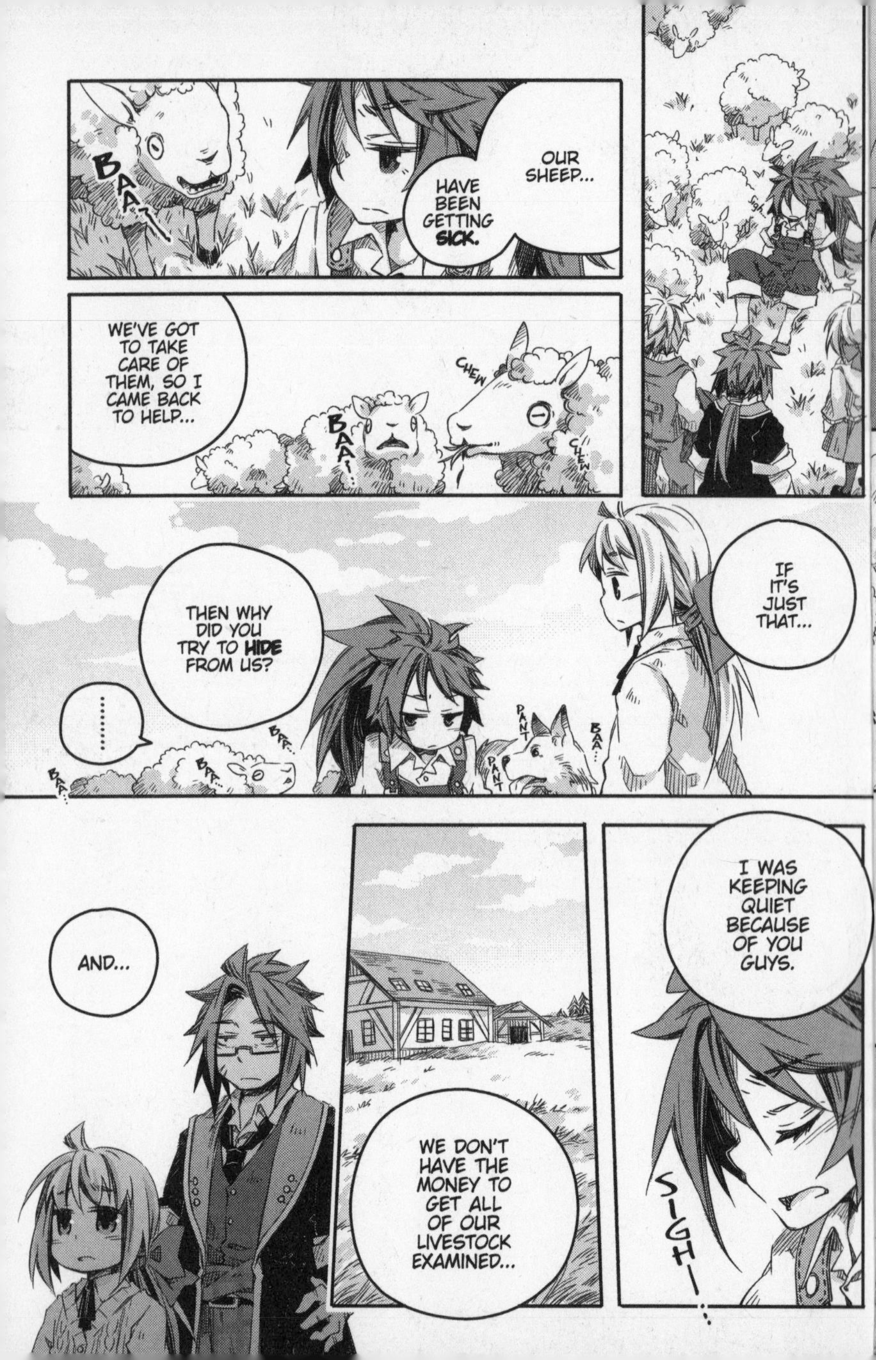
OUR SHEEP...
HAVE BEEN GETTING SICK.
BAA~!
WE'VE GOT TO TAKE CARE OF THEM, SO I CAME BACK TO HELP...
CHEW
CHEW
BAA!...
IF IT'S JUST THAT...
THEN WHY DID YOU TRY TO HIDE FROM US?
......
PANT
PANT
BAA...
I WAS KEEPING QUIET BECAUSE OF YOU GUYS.
SIGH...
WE DON'T HAVE THE MONEY TO GET ALL OF OUR LIVESTOCK EXAMINED...
AND...

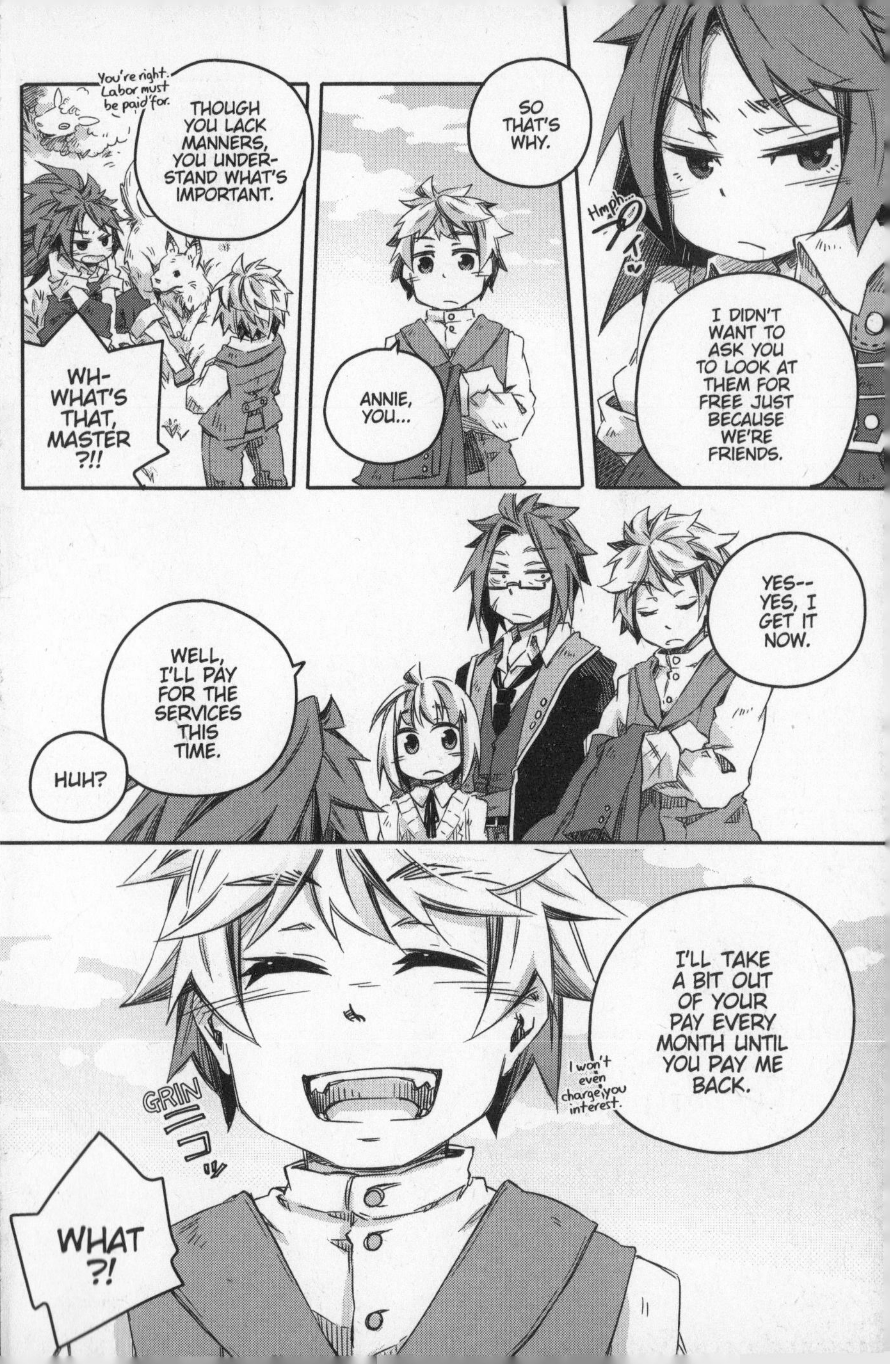
Hmph...
I DIDN'T WANT TO ASK YOU TO LOOK AT THEM FOR FREE JUST BECAUSE WE'RE FRIENDS.
SO THAT'S WHY.
ANNIE, YOU...
THOUGH YOU LACK MANNERS, YOU UNDERSTAND WHAT'S IMPORTANT.
You're right. Labor must be paid for.
WH-WHAT'S THAT, MASTER?!!
YES-- YES, I GET IT NOW.
WELL, I'LL PAY FOR THE SERVICES THIS TIME.
HUH?
I'LL TAKE A BIT OUT OF YOUR PAY EVERY MONTH UNTIL YOU PAY ME BACK.
I won't even charge you interest.
GRIN
WHAT?!
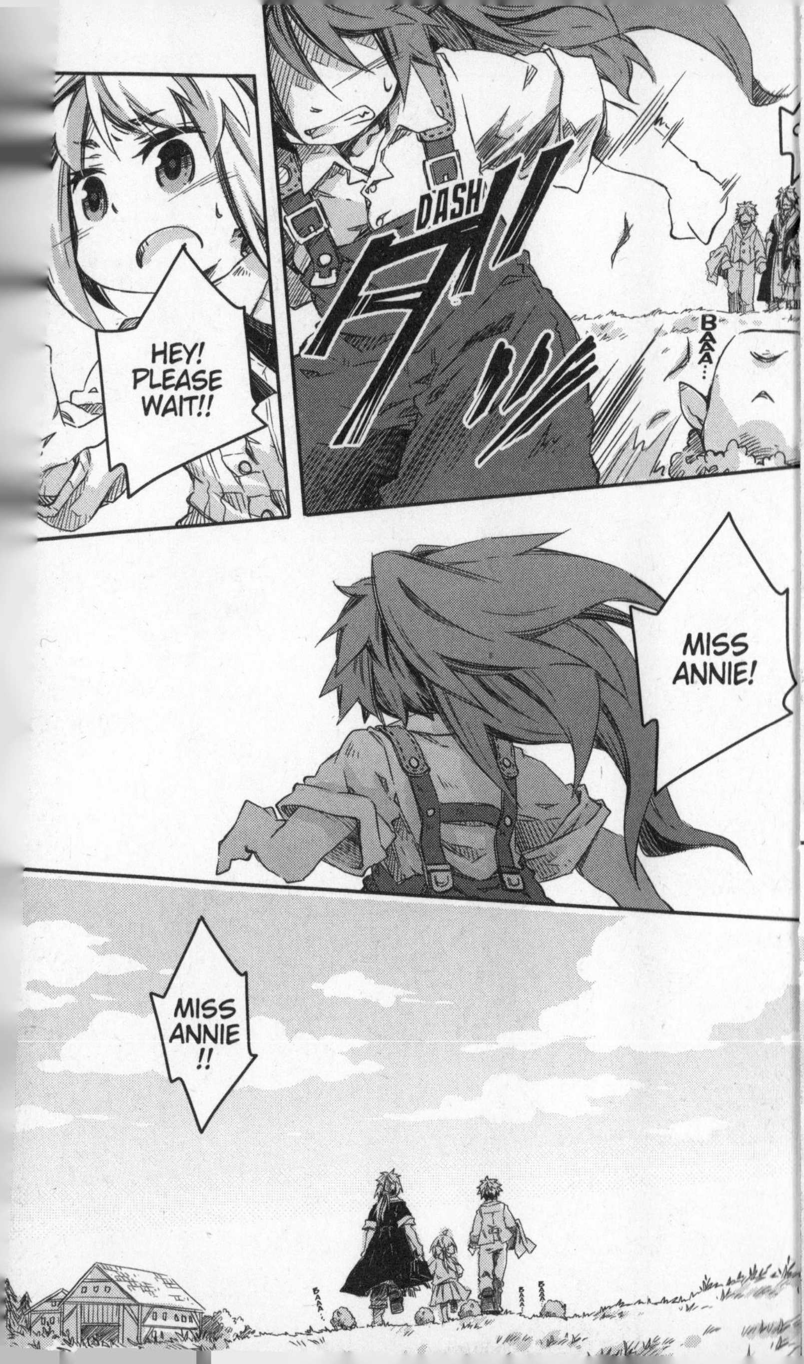
DASH
BAAA...
HEY! PLEASE WAIT!!
MISS ANNIE!
MISS ANNIE!!

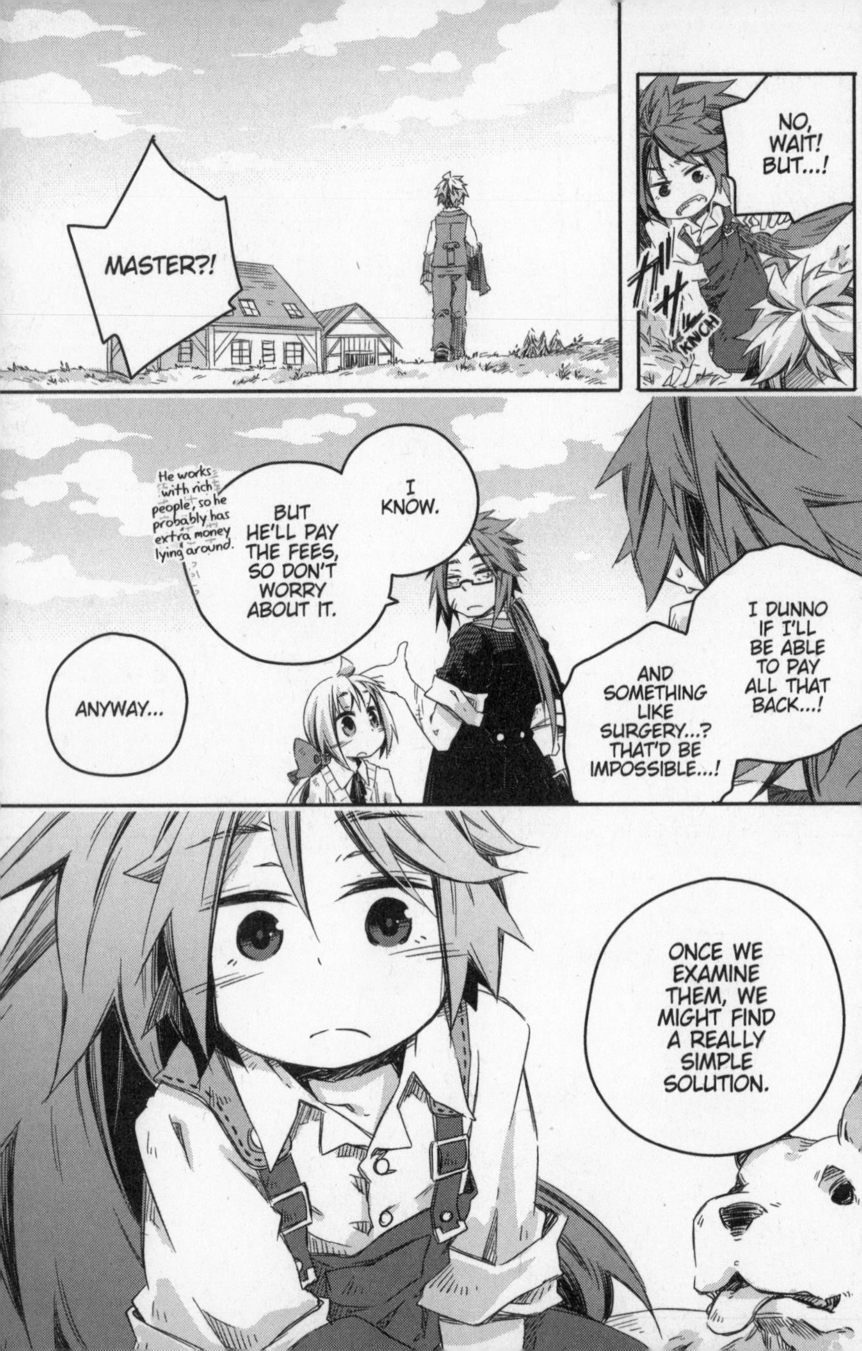
NO, WAIT! BUT...!
KNICH
MASTER?!
I DUNNO IF I'LL BE ABLE TO PAY ALL THAT BACK...!
AND SOMETHING LIKE SURGERY...? THAT'D BE IMPOSSIBLE...!
I KNOW.
BUT HE'LL PAY THE FEES, SO DON'T WORRY ABOUT IT.
He works with rich people, so he probably has extra money lying around.
ANYWAY...
ONCE WE EXAMINE THEM, WE MIGHT FIND A REALLY SIMPLE SOLUTION.

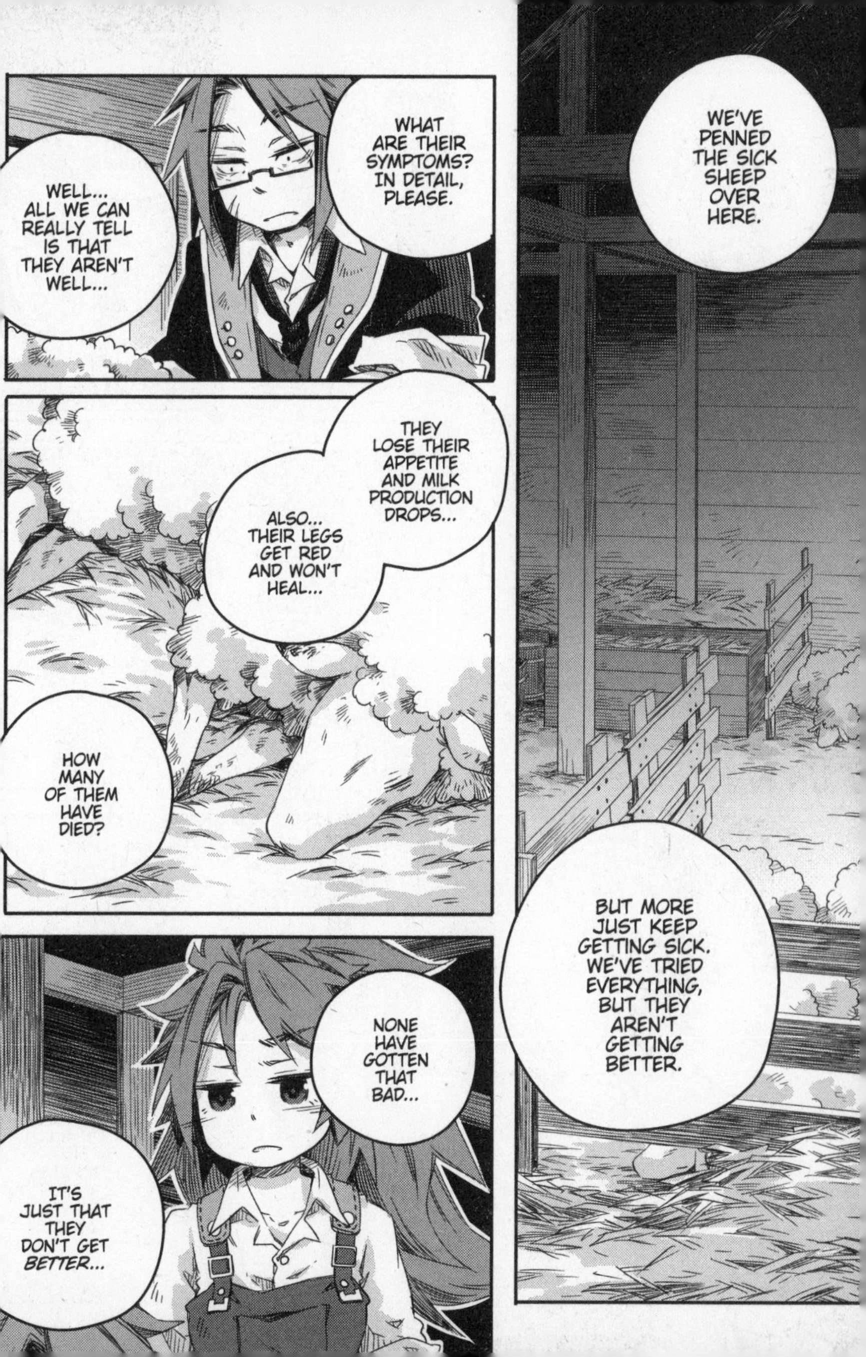
WE'VE PENNED THE SICK SHEEP OVER HERE.
BUT MORE JUST KEEP GETTING SICK. WE'VE TRIED EVERYTHING, BUT THEY AREN'T GETTING BETTER.
WHAT ARE THEIR SYMPTOMS? IN DETAIL, PLEASE.
WELL... ALL WE CAN REALLY TELL IS THAT THEY AREN'T WELL...
THEY LOSE THEIR APPETITE AND MILK PRODUCTION DROPS...
ALSO... THEIR LEGS GET RED AND WON'T HEAL...
HOW MANY OF THEM HAVE DIED?
NONE HAVE GOTTEN THAT BAD...
IT'S JUST THAT THEY DON'T GET *BETTER*...

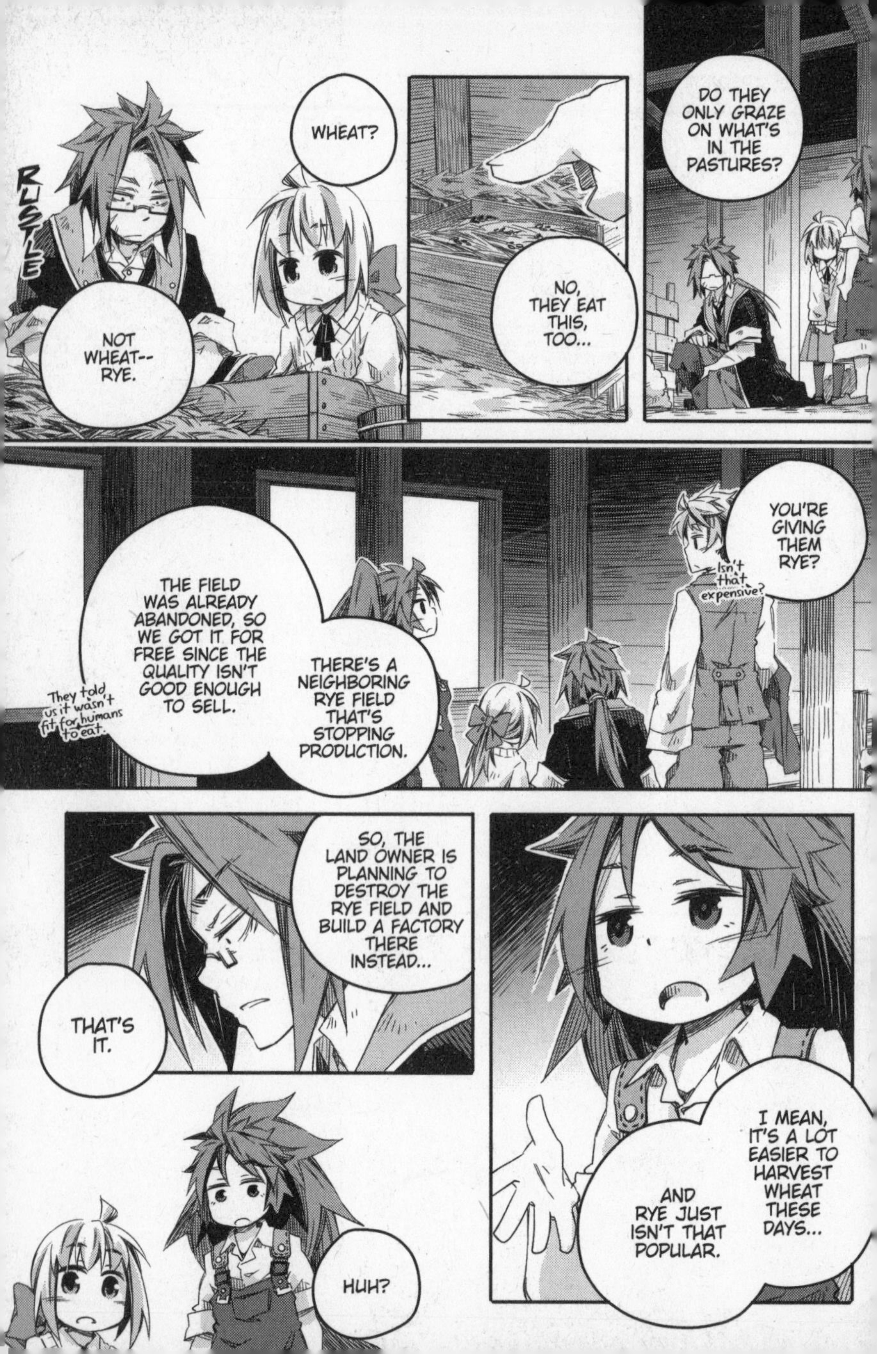
DO THEY ONLY GRAZE ON WHAT'S IN THE PASTURES?
NO, THEY EAT THIS, TOO...
WHEAT?
RUSTLE
NOT WHEAT-- RYE.
YOU'RE GIVING THEM RYE?
Isn't that expensive?
THERE'S A NEIGHBORING RYE FIELD THAT'S STOPPING PRODUCTION.
THE FIELD WAS ALREADY ABANDONED, SO WE GOT IT FOR FREE SINCE THE QUALITY ISN'T GOOD ENOUGH TO SELL.
They told us it wasn't fit for humans to eat.
I MEAN, IT'S A LOT EASIER TO HARVEST WHEAT THESE DAYS...
AND RYE JUST ISN'T THAT POPULAR.
SO, THE LAND OWNER IS PLANNING TO DESTROY THE RYE FIELD AND BUILD A FACTORY THERE INSTEAD...
THAT'S IT.
HUH?

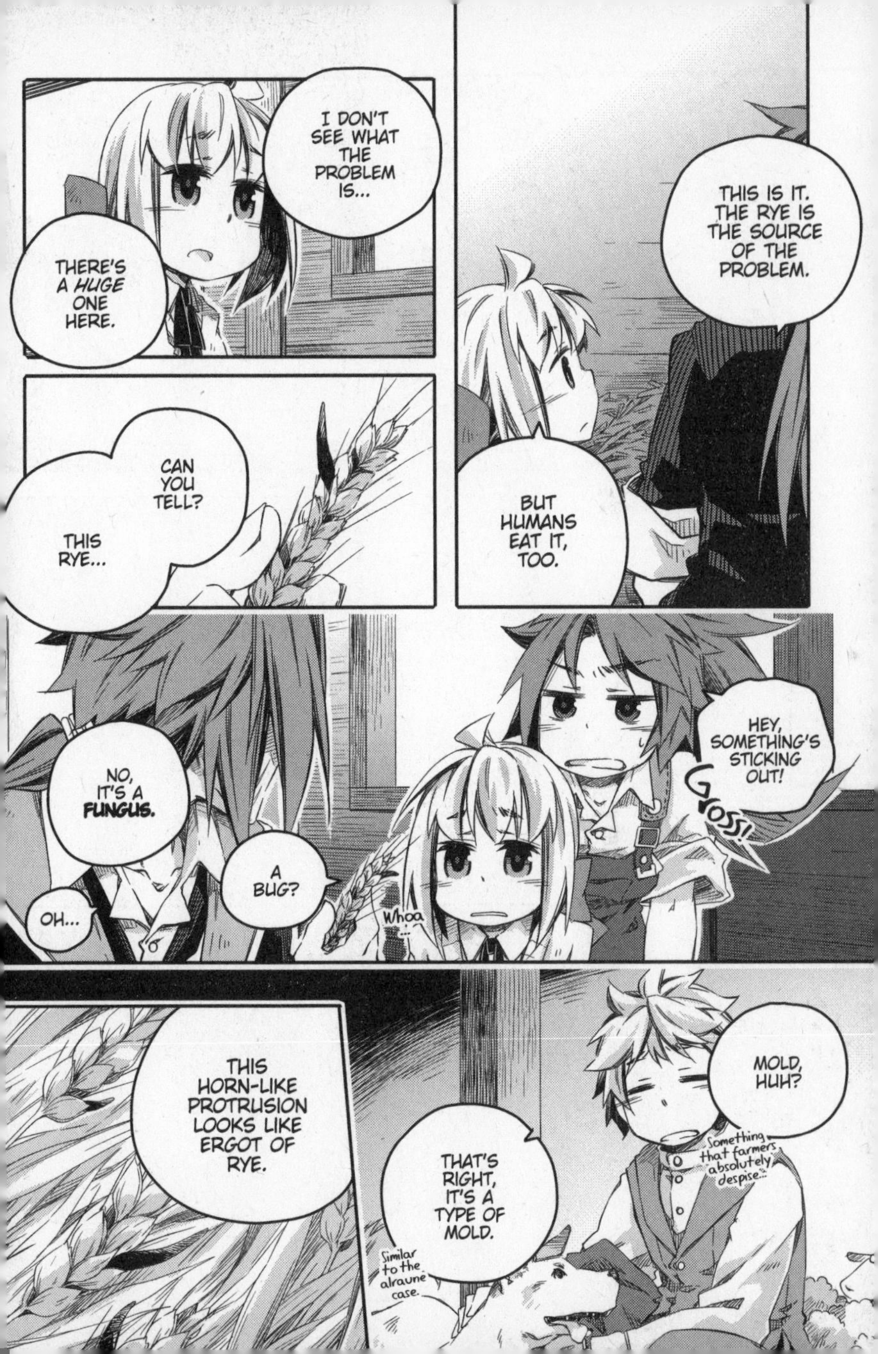
THIS IS IT. THE RYE IS THE SOURCE OF THE PROBLEM.
BUT HUMANS EAT IT, TOO.
I DON'T SEE WHAT THE PROBLEM IS...
THERE'S A HUGE ONE HERE.
CAN YOU TELL?
THIS RYE...
HEY, SOMETHING'S STICKING OUT!
GROSS!
Whoa...
A BUG?
NO, IT'S A FUNGUS.
OH...
MOLD, HUH?
Something that farmers absolutely despise...
THAT'S RIGHT, IT'S A TYPE OF MOLD.
THIS HORN-LIKE PROTRUSION LOOKS LIKE ERGOT OF RYE.
Similar to the alraune case.

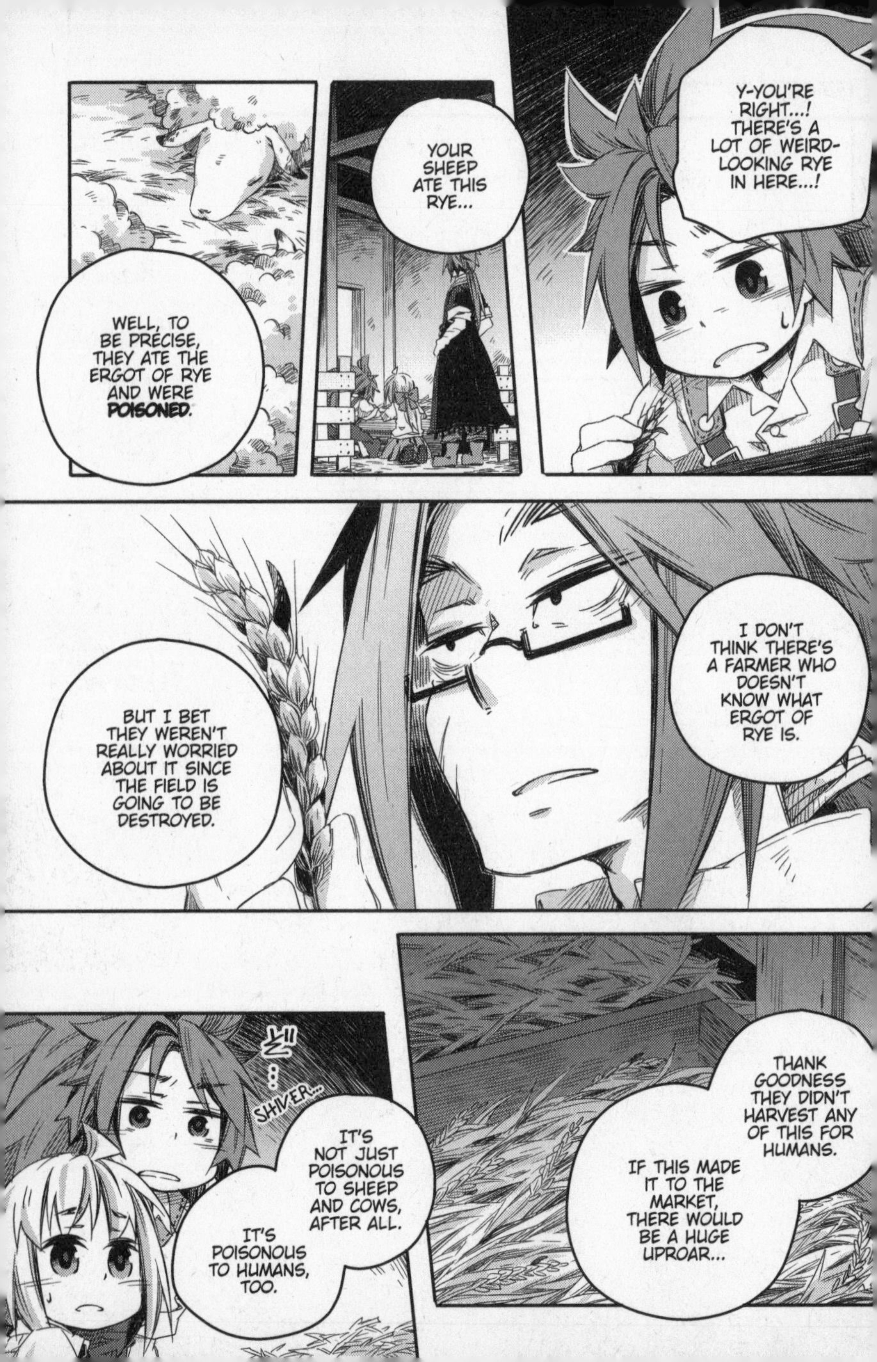
Y-YOU'RE RIGHT...! THERE'S A LOT OF WEIRD-LOOKING RYE IN HERE...!
YOUR SHEEP ATE THIS RYE...
WELL, TO BE PRECISE, THEY ATE THE ERGOT OF RYE AND WERE **POISONED**.
I DON'T THINK THERE'S A FARMER WHO DOESN'T KNOW WHAT ERGOT OF RYE IS.
BUT I BET THEY WEREN'T REALLY WORRIED ABOUT IT SINCE THE FIELD IS GOING TO BE DESTROYED.
THANK GOODNESS THEY DIDN'T HARVEST ANY OF THIS FOR HUMANS.
IF THIS MADE IT TO THE MARKET, THERE WOULD BE A HUGE UPROAR...
SHIVER...
IT'S NOT JUST POISONOUS TO SHEEP AND COWS, AFTER ALL.
IT'S POISONOUS TO HUMANS, TOO.

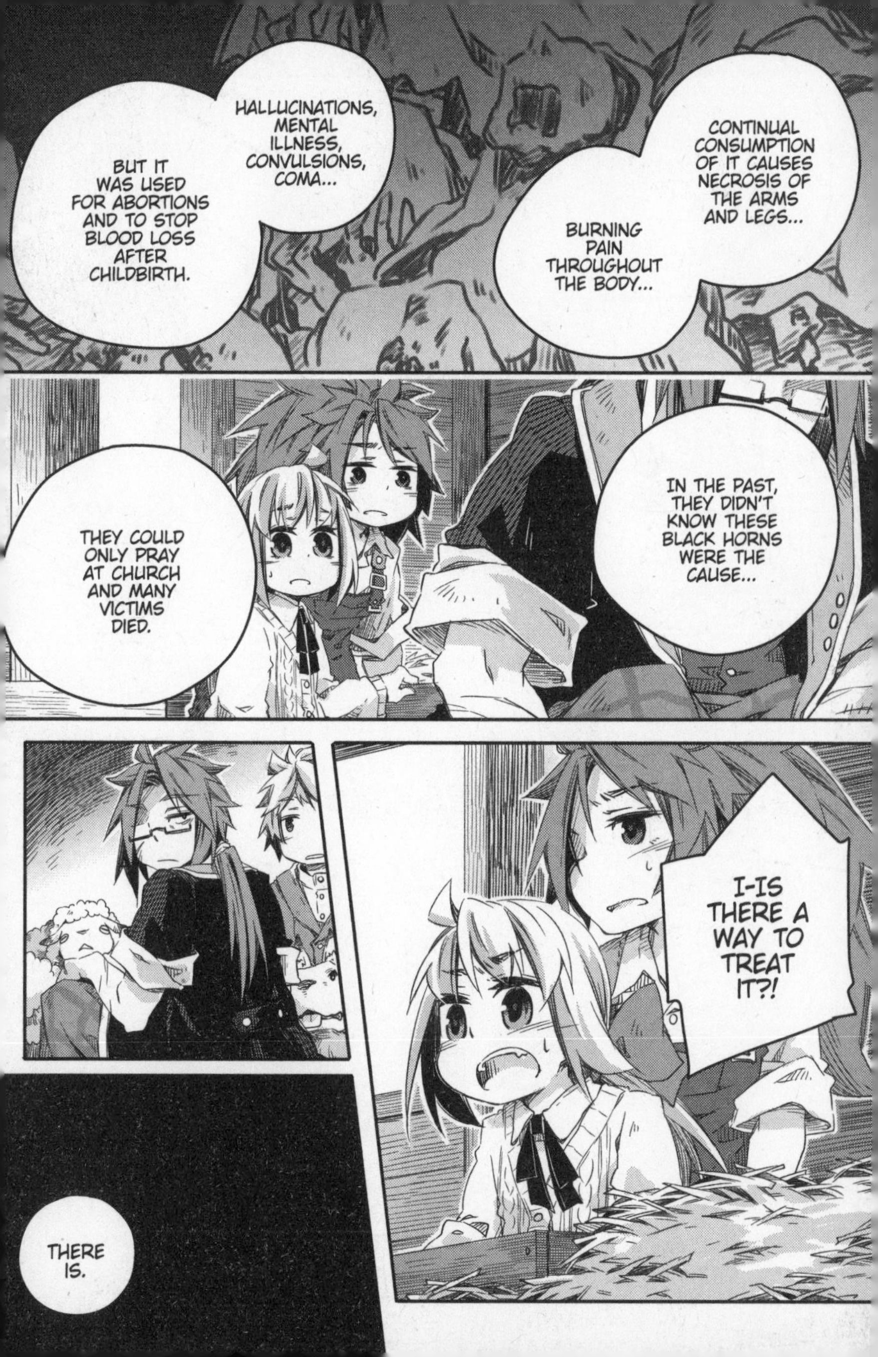
CONTINUAL CONSUMPTION OF IT CAUSES NECROSIS OF THE ARMS AND LEGS...
BURNING PAIN THROUGHOUT THE BODY...
HALLUCINATIONS, MENTAL ILLNESS, CONVULSIONS, COMA...
BUT IT WAS USED FOR ABORTIONS AND TO STOP BLOOD LOSS AFTER CHILDBIRTH.
IN THE PAST, THEY DIDN'T KNOW THESE BLACK HORNS WERE THE CAUSE...
THEY COULD ONLY PRAY AT CHURCH AND MANY VICTIMS DIED.
I-IS THERE A WAY TO TREAT IT?!
THERE IS.

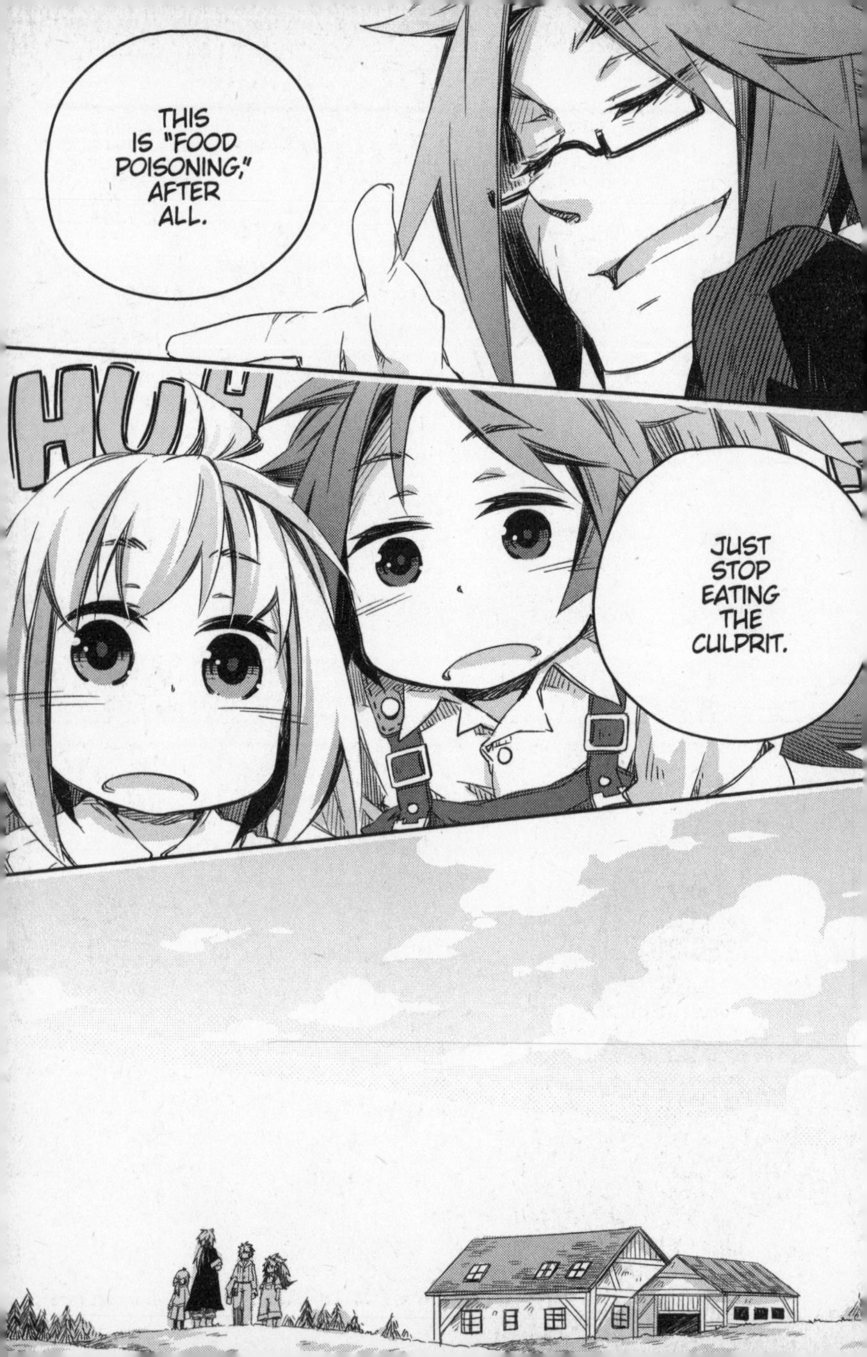
THIS IS "FOOD POISONING," AFTER ALL.
JUST STOP EATING THE CULPRIT.
HUH

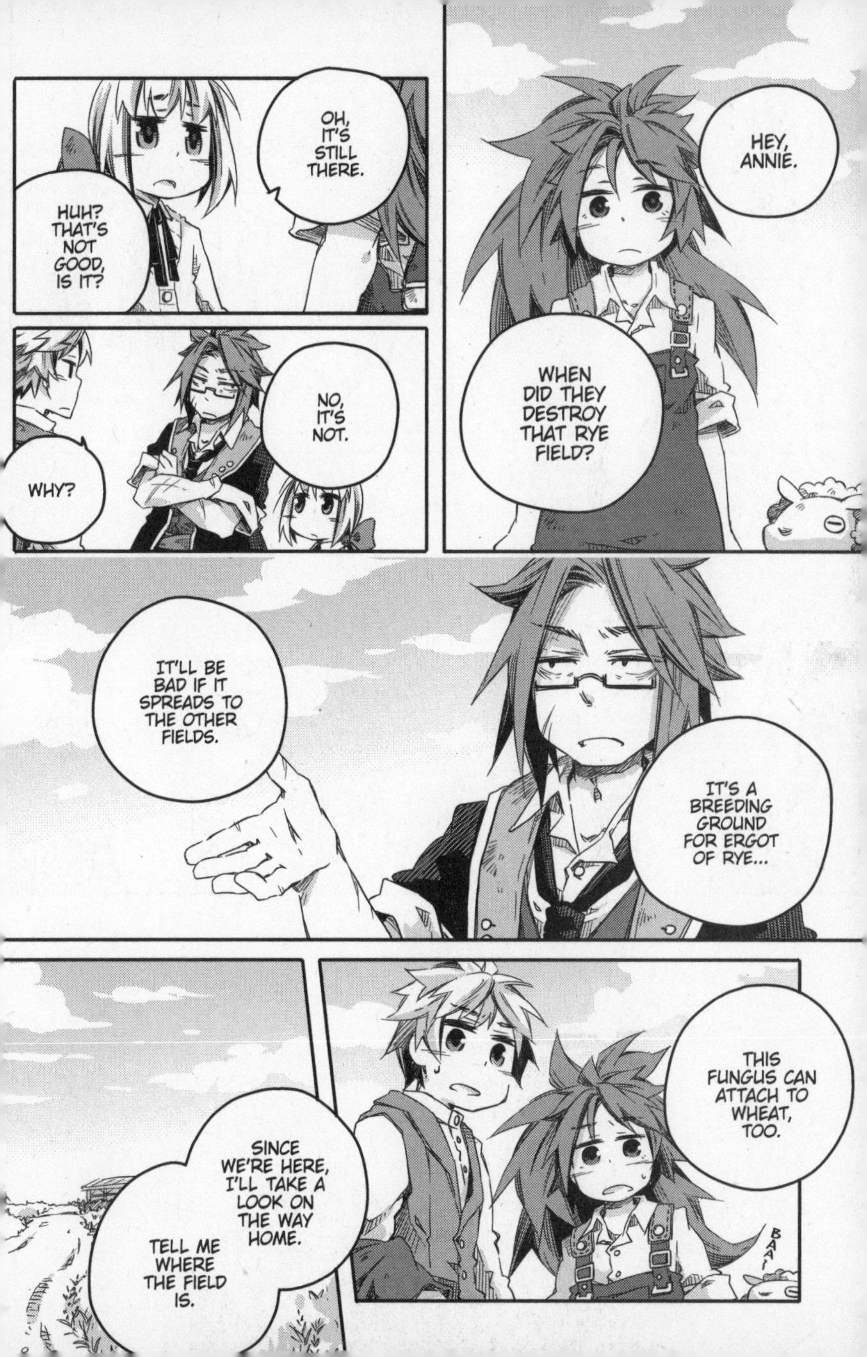
HEY, ANNIE.
WHEN DID THEY DESTROY THAT RYE FIELD?
OH, IT'S STILL THERE.
HUH? THAT'S NOT GOOD, IS IT?
NO, IT'S NOT.
WHY?
IT'S A BREEDING GROUND FOR ERGOT OF RYE...
IT'LL BE BAD IF IT SPREADS TO THE OTHER FIELDS.
THIS FUNGUS CAN ATTACH TO WHEAT, TOO.
BAA
SINCE WE'RE HERE, I'LL TAKE A LOOK ON THE WAY HOME.
TELL ME WHERE THE FIELD IS.

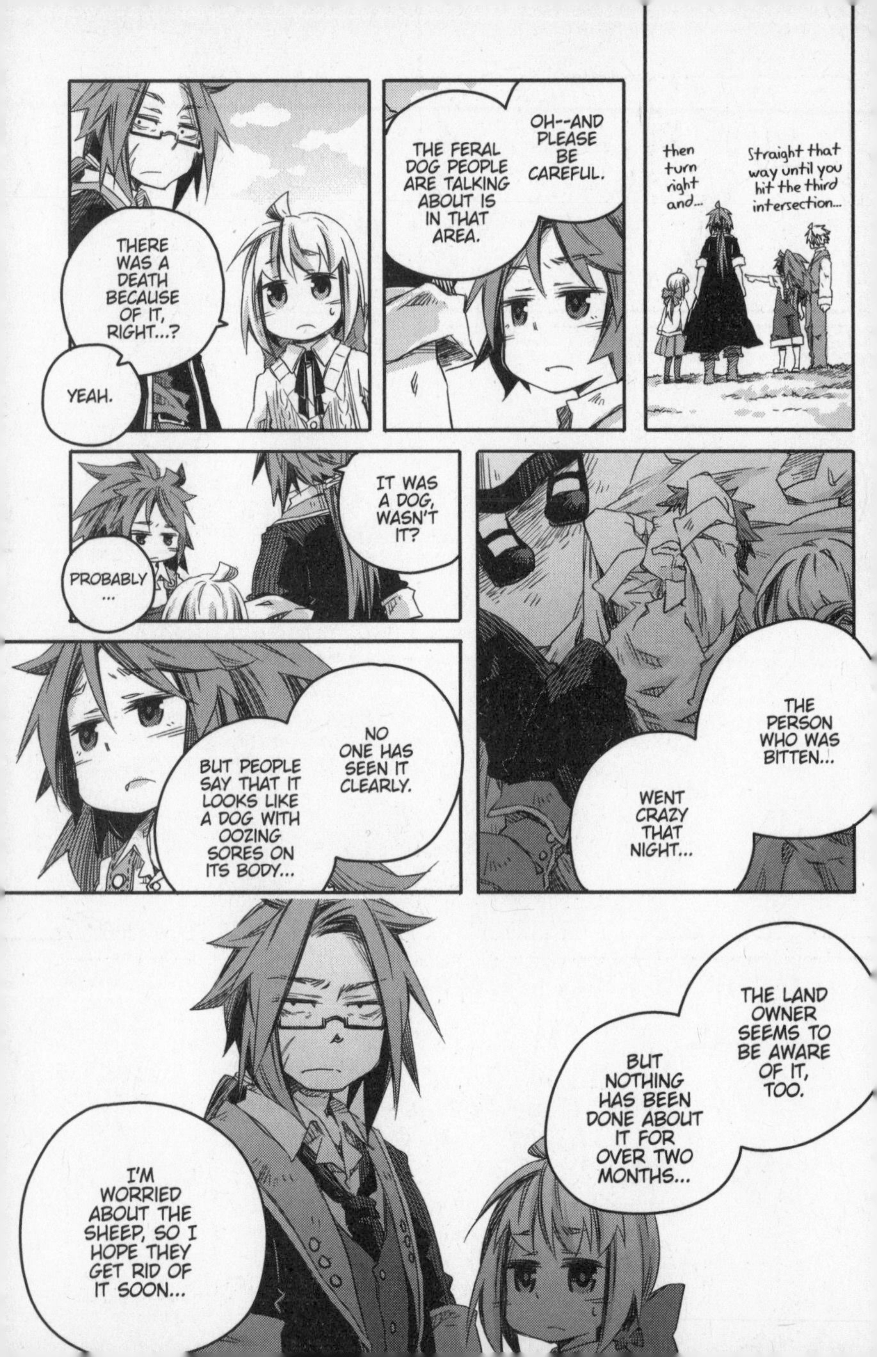
Straight that way until you hit the third intersection...
then turn right and...
OH--AND PLEASE BE CAREFUL.
THE FERAL DOG PEOPLE ARE TALKING ABOUT IS IN THAT AREA.
THERE WAS A DEATH BECAUSE OF IT, RIGHT...?
YEAH.
THE PERSON WHO WAS BITTEN...
WENT CRAZY THAT NIGHT...
IT WAS A DOG, WASN'T IT?
PROBABLY...
NO ONE HAS SEEN IT CLEARLY.
BUT PEOPLE SAY THAT IT LOOKS LIKE A DOG WITH OOZING SORES ON ITS BODY...
THE LAND OWNER SEEMS TO BE AWARE OF IT, TOO.
BUT NOTHING HAS BEEN DONE ABOUT IT FOR OVER TWO MONTHS...
I'M WORRIED ABOUT THE SHEEP, SO I HOPE THEY GET RID OF IT SOON...

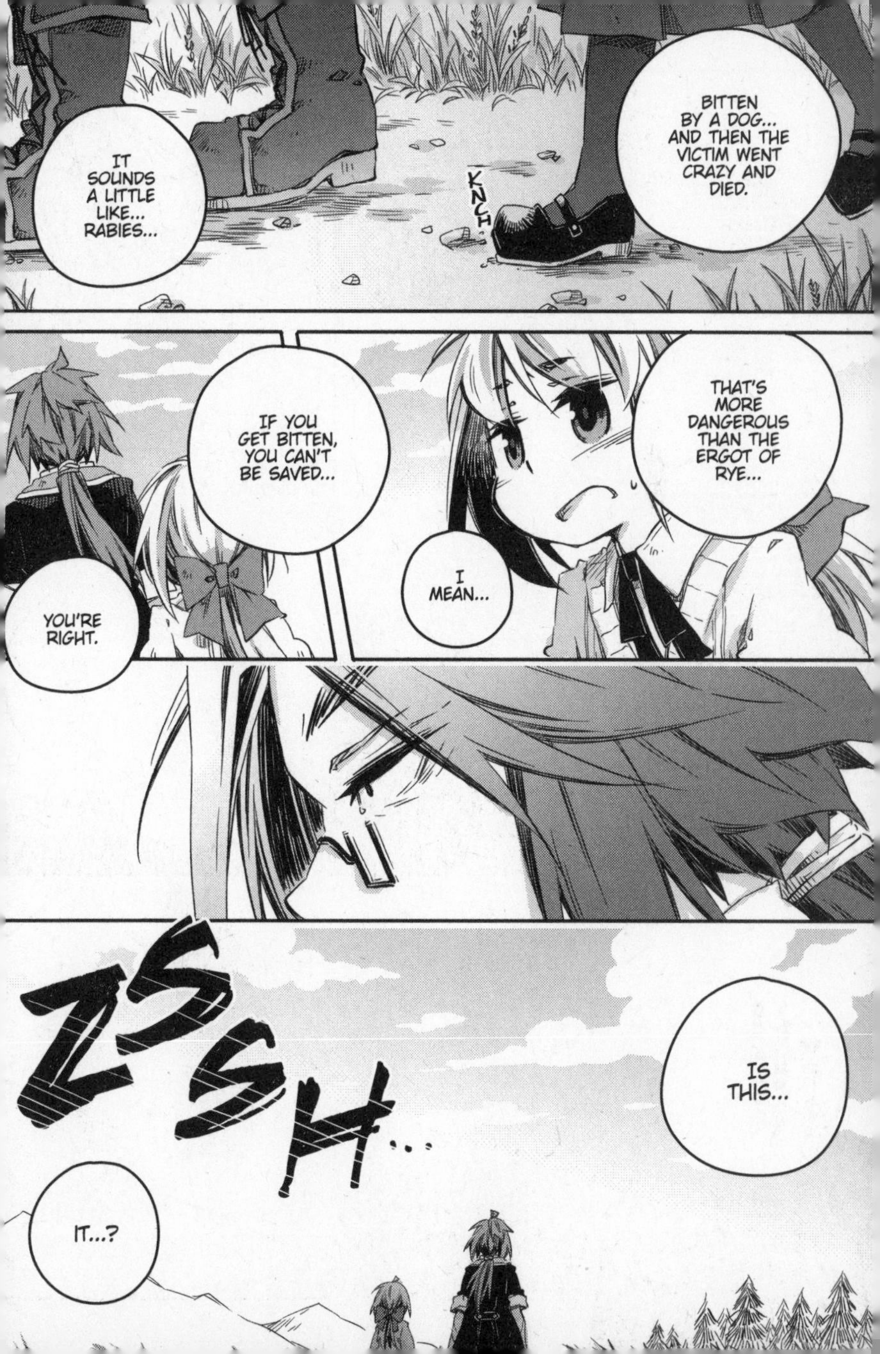
BITTEN BY A DOG... AND THEN THE VICTIM WENT CRAZY AND DIED.
KNCH
IT SOUNDS A LITTLE LIKE... RABIES...
THAT'S MORE DANGEROUS THAN THE ERGOT OF RYE...
I MEAN...
IF YOU GET BITTEN, YOU CAN'T BE SAVED...
YOU'RE RIGHT.
IS THIS...
ZSSH...
IT...?

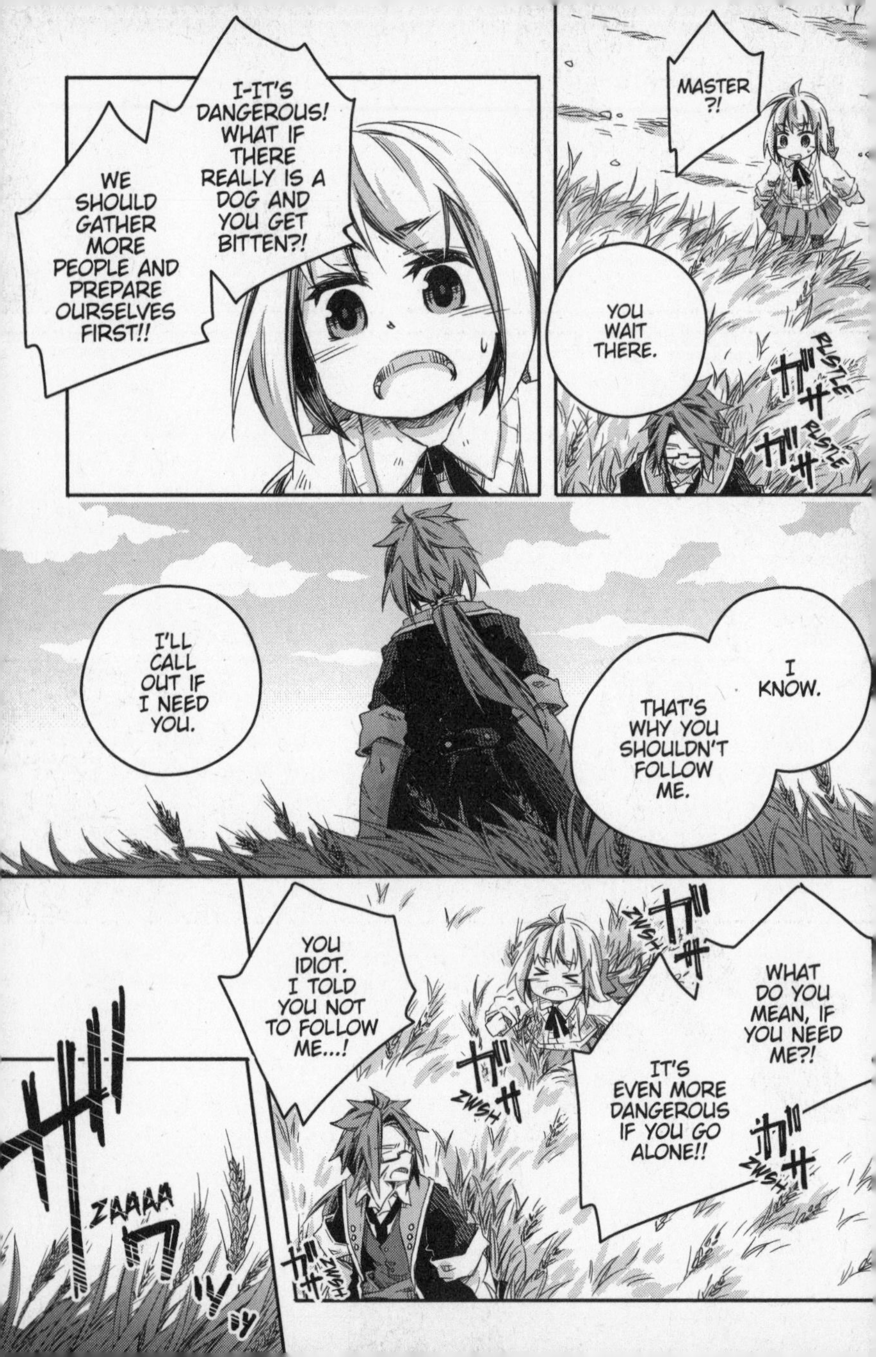
MASTER ?!
YOU WAIT THERE.
RUSTLE
RUSTLE
I-IT'S DANGEROUS! WHAT IF THERE REALLY IS A DOG AND YOU GET BITTEN?!
WE SHOULD GATHER MORE PEOPLE AND PREPARE OURSELVES FIRST!!
I KNOW.
THAT'S WHY YOU SHOULDN'T FOLLOW ME.
I'LL CALL OUT IF I NEED YOU.
WHAT DO YOU MEAN, IF YOU NEED ME?!
IT'S EVEN MORE DANGEROUS IF YOU GO ALONE!!
ZWSH
ZWSH
YOU IDIOT. I TOLD YOU NOT TO FOLLOW ME...!
ZWSH
ZWSH
ZAAAA

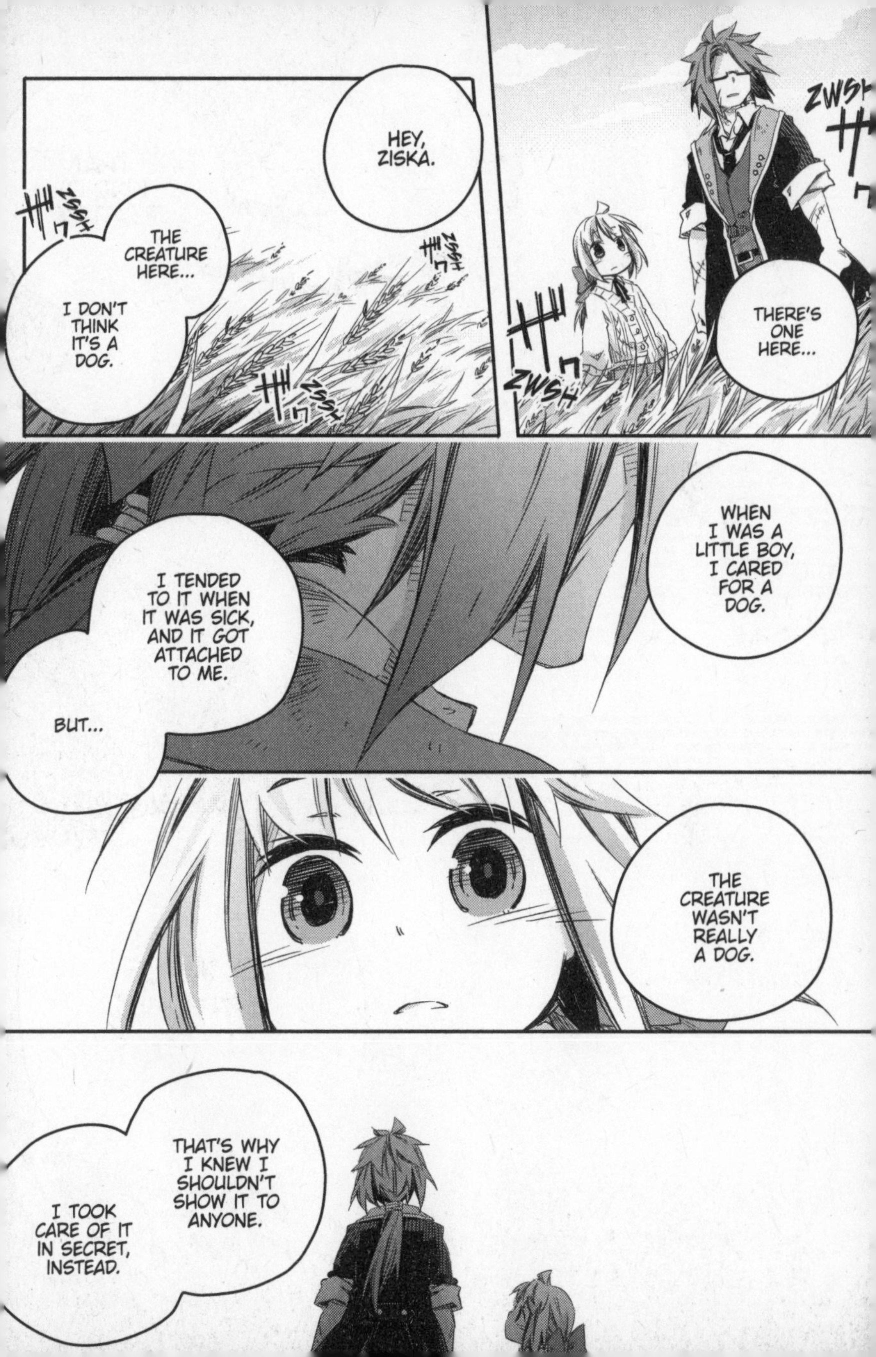
ZWSH
THERE'S ONE HERE...
ZWSH
HEY, ZISKA.
THE CREATURE HERE...
I DON'T THINK IT'S A DOG.
ZSSH
ZSSH
ZSSH
WHEN I WAS A LITTLE BOY, I CARED FOR A DOG.
I TENDED TO IT WHEN IT WAS SICK, AND IT GOT ATTACHED TO ME.
BUT...
THE CREATURE WASN'T REALLY A DOG.
THAT'S WHY I KNEW I SHOULDN'T SHOW IT TO ANYONE.
I TOOK CARE OF IT IN SECRET, INSTEAD.

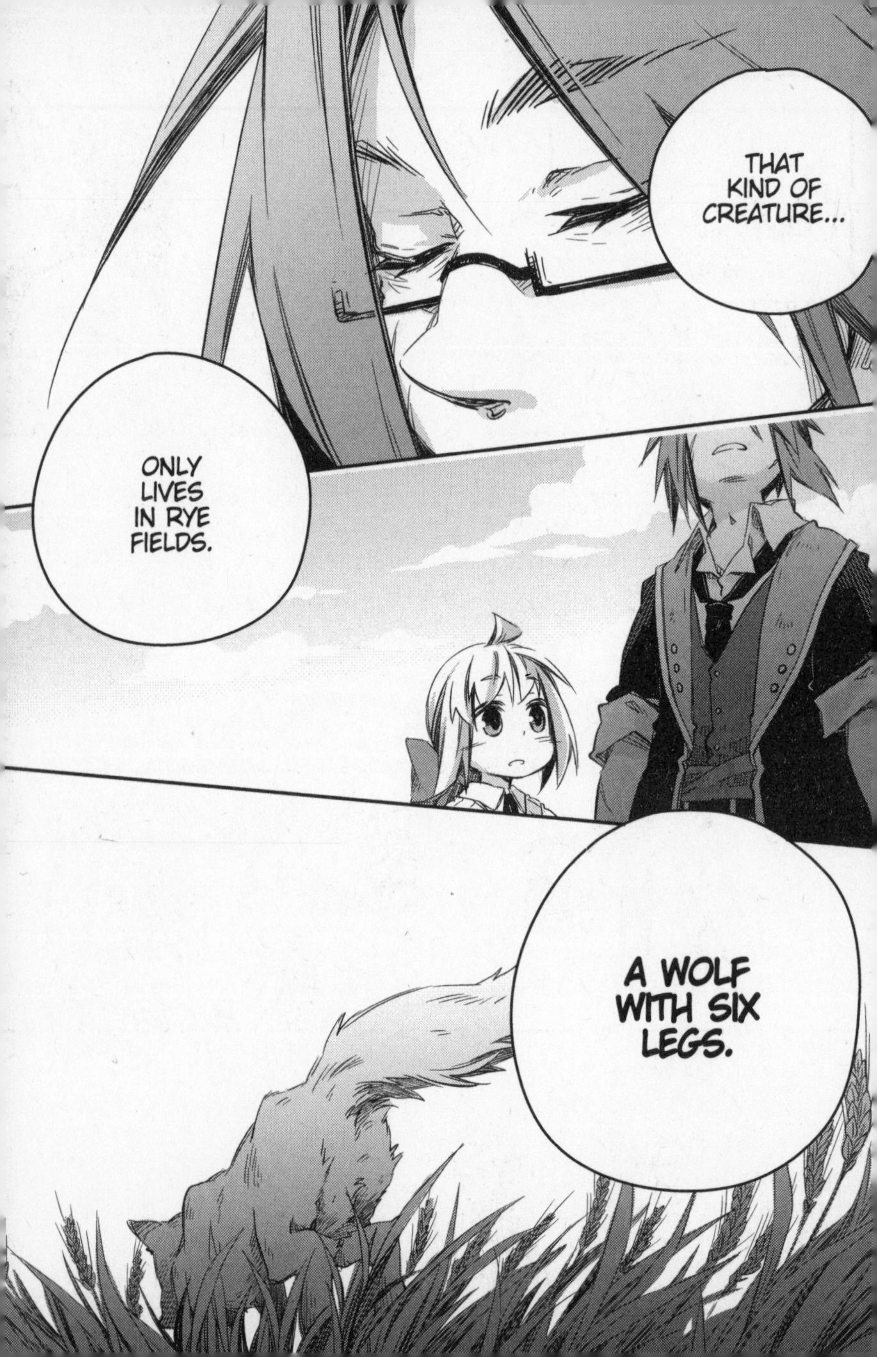
THAT KIND OF CREATURE...
ONLY LIVES IN RYE FIELDS.
A WOLF WITH SIX LEGS.

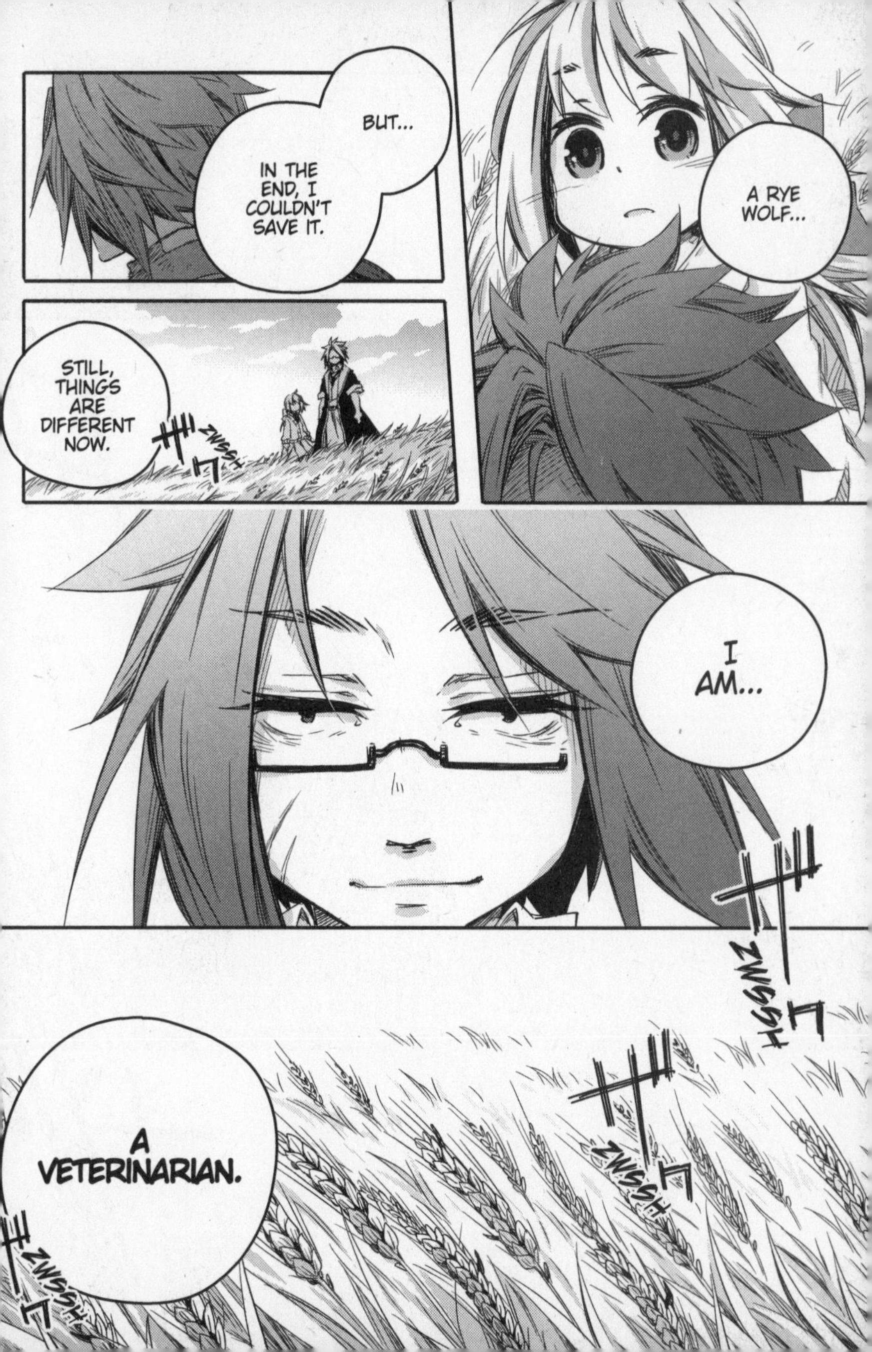
A RYE WOLF...
BUT...
IN THE END, I COULDN'T SAVE IT.
STILL, THINGS ARE DIFFERENT NOW.
ZWSSH
I AM...
ZWSSH
ZWSSH
A VETERINARIAN.
ZWSSH

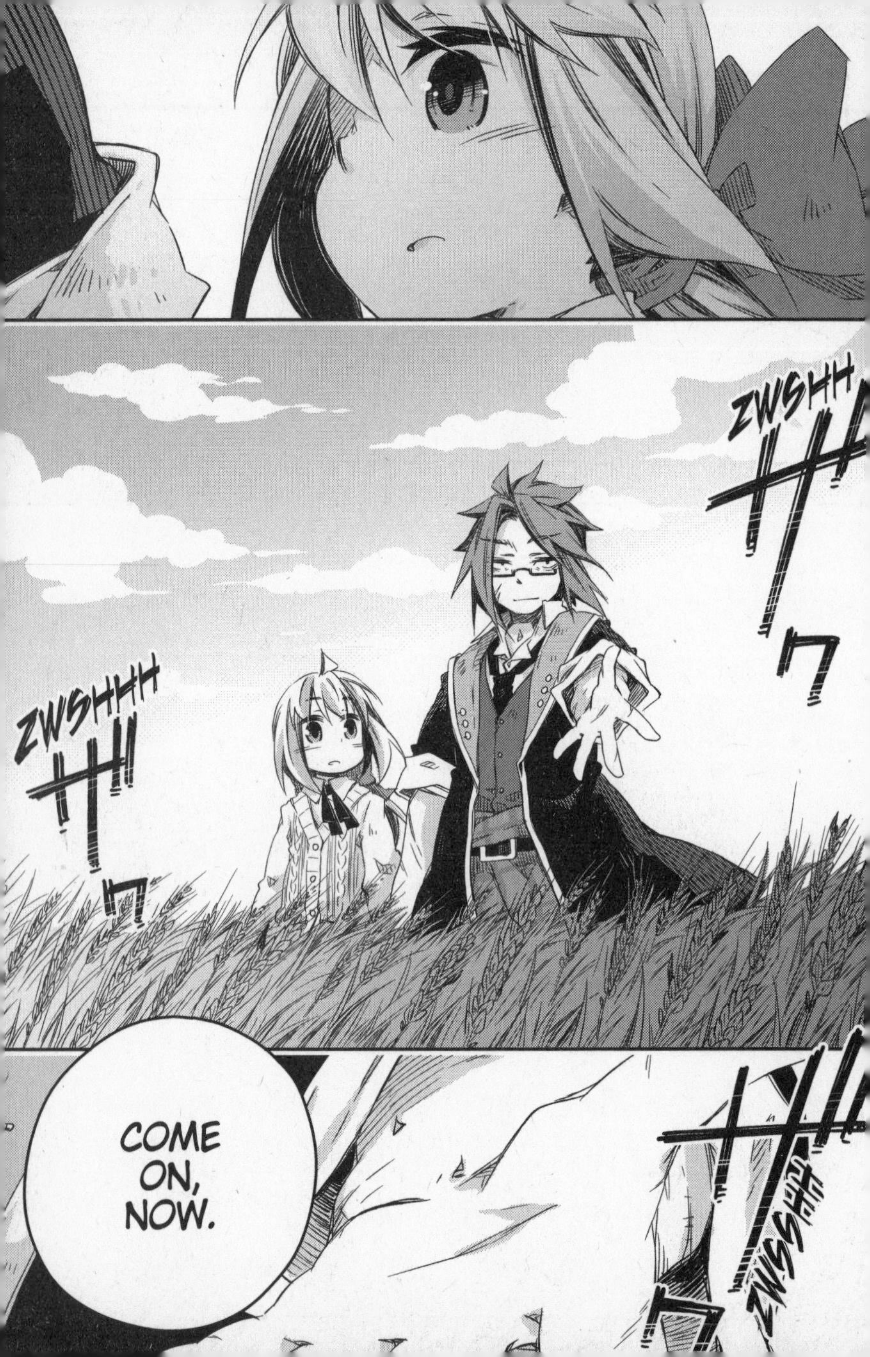
ZWSHH
ZWSHHH
ZWSSHHH
COME ON, NOW.

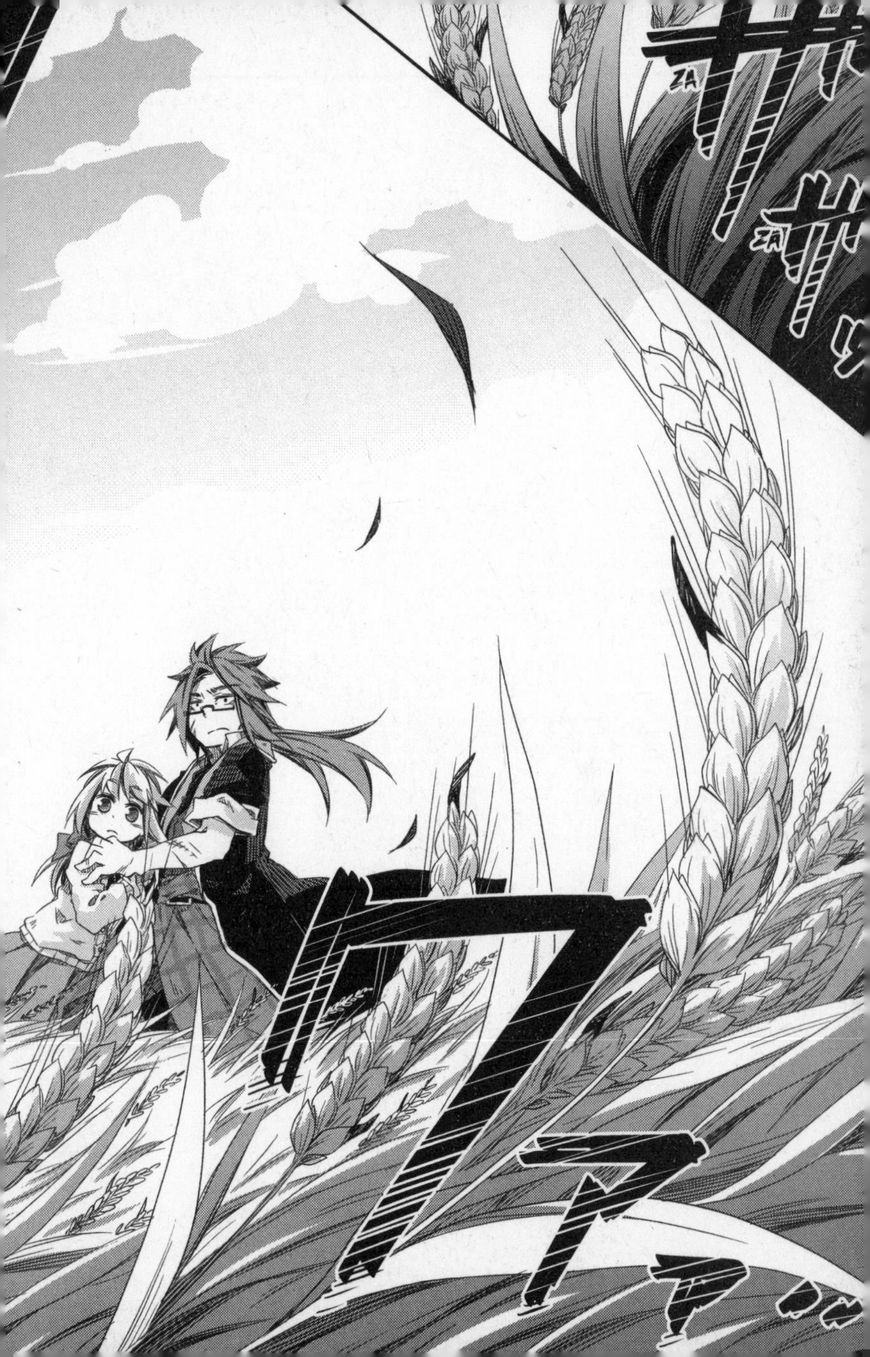
ZA
ZA

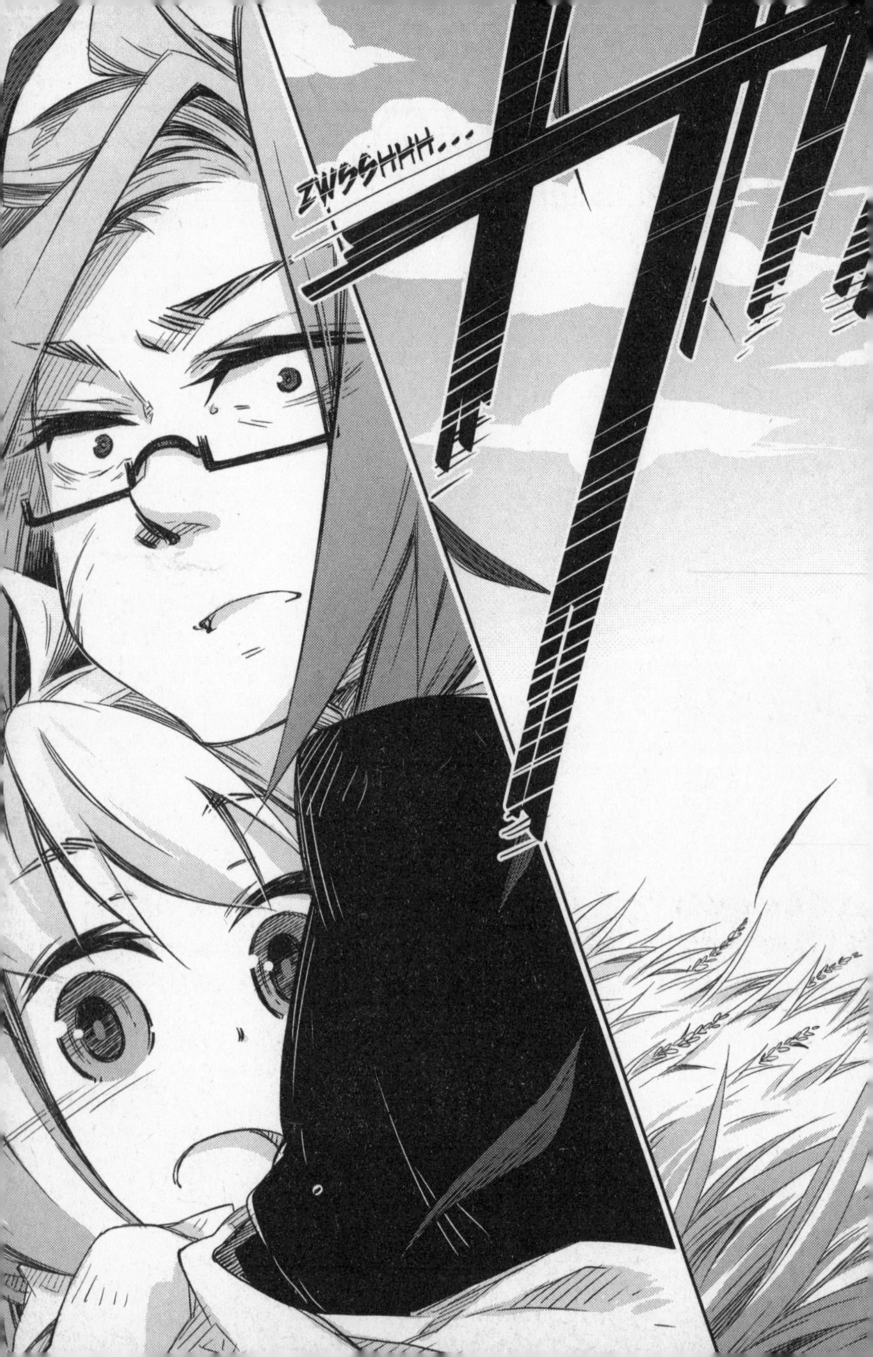
ZWSSHHH...

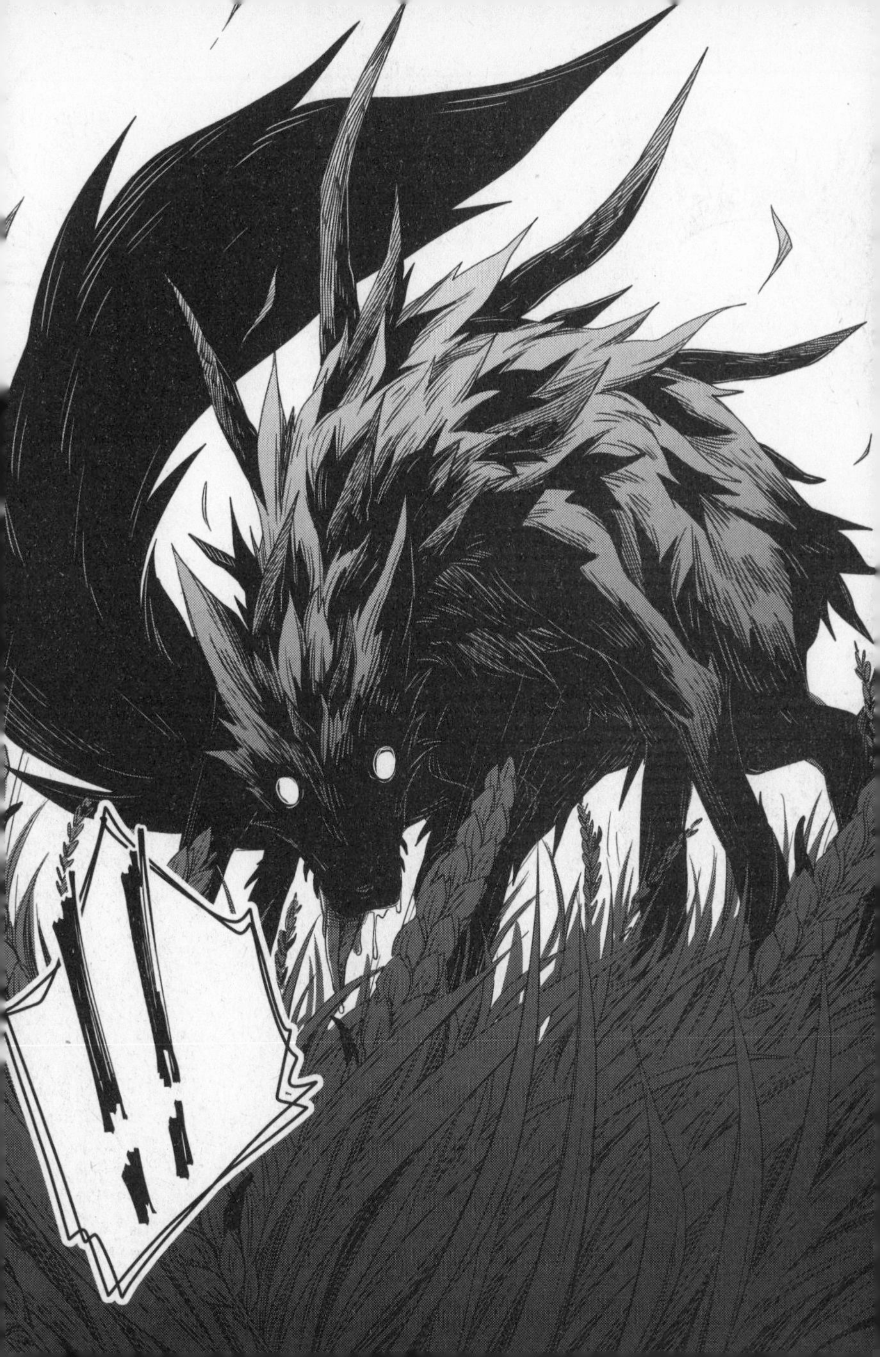
!!

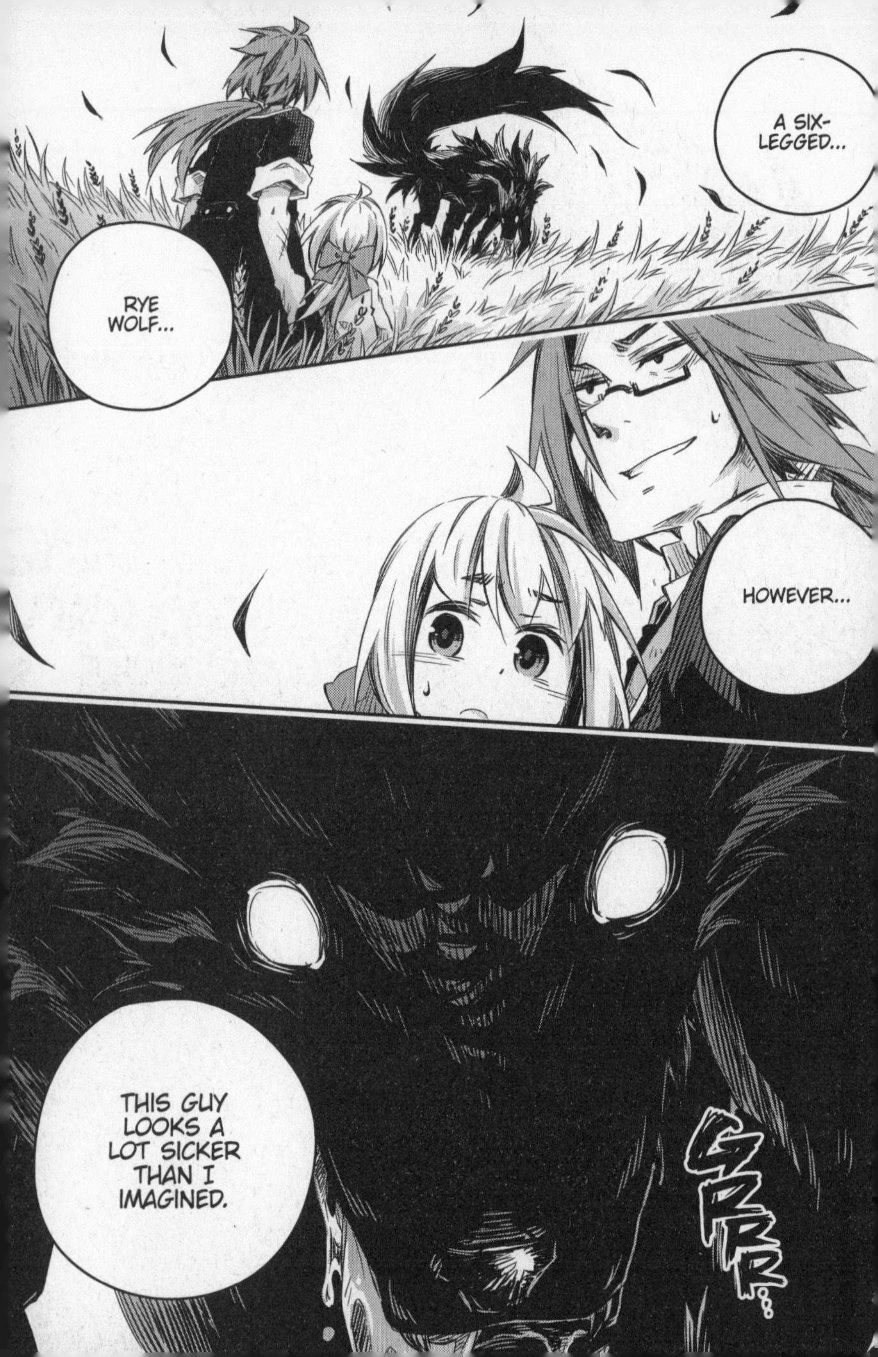
A SIX-LEGGED...
RYE WOLF...
HOWEVER...
THIS GUY LOOKS A LOT SICKER THAN I IMAGINED.
GRRR..

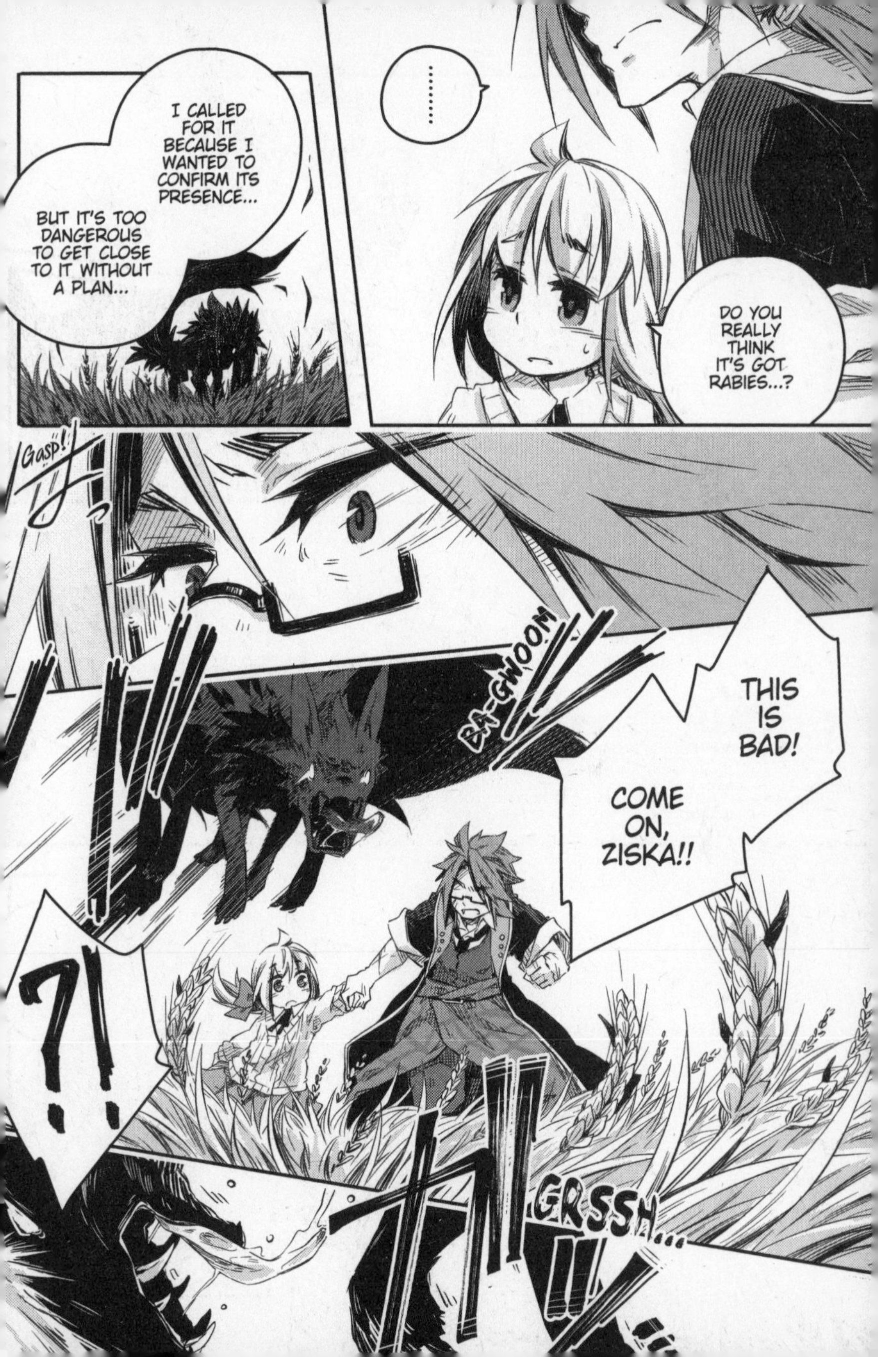
......
DO YOU REALLY THINK IT'S GOT RABIES...?
I CALLED FOR IT BECAUSE I WANTED TO CONFIRM ITS PRESENCE...
BUT IT'S TOO DANGEROUS TO GET CLOSE TO IT WITHOUT A PLAN...
Gasp!
BA-GWOOM
THIS IS BAD!
COME ON, ZISKA!!
?!
GRSSH...

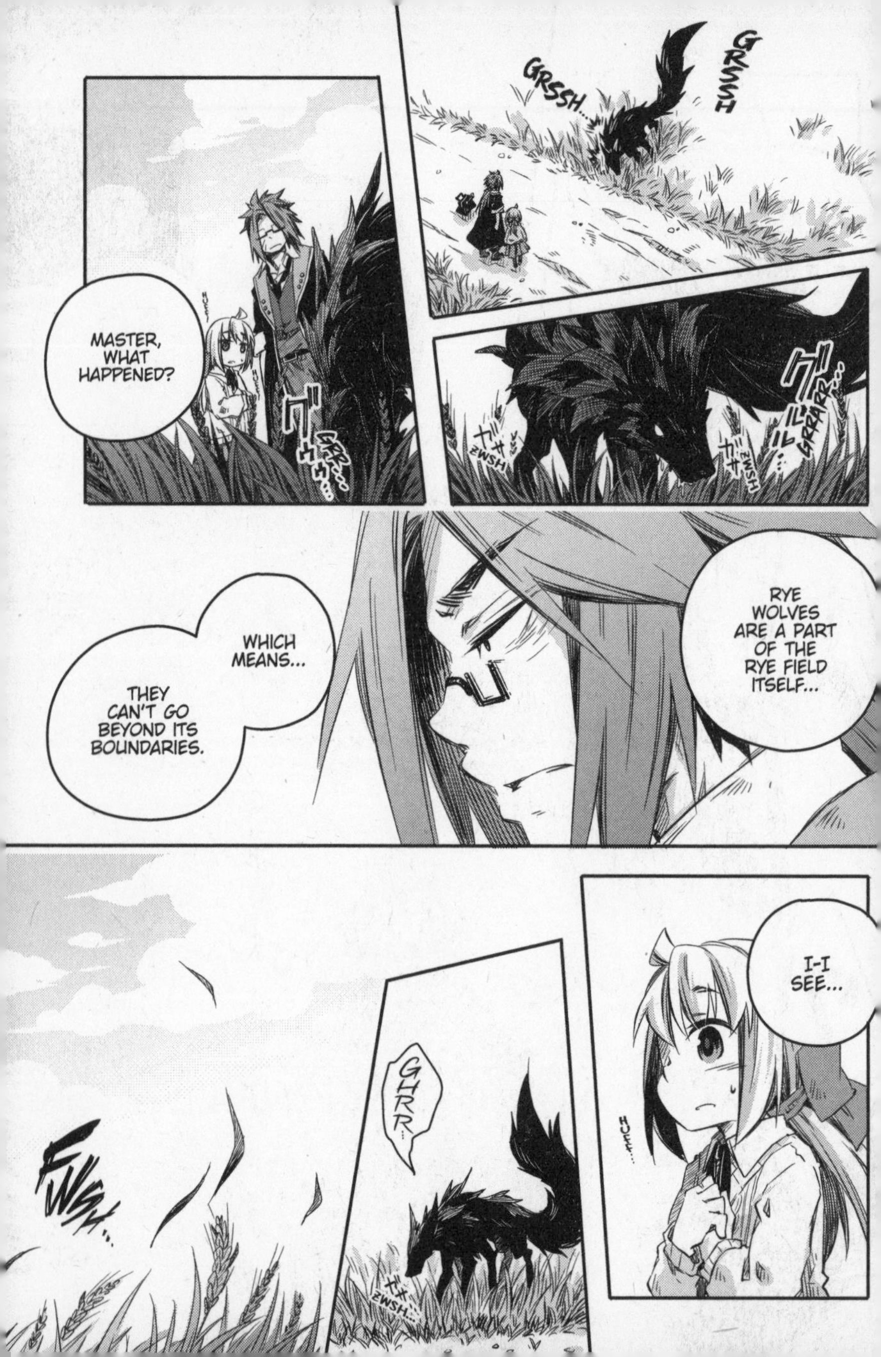
GRSSH...
GRSSH
GRRARR...
ZWSH
ZWSH
MASTER, WHAT HAPPENED?
HUFF
HUFF
GRRR...
RYE WOLVES ARE A PART OF THE RYE FIELD ITSELF...
WHICH MEANS...
THEY CAN'T GO BEYOND ITS BOUNDARIES.
I-I SEE...
HUFF...
GHRR...
ZWSH...
FWSH...

[Case 11: Rye Wolf]

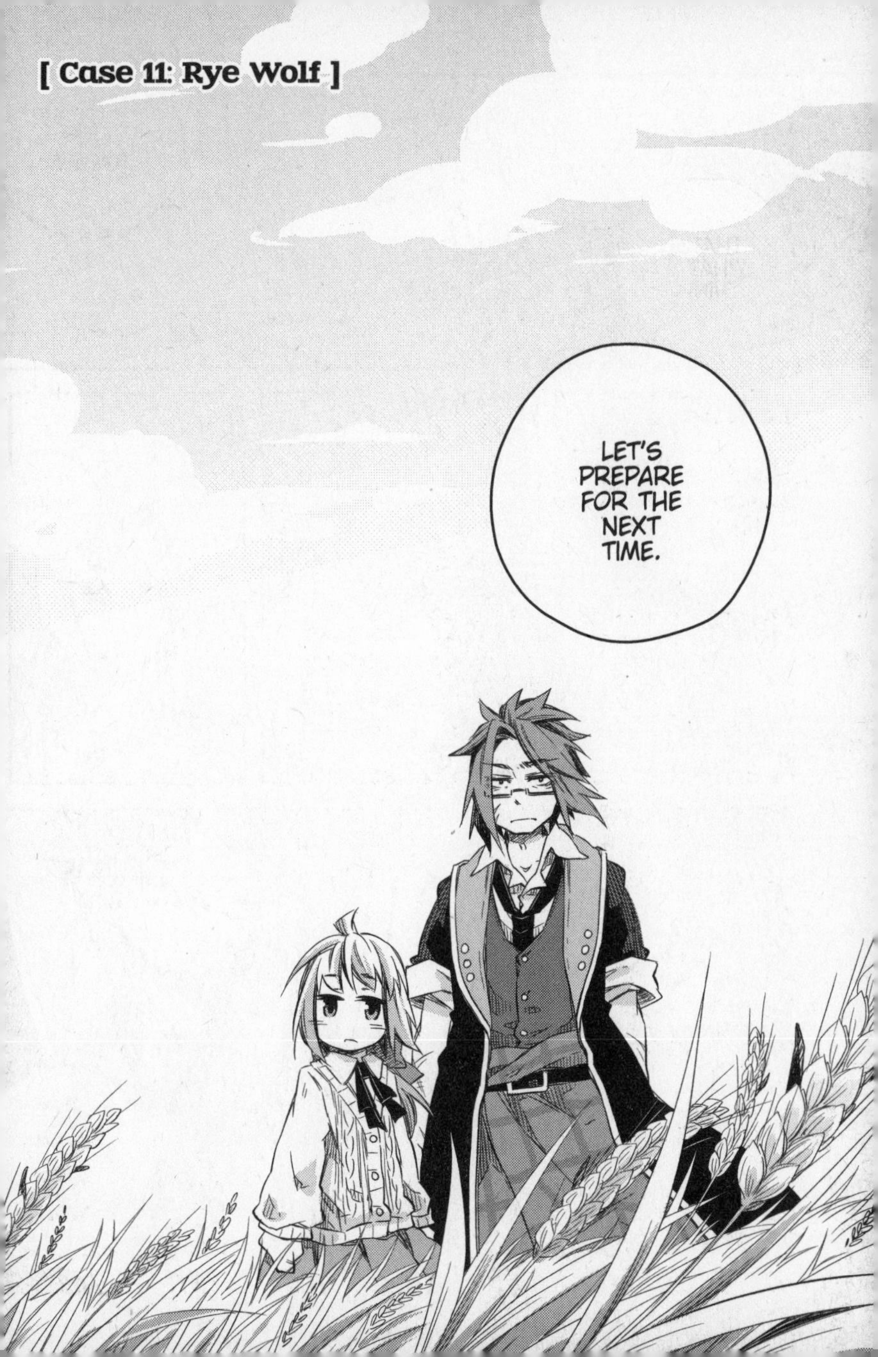
LET'S PREPARE FOR THE NEXT TIME.

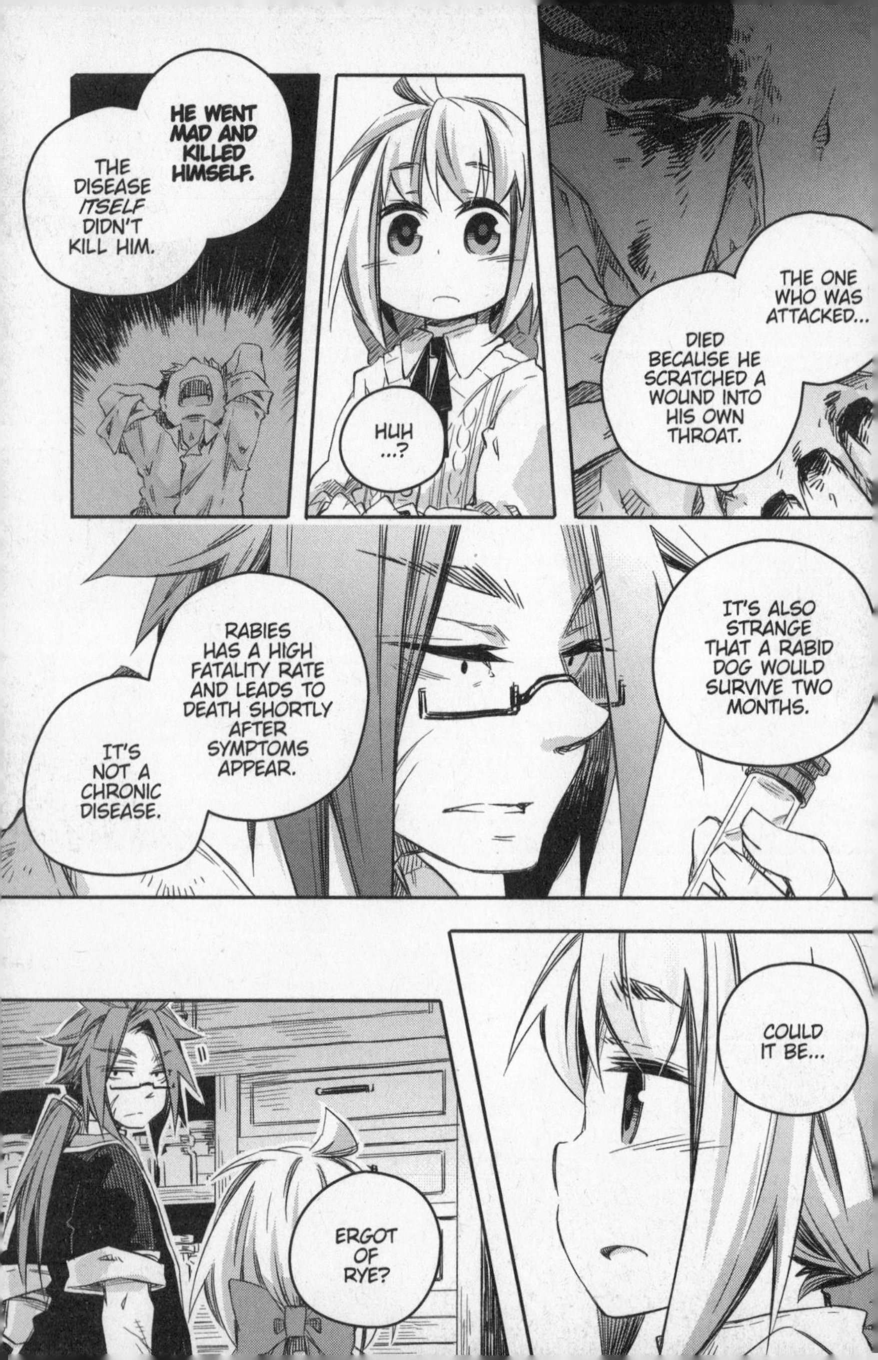
THE ONE WHO WAS ATTACKED...
DIED BECAUSE HE SCRATCHED A WOUND INTO HIS OWN THROAT.
HUH ...?
HE WENT MAD AND KILLED HIMSELF.
THE DISEASE *ITSELF* DIDN'T KILL HIM.
IT'S ALSO STRANGE THAT A RABID DOG WOULD SURVIVE TWO MONTHS.
RABIES HAS A HIGH FATALITY RATE AND LEADS TO DEATH SHORTLY AFTER SYMPTOMS APPEAR.
IT'S NOT A CHRONIC DISEASE.
COULD IT BE...
ERGOT OF RYE?

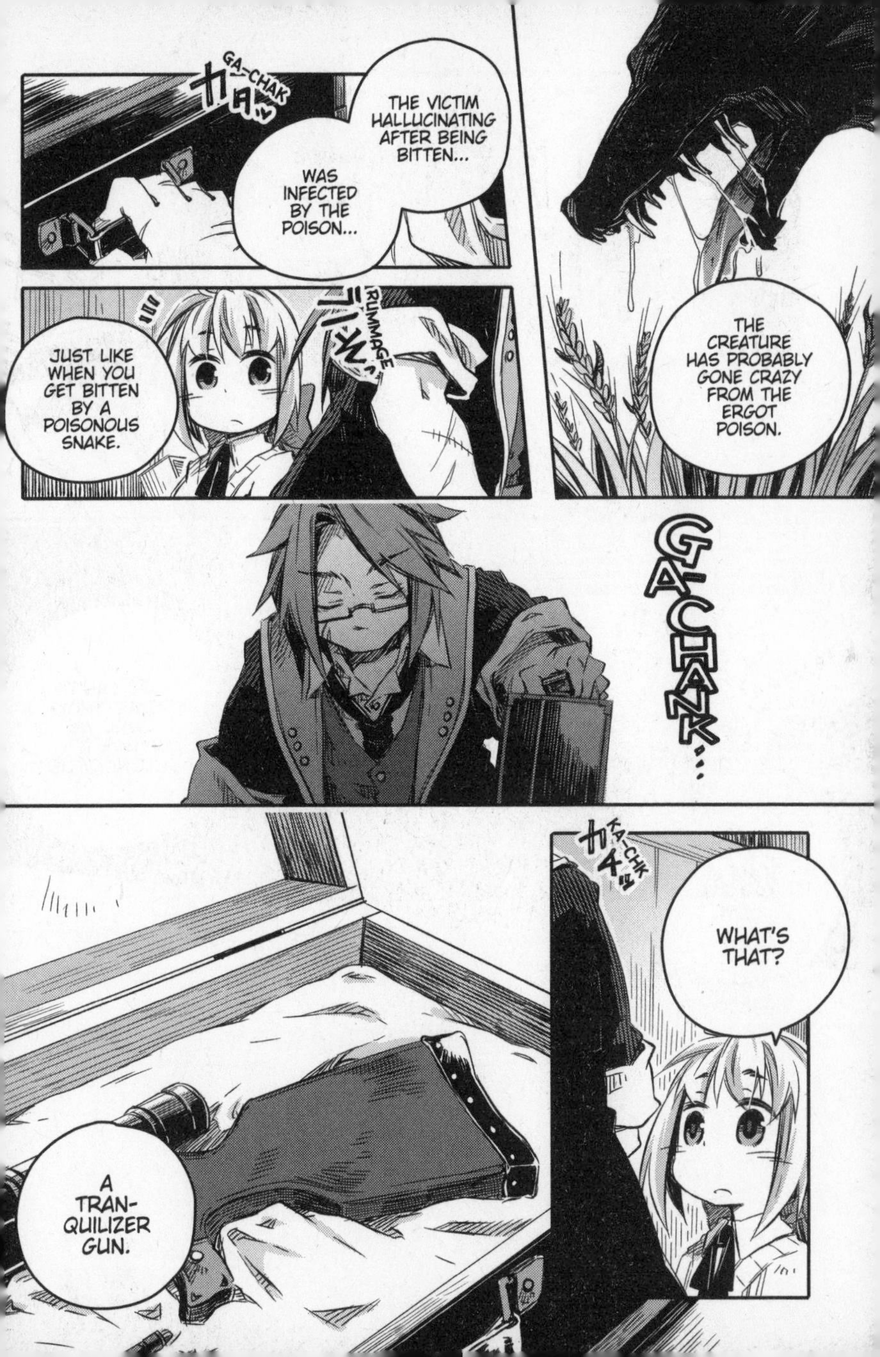

THE CREATURE HAS PROBABLY GONE CRAZY FROM THE ERGOT POISON.
GA-CHAK
THE VICTIM HALLUCINATING AFTER BEING BITTEN...
WAS INFECTED BY THE POISON...
RUMMAGE
JUST LIKE WHEN YOU GET BITTEN BY A POISONOUS SNAKE.
GA-CHAK...
KA-CHK
WHAT'S THAT?
A TRAN-QUILIZER GUN.

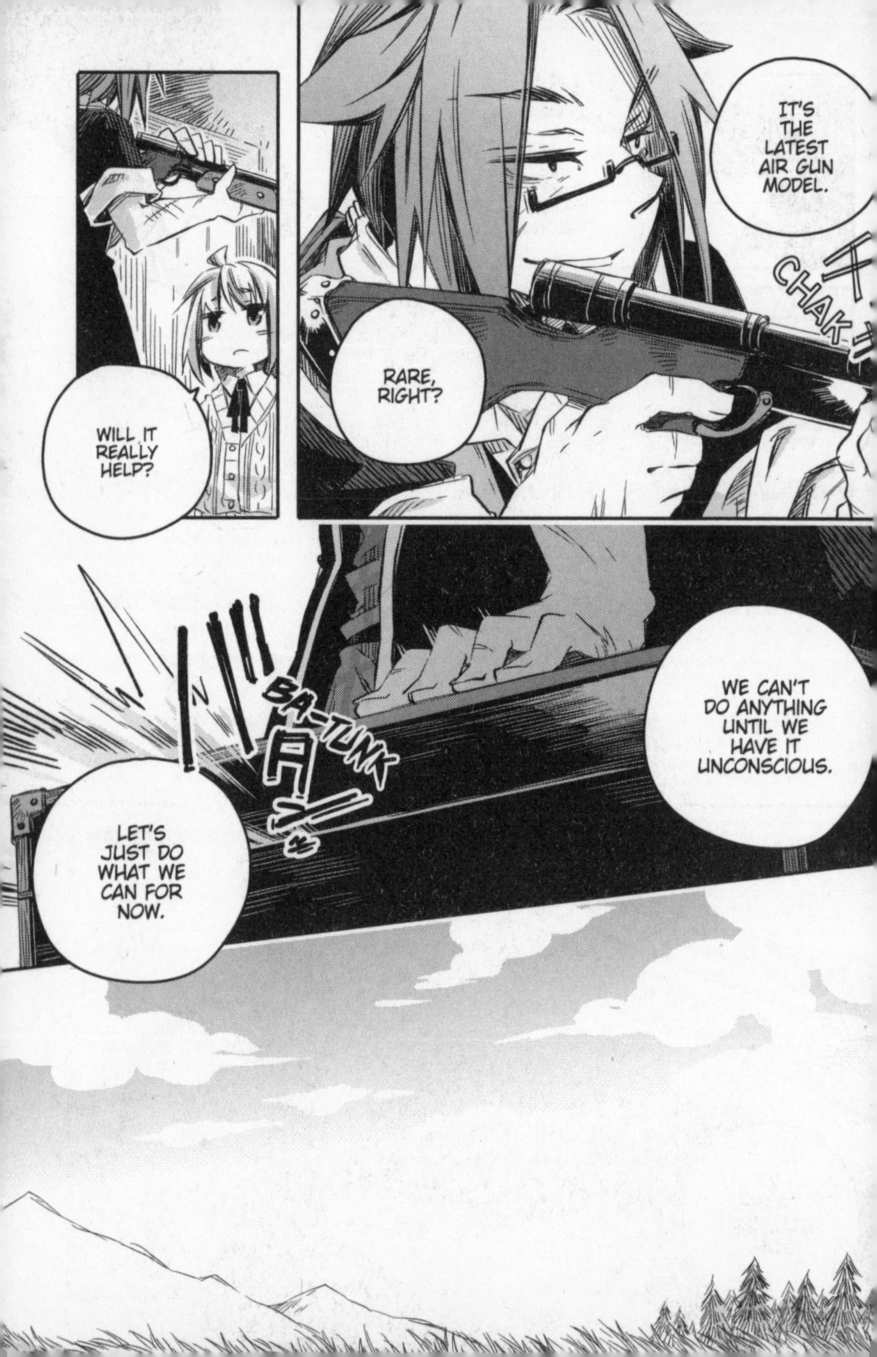
IT'S THE LATEST AIR GUN MODEL.
CHAK
RARE, RIGHT?
WILL IT REALLY HELP?
WE CAN'T DO ANYTHING UNTIL WE HAVE IT UNCONSCIOUS.
BA-TUNK
LET'S JUST DO WHAT WE CAN FOR NOW.

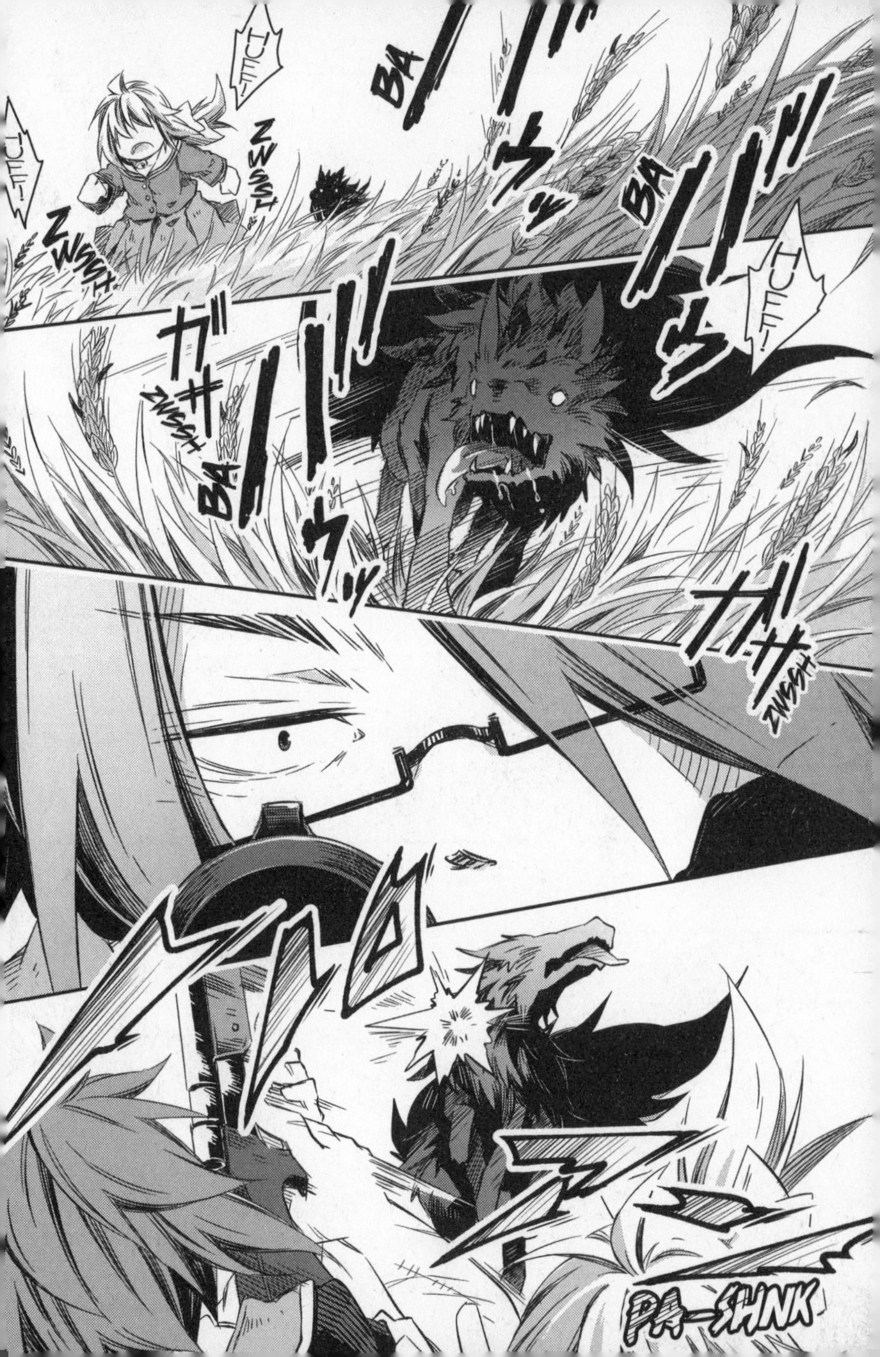
HUFF!
BA
BA
HUFF!
ZWSSSH
HUFF!
ZWSSSH
ZWSSSH
BA
ZWSSSH
PA-SHNK

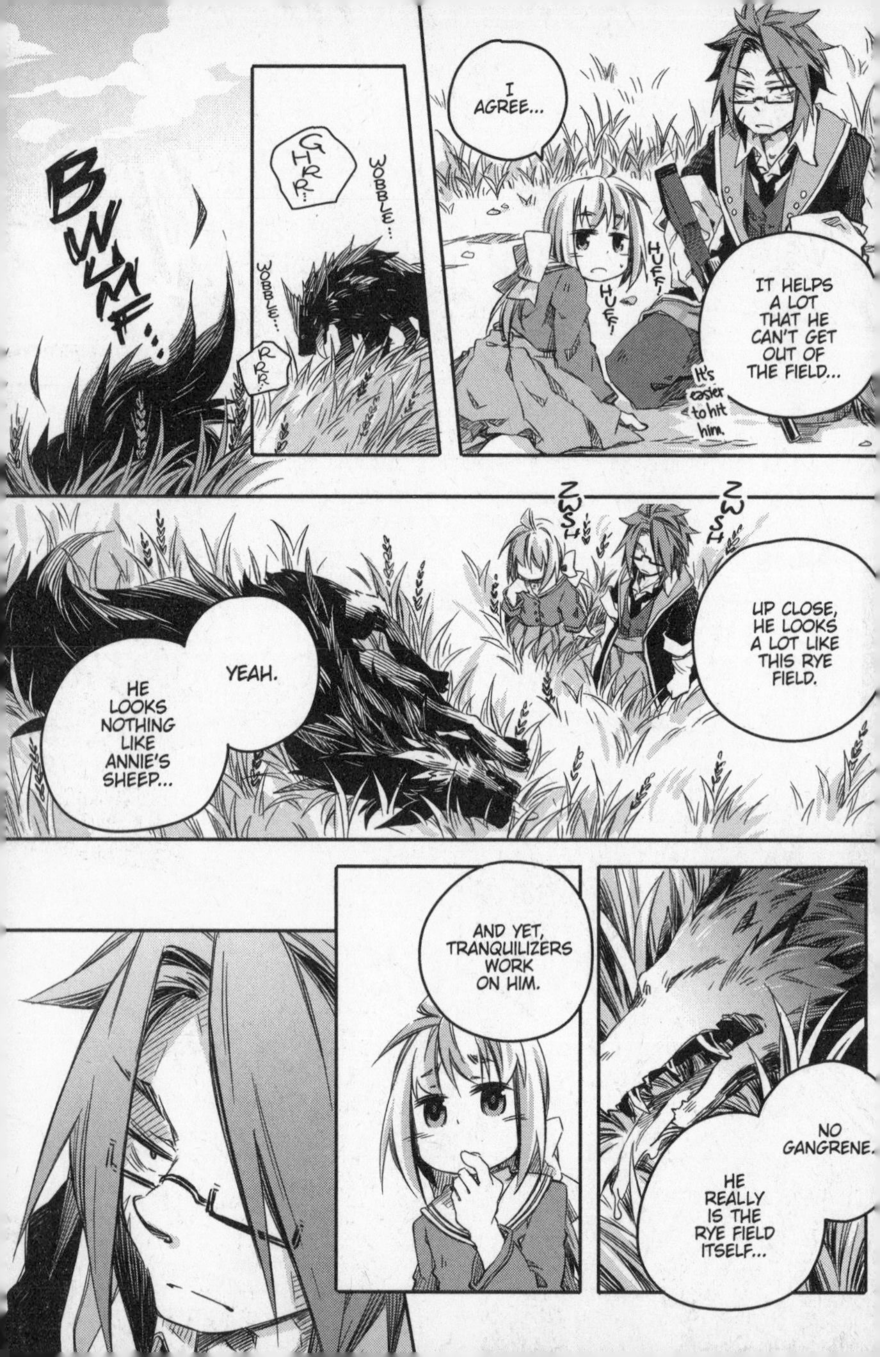
I AGREE...
HUFF! HUFF!
IT HELPS A LOT THAT HE CAN'T GET OUT OF THE FIELD...
It's easier to hit him.
GHRR...
WOBBLE...
WOBBLE...
RRR...
BWUMF...
ZWSH
ZWSH
UP CLOSE, HE LOOKS A LOT LIKE THIS RYE FIELD.
YEAH.
HE LOOKS NOTHING LIKE ANNIE'S SHEEP...
NO GANGRENE.
HE REALLY IS THE RYE FIELD ITSELF...
AND YET, TRANQUILIZERS WORK ON HIM.

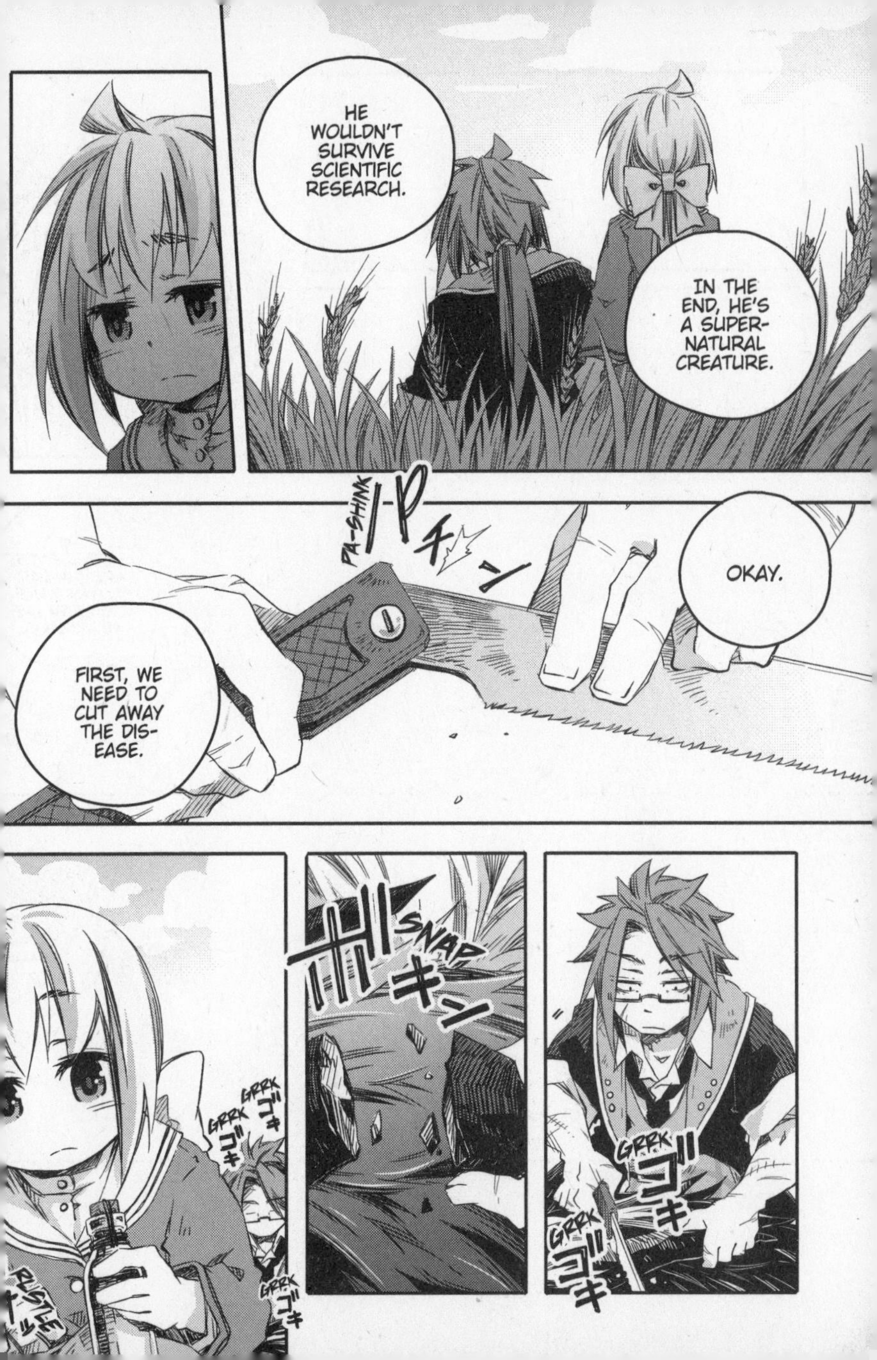
HE WOULDN'T SURVIVE SCIENTIFIC RESEARCH.
IN THE END, HE'S A SUPER-NATURAL CREATURE.
OKAY.
PA-SHINK
FIRST, WE NEED TO CUT AWAY THE DIS-EASE.
GRRK
GRRK
SNAP
GRRK
GRRK
GRRK
RUSTLE

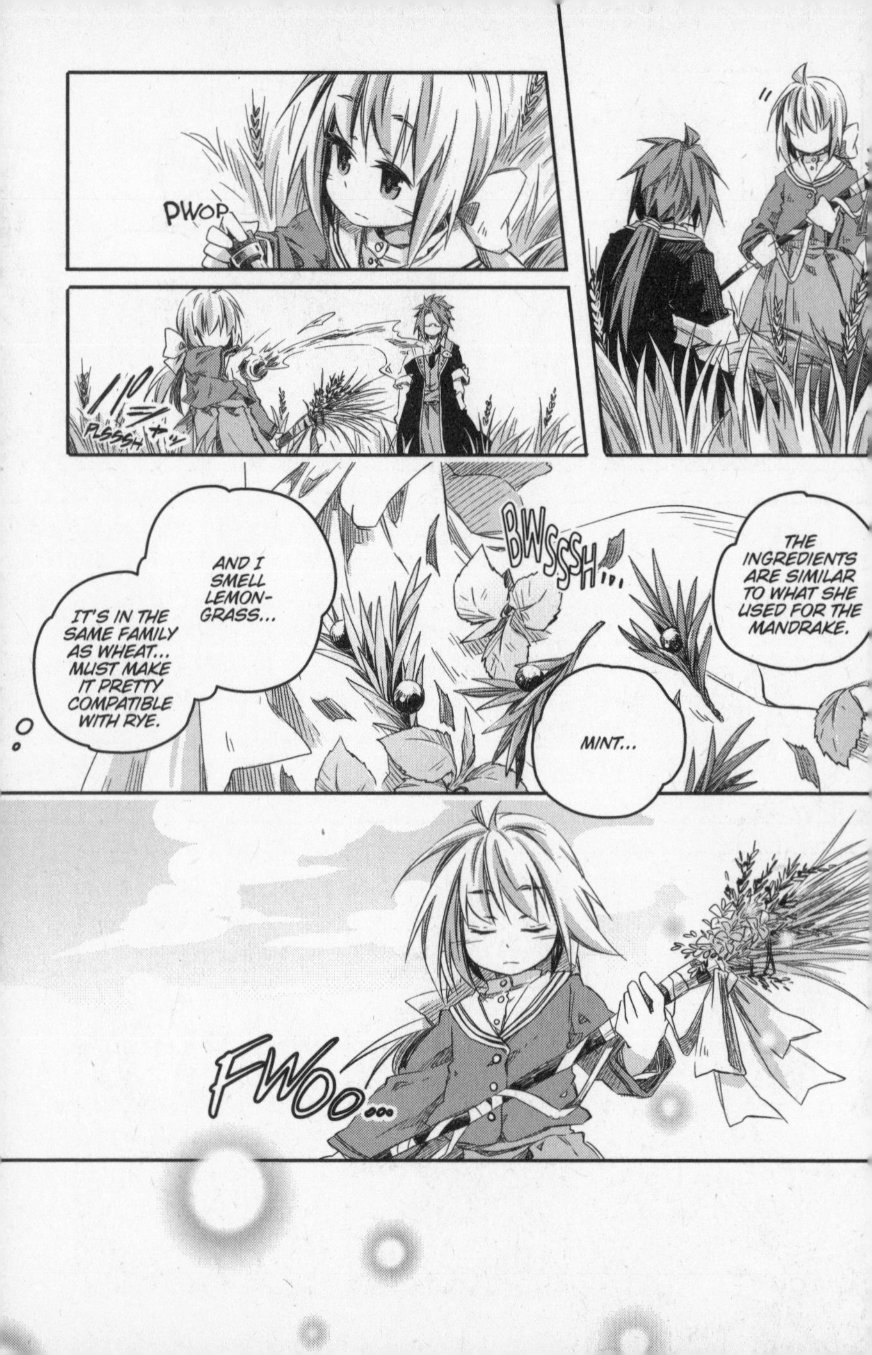
PWOP
PLSSSH
THE INGREDIENTS ARE SIMILAR TO WHAT SHE USED FOR THE MANDRAKE.
BWSSSH...
MINT...
AND I SMELL LEMON-GRASS...
IT'S IN THE SAME FAMILY AS WHEAT... MUST MAKE IT PRETTY COMPATIBLE WITH RYE.
FWOO...

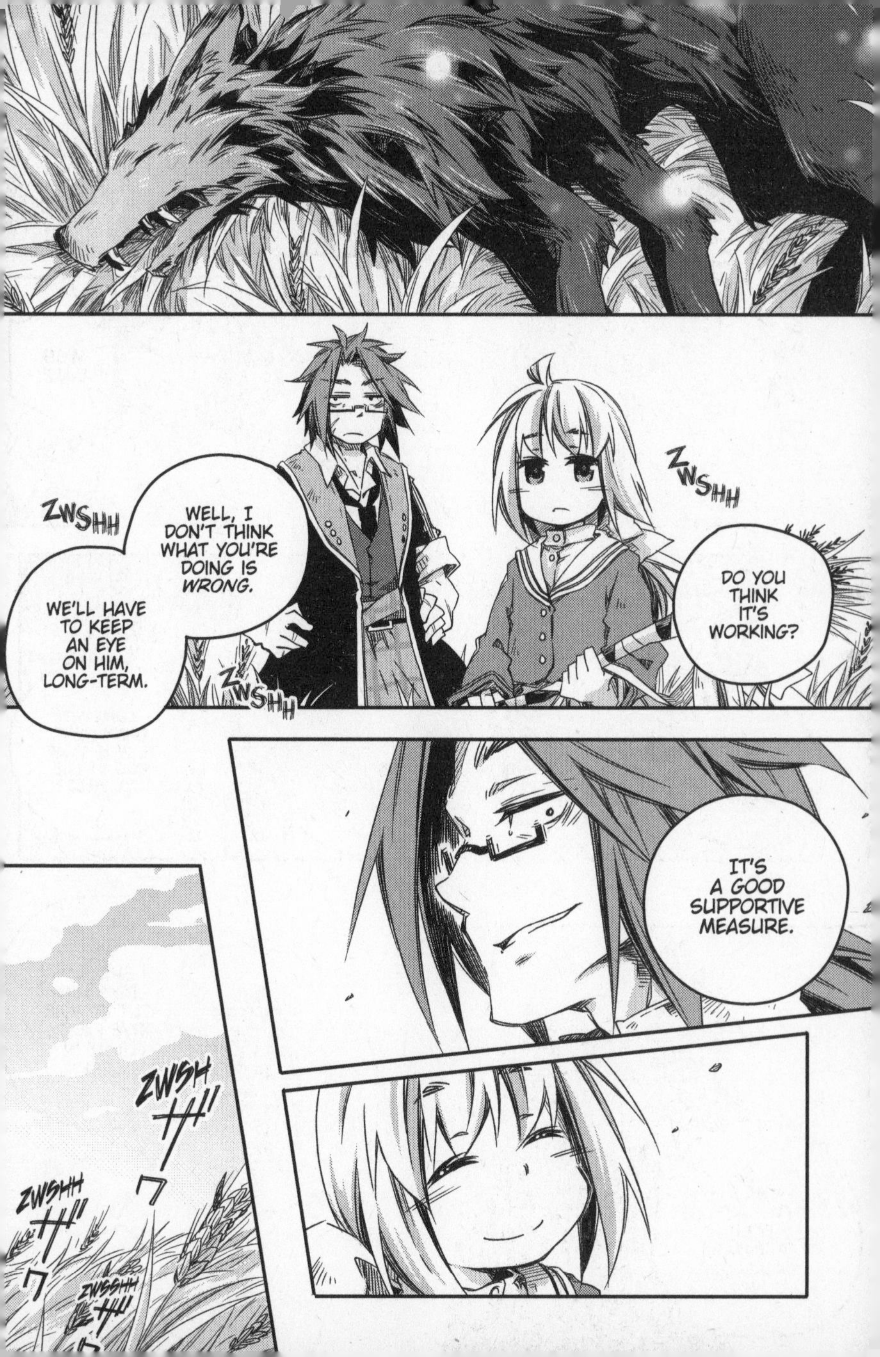
ZWSHH
DO YOU THINK IT'S WORKING?
WELL, I DON'T THINK WHAT YOU'RE DOING IS *WRONG.*
ZWSHH
WE'LL HAVE TO KEEP AN EYE ON HIM, LONG-TERM.
ZWSHH
IT'S A GOOD SUPPORTIVE MEASURE.
ZWSH
ZWSHH
ZWSSHH

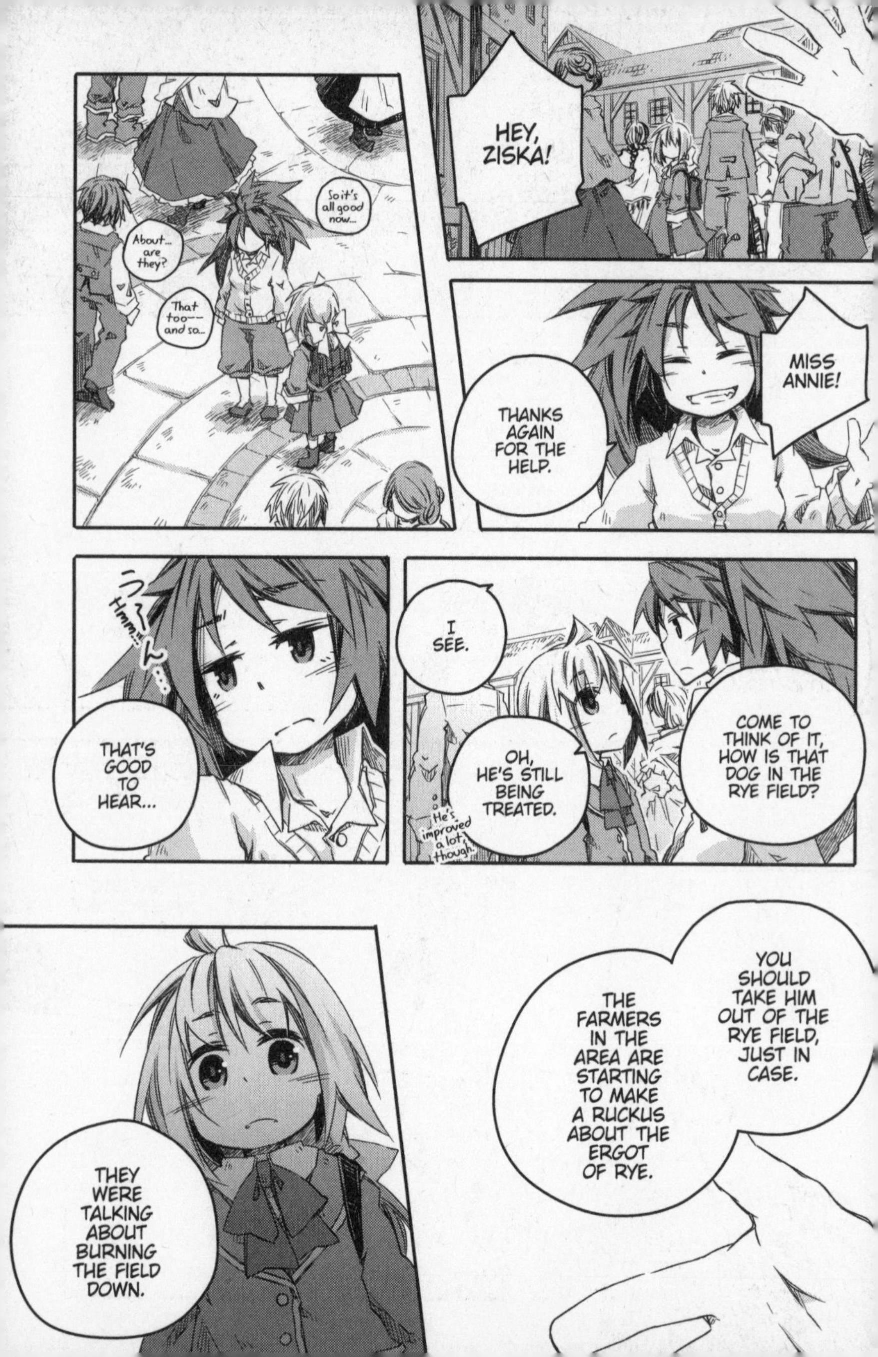
HEY, ZISKA!
So it's all good now...
About... are they?
That too--- and so...
MISS ANNIE!
THANKS AGAIN FOR THE HELP.
COME TO THINK OF IT, HOW IS THAT DOG IN THE RYE FIELD?
OH, HE'S STILL BEING TREATED.
He's improved a lot, though.
I SEE.
うーん…
Hmm...
THAT'S GOOD TO HEAR...
YOU SHOULD TAKE HIM OUT OF THE RYE FIELD, JUST IN CASE.
THE FARMERS IN THE AREA ARE STARTING TO MAKE A RUCKUS ABOUT THE ERGOT OF RYE.
THEY WERE TALKING ABOUT BURNING THE FIELD DOWN.

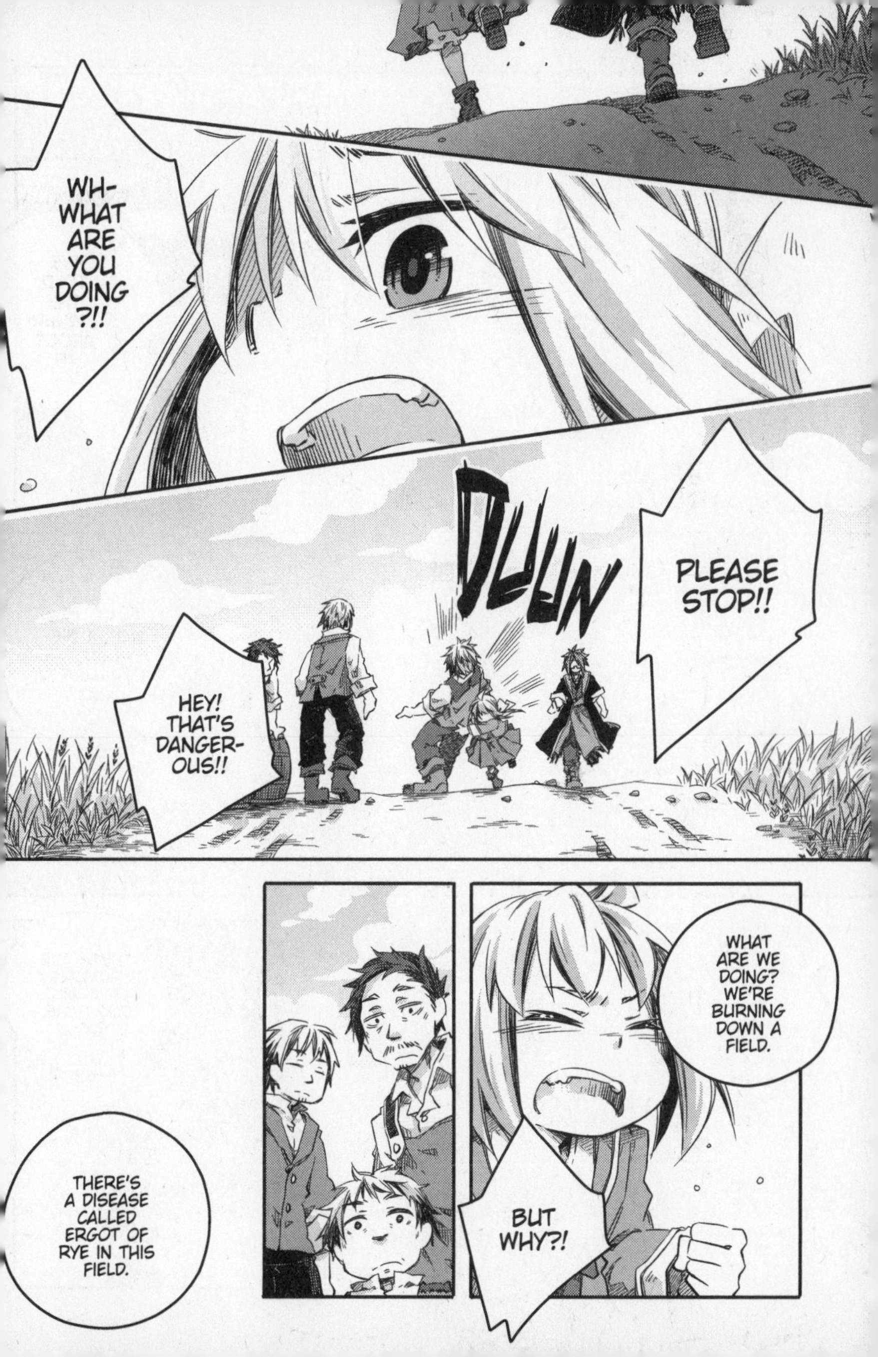
WH- WHAT ARE YOU DOING ?!!
PLEASE STOP!!
DUUN
HEY! THAT'S DANGER-OUS!!
WHAT ARE WE DOING? WE'RE BURNING DOWN A FIELD.
BUT WHY?!
THERE'S A DISEASE CALLED ERGOT OF RYE IN THIS FIELD.

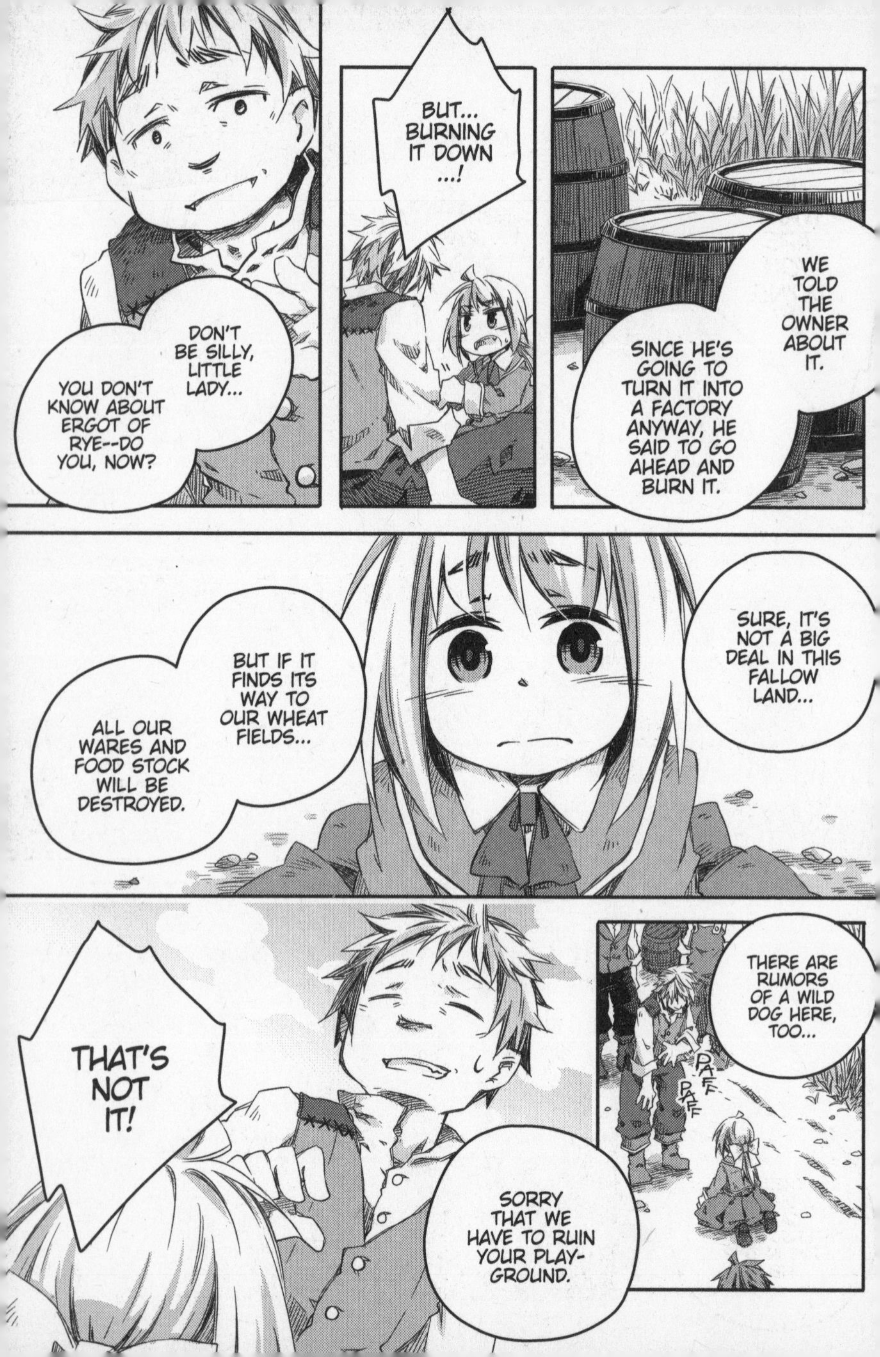
WE TOLD THE OWNER ABOUT IT.
SINCE HE'S GOING TO TURN IT INTO A FACTORY ANYWAY, HE SAID TO GO AHEAD AND BURN IT.
BUT... BURNING IT DOWN ...!
DON'T BE SILLY, LITTLE LADY...
YOU DON'T KNOW ABOUT ERGOT OF RYE--DO YOU, NOW?
SURE, IT'S NOT A BIG DEAL IN THIS FALLOW LAND...
BUT IF IT FINDS ITS WAY TO OUR WHEAT FIELDS...
ALL OUR WARES AND FOOD STOCK WILL BE DESTROYED.
THERE ARE RUMORS OF A WILD DOG HERE, TOO...
PAFF
PAFF
SORRY THAT WE HAVE TO RUIN YOUR PLAY-GROUND.
THAT'S NOT IT!

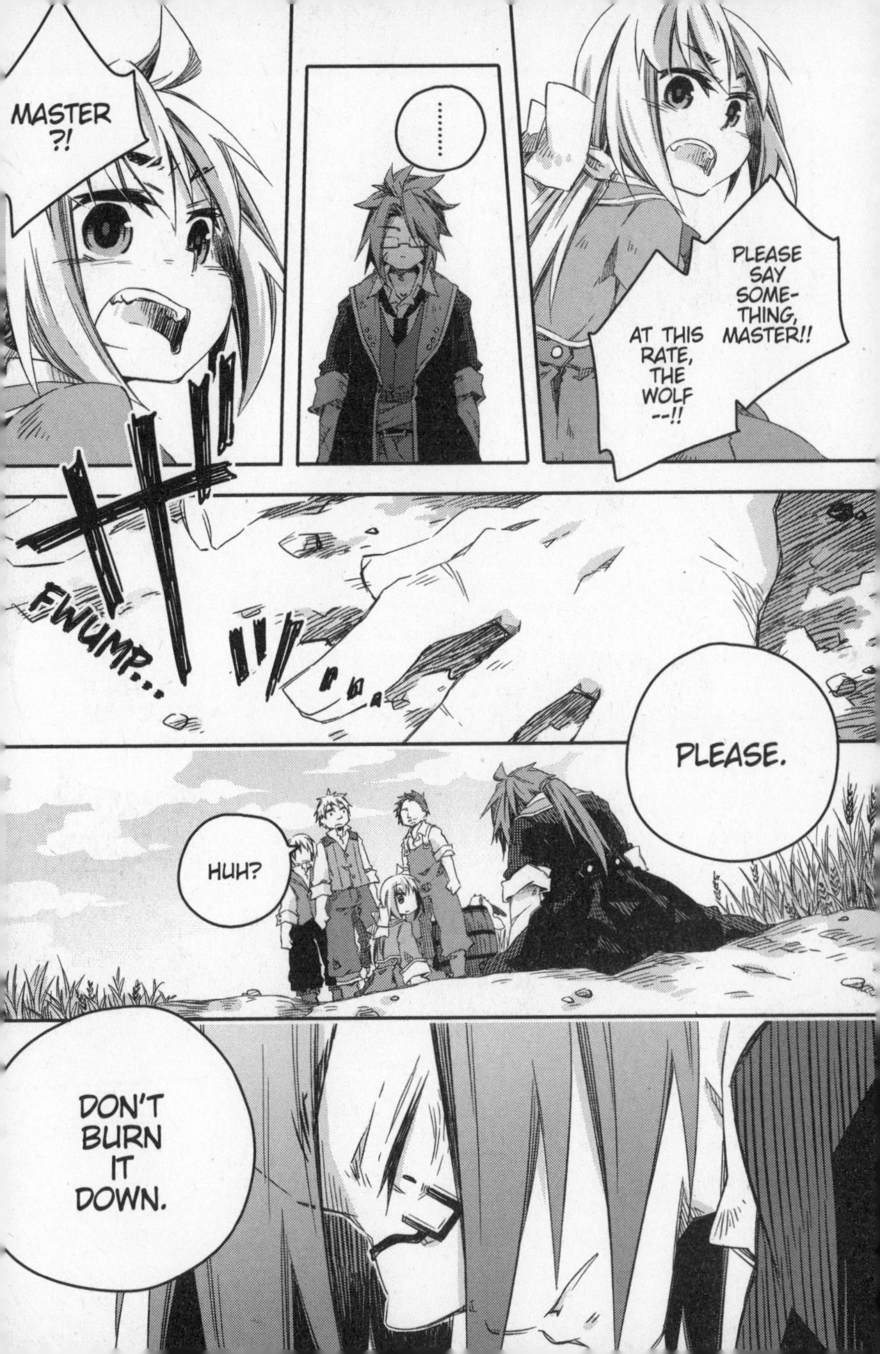
PLEASE SAY SOME-THING, MASTER!!
AT THIS RATE, THE WOLF --!!
......
MASTER ?!
FWUMP...
PLEASE.
HUH?
DON'T BURN IT DOWN.

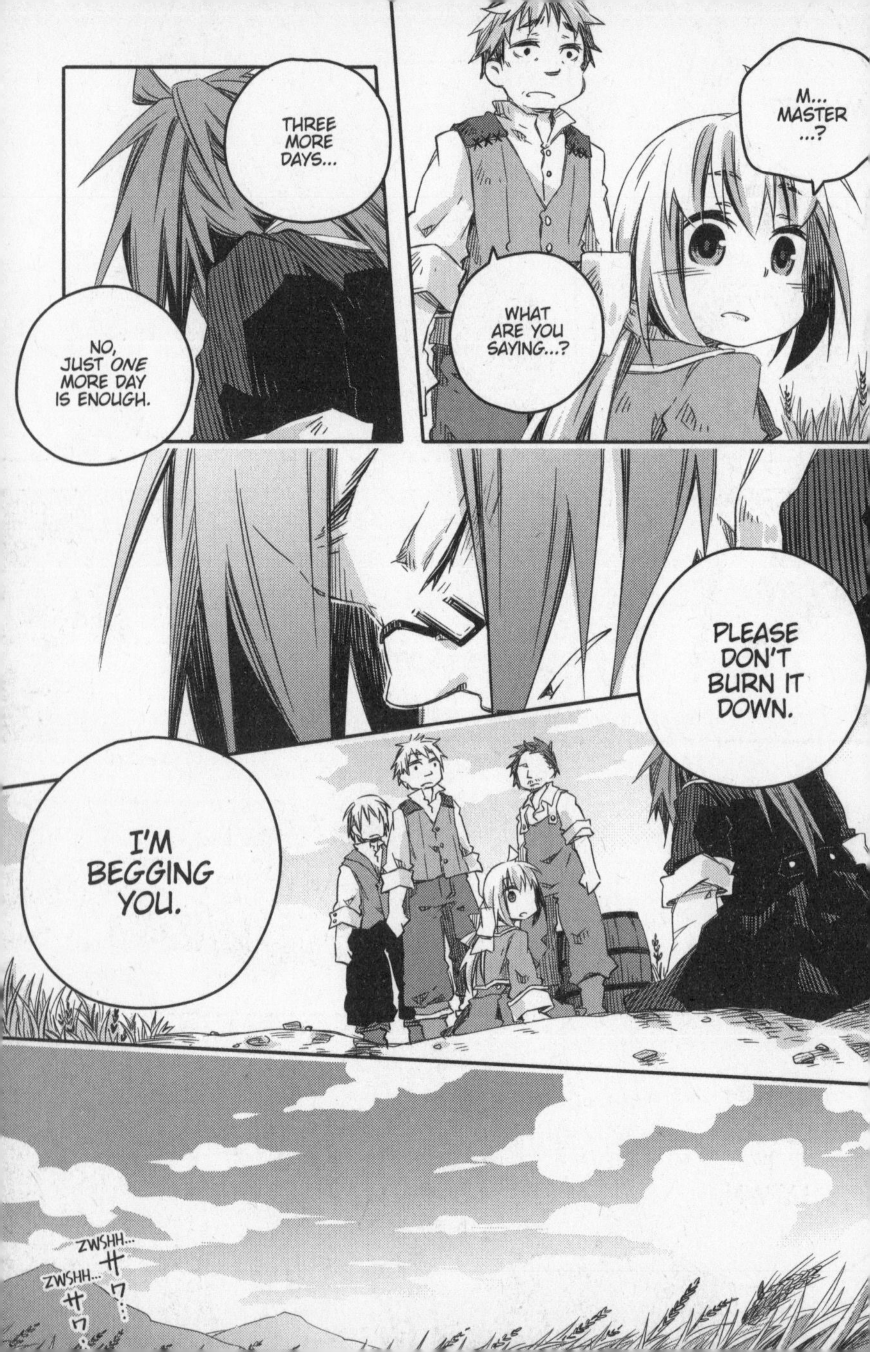

M... MASTER ...?
WHAT ARE YOU SAYING...?
THREE MORE DAYS...
NO, JUST ONE MORE DAY IS ENOUGH.
PLEASE DON'T BURN IT DOWN.
I'M BEGGING YOU.
ZWSHH...
サワ...
ZWSHH...
サワ...

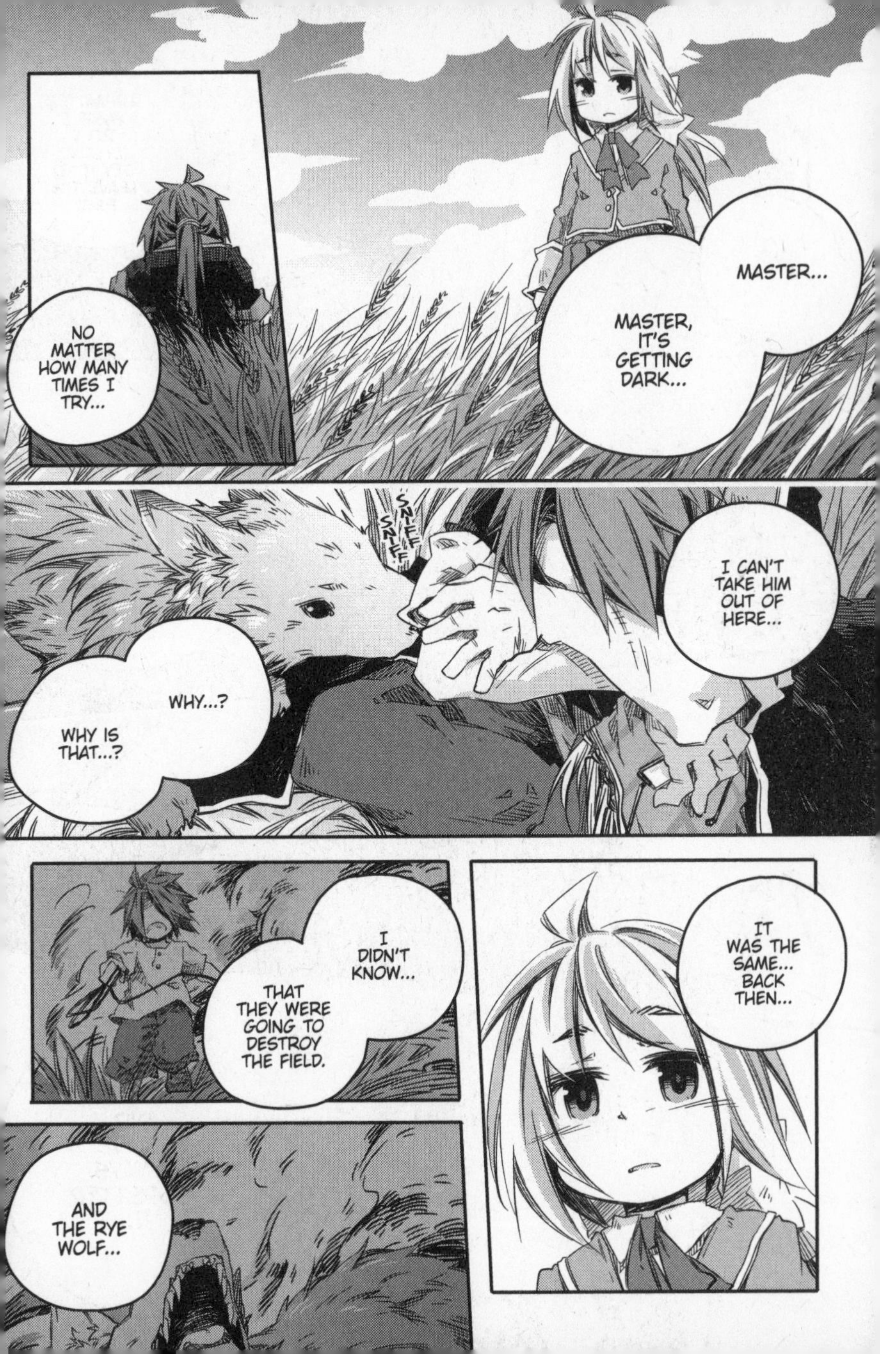
MASTER...
MASTER, IT'S GETTING DARK...
NO MATTER HOW MANY TIMES I TRY...
SNIFF SNIFF
I CAN'T TAKE HIM OUT OF HERE...
WHY...?
WHY IS THAT...?
IT WAS THE SAME... BACK THEN...
I DIDN'T KNOW...
THAT THEY WERE GOING TO DESTROY THE FIELD.
AND THE RYE WOLF...

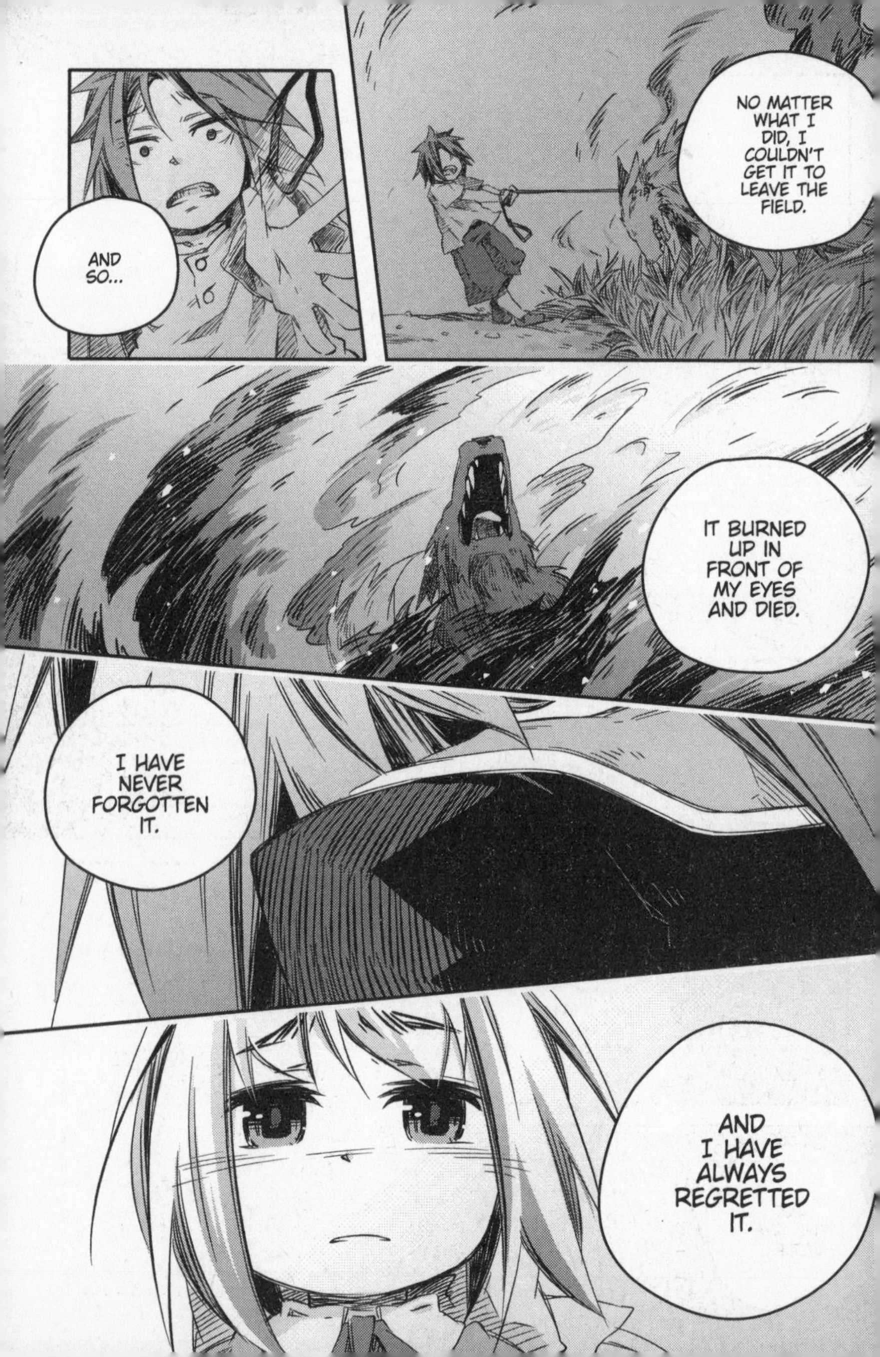
NO MATTER WHAT I DID, I COULDN'T GET IT TO LEAVE THE FIELD.
AND SO...
IT BURNED UP IN FRONT OF MY EYES AND DIED.
I HAVE NEVER FORGOTTEN IT.
AND I HAVE ALWAYS REGRETTED IT.

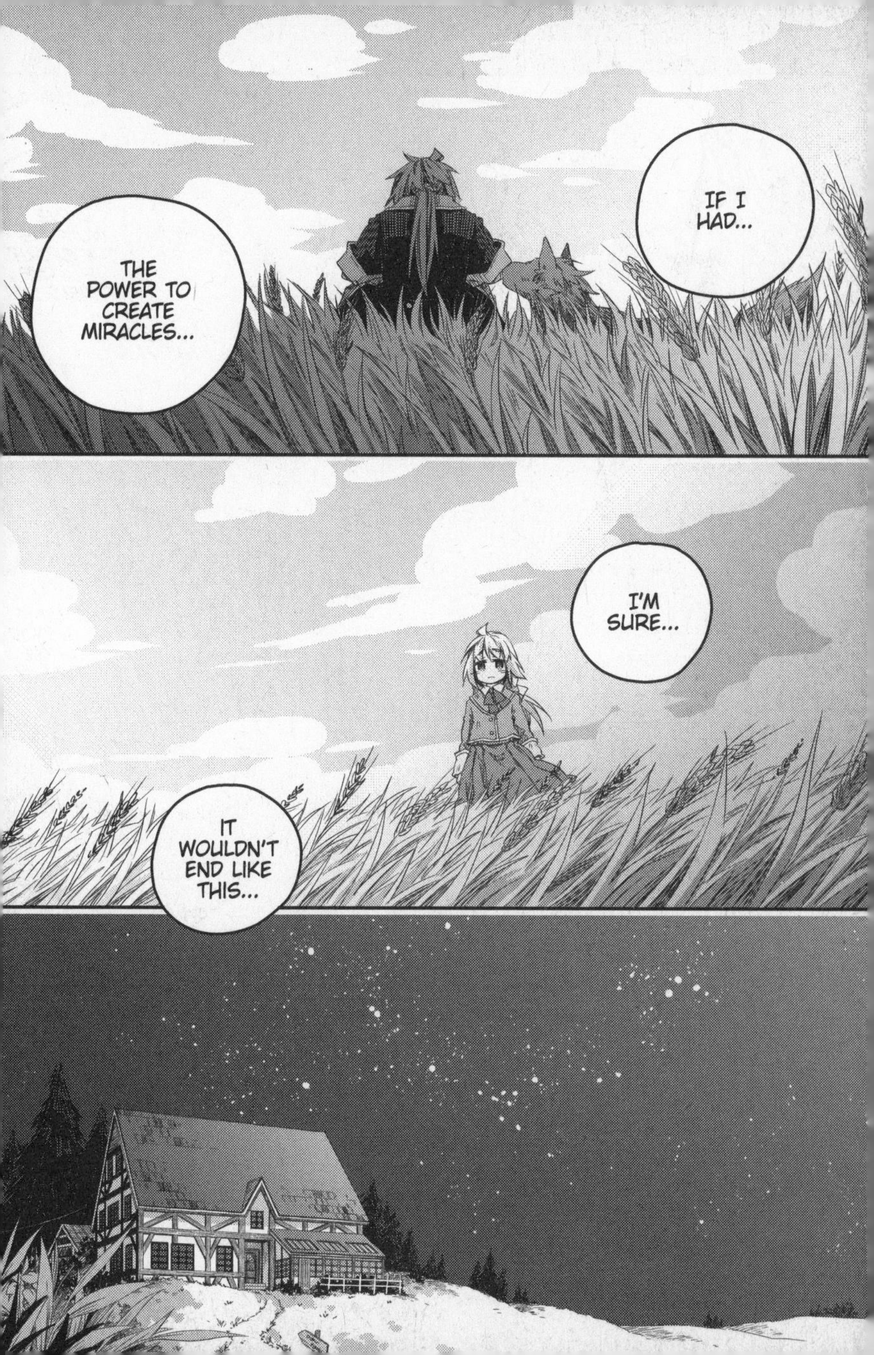
IF I HAD...
THE POWER TO CREATE MIRACLES...
I'M SURE...
IT WOULDN'T END LIKE THIS...

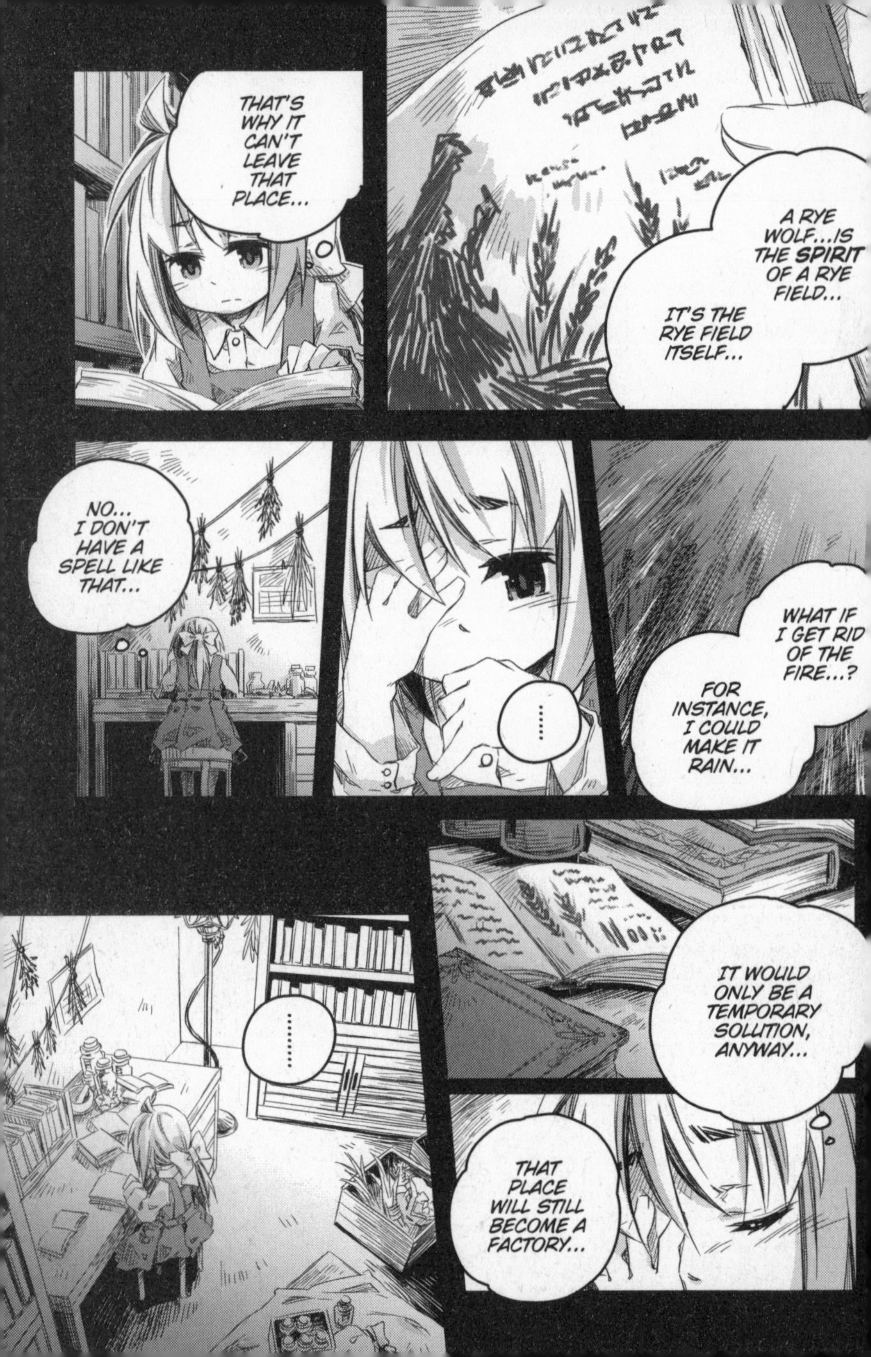
A RYE WOLF...IS THE SPIRIT OF A RYE FIELD...
IT'S THE RYE FIELD ITSELF...
THAT'S WHY IT CAN'T LEAVE THAT PLACE...
WHAT IF I GET RID OF THE FIRE...?
FOR INSTANCE, I COULD MAKE IT RAIN...
......
NO... I DON'T HAVE A SPELL LIKE THAT...
IT WOULD ONLY BE A TEMPORARY SOLUTION, ANYWAY...
THAT PLACE WILL STILL BECOME A FACTORY...
......

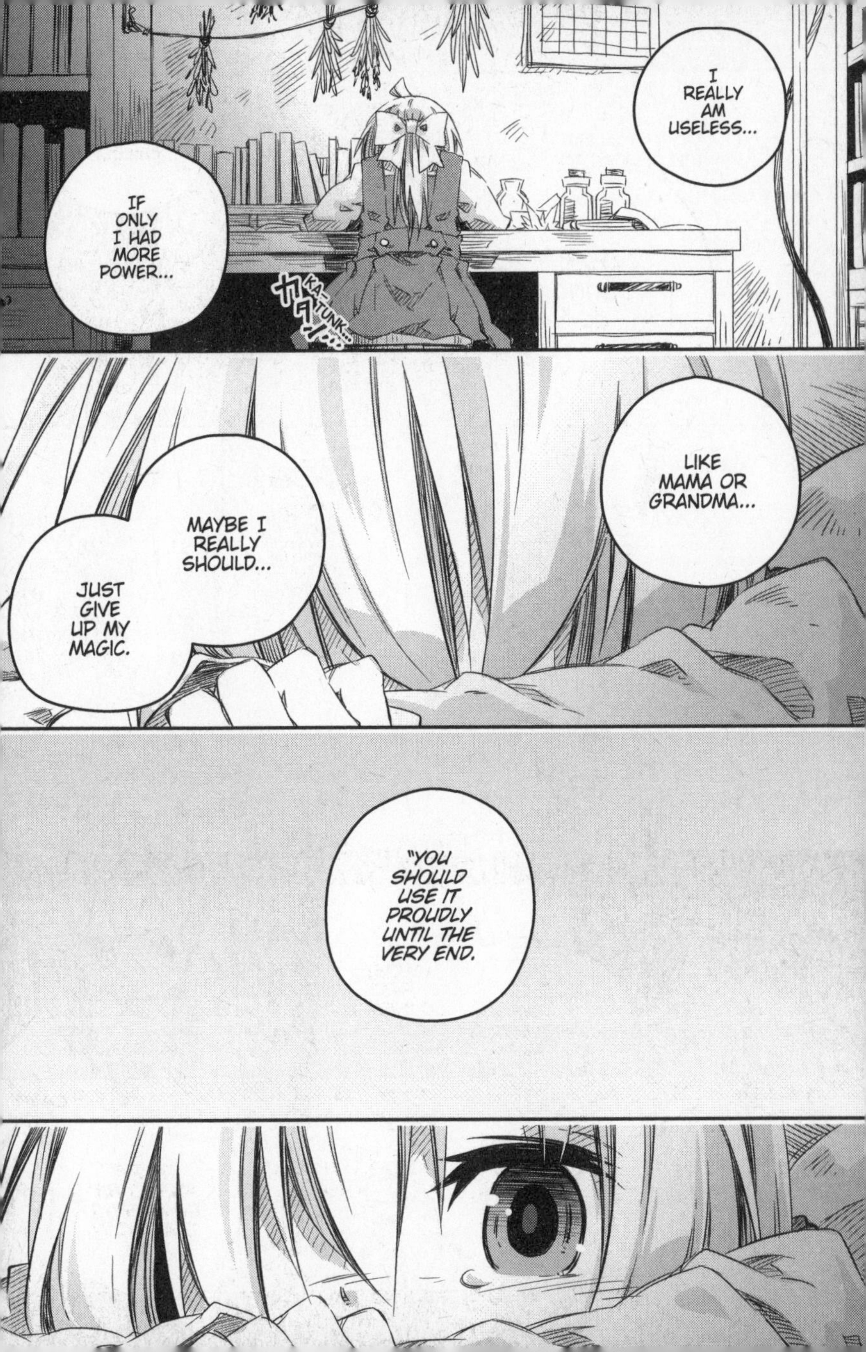

I REALLY AM USELESS...
IF ONLY I HAD MORE POWER...
KA-TUNK...
LIKE MAMA OR GRANDMA...
MAYBE I REALLY SHOULD...
JUST GIVE UP MY MAGIC.
"YOU SHOULD USE IT PROUDLY UNTIL THE VERY END.

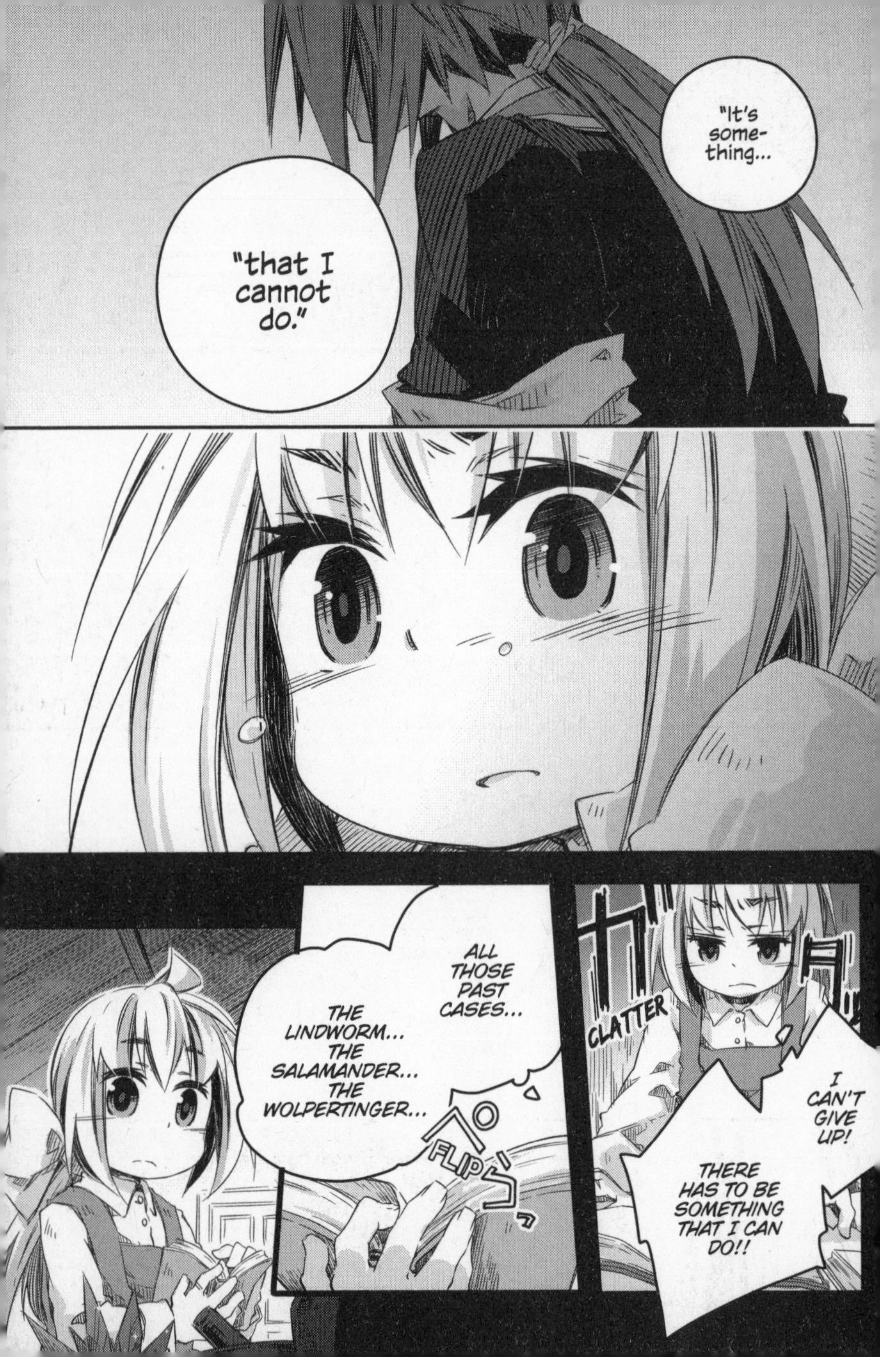
"It's some-thing...
"that I cannot do."
CLATTER
I CAN'T GIVE UP!
THERE HAS TO BE SOMETHING THAT I CAN DO!!
ALL THOSE PAST CASES...
THE LINDWORM... THE SALAMANDER... THE WOLPERTINGER...
FLIP

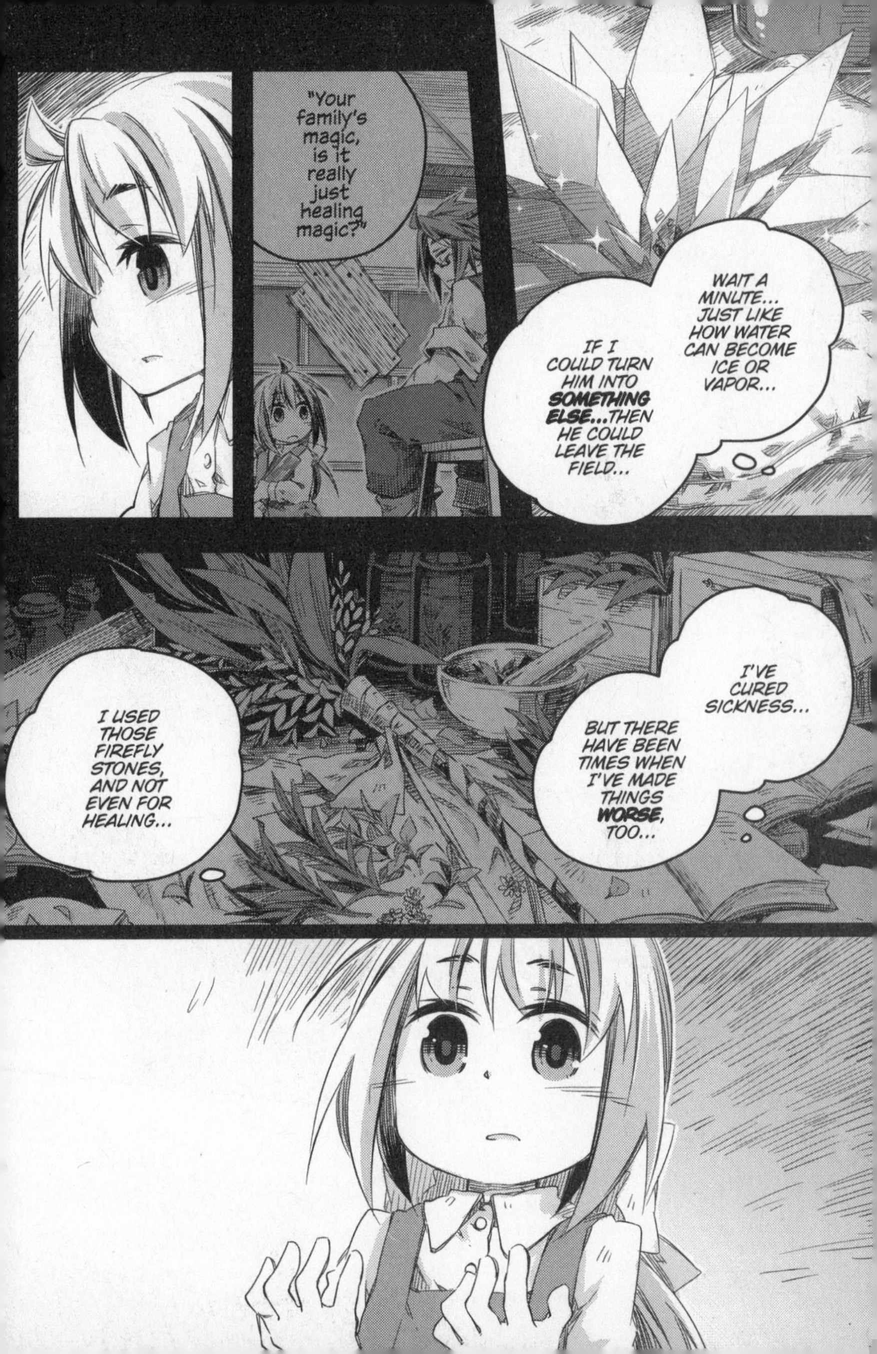
WAIT A MINUTE... JUST LIKE HOW WATER CAN BECOME ICE OR VAPOR...
IF I COULD TURN HIM INTO SOMETHING ELSE...THEN HE COULD LEAVE THE FIELD...
"Your family's magic, is it really just healing magic?"
I'VE CURED SICKNESS...
BUT THERE HAVE BEEN TIMES WHEN I'VE MADE THINGS WORSE, TOO...
I USED THOSE FIREFLY STONES, AND NOT EVEN FOR HEALING...

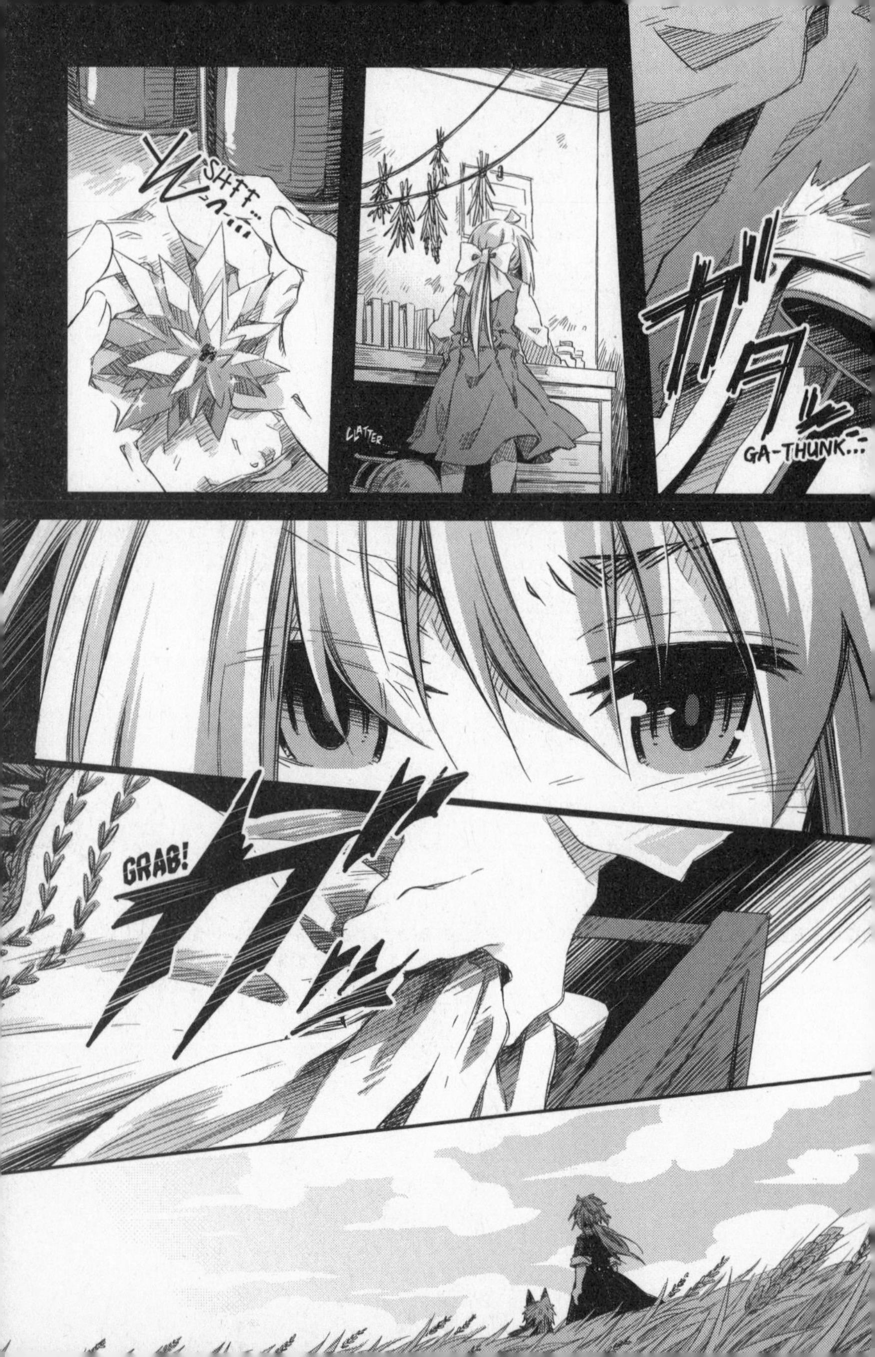
ガタッ
GA-THUNK...
CLATTER...
SHFF...
GRAB!

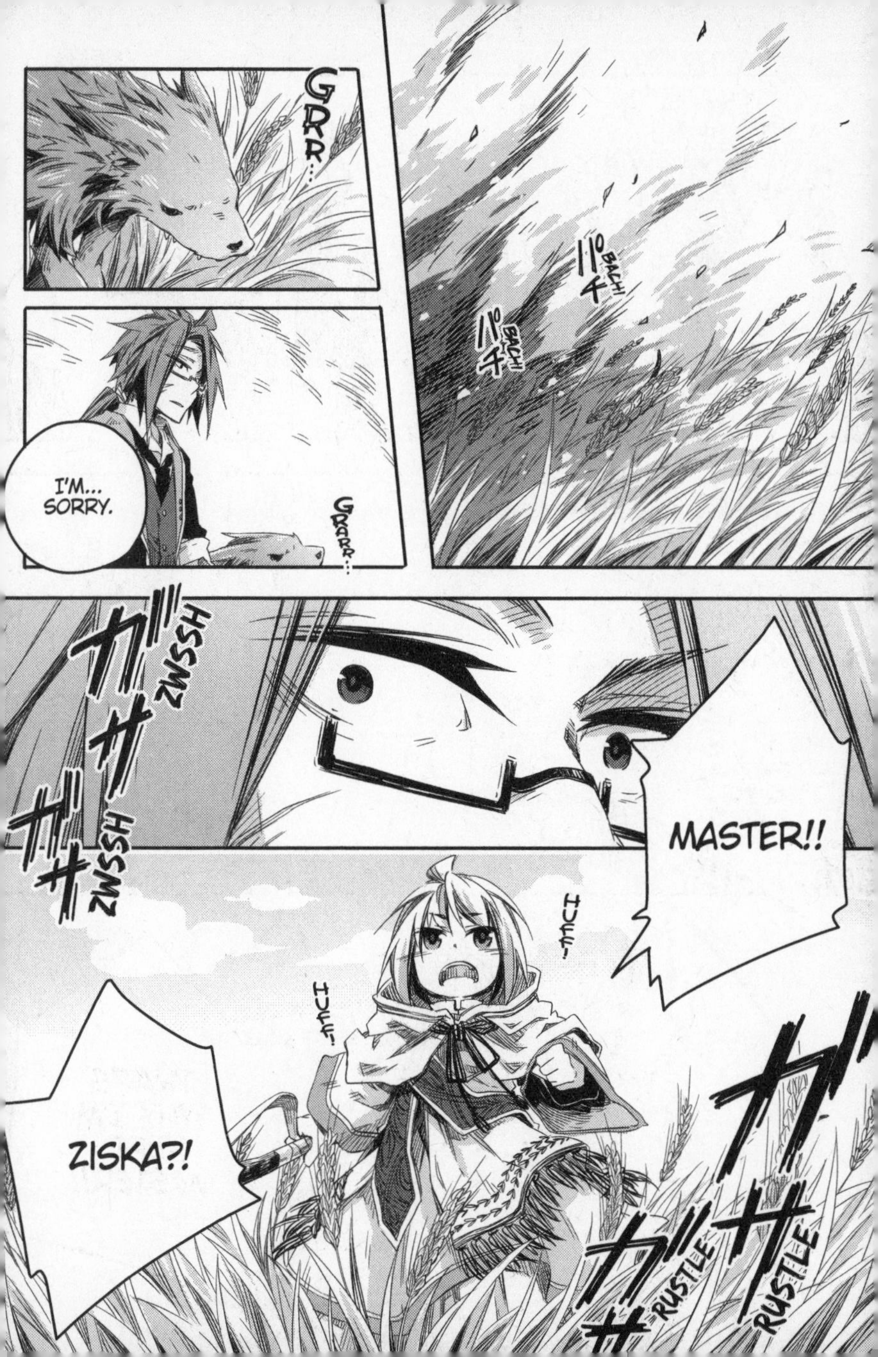
パチ BACHI
パチ BACHI
GRR...
I'M... SORRY.
GRARR...
ガサ ZWSSH
ガサ ZWSSH
MASTER!!
HUFF!
HUFF!
ガサ RUSTLE
ガサ RUSTLE
ZISKA?!

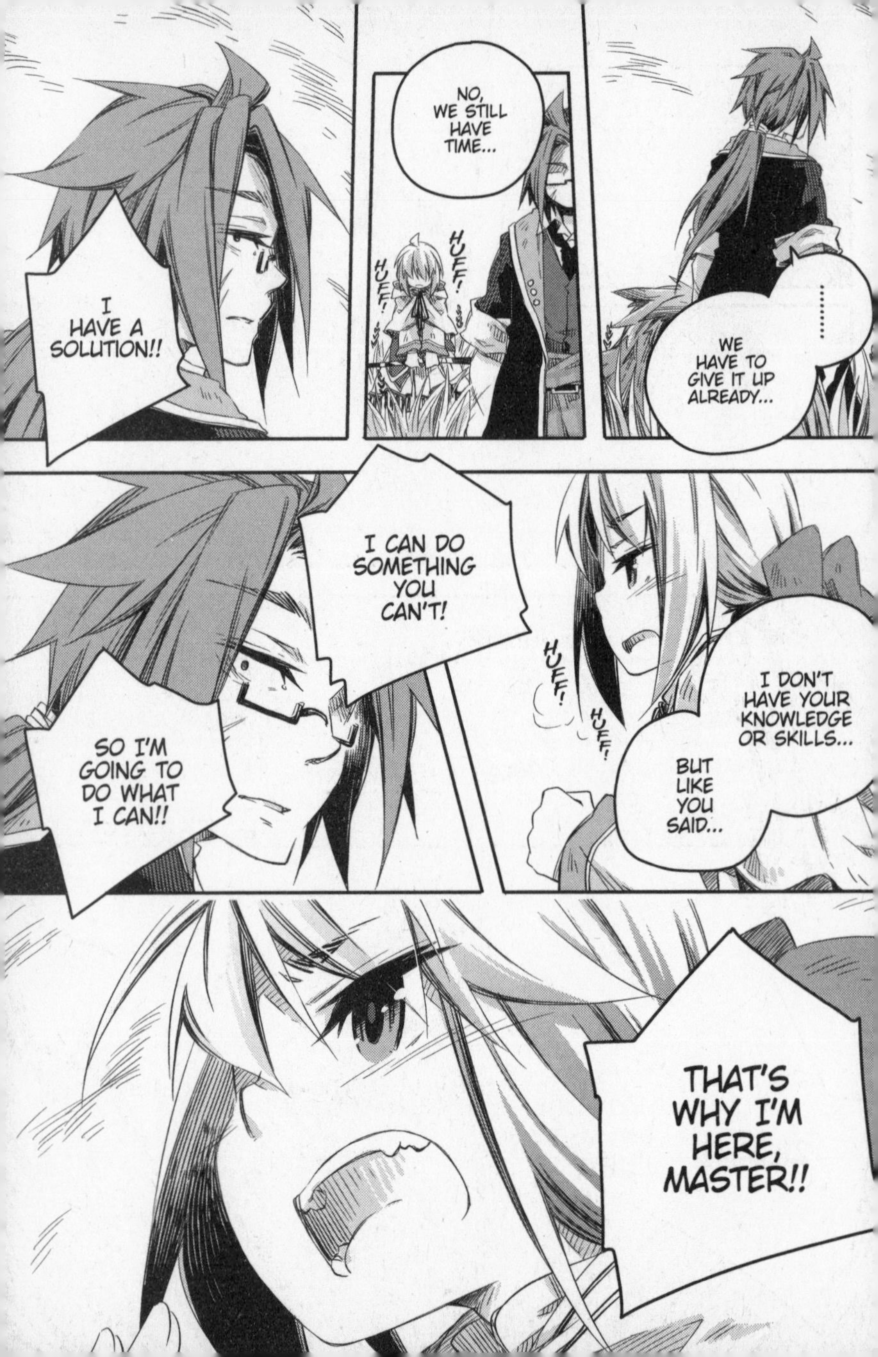
......
WE HAVE TO GIVE IT UP ALREADY...
NO, WE STILL HAVE TIME...
HUFF! HUFF!
I HAVE A SOLUTION!!
HUFF! HUFF!
I DON'T HAVE YOUR KNOWLEDGE OR SKILLS...
BUT LIKE YOU SAID...
I CAN DO SOMETHING YOU CAN'T!
SO I'M GOING TO DO WHAT I CAN!!
THAT'S WHY I'M HERE, MASTER!!

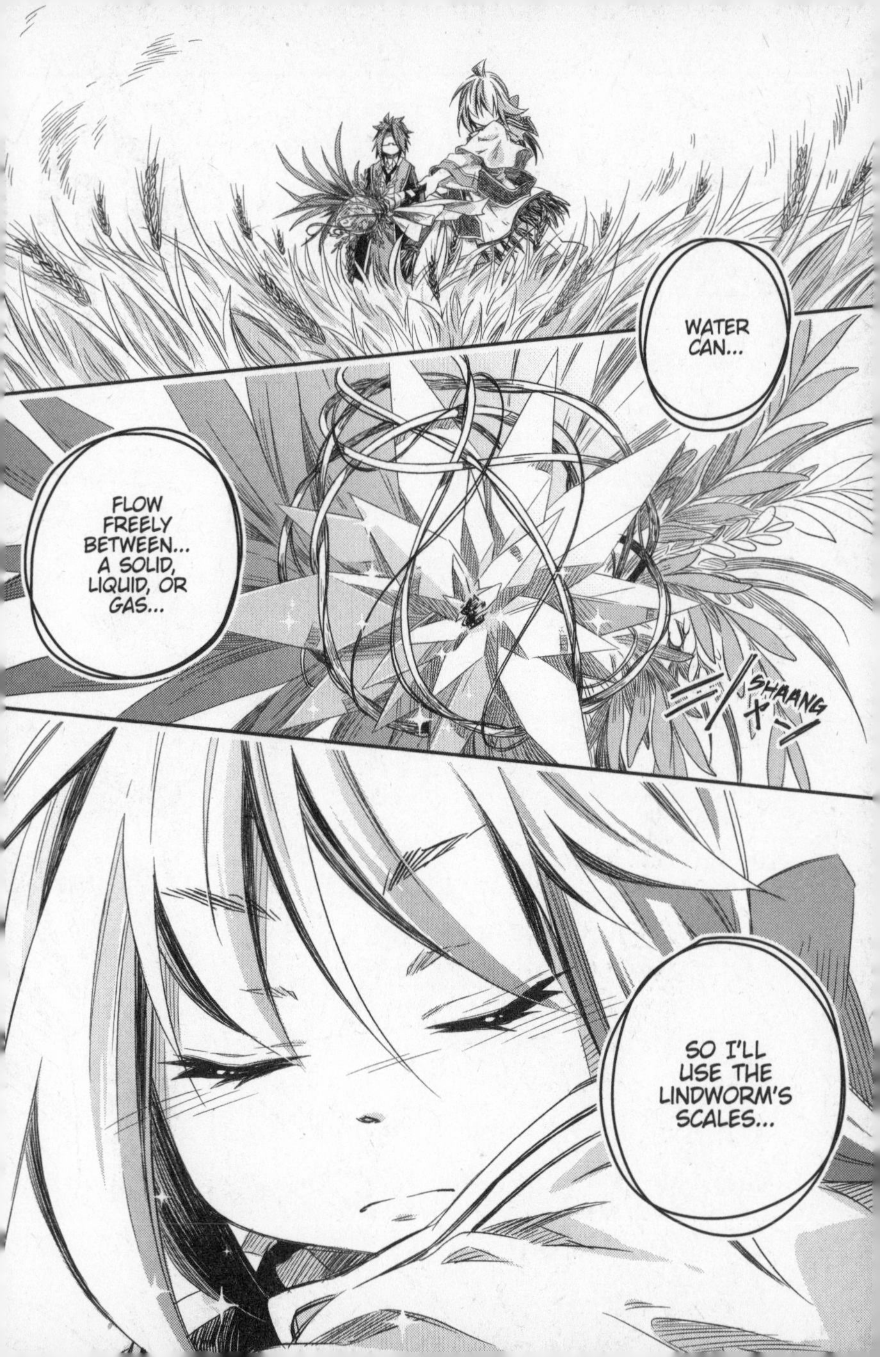
WATER CAN...
FLOW FREELY BETWEEN... A SOLID, LIQUID, OR GAS...
SHAANG
SO I'LL USE THE LINDWORM'S SCALES...

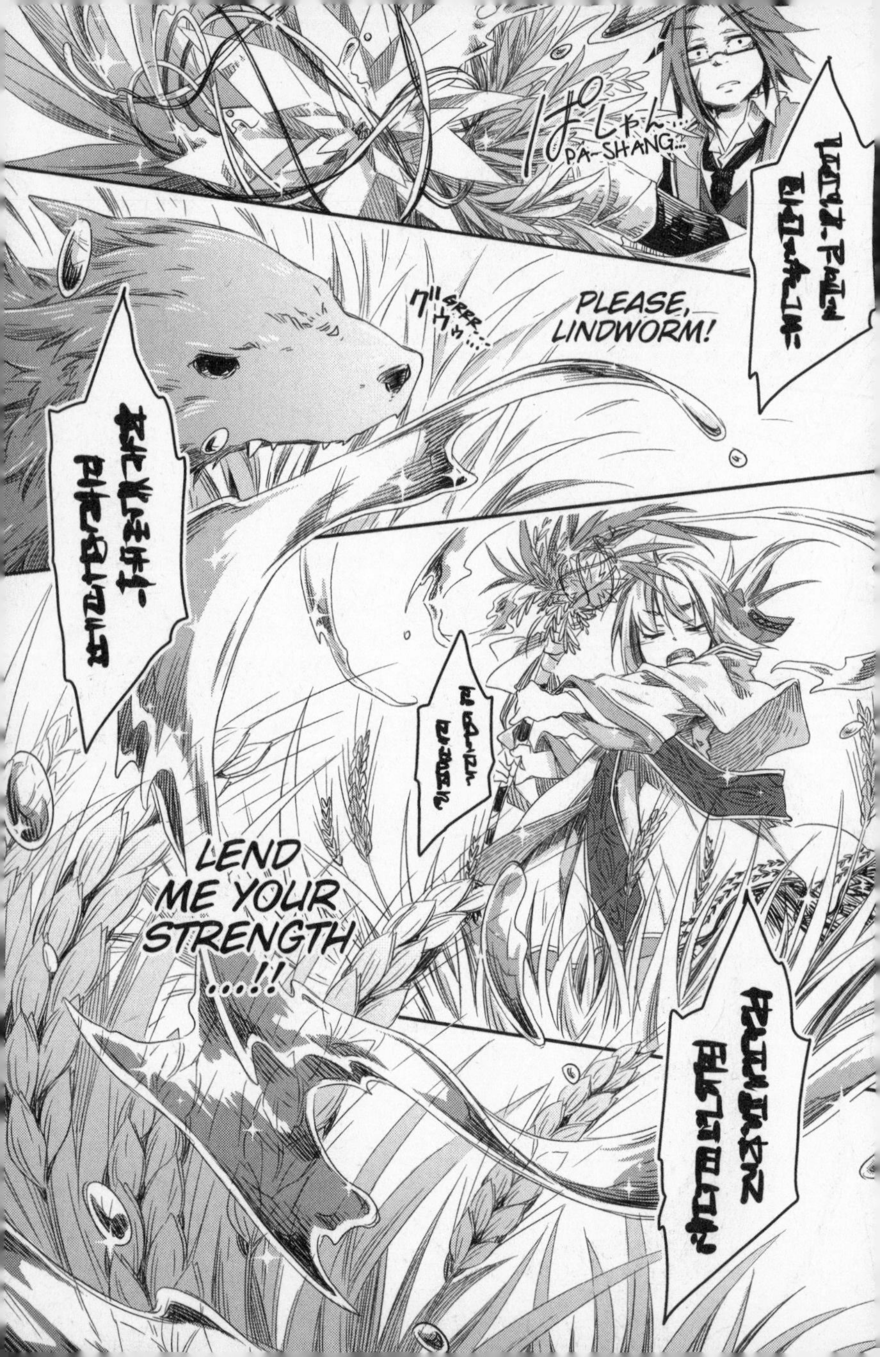
ぱしゃん...
PA-SHANG...
PLEASE, LINDWORM!
グゥゥ...
GRRR...
LEND ME YOUR STRENGTH ...!!

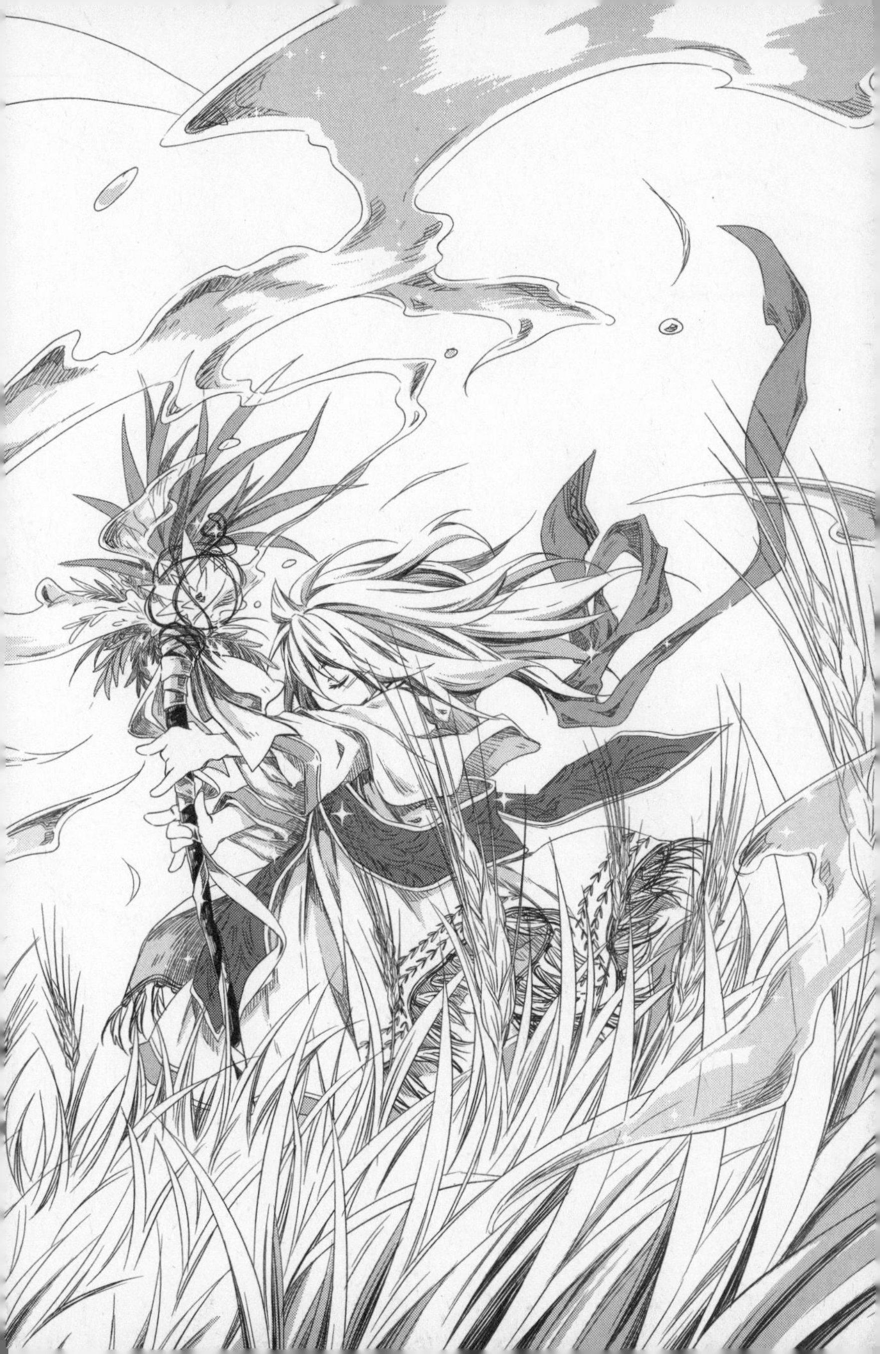

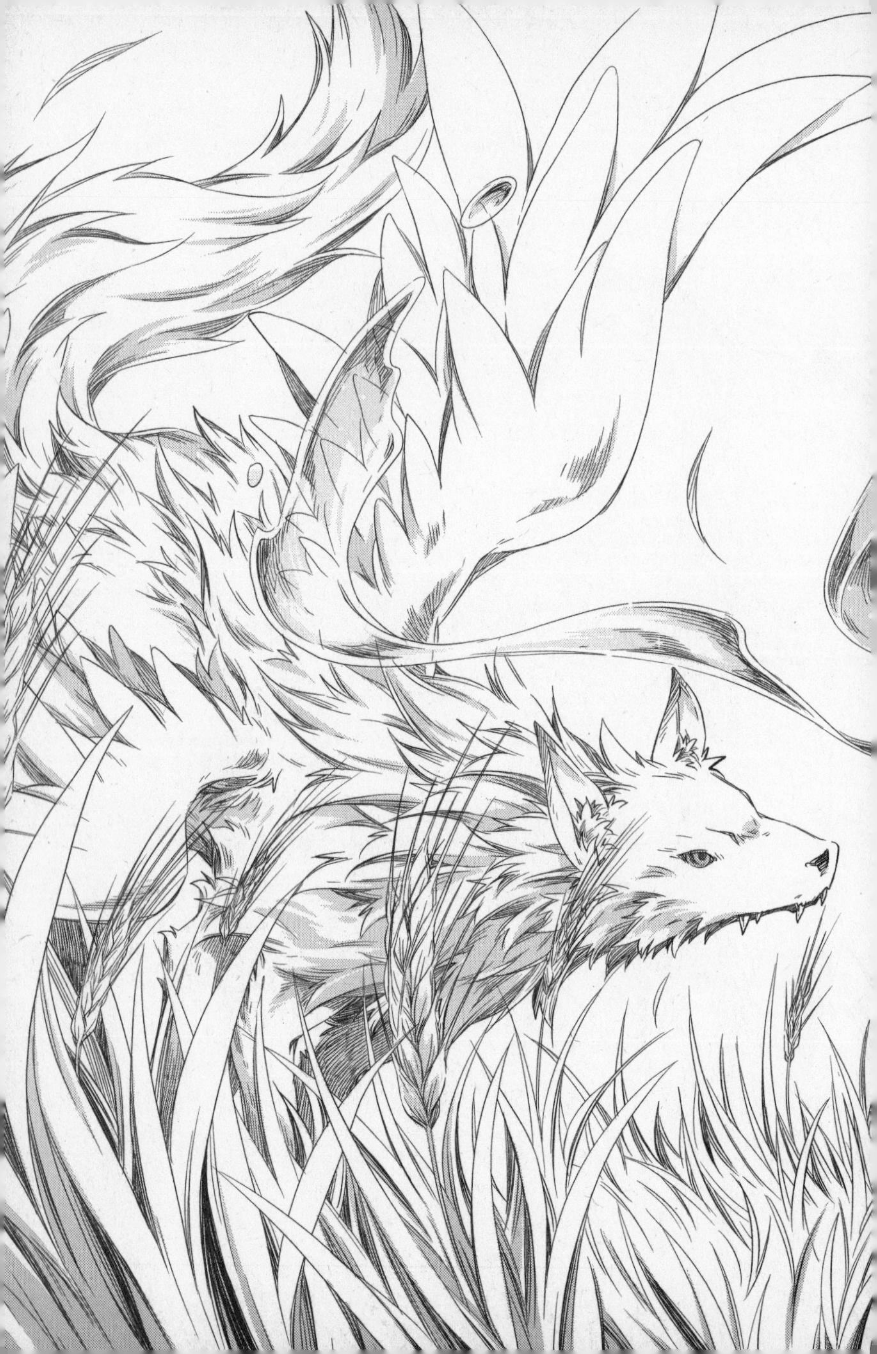

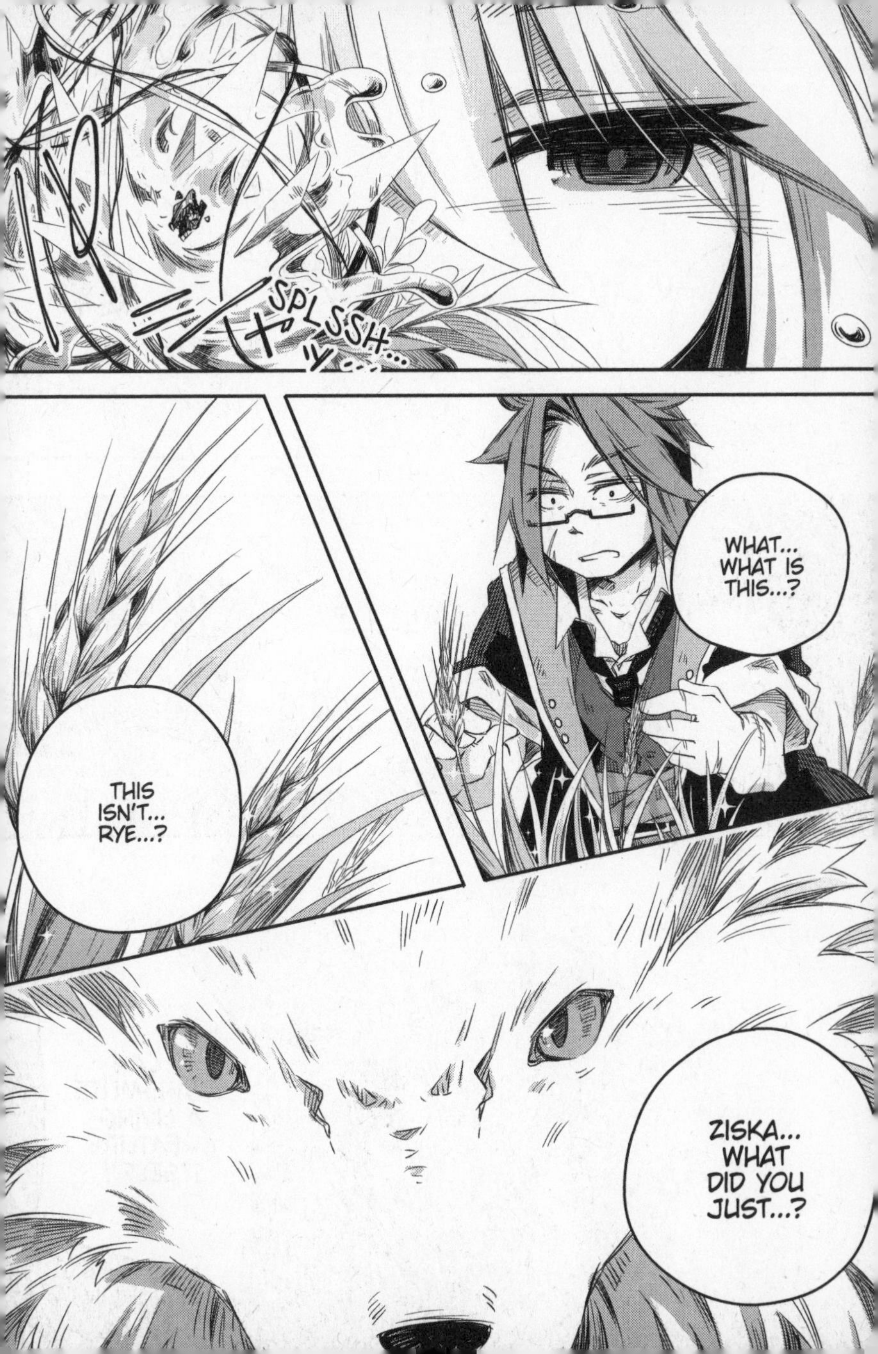
SPLSSH...
WHAT... WHAT IS THIS...?
THIS ISN'T... RYE...?
ZISKA... WHAT DID YOU JUST...?

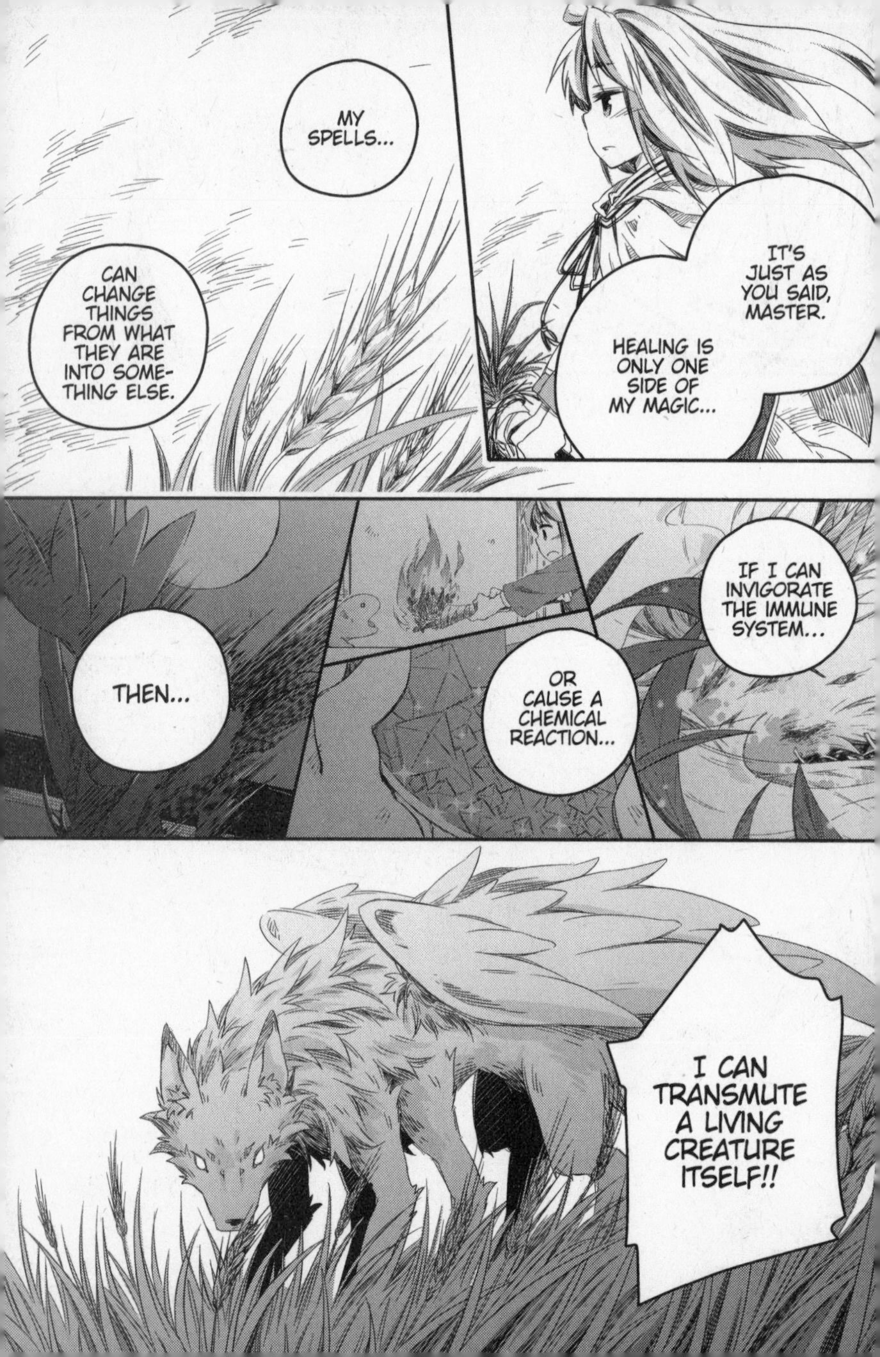
IT'S JUST AS YOU SAID, MASTER.
HEALING IS ONLY ONE SIDE OF MY MAGIC...
MY SPELLS...
CAN CHANGE THINGS FROM WHAT THEY ARE INTO SOME-THING ELSE.
IF I CAN INVIGORATE THE IMMUNE SYSTEM...
OR CAUSE A CHEMICAL REACTION...
THEN...
I CAN TRANSMUTE A LIVING CREATURE ITSELF!!

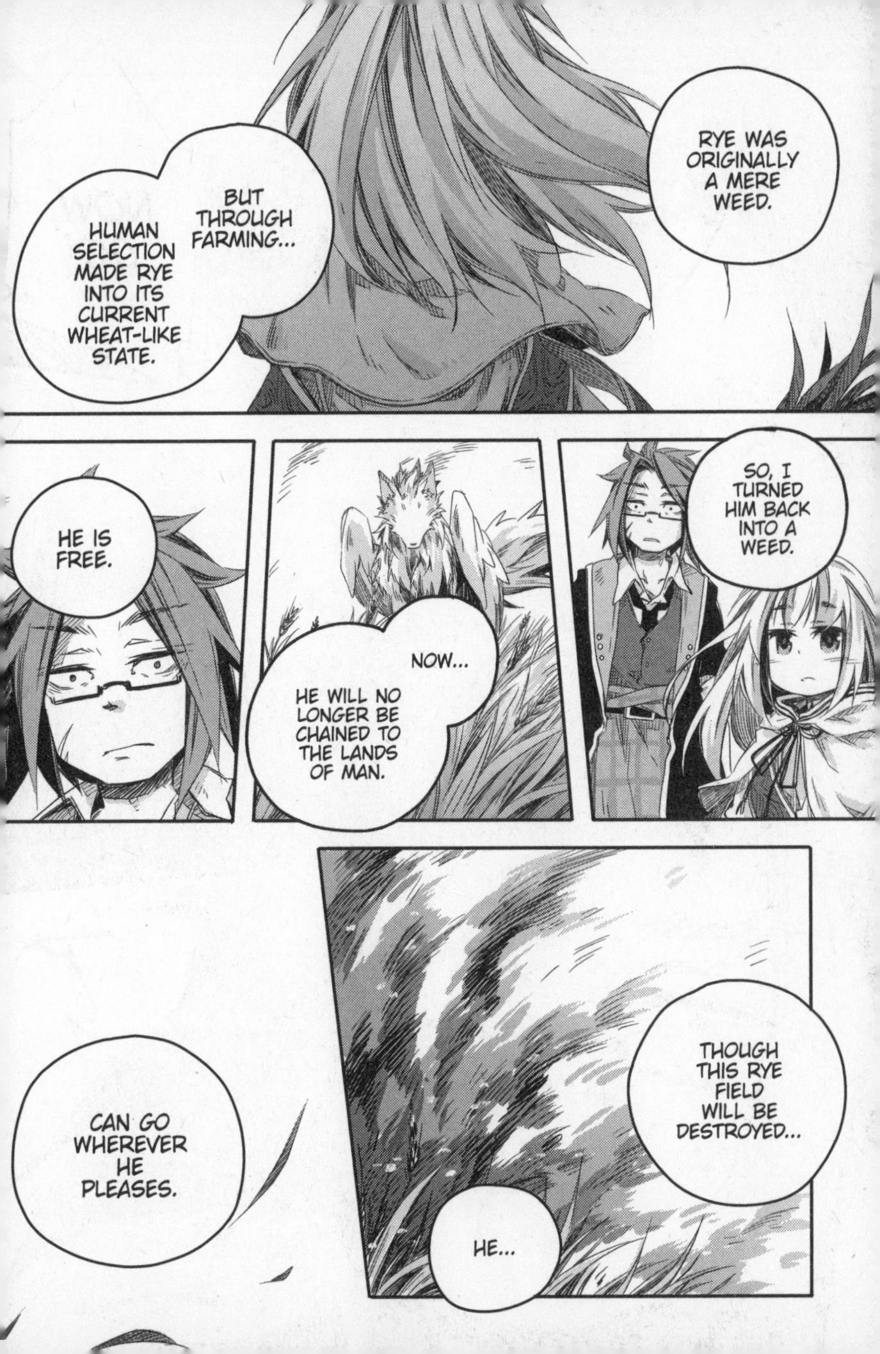
RYE WAS ORIGINALLY A MERE WEED.
BUT THROUGH FARMING...
HUMAN SELECTION MADE RYE INTO ITS CURRENT WHEAT-LIKE STATE.
SO, I TURNED HIM BACK INTO A WEED.
NOW...
HE WILL NO LONGER BE CHAINED TO THE LANDS OF MAN.
HE IS FREE.
THOUGH THIS RYE FIELD WILL BE DESTROYED...
HE...
CAN GO WHEREVER HE PLEASES.

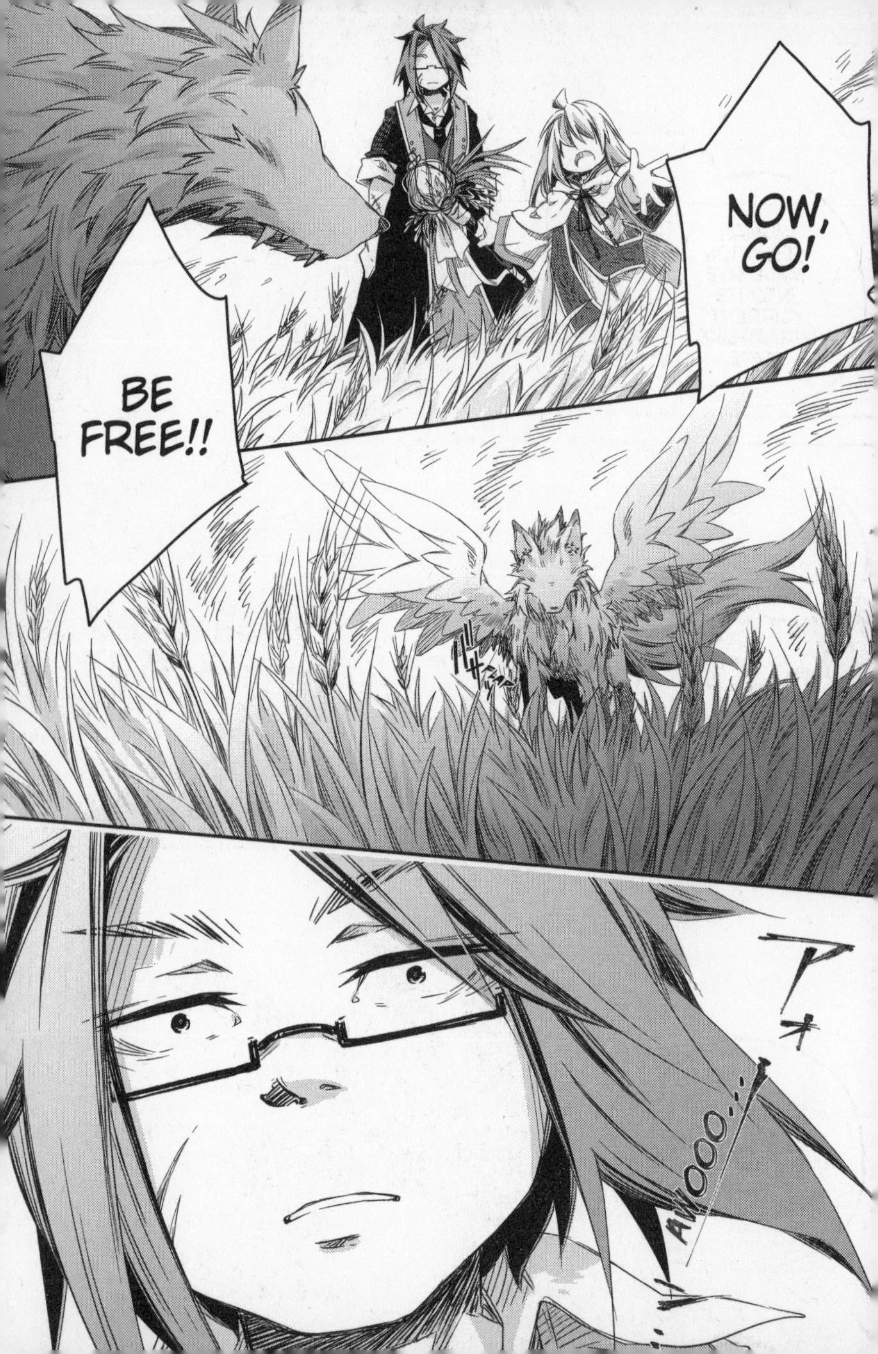
NOW, GO!
BE FREE!!
FLAP
AWOOO...!

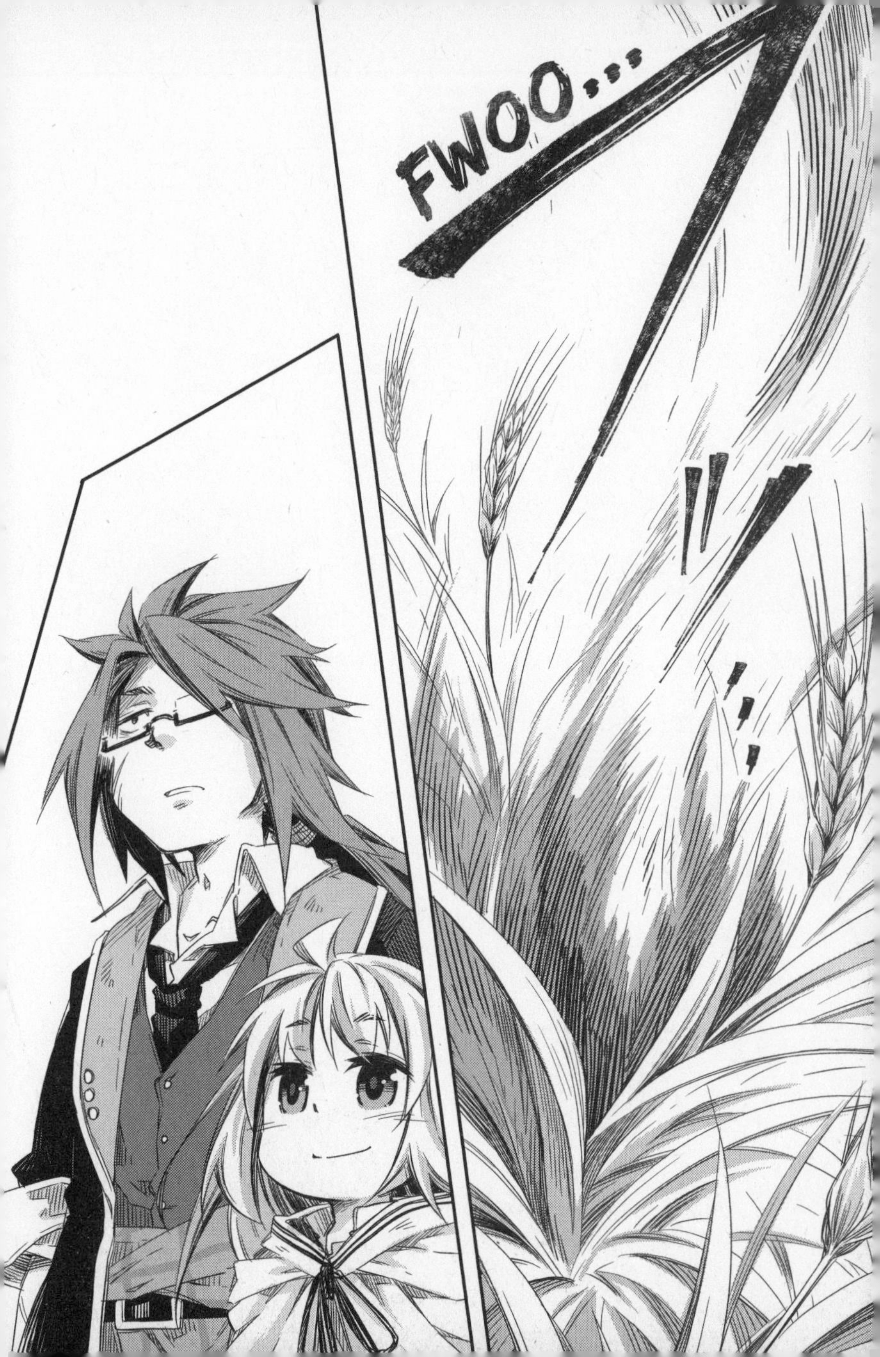
FWOO...

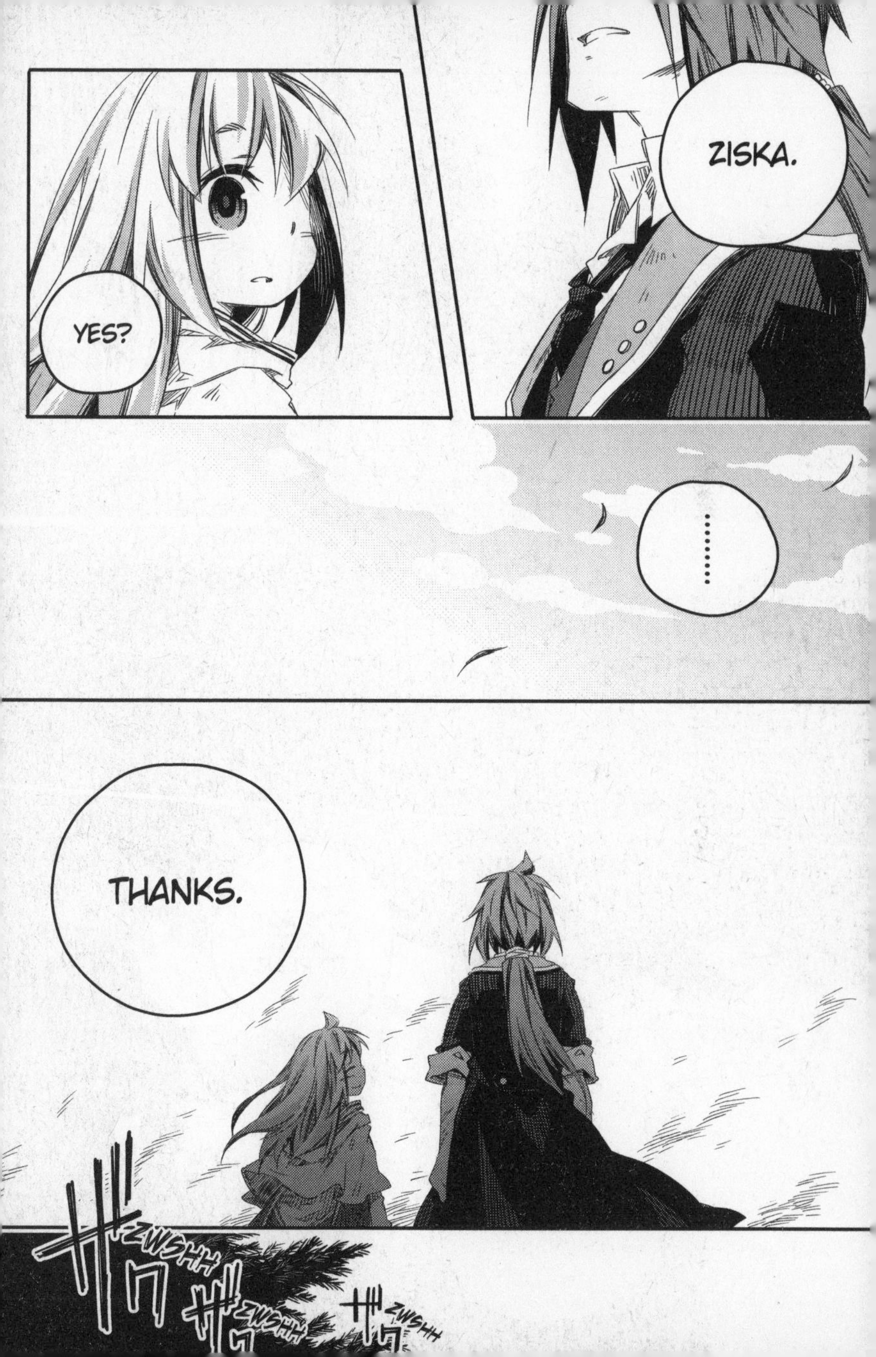
ZISKA.
YES?
......
THANKS.
ZWSHH
ZWSHH
ZWSHH

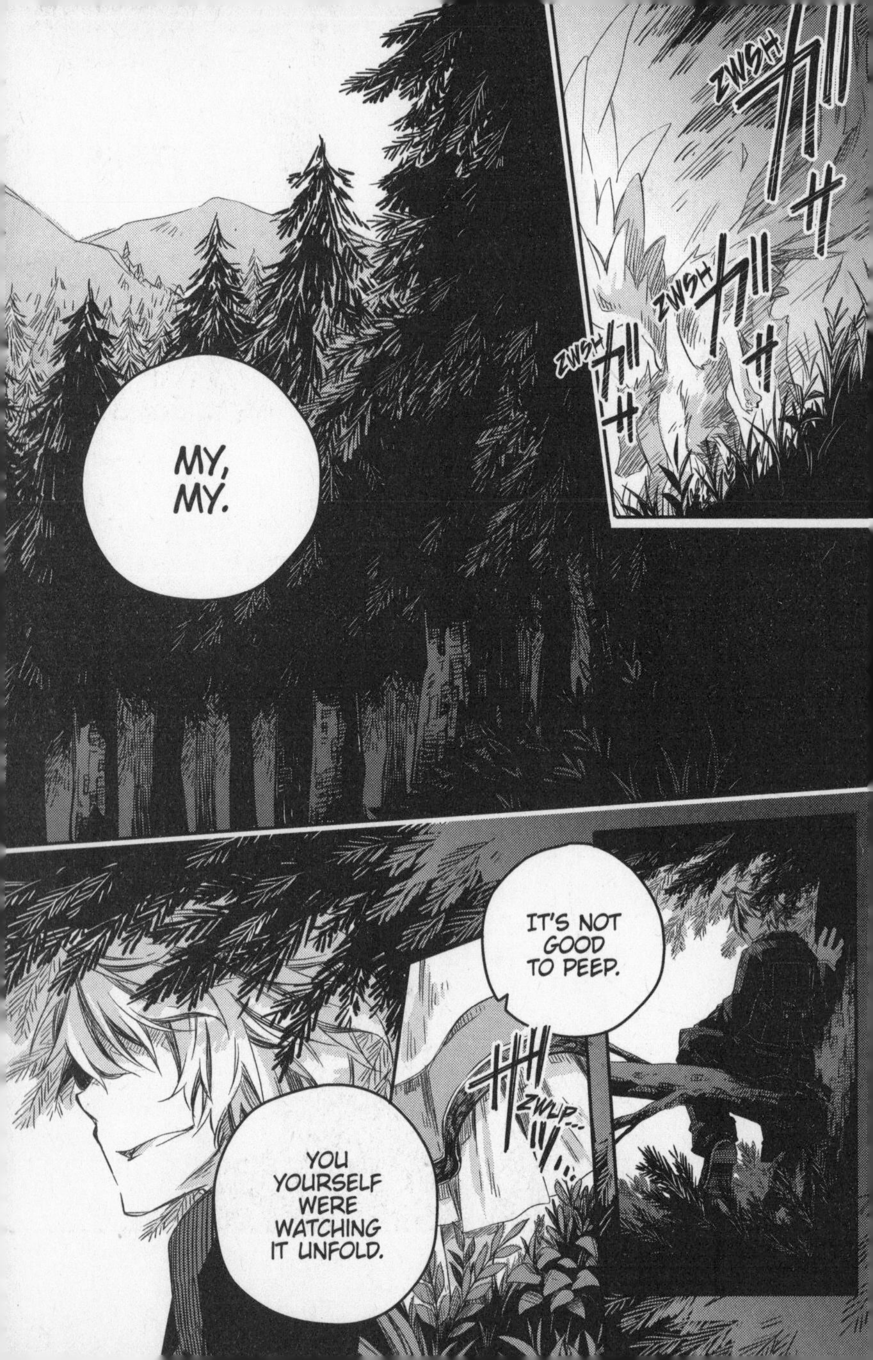
ZWSH
ZWSH
ZWSH
MY, MY.
IT'S NOT GOOD TO PEEP.
ZWLP...
YOU YOURSELF WERE WATCHING IT UNFOLD.

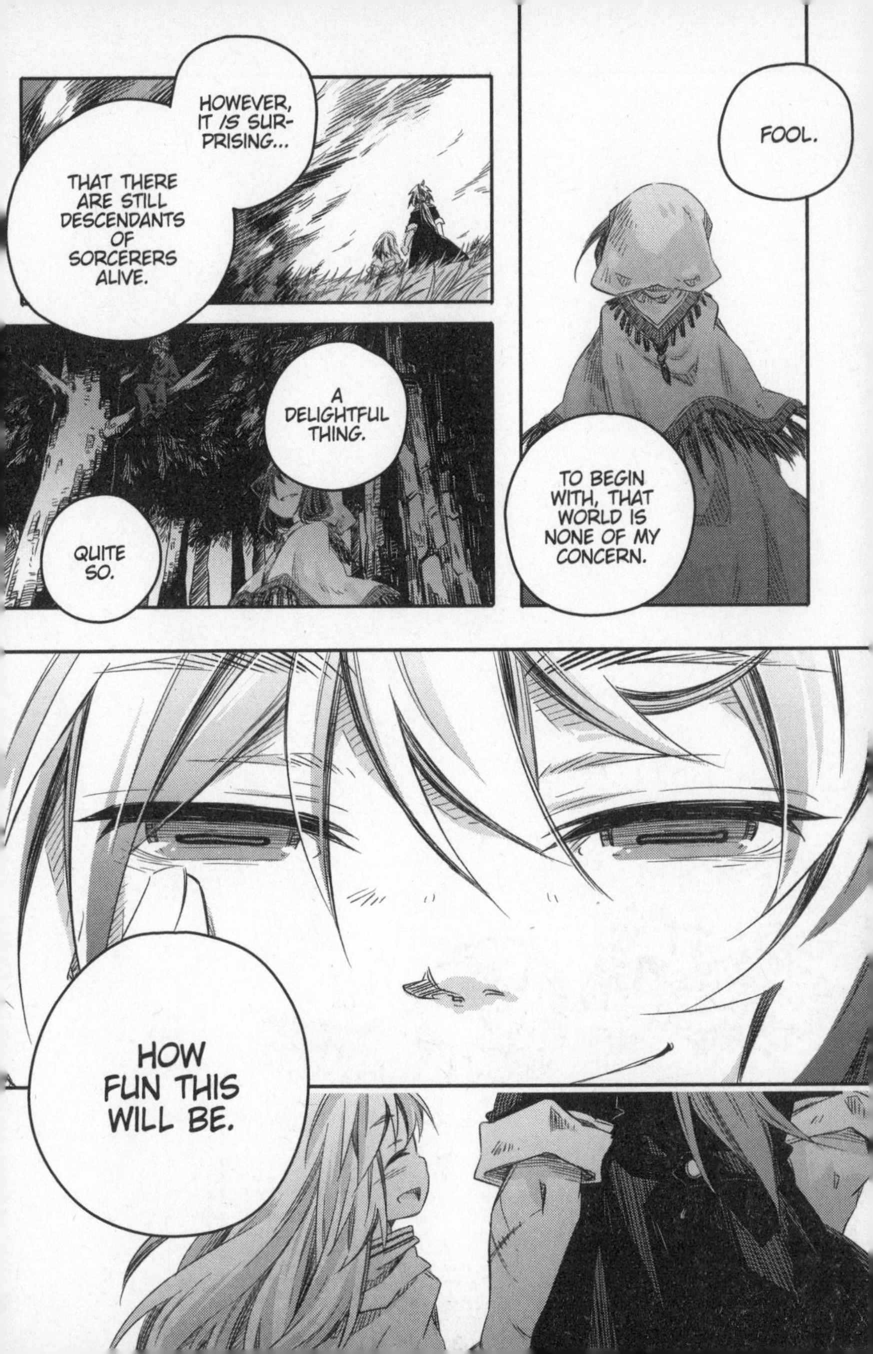
FOOL.
TO BEGIN WITH, THAT WORLD IS NONE OF MY CONCERN.
HOWEVER, IT IS SURPRISING...
THAT THERE ARE STILL DESCENDANTS OF SORCERERS ALIVE.
A DELIGHTFUL THING.
QUITE SO.
HOW FUN THIS WILL BE.

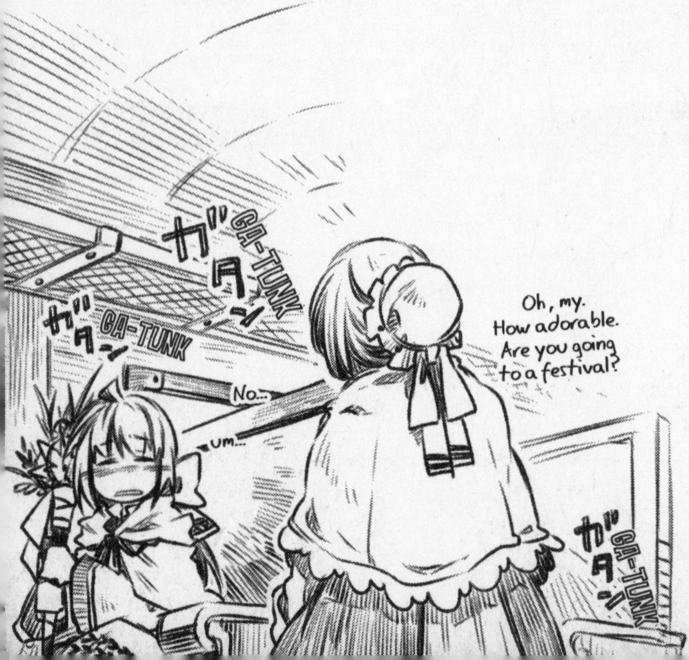

GA-TUNK
Oh, my. How adorable. Are you going to a festival?
GA-TUNK
No...
um...
GA-TUNK

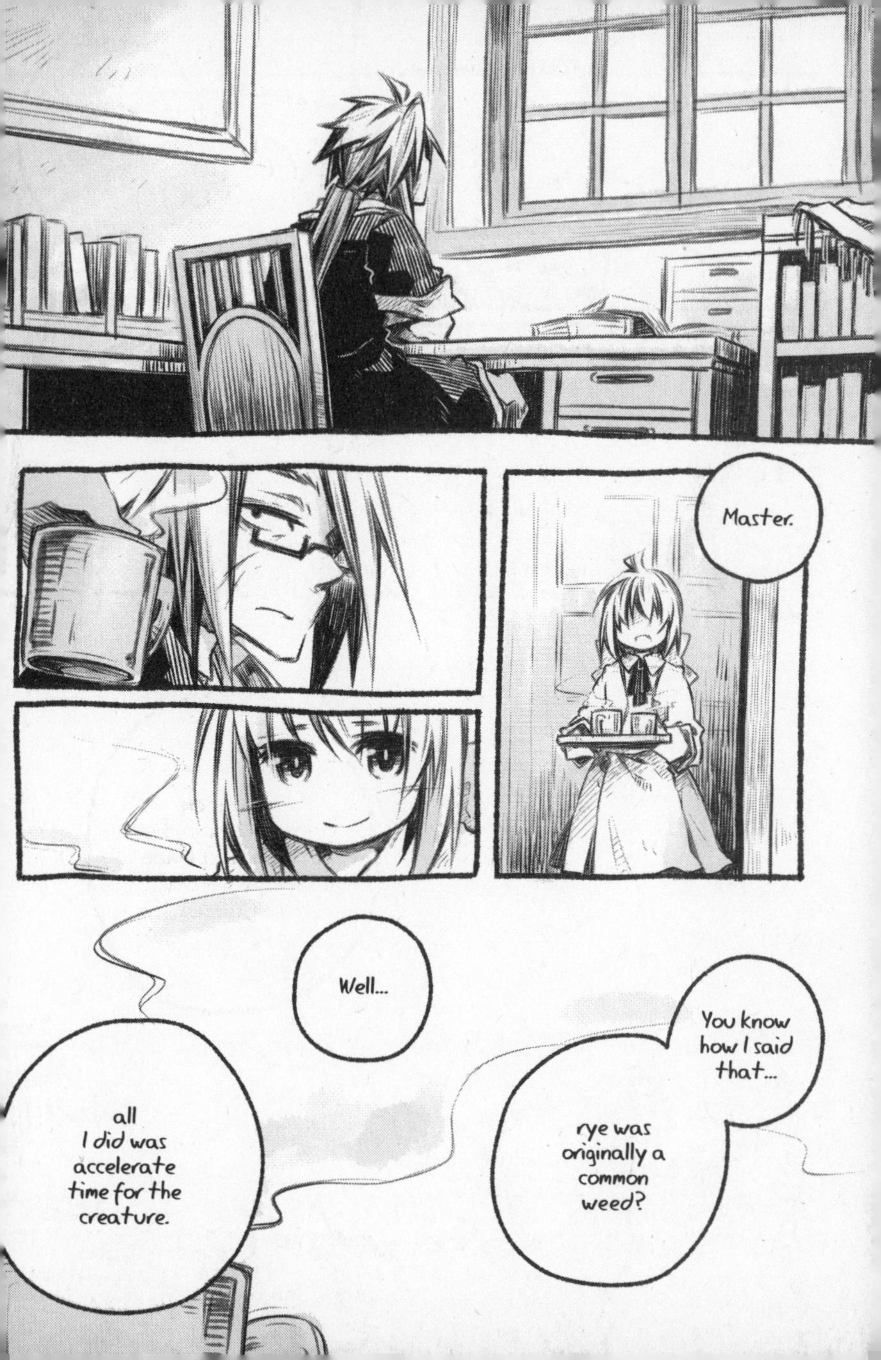
Master.
Well...
You know how I said that...
rye was originally a common weed?
all I did was accelerate time for the creature.

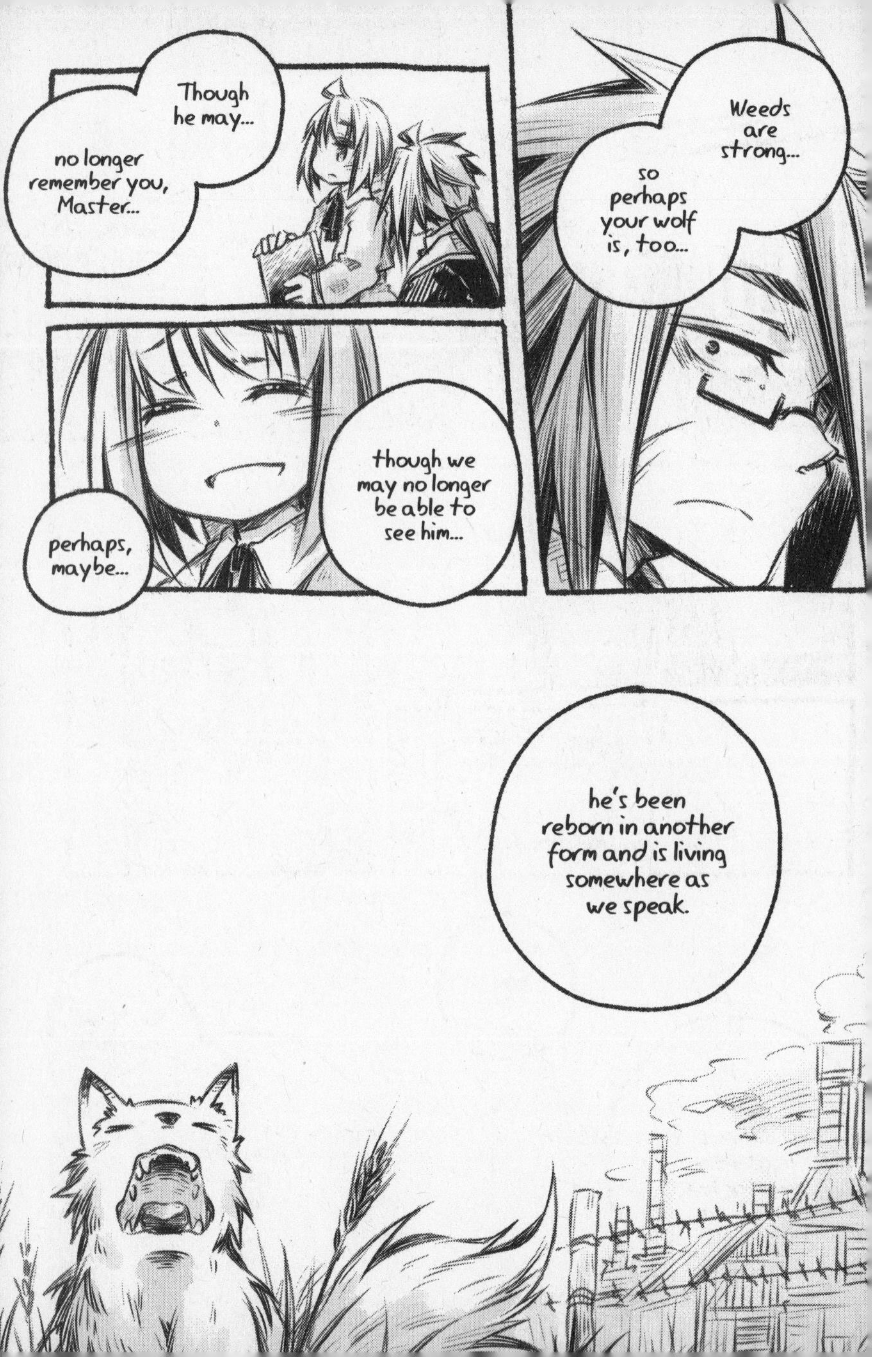
Weeds are strong...
so perhaps your wolf is, too...
Though he may...
no longer remember you, Master...
though we may no longer be able to see him...
perhaps, maybe...
he's been reborn in another form and is living somewhere as we speak.

SEVEN SEAS ENTERTAINMENT PRESENTS

How to Treat Magical Beasts
Mine and Master's Medical Journal

story and art by **KAZIYA**

VOLUME 2

TRANSLATION
Angela Liu

ADAPTATION
Jaymee Goh

LETTERING AND RETOUCH
Annaliese Christman

COVER DESIGN
KC Fabellon

PROOFREADER
Cae Hawksmoor
Holly Kolodziejczak

EDITOR
Jenn Grunigen

PRODUCTION ASSISTANT
CK Russell

PRODUCTION MANAGER
Lissa Pattillo

EDITOR-IN-CHIEF
Adam Arnold

PUBLISHER
Jason DeAngelis

WATASHI TO SENSEI NO GENJUU SHINRYOUROKU VOL. 2

Originally published in Japan in 2017 by MAG Garden Corporation, Tokyo.
English translation rights arranged through TOHAN CORPORATION, Tokyo.

Seven Seas books may be purchased in bulk for promotional, educational, or business use. Please contact your local bookseller or the Macmillan Corporate and Premium Sales Department at 1-800-221-7945, extension 5442, or by e-mail at MacmillanSpecialMarkets@macmillan.com.

ISBN: 978-1-626929-13-5

Printed in Canada

First Printing: October 2018

10 9 8 7 6 5 4 3 2 1

FOLLOW US ONLINE: ***www.sevenseasentertainment.com***

READING DIRECTIONS

This book reads from ***right to left***, Japanese style. If this is your first time reading manga, you start reading from the top right panel on each page and take it from there. If you get lost, just follow the numbered diagram here. It may seem backwards at first, but you'll get the hang of it! Have fun!!

1
2
3
4
5
6
7
8
9

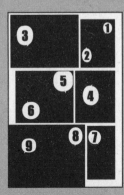